Praise for *C. S. Lewis—A Life*

Alister McGrath sheds new light on the life of the incomparable
C. S. Lewis. This is an important book.

ERIC METAXAS
New York Times bestselling author of *Bonhoeffer: Pastor, Martyr, Prophet, Spy*

Alister McGrath's new biography of C. S. Lewis is excellent. It's filled
with information based on extensive scholarship but is nonetheless
extremely readable. It not only devotes great attention to the
formation and character of Lewis the man, it offers incisive and
balanced analyses of all his main literary works. I was one of those
newly converted American evangelicals who hungrily devoured
Lewis's works in the late 1960s and early '70s. His impact on me was
profound and lasting, and Dr. McGrath clearly explains why so many
believers and Christian leaders today can say the same thing.

TIMOTHY KELLER
Bestselling author of *The Reason for God* and senior pastor of Redeemer
Presbyterian Church

Many of us thought we knew most of what there was to know about
C. S. Lewis. Alister McGrath's new biography makes use of archives
and other material that clarify, deepen, and further explain the many
sides of one of Christianity's most remarkable apologists. This is a
penetrating and illuminating study.

N. T. WRIGHT
Bestselling author of *Simply Christian*

Alister McGrath has written a meticulously researched, insightful, fair-minded, and honest account of a fascinating man's life. His book is especially distinctive in its placing of Lewis in his vocational and social contexts, but it also provides a compelling account of the development of Lewis's Christian mind. This will be an indispensable resource for fans and scholars of Lewis.

ALAN JACOBS
Bestselling author of *The Narnian*

For people who might wonder if we need another biography of C. S. Lewis, McGrath's crisp, insightful, and at times quite original portrait of the celebrated Oxford Christian will change their minds.

LYLE W. DORSETT
Editor of *The Essential C. S. Lewis*

A welcome addition to the biographical literature on C. S. Lewis, which includes several valuable new perspectives. McGrath's book will gain a permanent position in Lewis scholarship for his brilliant and, to my mind, undeniable re-dating of Lewis's conversion to Theism. How we all missed this for so long is astonishing!

MICHAEL WARD
Author of *Planet Narnia*

ECCENTRIC GENIUS. RELUCTANT PROPHET.

C.S. LEWIS

A LIFE

ALISTER McGRATH

HODDER

Scripture quotations are taken from
the Holy Bible, King James Version

First published in Great Britain in 2013 by Hodder & Stoughton
An Hachette UK company

This paperback edition first published in 2013.

2

ISBN 978 1 444 74554 2
eBook ISBN 978 1 444 74553 5

Printed and bound in the UK by CPI Group (UK) Ltd, Croydon CR0 4YY

Hodder & Stoughton policy is to use papers that are natural, renewable
and recyclable products and made from wood grown in sustainable
forests. The logging and manufacturing processes are expected to conform
to the environmental regulations of the country of origin.

Hodder & Stoughton Ltd
338 Euston Road
London NW1 3BH

www.hodderfaith.com

Contents

PART 2: OXFORD

List of Illustrations

Preface

Who is C. S. Lewis (1898–1963)? For many, probably most, Lewis is the creator of the fabulous world of Narnia, the author of some of the best-known and most discussed children's books of the twentieth century, which continue to attract enthusiastic readers and sell in the millions. Fifty years after his death, Lewis remains one of the most influential popular writers of our age. Alongside his equally famous Oxford colleague and friend J. R. R. Tolkien (1892–1973), author of *The Lord of the Rings*, Lewis is widely seen as a literary and cultural landmark. The worlds of literature and cinema have been deeply shaped by both of these Oxford authors. Yet without Lewis, *The Lord of the Rings* might never have been written. Lewis may have created his own bestsellers, but he was also midwife to Tolkien's masterpiece, even proposing Tolkien for the 1961 Nobel Prize in Literature on the basis of this epic work. For these reasons alone, the story of C. S. Lewis is worth telling.

But there is far more to C. S. Lewis than this. As Lewis's long-term friend Owen Barfield (1898–1997) once remarked, there were really three C. S. Lewises. Alongside Lewis the author of bestselling novels, there is a second, less well-known persona: Lewis the Christian writer and apologist, concerned to communicate and share his rich vision of the intellectual and imaginative power of the Christian faith—a faith he discovered in the middle of his life and found rationally and spiritually compelling.

Much to the annoyance of some, his *Mere Christianity* is now often cited as the most influential religious work of the twentieth century.

Perhaps on account of his very public commitment to Christianity, Lewis remains a controversial figure, who elicits affection and admiration from some of those who share his delight in the Christian faith, and ridicule and contempt from some of those who do not. Yet whether one thinks Christianity is good or bad, it is clearly *important*—and Lewis is perhaps the most credible and influential popular representative of the "mere Christianity" that he himself championed.

Yet there is a third aspect to Lewis, perhaps the least familiar to most of his admirers and critics: the distinguished Oxford don and literary critic who packed lecture theatres with his unscripted reflections on English literature, and who went on to become the first occupant of the Chair of Medieval and Renaissance English at the University of Cambridge. Few might now read his *Preface to "Paradise Lost"* (1942); in its day, however, it set a new standard through its clarity and insight.

Lewis's professional calling was to the "groves of Academe." His election as a fellow of the British Academy in July 1955 was a public demonstration of his high scholarly repute. Yet some in the academic world regarded his commercial and popular success as being inconsistent with any claim on his part to be a serious scholar. From 1942 onwards, Lewis struggled to maintain his academic credibility in the light of his more popular works, above all his lighthearted musings on the diabolical world of Screwtape.

So how do these three Lewises relate to each other? Are they separate compartments of his life, or are they somehow interconnected? And how did they each develop? This book aims to tell the story of the shaping and expressing of Lewis's mind, focussing on his writings. It is not concerned with documenting every aspect of Lewis's life, but with exploring the complex and fascinating connections between Lewis's external and internal worlds. This biography is thus organised around the real and imaginary worlds that Lewis inhabited—primarily Oxford, Cambridge, and Narnia. How does the development of his ideas and his imagination map onto the physical worlds he inhabited? Who helped him craft his intellectual and imaginative vision of reality?

In our discussion, we shall consider Lewis's rise to fame, and some of the factors that lay behind this. Yet it is one thing for Lewis to have become famous; it is another for him to remain so fifty years after his death. Many commentators back in the 1960s believed that Lewis's fame was transitory. His inevitable decline into obscurity, many then believed, was just a matter of time—a decade at most. It is for this reason that the final chapter of this work tries to explain, not simply why Lewis became such a figure of authority and influence, but why he remains so today.

Some of the more important early biographies were written by those who knew Lewis personally. These continue to be invaluable as descriptions of what Lewis was *like* as a human being, as well as offering some important judgements concerning his character. However, the vast scholarly endeavours of the last two decades have clarified questions of historical importance (such as Lewis's role in the Great War), explored aspects of Lewis's intellectual development, and provided critical readings of his major works. This biography tries to weave these strands together, presenting an understanding of Lewis firmly grounded in earlier studies, yet able to go beyond them.

Any attempt to deal with Lewis's rise to prominence has to acknowledge his misgivings about assuming a public role. Lewis was indeed a prophet to his own day and age, and beyond; yet it must be said that he was a *reluctant* prophet. Even his own conversion seemed to take place against his better judgement; and having been converted to Christianity, Lewis spoke out on its themes largely because of the silence or unintelligibility of those he believed were better placed than he was to engage religious and theological questions publicly.

Lewis also comes across as something of an eccentric, in the proper sense of that term—someone who departs from recognised, conventional, or established norms or patterns, or who is displaced from the centre of things. His curious relationship with Mrs. Moore, to be discussed in some detail in this work, placed him well outside the British social norms of the 1920s. Many of Lewis's academic colleagues at Oxford came to regard him as an outsider from about 1940, both on account of his openly Christian views and his unscholarly habit of writing popular works of fiction and apologetics. Lewis famously described his distance from the prevailing academic trends of his day when he referred to himself as a "dinosaur" in his inaugural lecture at Cambridge University in 1954.

This sense of distance from the centre is also evident in Lewis's religious life. Although Lewis became a highly influential voice within British Christianity, he operated from its margins rather than its centre, and had no time for the cultivation of relationships with leading figures of the religious establishment. It was perhaps this trait that endeared him to some in the media, anxious to find an authentic religious voice outside the power structures of the mainstream churches.

This biography sets out, not to praise Lewis or condemn him, but to *understand* him—above all, his ideas, and how these found expression in his writings. This task has been made easier by the publication of virtually all that is known to remain of Lewis's writings, as well as a significant body of critical scholarly literature dealing with his works and ideas.

The vast amount of biographical and scholarly material now available concerning Lewis and his circle threatens to overwhelm the reader with fine detail. Those trying to make sense of Lewis find themselves bombarded with what the American poet Edna St. Vincent Millay (1892–1950) called "a meteoric shower of facts," raining from the sky.[1] How, she asked, might these be combined to disclose meaning, rather than remaining a mere accumulation of information? This biography adds to what is known about Lewis's life, while also trying to make sense of it. How are these facts to be woven together, so that they may disclose a pattern? This biography of Lewis is not another rehearsal of the vast army of facts and figures concerning his life, but an attempt to identify its deeper themes and concerns, and assess its significance. This is not a work of synopsis, but of analysis.

The publication of the collected letters of C. S. Lewis, carefully annotated and cross-referenced by Walter Hooper during the period 2000–2006, is of landmark importance for Lewis studies. These letters, taking up some 3,500 pages of text, offer insights into Lewis that were simply not available to an earlier generation of Lewis biographers. Perhaps most important, they provide a continuous narrative backbone for an account of Lewis's life. For this reason, these letters are cited more than any other source throughout this biography. As will become clear, a close reading of these letters forces review and possibly revision of some widely accepted dates in Lewis's life.

This is a critical biography, which examines the evidence for existing assumptions and approaches, and corrects them where necessary. In most cases, this can be done simply and subtly, and I have seen no reason to draw attention to those corrections. On the other hand, it is only fair to tell readers from the outset that this wearying yet necessary process of checking everything against documentary evidence has led me to one conclusion in particular that pits me, not simply against every Lewis scholar I know, but against Lewis himself. I refer to the date of his "conversion" or recovery of belief in God, which Lewis himself, in his book *Surprised by Joy* (1955), locates in "Trinity Term 1929" (that is, at some point between 28 April and 22 June 1929).[2]

This date is faithfully repeated in every major study of Lewis to have appeared recently. Yet my close reading of the documentary material points unequivocally to a later date, possibly as early as March 1930, but more likely in the Trinity Term of that year. On this point, I stand entirely alone in Lewis scholarship, and the reader has a right to know that I am completely isolated on this question.

From what has been said already, it will be clear that there is no need to justify a new biography of Lewis to mark the fiftieth anniversary of his death in 1963. Yet perhaps there is a need to offer a small defence of myself as his biographer. Unlike his earlier biographers—such as his longtime friends George Sayer (1914–2005) and Roger Lancelyn Green (1918–1987)—I never knew Lewis personally. He was someone I discovered through his writings in my early twenties, a decade after his death, and who, over a period of twenty years, gradually came to win my respect and admiration, though mingled with continuing curiosity and abiding concerns. I have no illuminating memories, no privileged disclosures, and no private documents on which to draw. Every resource used in this biography is either already in the public domain or available to public scrutiny and inspection.

This is a book written by someone who discovered Lewis through his writings, for others who have come to know Lewis in the same way. The Lewis I have come to know is mediated through his words, not through any personal acquaintance. Where other biographers refer to Lewis as "Jack" in their works, I have felt it right to call him "Lewis" throughout, mainly to emphasise my personal and critical distance from him. I believe that this is the Lewis whom he himself would wish future generations to know.

Why so? As Lewis emphasised throughout the 1930s, the important thing about authors is the *texts* that they write. What really matters is what those texts themselves say. Authors should not themselves be a "spectacle"; they are rather the "set of spectacles" through which we as readers see ourselves, the world, and the greater scheme of things of which we are a part. Lewis thus had surprisingly little interest in the personal history of the great English poet John Milton (1608–1674), or the political and social context within which he wrote. What really mattered were Milton's writings—his *ideas*. The way Lewis believed we should approach Milton must be allowed to shape the way we in turn approach Lewis. Throughout this work, wherever possible, I have tried to engage with his writings, exploring what they say, and assessing their significance.

Though I did not know Lewis as a person, I can relate well—perhaps better than most—to at least some aspects of Lewis's worlds. Like Lewis, I spent my childhood in Ireland, mainly in Downpatrick, the county town of County Down, whose "long, soft hills" Lewis knew and loved, and described so beautifully. I have walked where he walked, paused where he paused, and marvelled where he marvelled. I, too, felt that twinge of yearning at seeing the distant blue Mountains of Mourne from my childhood home. Like Lewis's mother, Flora, I also was a pupil at the Methodist College, Belfast.

I also know Lewis's Oxford well, having been a student there for seven years, before—after a brief spell at Lewis's other university, Cambridge—returning to teach and write there for twenty-five years, ending up as Oxford University's chair in historical theology, as well as becoming what Oxford calls a "Head of House." Like Lewis, I was an atheist as a younger man, before discovering the intellectual riches of the Christian faith. Like Lewis, I chose to express and enact that faith in the specific form found in the Church of England. And finally, as someone who is often called upon to offer a public defence of the Christian faith against its critics, I find myself both appreciating and using Lewis's ideas and approaches, many—but not all—of which seem to me to retain at least something of their sparkle and power.

Finally, a word about the method used in writing this biography. The core research began with a close reading of Lewis's entire published output (including his letters) in strictly chronological order of writing, so that the development of his thought and writing style could be appreciated. *The Pilgrim's Regress* was thus assigned to August 1932, when it was written, rather than May 1933, when it was published. This process of intense engagement with primary sources, which took fifteen months, was followed by a reading—in some cases a somewhat critical rereading—of the substantial secondary literature concerning Lewis, his circle of friends, and the intellectual and cultural context in which they lived, thought, and wrote. Finally, I examined unpublished archive material, much of which is held in Oxford, which casts further light on the shaping of Lewis's mind and on the intellectual and institutional context within which he worked.

It became clear at an early stage that a more academic study would be necessary to engage some of the scholarly questions that emerged from this detailed research. This biography avoids such details of scholarly engagement; notes and bibliography have been kept to the bare minimum. My concern in this volume is to tell a story, not to settle occasionally arcane and invariably detailed academic debates. Readers may, however, like to know that a more academic volume will be published shortly, offering scholarly exploration and justification of some of the assertions and conclusions of this biography.[3]

But enough of apologies and preliminaries. Our story begins in a world of long ago and far away—the Irish city of Belfast in the 1890s.

Alister E. McGrath
London

PART 1

PRELUDE

THE SOFT HILLS OF DOWN: AN IRISH CHILDHOOD

"I was born in the winter of 1898 at Belfast, the son of a solicitor and of a clergyman's daughter."[1] On 29 November 1898, Clive Staples Lewis was plunged into a world that was simmering with political and social resentment and clamouring for change. The partition of Ireland into Northern Ireland and the Republic of Ireland was still two decades away. Yet the tensions that would lead to this artificial political division of the island were obvious to all. Lewis was born into the heart of the Protestant establishment of Ireland (the "Ascendancy") at a time when every one of its aspects—political, social, religious, and cultural—was under threat.

Ireland was colonised by English and Scottish settlers in the sixteenth and seventeenth centuries, leading to deep political and social resentment on the part of the dispossessed native Irish towards the incomers. The Protestant colonists were linguistically and religiously distinct from the native Catholic Irish. Under Oliver Cromwell, "Protestant plantations" developed during the seventeenth century—English Protestant islands in an Irish Catholic sea. The native Irish ruling classes were quickly displaced by a new Protestant establishment. The 1800 Act of Union saw Ireland become part of the United Kingdom, ruled directly from London. Despite being a numerical minority, located primarily in the northern counties of Down and Antrim, including the industrial city of Belfast, Protestants dominated the cultural, economic, and political life of Ireland.

Yet all this was about to change. In the 1880s, Charles Stewart Parnell (1846–1891) and others began to agitate for "Home Rule" for Ireland. In the 1890s, Irish nationalism began to gain momentum, creating a sense of Irish cultural identity that gave new energy to the Home Rule movement. This was strongly shaped by Catholicism, and was vigorously opposed to all forms of English influence in Ireland, including games such as rugby and cricket. More significantly, it came to consider the English language as an agent of cultural oppression. In 1893 the Gaelic League (*Conradh na Gaeilge*) was founded to promote the study and use of the Irish language. Once more, this was seen as an assertion of Irish identity over and against what were increasingly regarded as alien English cultural norms.

As demands for Home Rule for Ireland became increasingly forceful and credible, many Protestants felt threatened, fearing the erosion of privilege and the possibility of civil strife. Perhaps unsurprisingly, the Protestant community in Belfast in the early 1900s was strongly insular, avoiding social and professional contact with their Catholic neighbours wherever possible. (C. S. Lewis's older brother, Warren ["Warnie"], later recalled that he never spoke to a Catholic from his own social background until he entered the Royal Military College at Sandhurst in 1914.)[2] Catholicism was "the Other"—something that was strange, incomprehensible, and above all *threatening*. Lewis absorbed such hostility towards—and isolation from—Catholicism with his mother's milk. When the young Lewis was being toilet trained, his Protestant nanny used to call his stools "wee popes." Many regarded, and still regard, Lewis as lying outside the pale of true Irish cultural identity on account of his Ulster Protestant roots.

THE LEWIS FAMILY

The 1901 Census of Ireland recorded the names of everyone who "slept or abode" at the Lewis household in East Belfast on the night of Sunday, 31 March 1901. The record included a mass of personal details—relationship to one another, religion, level of education, age, sex, rank or occupation, and place of birth. Although most biographies refer to the Lewis household as then residing at "47 Dundela Avenue," the Census records them as living at "House 21 in Dundella [sic] Avenue (Victoria, Down)." The entry for the Lewis household provides an accurate snapshot of the family at the opening of the twentieth century:

Albert James Lewis, Head of Family, Church of Ireland, Read &
    Write, 37, M, Solicitor, Married, City of Cork
Florence Augusta Lewis, Wife, Church of Ireland, Read & Write,
    38, F, Married, County Cork
Warren Hamilton Lewis, Son, Church of Ireland, Read, 5, M,
    Scholar, City of Belfast
Clive Staples Lewis, Son, Church of Ireland, Cannot Read, 2, M,
    City of Belfast
Martha Barber, Servant, Presbyterian, Read & Write, 28, F, Nurse—
    Domestic Servant, Not Married, County Monaghan
Sarah Ann Conlon, Servant, Roman Catholic, Read & Write, 22, F,
    Cook—Domestic Servant, Not Married, County Down[3]

As the Census entry indicates, Lewis's father, Albert James Lewis (1863–1929), was born in the city and county of Cork, in the south of Ireland. Lewis's paternal grandfather, Richard Lewis, was a Welsh boilermaker who had immigrated to Cork with his Liverpudlian wife in the early 1850s. Soon after Albert's birth, the Lewis family moved to the northern industrial city of Belfast, so that Richard could go into partnership with John H. MacIlwaine to form the successful firm MacIlwaine, Lewis & Co., Engineers and Iron Ship Builders. Perhaps the most interesting ship to be built by this small company was the original *Titanic*—a small steel freight steamer built in 1888, weighing a mere 1,608 tons.[4]

Yet the Belfast shipbuilding industry was undergoing change in the 1880s, with the larger yards of Harland and Wolff and Workman Clark achieving commercial dominance. It became increasingly difficult for the "wee yards" to survive economically. In 1894, Workman Clark took over MacIlwaine, Lewis & Co. The rather more famous version of the *Titanic*—also built in Belfast—was launched in 1911 from the shipyard of Harland and Wolff, weighing 26,000 tons. Yet while Harland and Wolff's liner famously sank on its maiden voyage in 1912, MacIlwaine and Lewis's much smaller ship continued to ply its trade in South American waters under other names until 1928.

1.1 Royal Avenue, one of the commercial hubs of the city of Belfast, in 1897. Albert Lewis established his solicitor's practice at 83 Royal Avenue in 1884, and continued working from these offices until his final illness in 1929.

Albert showed little interest in the shipbuilding business, and made it clear to his parents that he wanted to pursue a legal career. Richard Lewis, knowing of the excellent reputation of Lurgan College under its head-master, William Thompson Kirkpatrick (1848–1921), decided to enrol Albert there as a boarding pupil.[5] Albert formed a lasting impression of Kirkpatrick's teaching skills during his year there. After Albert graduated in 1880, he moved to Dublin, the capital city of Ireland, where he worked for five years for the firm of Maclean, Boyle, and Maclean. Having gained the necessary experience and professional accreditation as a solicitor, he moved back to Belfast in 1884 to establish his own practice with offices on Belfast's prestigious Royal Avenue.

The Supreme Court of Judicature (Ireland) Act of 1877 followed the English practice of making a clear distinction between the legal role of "solicitors" and "barristers," so that aspiring Irish lawyers were required to decide which professional position they wished to pursue. Albert Lewis chose to become a solicitor, acting directly on behalf of clients, including representing them in the lower courts. A barrister specialised in court-room advocacy, and would be hired by a solicitor to represent a client in the higher courts.[6]

Lewis's mother, Florence ("Flora") Augusta Lewis (1862–1908), was born in Queenstown (now Cobh), County Cork. Lewis's maternal grand-father, Thomas Hamilton (1826–1905), was a Church of Ireland clergy-man—a classic representative of the Protestant Ascendancy that came under threat as Irish nationalism became an increasingly significant and cultural force in the early twentieth century. The Church of Ireland had been the established church throughout Ireland, despite being a minority faith in at least twenty-two of the twenty-six Irish counties. When Flora was eight, her father accepted the post of chaplain to Holy Trinity Church in Rome, where the family lived from 1870 to 1874.

In 1874, Thomas Hamilton returned to Ireland to take up the position of curate-in-charge of Dundela Church in the Ballyhackamore area of East Belfast. The same temporary building served as a church on Sundays and a school during weekdays. It soon became clear that a more perma-nent arrangement was required. Work soon began on a new, purpose-built church, designed by the famous English ecclesiastical architect William Butterfield. Hamilton was installed as rector of the newly built parish church of St. Mark's, Dundela, in May 1879.

Irish historians now regularly point to Flora Hamilton as illustrating the increasingly significant role of women in Irish academic and cultural life in the final quarter of the nineteenth century.[7] She was enrolled as a day pupil at the Methodist College, Belfast—an all-boys school, founded in 1865, at which "Ladies' Classes" had been established in response to popular demand in 1869.[8] She attended for one term in 1881, and went on to study at the Royal University of Ireland in Belfast (now Queen's University, Belfast), gaining First Class Honours in Logic and Second Class Honours in Mathematics in 1886.[9] (As will become clear, Lewis failed to inherit anything of his mother's gift for mathematics.)

When Albert Lewis began to attend St. Mark's, Dundela, his eye was caught by the rector's daughter. Slowly but surely, Flora appears to have been drawn to Albert, partly on account of his obvious literary interests. Albert had joined the Belmont Literary Society in 1881, and was soon considered one of its best speakers. His reputation as a man of literary inclinations would remain with him for the rest of his life. In 1921, at the height of Albert Lewis's career as a solicitor, *Ireland's Saturday Night* newspaper featured him in a cartoon. Dressed in the garb of a court solicitor of the period, he is depicted as holding a mortarboard under one arm and a volume of English literature under the other. Years later, Albert Lewis's obituary in the *Belfast Telegraph* described him as a "well read and erudite man," noted for literary allusions in his presentations in court, and who "found his chief recreation away from the courts of law in reading."[10]

After a suitably decorous and extended courtship, Albert and Flora were married on 29 August 1894 at St. Mark's Church, Dundela. Their first child, Warren Hamilton Lewis, was born on 16 June 1895 at their home, "Dundela Villas," in East Belfast. Clive was their second and final child. The Census return of 1901 indicates that the Lewis household then had two servants. Unusual for a Protestant family, the Lewises employed a Catholic housemaid, Sarah Ann Conlon. Lewis's long-standing aversion to religious sectarianism—evident in his notion of "mere Christianity"—may have received a stimulus from memories of his childhood.

From the outset, Lewis developed a close relationship with his elder brother, Warren, which was reflected in their nicknames for each other. C. S. Lewis was "Smallpigiebotham" (SPB) and Warnie "Archpigiebotham" (APB), affectionate names inspired by their childhood nurse's frequent (and apparently real) threats to smack their "piggybottoms" unless they behaved properly. The brothers referred to their father as the "Pudaitabird" or "P'dayta" (because of his Belfast pronunciation of *potato*). These childhood nicknames would become important once more as the brothers reconnected and reestablished their intimacy in the late 1920s.[11]

Lewis himself was known as "Jack" to his family and friends. Warnie dates his brother's rejection of the name *Clive* to a summer holiday in 1903 or 1904, when Lewis suddenly declared that he now wished to be known as "Jacksie." This was gradually abbreviated to "Jacks," and finally to "Jack."[12] The reason for this choice of name remains obscure. Although some sources suggest that the name "Jacksie" was taken from a family dog that died in an accident, there is no documentary evidence in support of this.

THE AMBIVALENT IRISHMAN: THE ENIGMA OF IRISH CULTURAL IDENTITY

Lewis was Irish—something that some Irish seem to have forgotten, if they knew it at all. While I myself was growing up in Northern Ireland during the 1960s, my recollection is that when Lewis was referred to at all, it was as an "English" writer. Yet Lewis never lost sight of his Irish roots. The sights, sounds, and fragrances—not, on the whole, the *people*—of his native Ireland evoked nostalgia for the later Lewis, just as they subtly but powerfully moulded his descriptive prose. In a letter of 1915, Lewis fondly recalls his memories of Belfast: "the distant murmuring of the 'yards,'" the broad sweep of Belfast Lough, the Cave Hill Mountain, and the little glens, meadows, and hills around the city.[13]

Yet there is more to Lewis's Ireland than its "soft hills." Its culture was marked by a passion for storytelling, evident both in its mythology and its historical narratives, and in its love of language. Yet Lewis never made his Irish roots into a fetish. They were simply part of who he was, not his defining feature. As late as the 1950s, Lewis regularly spoke of Ireland as his "home," calling it "my country," even choosing to spend his belated honeymoon with Joy Davidman there in April 1958. Lewis had inhaled the soft, moist air of his homeland, and never forgot its natural beauty.

Few who know County Down can fail to recognise the veiled Irish originals which may have inspired some of Lewis's beautifully crafted literary landscapes. Lewis's depiction of heaven in *The Great Divorce* as an "emerald green" land echoes his native country, just as the dolmens at Legananny in County Down, Belfast's Cave Hill Mountain, and the Giant's Causeway all seem to have their Narnian equivalents—perhaps softer and brighter than their originals, but still bearing something of their imprint.

Lewis frequently referred to Ireland as a source of literary inspiration, noting how its landscapes were a powerful stimulus to the imagination. Lewis disliked Irish politics and was prone to imagine a pastoral Ireland composed solely of soft hills, mists, loughs, and woods. Ulster, he once confided to his diary, "is very beautiful and if only I could deport the Ulstermen and fill their land with a populace of my own choosing, I should ask for no better place to live in."[14] (In certain ways, Narnia can be seen as an imaginary and idealised Ulster, populated with creatures of Lewis's imagination, rather than Ulstermen.)

The term *Ulster* needs further explanation. Just as the English county of Yorkshire was divided into three parts (the "Ridings," from the Old Norse word for "a third part," *thrithjungr*), the island of Ireland was originally divided into five regions (Gaelic *cúigí*, from *cóiced*, "a fifth part"). After the Norman conquest of 1066, these were reduced to four: Connaught, Leinster, Munster, and Ulster. The term *province* now came to be preferred to the Gaelic *cúige*. The Protestant minority in Ireland was concentrated in the northern province of Ulster, which consisted of nine counties. When Ireland was partitioned, six of these nine counties formed the new political entity of Northern Ireland. The term *Ulster* is today often used as synonymous with Northern Ireland, with the term *Ulsterman* tending to be used—though not consistently—to designate "a Protestant inhabitant of Northern Ireland." This is done despite the fact that the original *cúige* of Ulster also included the three counties of Cavan, Donegal, and Monaghan, now part of the Republic of Ireland.

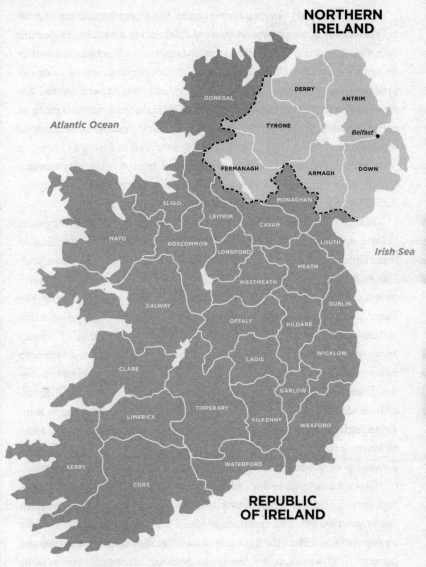

NORTHERN IRELAND

DONEGAL

DERRY

ANTRIM

Atlantic Ocean

TYRONE

Belfast

FERMANAGH

ARMAGH

DOWN

MONAGHAN

SLIGO

LEITRIM

CAVAN

LOUTH

Irish Sea

MAYO

ROSCOMMON

LONGFORD

MEATH

WESTMEATH

GALWAY

OFFALY

KILDARE

DUBLIN

WICKLOW

LAOIS

CLARE

CARLOW

LIMERICK

TIPPERARY

KILKENNY

WEXFORD

KERRY

WATERFORD

CORK

REPUBLIC OF IRELAND

1.2 C. S. Lewis's Ireland.

Lewis returned to Ireland for his annual vacation almost every year of his life, except when prevented by war or illness. He invariably visited the counties of Antrim, Derry, Down (his favourite), and Donegal—all within the province of Ulster, in its classic sense. At one point, Lewis even considered permanently renting a cottage in Cloghy, County Down,[15] as the base for his annual walking holidays, which often included strenuous hikes in the Mountains of Mourne. (In the end, he decided that his finances would not stretch to this luxury.) Although Lewis worked in England, his heart was firmly fixed in the northern counties of Ireland, especially County Down. As he once remarked to his Irish student David Bleakley, "Heaven is Oxford lifted and placed in the middle of County Down."[16]

Where some Irish writers found their literary inspiration in the political and cultural issues surrounding their nation's quest for independence from Great Britain, Lewis found his primarily in the landscapes of Ireland. These, he declared, had inspired and shaped the prose and poetry of many before him—perhaps most important, Edmund Spenser's classic *The Faerie Queene*, an Elizabethan work that Lewis regularly expounded in his lectures at Oxford and Cambridge. For Lewis, this classic work of "quests and wanderings and inextinguishable desires" clearly reflected Spenser's many years spent in Ireland. Who could fail to detect "the soft, wet air, the loneliness, the muffled shapes of the hills" or "the heart-rending sunsets" of Ireland? For Lewis—who here identifies himself as someone who actually is "an Irishman"—Spenser's subsequent period in England led to a loss of his imaginative power. "The many years in Ireland lie behind Spenser's greatest poetry, and the few years in England behind his minor poetry."[17]

Lewis's language echoes his origins. In his correspondence, Lewis regularly uses Anglo-Irish idioms or slang derived from Gaelic, without offering a translation or explanation—for example, the phrases to "make a poor mouth" (from the Gaelic *an béal bocht*, meaning "to complain of poverty"), or "whisht, now!" (meaning "be quiet," derived from the Gaelic *bí i do thost*). Other idioms reflect local idiosyncrasies, rather than Gaelic linguistic provenance, such as the curious phrase "as long as a Lurgan spade" (meaning "looking gloomy" or "having a long face").[18] Although

Lewis's voice in his "broadcast talks" of the 1940s is typical of the Oxford academic culture of his day, his pronunciation of words such as *friend*, *hour*, and *again* betrays the subtle influence of his Belfast roots.

So why is Lewis not celebrated as one of the greatest Irish writers of all time? Why is there no entry for "Lewis, C. S." in the 1,472 pages of the supposedly definitive *Dictionary of Irish Literature* (1996)? The real issue is that Lewis does not fit—and, indeed, must be said partly to have *chosen* not to fit—the template of Irish identity that has dominated the late twentieth century. In some ways, Lewis represents precisely the forces and influences which the advocates of a stereotypical Irish literary identity wished to reject. If Dublin stood at the centre of the demands for Home Rule and the reassertion of Irish culture in the early twentieth century, Lewis's home city of Belfast was the heart of opposition to any such developments.

One of the reasons why Ireland has largely chosen to forget about Lewis is that he was the wrong kind of Irishman. In 1917, Lewis certainly saw himself as sympathetic to the "New Ireland School," and was considering sending his poetry to Maunsel and Roberts,[19] a Dublin publisher with strong links to Irish nationalism, having published the collected works of the great nationalist writer Patrick Pearse (1879–1916) that same year. Conceding that they were "only a second-rate house," Lewis expressed the hope that this might mean they would take his submission seriously.[20]

Yet a year later, things seemed very different to Lewis. Writing to his longtime friend Arthur Greeves, Lewis expressed his fear that the New Ireland School would end up as little more than "a sort of little by-way of the intellectual world, off the main track." Lewis now recognised the importance of keeping "in the broad highway of thought," writing for a broad readership rather than one narrowly defined by certain cultural and political agendas. To be published by Maunsel would, Lewis declared, be tantamount to associating himself with what was little more than a "cult." His Irish identity, inspired by Ireland's landscape rather than its political history, would find its expression in the literary mainstream, not one of its "side-tracks."[21] Lewis may have chosen to rise above the provinciality of Irish literature; he nevertheless remains one of its most luminous and famous representatives.

SURROUNDED BY BOOKS: HINTS OF A LITERARY VOCATION

The physical landscape of Ireland was unquestionably one of the influences that shaped Lewis's fertile imagination. Yet there is another source which did much to inspire his youthful outlook—literature itself. One of Lewis's most persistent memories of his youth is that of a home packed with books. Albert Lewis might have worked as a police solicitor to earn his keep, but his heart lay in the reading of literature.

In April 1905, the Lewis family moved to a new and more spacious home that had just been constructed on the outskirts of the city of Belfast—"Leeborough House" on the Circular Road in Strandtown, known more informally as "Little Lea" or "Leaboro." The Lewis brothers were free to roam this vast house, and allowed their imaginations to transform it into mysterious kingdoms and strange lands. Both brothers inhabited imaginary worlds, and committed something of these to writing. Lewis wrote about talking animals in "Animal-Land," while Warnie wrote about "India" (later combined into the equally imaginary land of Boxen).

As Lewis later recalled, wherever he looked in this new house, he saw stacks, piles, and shelves of books.[22] On many rainy days, he found solace and company in reading these works and roaming freely across imagined literary landscapes. The books so liberally scattered throughout the "New House" included works of romance and mythology, which opened the windows of Lewis's young imagination. The physical landscape of County Down was seen through a literary lens, becoming a gateway to distant realms. Warren Lewis later reflected on the imaginative stimulus offered to him and his brother by wet weather and a sense of longing for something more satisfying.[23] Might his brother's imaginative wanderings have been prompted by his childhood "staring out to unattainable hills," seen through rain and under grey skies?

1.3 The Lewis family at Little Lea in 1905. *Back Row* (left to right): Agnes Lewis (aunt), two maids, Flora Lewis (mother). *Front Row* (left to right): Warnie, C. S. Lewis, Leonard Lewis (cousin), Eileen Lewis (cousin), and Albert Lewis (father), holding Nero (dog).

Ireland is the "Emerald Isle" precisely on account of its high levels of rainfall and mist, which ensure moist soils and lush green grass. It was natural for Lewis to later transfer this sense of confinement by rain to four young children, trapped in an elderly professor's house, unable to explore outside because of a "steady rain falling, so thick that when you looked out of the window you could see neither the mountains nor the woods nor even the stream in the garden."[24] Is the professor's house in *The Lion, the Witch and the Wardrobe* modelled on Leeborough?

From Little Lea, the young Lewis could see the distant Castlereagh Hills, which seemed to speak to him of something of heartrending significance, lying tantalizingly beyond his reach. They became a symbol of liminality, of standing on the threshold of a new, deeper, and more satisfying way of thinking and living. An unutterable sense of intense longing arose within him as he contemplated them. He could not say exactly *what* it was that he longed for, merely that there was a sense of emptiness within him, which the mysterious hills seemed to heighten without satisfying. In *The Pilgrim's Regress* (1933), these hills reappear as a symbol of the heart's unknown desire. But if Lewis was standing on the threshold of something wondrous and enticing, how could he enter this mysterious realm? Who would open the door and allow him through? Perhaps unsurprisingly, the image of a door became increasingly significant to Lewis's later reflections on the deeper questions of life.

The low, green line of the Castlereagh Hills, though actually quite close, thus came to be a symbol of something distant and unattainable. These hills were, for Lewis, distant objects of desire, marking the end of his known world, from which the whisper of the haunting "horns of elfland" could be heard. "They taught me longing—*Sehnsucht*; made me for good or ill, and before I was six years old, a votary of the Blue Flower."[25]

We must linger over this statement. What does Lewis mean by *Sehnsucht*? The German word is rich with emotional and imaginative associations, famously described by the poet Matthew Arnold as a "wistful, soft, tearful longing." And what of the "Blue Flower"? Leading German Romantic writers, such as Novalis (1772–1801) and Joseph von Eichendorff (1788–1857), used the image of a "Blue Flower" as a symbol of the wanderings and yearnings of the human soul, especially as this sense of longing is evoked—though not satisfied—by the natural world.

Even at this early stage, then, Lewis was probing and questioning the limits of his world. What lay beyond its horizons? Yet Lewis could not answer the questions that these longings so provocatively raised in his youthful mind. To what did they point? Was there a doorway? And if so, where was it to be found? And what did it lead to? Finding answers to these questions would preoccupy Lewis for the next twenty-five years.

SOLITUDE: WARNIE GOES TO ENGLAND

Everything we know about Lewis around 1905 suggests a lonely, introverted boy with hardly any friends, who found pleasure and fulfilment in the solitary reading of books. Why solitary? Having secured a new house for his family, Albert Lewis now turned his attention to ensuring the future prospects of his sons. As a pillar of the Protestant establishment in Belfast, Albert Lewis took the view that the interests of his sons would be best advanced by sending the boys to boarding school in England. Albert's brother William had already sent his son to an English school, seeing this as an acceptable route to social advancement. Albert decided to do the same, and took professional advice about which school would best suit his needs.

The London educational agents Gabbitas & Thring had been founded in 1873 to recruit suitable schoolmasters for leading English schools and provide guidance for parents wanting to secure the best possible education for their children. Schoolmasters whom they helped to find suitable positions included such future stars—now, it must be said, not chiefly remembered for having ever been schoolmasters—as W. H. Auden, John Betjeman, Edward Elgar, Evelyn Waugh, and H. G. Wells. By 1923, when the firm celebrated the fiftieth anniversary of its founding, over 120,000 teaching vacancies had been negotiated and no fewer than 50,000 parents had sought their counsel on the best school for their children. This included Albert Lewis, who asked their advice on where to send his elder son, Warren.

Their recommendation duly came through. It turned out to be stunningly bad advice. In May 1905, without making the more critical and thorough inquiries some would have expected of a man in his position, Albert Lewis packed the nine-year-old Warren off to Wynyard School in Watford, north of London. It was perhaps the first of many mistakes that Lewis's father would make concerning his relationship with his sons.

Jacks—as Lewis now preferred to be called—and his brother, Warnie, had lived together in Little Lea for only a month, sharing a "Little End Room" in the top floor of the rambling house as their haven. Now, they were separated. C. S. Lewis remained at home, and was taught privately by his mother and a governess, Annie Harper. But perhaps his best teachers were the burgeoning stacks of books, none of which were forbidden to him.

For two years, the solitary Lewis roamed the large house's long, creaking corridors and roomy attics, with vast quantities of books as his companions.

Lewis's inner world began to take shape. Where other boys of his age were playing games on the streets or in the countryside around Belfast, Lewis constructed, inhabited, and explored his own private worlds. He was forced to become a loner—something that unquestionably catalysed his imaginative life. In Warnie's absence, he had nobody as a soul mate with whom he could share his dreams and longings. The school vacations became of supreme importance to him. They were when Warnie came home.

FIRST ENCOUNTERS WITH JOY

At some point around this time, Lewis's already rich imaginative life took a new turn. Lewis later recalled three early experiences which he regarded as shaping one of his life's chief concerns. The first of these took place when the fragrance of a "flowering currant bush" in the garden at Little Lea triggered a memory of his time in the "Old House"—Dundela Villas, which Albert Lewis had then rented from a relative.[26] Lewis speaks of experiencing a transitory, delectable sense of desire, which overwhelmed him. Before he had worked out what was happening, the experience had passed, leaving him "longing for the longing that had just ceased." It seemed to Lewis to be of enormous importance. "Everything else that had ever happened to me was insignificant in comparison." But what did it mean?

The second experience came when reading Beatrix Potter's *Squirrel Nutkin* (1903). Though Lewis admired Potter's books in general at this time, something about this work sparked an intense longing for something he clearly struggled to describe—"the Idea of Autumn."[27] Once more, Lewis experienced the same intoxicating sense of "intense desire."

The third came when he read Henry Wadsworth Longfellow's poem written in the style of the Swedish poet Esaias Tegnér (1782–1846):[28]

I heard a voice that cried,
Balder the beautiful
Is dead, is dead—

Lewis found the impact of these words devastating. It was as if they opened a door that he did not know existed, allowing him to see a new realm beyond his own experience, which he longed to enter and possess. For a moment, nothing else seemed to matter. "I knew nothing of Balder," he recalled, "but instantly I was uplifted into huge regions of northern sky, [and] I desired with almost sickening intensity something never to be described (except that it is cold, spacious, severe, pale, and remote)."[29] Yet even before Lewis had realised what was happening to him, the experience passed, and left him longing to be able to reenter it.

Looking back on these three experiences, Lewis understood that they could be seen as aspects or manifestations of the same thing: "an unsatisfied desire which is itself more desirable than any other satisfaction. I call it Joy."[30] The quest for that Joy would become a central theme of Lewis's life and writing.

So how are we to make sense of these experiences, which played such a significant role in Lewis's development, especially the shaping of his "inner life"? Perhaps we can draw on the classic study *The Varieties of Religious Experience* (1902), in which the Harvard psychologist William James (1842–1910) tried to make sense of the complex, powerful experiences that lay at the heart of the lives of so many religious thinkers. Drawing extensively on a wide range of published writings and personal testimonies, James identified four characteristic features of such experiences.[31] In the first place, such experiences are "ineffable." They defy expression, and cannot be described adequately in words.

In the second place, James suggests that those who experience them achieve "insight into depths of truth unplumbed by the discursive intellect." In other words, they are experienced as "illuminations, revelations, full of significance and importance." They evoke an "enormous sense of inner authority and illumination," transfiguring the understanding of those who experience them, often evoking a deep sense "of being revelations of new depths of truth." These themes clearly underlie Lewis's early desriptions of "Joy," such as his statement that "everything else that had ever happened to me was insignificant in comparison."

19

Third, James goes on to emphasise that these experiences are transient; they "cannot be sustained for long." Usually they last from a few seconds to just minutes, and their quality cannot be accurately remembered, though the experience is recognised if it recurs. "When faded, their quality can but imperfectly be reproduced in memory." This aspect of James's typology of religious experience is clearly reflected in Lewis's prose.

Finally, James suggests that those who have had such an experience feel as if they have been "grasped and held by a superior power." Such experiences are not created by active subjects; they come upon people, often with overwhelming power.

Lewis's eloquent descriptions of his experience of "Joy" clearly fit into James's characterisation. Lewis's experiences were perceived as deeply meaningful, throwing open the doors of another world, which then shut almost immediately, leaving him exhilarated at what had happened, yet longing to recover it. They are like momentary and transient epiphanies, when things suddenly seem to come acutely and sharply into focus, only for the light to fade and the vision to recede, leaving nothing but a memory and a longing.

Lewis was left with a sense of loss, even of betrayal, in the aftermath of such experiences. Yet as frustrating and disconcerting as they may have been, they suggested to him that the visible world might be only a curtain that concealed vast, uncharted realms of mysterious oceans and islands. It was an idea that, once planted, never lost its imaginative appeal or its emotional power. Yet, as we shall see, Lewis would soon come to believe it was illusory, a childhood dream which the dawning of adult rationality exposed as a cruel delusion. Ideas of a transcendent realm or of a God might be "lies breathed through silver,"[32] but they remained lies nevertheless.

THE DEATH OF FLORA LEWIS

Edward VII came to the English throne after the death of Victoria in 1901 and reigned until 1910. The Edwardian Age is now often seen as a golden period of long summer afternoons and elegant garden parties, an image which was shattered by the Great War of 1914–1918. While this highly romanticised view of the Edwardian Age largely reflects the postwar nostalgia of the 1920s, there is no doubt that many at the time saw it as a settled and secure age. There were troubling developments afoot—above all, the growing military and industrial power of Germany and the economic strength of the United States, which some realised posed significant threats to British imperial interests. Yet the dominant mood was that of an empire which was settled and strong, its trade routes protected by the greatest navy the world had ever known.

This sense of stability is evident in Lewis's early childhood. In May 1907, Lewis wrote to Warnie, telling him that it was nearly settled that they were going to spend part of their holidays in France. Going abroad was a significant departure for the Lewis family, who normally spent up to six weeks during the summer at northern Irish resorts such as Castlerock or Portrush. Their father, preoccupied with his legal practice, was often an intermittent presence on these occasions. As things turned out, he would not join them in France at all.

1.4 Pension le Petit Vallon, Berneval-le-Grand, Seine-Maritime, France. Postcard dating from around 1905.

In the event, Lewis enjoyed an intimate and tranquil holiday with his brother and mother. On 20 August 1907, Flora Lewis took her two sons to the Pension le Petit Vallon, a family hotel in the small town of Berneval-le-Grand in Normandy, not far from Dieppe, where they would remain until 18 September. A picture postcard of the early 1900s perhaps helps us understand Flora's choice: the reassuring words "English spoken" feature prominently above a photograph of Edwardian families relaxing happily on its grounds. Any hopes that Lewis had of learning some French were dashed when he discovered that all the other guests were English.

It was to be an idyllic summer of the late Edwardian period, with no hints of the horrors to come. When hospitalised in France during the Great War a mere eighteen miles (29 kilometres) east of Berneval-le-Grand, Lewis found himself wistfully recalling those precious, lost golden days.[33] Nobody had foreseen the political possibility of such a war, nor the destruction it would wreak—just as nobody in the Lewis family could have known that this would be the last holiday they would spend together. A year later, Flora Lewis was dead.

Early in 1908, it became clear that Flora was seriously ill. She had developed abdominal cancer. Albert Lewis asked his father, Richard, who had been living in Little Lea for some months, to move out. They needed the space for the nurses who would attend Flora. It was too much for Richard Lewis. He suffered a stroke in late March, and died the following month.

When it became clear that Flora was in terminal decline, Warnie was summoned home from school in England to be with his mother in her final weeks. Their mother's illness brought the Lewis brothers even closer together. One of the most touching photographs of this period shows Warnie and C. S. Lewis standing by their bicycles, outside Glenmachan House, close to Little Lea, early in August 1908. Lewis's world was about to change, drastically and irreversibly.

Flora died in her bed at home on 23 August 1908—Albert Lewis's forty-fifth birthday. The somewhat funereal quotation for that day on her bedroom calendar was from Shakespeare's *King Lear*: "Men must endure their going hence." For the rest of Albert Lewis's life, Warnie later discovered, the calendar remained open at that page.[34]

1.5 Lewis and Warnie with their bicycles in front of the Ewart family home, Glenmachan House, in August 1908.

Following the custom of the day, Lewis was obliged to view the dead body of his mother lying in an open coffin, the gruesome marks of her illness all too visible. It was a traumatic experience for him. "With my mother's death all settled happiness, all that was tranquil and reliable, disappeared from my life."[35]

In *The Magician's Nephew*, Digory Kirke's mother is lovingly described on her deathbed, in terms that seem to echo Lewis's haunting memories of Flora: "There she lay, as he had seen her lie so many other times, propped up on the pillows, with a thin, pale face that would make you cry to look at."[36] There is little doubt that this passage recalls Lewis's own distress at the death of his mother, especially the sight of her emaciated body in an open coffin. In allowing Digory's mother to be cured of her terminal illness by the magic apple from Narnia, Lewis seems to be healing his own deep emotional wounds with an imaginative balm, trying to deal with what really happened by imagining what might have happened.

While Lewis was clearly distressed at his mother's death, his memories of this dark period often focus more on its broader implications for his family. As Albert Lewis tried to come to terms with his wife's illness, he seems to have lost an awareness of the deeper needs of his sons. C. S. Lewis depicts this period as heralding the end of his family life, as the seeds of alienation were sown. Having lost his wife, Albert Lewis was in danger of losing his sons as well.[37] Two weeks after Flora's death, Albert's elder brother, Joseph, died. The Lewis family, it seemed, was in crisis. The father and his two sons were on their own. "It was sea and islands now; the great continent had sunk like Atlantis."[38]

This could have been a time for the rebuilding of paternal affection and rekindling of filial devotion. Nothing of the sort happened. That Albert's judgement failed him at this critical time is made abundantly clear in his decision concerning the future of his sons at this crisis in their young lives. A mere two weeks after the traumatic death of his mother, C. S. Lewis found himself standing on the Belfast quayside with Warnie, preparing to board the overnight steamer to the Lancashire port of Fleetwood. An emotionally unintelligent father bade his emotionally neglected sons an emotionally inadequate farewell. Everything that gave the young Lewis his security and identity seemed to be vanishing around him. Lewis was being sent away from Ireland—from his home and from his books—to a strange place where he would live among strangers, with his brother, Warnie, as his only companion. He was being sent to Wynyard School—the "Belsen" of *Surprised by Joy*.

THE UGLY COUNTRY
OF ENGLAND: SCHOOLDAYS

In 1962, Francine Smithline—a schoolgirl from New York—wrote to C. S. Lewis, telling him how much she had enjoyed his *Narnia* books and asking him for information about his own schooldays. In reply, Lewis informed her that he had attended three boarding schools, "of which two were very horrid."[1] In fact, Lewis continues, he "never hated anything as much, not even the front line trenches in World War I." Even the most casual reader of *Surprised by Joy* is struck by both the vehemence of Lewis's hatred for the schools he attended in England and the implausibility that they were worse than the death-laden trenches of the Great War.

One of the significant sources of tension between C. S. Lewis and his brother in the late 1950s was Warnie's belief that Lewis had significantly misrepresented his time at Malvern College in *Surprised by Joy* (1955). George Sayer (1914–2005), a close friend who penned one of the most revealing and perceptive biographies of Lewis, recalls Lewis admitting later in life that his account of his time at Malvern was "lies," reflecting the complex interaction of two strands of his identity at that time.[2] Sayer's recollection leaves readers of *Surprised by Joy* wondering about both the extent and motivation of Lewis's reconstruction of his past.

Perhaps Lewis's judgement here may have been clouded by his overwhelmingly negative initial impressions of England, which spilled over into his educational experience. As he later remarked, he "conceived a hatred for England which took many years to heal."[3] His aversion to English schools possibly reflects a deeper cultural dislike of England itself at this time, evident in some of his correspondence. In June 1914, for example, Lewis complained about being "cooped up in this hot, ugly country of England" when he could have been roaming the cool, lush countryside of County Down.[4]

Yet there is clearly something deeper and more visceral here. Lewis simply does not seem to have fitted in to the public school culture of the Edwardian Age. What others saw as a necessary, if occasionally distasteful, preparation for the rigours of life in the real world was dismissed and vilified by Lewis as a "concentration camp." What his father hoped would make him into a successful citizen came close to breaking him instead.

Lewis's experience of British schools, following the death of his mother, can be summarised as follows:

Wynyard School, Watford ("Belsen"): September 1908–June 1910
Campbell College, Belfast: September–December 1910
Cherbourg School, Malvern ("Chartres"): January 1911–June 1913
Malvern College ("Wyvern"): September 1913–March 1914
Private tuition at Great Bookham: September 1914–June 1917

The three English schools to which Lewis took exception are presumably those he chose to identify by pseudonyms: Wynyard School, Cherbourg School, and Malvern College. As we shall see, his memories of his time at Great Bookham were much more positive, as was his view of its impact on the shaping of his mind.

WYNYARD SCHOOL, WATFORD: 1908–1910

Lewis's first educational experience in England was at Wynyard School, a converted pair of dreary yellow-brick houses on Langley Road, Watford. This small private boarding school had been established by Robert "Oldie" Capron in 1881, and appears to have enjoyed some small success in its early years. By the time Lewis arrived, however, it had fallen on hard times, having only about eight or nine boarders, and about the same number of "day-boys." His brother had already studied there for two years, and had adjusted to its brutal regime with relative ease. Lewis, with little experience of the world outside the gentle cocoon of Little Lea, was shocked by Capron's brutality, and later dubbed the school "Belsen" after the infamous Nazi concentration camp.

While initially hoping that things would work out well, Lewis rapidly came to hate Wynyard, and regarded his period there as an almost total waste of time. Warnie left Wynyard in the summer of 1909 and went on to Malvern College, leaving his younger brother alone to cope with an institution that was clearly in terminal decline. Lewis recalled his education at Wynyard as the forced feeding and rote learning of "a jungle of dates, battles, exports, imports and the like, forgotten as soon as learned and perfectly useless had they been remembered."[5] Warnie concurred in this judgement: "I cannot remember one single piece of instruction that was imparted to me at Wynyard."[6] Nor was there any library by which Lewis might nourish the imaginative side of his life. In the end, the school was closed down in the summer of 1910 when Capron was finally certified as being insane.

Albert Lewis was now forced to review his arrangements for his younger son's education. While Warnie went off to resume his education at Malvern College, Lewis was sent to Campbell College, a boarding school in the city of Belfast, only a mile from Little Lea. As Lewis later remarked, Campbell had been founded to allow "Ulster boys all the advantages of a public-school education without the trouble of crossing the Irish Sea."[7] It is not clear whether his father intended this to be a permanent arrangement. In the event, Lewis developed a serious respiratory

27

illness while at Campbell, and his father reluctantly withdrew him. It was not an unhappy time for Lewis. Indeed, Lewis seems to have wished that the arrangement could have been continued. His father, however, had other plans. Unfortunately, they turned out not to be very good.

CHERBOURG SCHOOL, MALVERN: 1911–1913

After further consultation with Gabbitas & Thring, Lewis was sent to Cherbourg School ("Chartres" in *Surprised by Joy*) in the English Victorian spa town of Great Malvern.[8] During the nineteenth century, Malvern became popular as a hydrotherapy spa on account of its spring waters. As spa tourism declined towards the end of the century, many former hotels and villas were converted to small boarding schools, such as Cherbourg. This small preparatory school, which had about twenty boys between the ages of eight and twelve during Lewis's time, was located next to Malvern College, where Warnie was already ensconced as a student. The two brothers would at least be able to see each other once more.

The most important outcome of Lewis's time at Cherbourg was that he won a scholarship to Malvern College. Yet Lewis recalls a number of developments in his inner life to which his schooling at Cherbourg was essentially a backdrop, rather than a cause or stimulus. One of the most important was his discovery of what he termed "Northernness," which took place "fairly early" during his time at Cherbourg. Lewis regarded this discovery as utterly and gloriously transformative, comparable to a silent and barren Arctic icescape turning into "a landscape of grass and primroses and orchards in bloom, deafened with bird songs and astir with running water."[9]

Lewis's recollections of this development are as imaginatively precise as they are chronologically vague. "I can lay my hand on the very moment; there is hardly any fact I know so well, though I cannot date it."[10] The stimulus was a "literary periodical" which had been left lying around in the schoolroom. This can be identified as the Christmas edition of *The Bookman*, published in December 1911. This magazine included a coloured supplement reproducing some of Arthur Rackham's suite of thirty illustrations to an English translation by Margaret Armour of the libretto of Richard Wagner's operas *Siegfried* and *The Twilight of the Gods*, which had been published earlier that year.[11]

Rackham's highly evocative illustrations proved to be a powerful imaginative stimulus to Lewis, causing him to be overwhelmed by an experience of desire. He was engulfed by "pure 'Northernness'"—by "a vision of huge, clear spaces hanging above the Atlantic in the endless twilight of Northern summer."[12] Lewis was thrilled to be able to experience again something that he had believed he had permanently lost. This was no "wish fulfilment and fantasy";[13] this was a vision of standing on the threshold of another world, and peering within. Hoping to recapture something of this sense of wonder, Lewis indulged his growing passion in Wagner, spending his pocket money on recordings of Wagner's operas, and even managing to buy a copy of the original text from which the Rackham illustrations had been extracted.

Although Lewis's letters of his Malvern period probably conceal as much as they reveal, they nevertheless hint of some of the themes that would recur throughout his career. One of those is Lewis's sense of being an Irishman in exile in a strange land. Lewis had not simply lost his paradise; he had been expelled from his Eden. Lewis might live in England; he did not, however, see himself as English. Even in his final days at Cherbourg, Lewis had become increasingly aware of having been "born in a race rich in literary feeling and mastery of their own tongue."[14] In the 1930s, Lewis found the physical geography of his native Ireland to be a stimulus to his own literary imagination, and that of others—such as the poet Edmund Spenser. The seeds of this development can be seen in his letters home in 1913.

A significant intellectual development which Lewis attributes to this period in his life was his explicit loss of any remnants of a Christian faith. Lewis's account of this final erosion of faith in *Surprised by Joy* is less satisfactory than one might like, particularly given the importance of faith in his later life. While unable to give "an accurate chronology" of his "slow apostasy," Lewis nevertheless identifies a number of factors that moved him in that direction.

Perhaps the most important of these, as judged by its lingering presence in his subsequent writings, was raised by his reading of Virgil and other classical authors. Lewis noted that their religious ideas were treated by both scholars and teachers as "sheer illusion." So what of today's religious ideas? Were they not simply *modern* illusions, the contemporary counterpart to their ancient forebears? Lewis came to the view that religion, though "utterly false," was a natural development, "a kind of endemic nonsense into which humanity tended to blunder."[15] Christianity was just one of a thousand religions, all claiming to be true. So why should he believe this one to be right, and the others wrong?

By the spring of 1913, Lewis had decided where he wished to go after Cherbourg. In a letter to his father of June 1913, he declares his time at Cherbourg—though initially something of a "leap in the dark"—to have been a "success."[16] He liked Great Malvern as a town, and would like to proceed to "the Coll."—in other words, to Malvern College, where he could join his older brother, Warnie. In late May, Warnie announced that he wanted to pursue a military career, and would spend the autumn of 1913 at Malvern College, preparing for the entrance examination at the Royal Military College at Sandhurst.

However, things did not work out quite as expected. In June, Lewis won a scholarship to Malvern College beginning in September, despite being ill and having to take the examination in Cherbourg's sickroom. But Warnie would no longer be there. He had been asked to leave by the headmaster after being caught smoking on school premises. (Both Lewis brothers had developed their lifelong habit of smoking by this stage.) Albert Lewis now had to work out how to prepare Warnie for the Sandhurst entrance examinations without any assistance from the masters of Malvern College. He found an answer—a brilliant answer, that would have significant and positive implications for his younger son a year later.

Albert Lewis had been a pupil at Lurgan College in Ireland's County Armagh from 1877–1879, and had developed a great respect for his former headmaster, William Thompson Kirkpatrick (1848–1921).[17] Kirkpatrick had arrived at Lurgan College in 1876, at which time it had only sixteen pupils. A decade later, it was regarded as one of the premier schools in Ireland. Kirkpatrick retired in 1899, and moved with his wife to Sharston House in Northenden, Cheshire, to be near their son, George, who was then working for Browett, Lindley & Co., Engine Makers of Patricroft, Manchester. However, it seems that Kirkpatrick's wife had little enthusiasm for the industrialised Northwest of England, and the couple soon moved to Great Bookham in the "Stockbroker Belt" of the southern county of Surrey, where Kirkpatrick set himself up as a private tutor.

Albert Lewis acted as Kirkpatrick's solicitor, and the two had occasion to correspond over what should be done with parents who refused to pay their sons' school fees. Albert Lewis had asked Kirkpatrick's advice on educational matters in the past, and he now asked for something more specific and personal: would Kirkpatrick prepare Warnie for the entrance examination to Sandhurst? The deal was done, and Warnie began his studies at Great Bookham on 10 September 1913. Eight days later, his younger brother started at Malvern College—the "Wyvern" of *Surprised by Joy*—without his older brother as his mentor and friend. Lewis was on his own.

MALVERN COLLEGE: 1913-1914

Lewis presents Malvern College as a disaster. *Surprised by Joy* devotes three of its fifteen chapters to railing against his experiences at "the Coll," faulting it at point after point. Yet this accumulation of Lewis's vivid and harsh memories curiously fails to advance his narrative of the pursuit of Joy. Why spend so much time recounting such painful and subjective memories, which others who knew the college at that time (including Warnie) criticised as distorted and unrepresentative? Perhaps Lewis saw the writing of these sections of *Surprised by Joy* as a cathartic exercise, allowing him to purge his painful memories by writing about them at greater length than required. Yet even a sympathetic reader of this work cannot fail to see that the pace of the book slackens in the three chapters devoted to Malvern, where the narrative detail obscures the plotline.[18]

2.1 William Thompson Kirkpatrick (1848–1921), at his home in Great Bookham in 1920, photographed by Warren Lewis during his visit when on leave from the British army. This is the only known photograph of Kirkpatrick.

Lewis declares that he became a victim of the "fagging" system, by which younger pupils were expected to act as errand boys for the older pupils (the "Bloods"). The more a boy was disliked by his peers and elders, the more he would be picked on and exploited in this way. This was customary in English public schools of this age. What most boys accepted as part of a traditional initiation rite into adulthood was seen by Lewis as a form of forced labour. Lewis suggested that the forms of service that younger boys were expected to provide to their seniors were rumoured (but never proved) to include sexual favours—something which Lewis found horrifying.

Perhaps more significantly, Lewis found himself excluded from the value system of Malvern College, which was heavily influenced by the then dominant educational philosophy of the English public school system—athleticism.[19] By the end of the Edwardian era, the "games cult" had assumed an almost unassailable position as the centrepiece of an English public school education. Athleticism was an ideology with a darker side. Boys who were not good at games were ridiculed and bullied by their peers. Athleticism devalued intellectual and artistic achievement and turned many schools into little more than training camps for the glorification of physicality. Yet the cultivation of "manliness" was seen as integral to the development of "character"—an essential trait that dominated the educational theories of this period in British culture.[20] In all these respects, Malvern was typical of the Edwardian age. It provided what it believed was needed, and what parents clearly wanted.

But it was not what *Lewis* wanted. His "native clumsiness," partly arising from having only one joint in his thumbs, made excelling in anything physical a total impossibility.[21] Lewis seems to have made little attempt to fit into the school's culture. His refusal to conform simply created the impression that Lewis was socially withdrawn and academically arrogant. As Lewis wryly remarked in a letter, Malvern helped him discover what he did *not* want to be: "If I had never seen the horrible spectacle which these coarse, brainless English schoolboys present, there might be a danger of my sometimes becoming like that myself."[22] To many, these remarks simply sound arrogant and condescending. Yet Lewis was clear that one of Malvern's relatively few positive achievements was to help him realise that he *was* arrogant.[23] It was an aspect of his character that he would have to deal with in the coming years.

Lewis frequently sought refuge in the school library, finding solace in books. He also developed a friendship with the classics master, Harry Wakelyn Smith ("Smewgy"). Smith worked with Lewis on his Latin and helped him begin his serious study of Greek. Perhaps more important, he taught Lewis how to analyse poetry properly, allowing its aesthetic qualities to be appreciated. Furthermore, he helped Lewis realise that poetry was to be read in such a way that its rhythm and musical qualities could be appreciated. Lewis later expressed his gratitude in a poem explaining how Smith—an "old man with a honey-sweet and singing voice"—taught him to love the "Mediterranean metres" of classical poetry.[24]

Important though such positive encounters may have been for Lewis's later scholarly and critical development, at the time they were ultimately intellectual diversions, designed to take Lewis's mind off what he regarded as an insufferable school culture. Warnie took the view that his brother was simply a "square peg in a round hole." With the benefit of hindsight, he believed that Lewis ought not to have been sent to a public school at all. Lewis's lack of athletic prowess and his strong intellectual leanings immediately identified him as a "misfit, a heretic, an object of suspicion within the collective-minded and standardizing Public School system."[25] But at the time, Warnie was clear that the fault, if fault there were, lay in Lewis himself, not in the school.

It remains unclear why Lewis spends so much of *Surprised by Joy* dealing with his time at Malvern. It is true that he was invited to be a governor of the college in 1929, an invitation which caused him some amusement.[26] Yet there is no doubt of Lewis's despair at the time concerning his circumstances there, and his desperate attempts to persuade his father to move him to a more congenial place. "Please take me out of this as soon as possible," he wrote imploringly to his father in March 1914, as he prepared to return to Belfast for the school holidays.[27]

Albert Lewis finally realised things were not working out for his younger son. He consulted with Warnie, who was by then in his second month of training as a British army officer at Sandhurst. Warnie took the view that his younger brother had contributed significantly to his own deteriorating situation. He had hoped, he told his father, that Malvern would provide his brother with the same "happy years and memories and friendships that he would carry with him to the grave." But it hadn't worked out like that. Lewis had made Malvern "too hot to hold him."[28] A radical rethink was required. Since Warnie had benefitted from personal tuition from Kirkpatrick, Lewis should be offered the same. It is not difficult to discern Warnie's irritation with his brother when he tells his father that "he could amuse himself by detonating his cheap little stock of intellectual fireworks under old K[irkpatrick]'s nose."[29]

Albert Lewis then wrote to Kirkpatrick, asking him for his advice. Kirkpatrick initially suggested that Lewis should resume his studies at Campbell College. But as the two men wrestled with the problem, another solution began to emerge. Albert persuaded Kirkpatrick to become Lewis's personal tutor effective September 1914. Kirkpatrick professed himself overwhelmed by this compliment: "To have been the teacher of the father and his two sons is surely a unique experience." It was still risky. Warnie had loved Malvern, yet Lewis had detested it. What would Lewis make of Kirkpatrick, who had been so good for Warnie? Kirkpatrick's efforts had led to Warnie's being ranked twenty-second out of more than two hundred successful candidates in the highly competitive entrance examination. Warnie's military record shows that he entered Sandhurst on 4 February 1914 as a "Gentleman Cadet," being awarded a "Prize Cadetship with emoluments." His military career was off to a flying start.

Meanwhile, Lewis had returned home to Belfast for the vacation. In mid-April 1914, shortly before he was due to return for his final term at Malvern College, he received a message. Arthur Greeves (1895–1966) was in bed recovering from an illness and would welcome a visit. Greeves, who was the same age as Warnie, was the youngest son of Joseph Greeves, one of Belfast's most wealthy flax-spinners. The family lived at "Bernagh," a large house just over the road from Little Lea.

2.2 A tennis party at Glenmachan House, the Ewart family home, close to Little Lea, in the summer of 1910. Arthur Greeves is on the far left in the back row, with C. S. Lewis to the far right. Lily Greeves, Arthur's sister, is seated second from the right, in front of Lewis

In *Surprised by Joy*, Lewis recalls that Greeves had been trying to initiate a friendship with him for some time, but that they had never met.[30] Yet there is evidence that Lewis's memory may not be entirely correct here. In one of his earliest surviving letters of May 1907, Lewis informed Warnie that a telephone had just been installed at Little Lea. He had used this new piece of technology to call Arthur Greeves, but had not been able to speak to him.[31] This hints at a childhood acquaintance of some sort. If Lewis and Greeves had been friends around this time, it seems likely that Lewis's enforced absence from Belfast at English schools had caused the existing relationship to wither.

Lewis agreed to visit Greeves with some reluctance. He found him sitting up in bed, with a book beside him: H. M. A. Guerber's *Myths of the Norsemen* (1908). Lewis, whose love of "Northernness" now knew few bounds, looked at the book in astonishment: "Do *you* like that?" he asked— only to receive the same excited reply from Greeves.[32] Lewis had finally found a soul mate. They would remain in touch regularly until Lewis's death, nearly fifty years later.

As his final term at Malvern drew to an end, Lewis wrote his first letter to Greeves, planning a walk together. Though he was "cooped up" in the "hot, ugly country of England," they could watch the sun rise over the Holywood Hills and see Belfast Lough and Cave Hill.[33] Yet a month later, Lewis's view of England had changed. "Smewgy" had invited him and another boy to drive into the country, leaving behind the "flat, plain, and ugly hills of Malvern." In their place, Lewis discovered an "enchanted ground" of "rolling hills and valleys," with "mysterious woods and cornfields."[34] Perhaps England was not so bad; maybe he might stay there after all.

BOOKHAM AND THE "GREAT KNOCK": 1914–1917

On 19 September 1914, Lewis arrived at Great Bookham to begin his studies with Kirkpatrick—the "Great Knock." Yet the world around Lewis had changed irreversibly since he had left Malvern. On 28 June, Archduke Franz Ferdinand of Austria was assassinated in Sarajevo, creating ripples of tension and instability which gradually escalated. Grand alliances were formed. If one great nation went to war, all would follow. A month later, on 28 July, Austria launched an attack against Serbia. Germany immediately launched an attack against France. It was inevitable that Britain would be drawn into the conflict. Britain eventually declared war against Germany and the Austro-Hungarian Empire on 4 August.

It was Warnie who was affected most immediately by this development. His period of training was reduced from eighteen months to nine, to allow him to enter active military service as soon as possible. He was commissioned as a second lieutenant in the Royal Army Service Corps on 29 September 1914, and was on active service in France with the British Expeditionary Force by 4 November. Meanwhile, Lord Kitchener (1850–1916), Secretary of State for War, set out to organise the recruitment of the largest volunteer army that the nation had ever seen. His famous recruiting poster declaring "Your country needs you!" became one of the most familiar images of the war. Lewis could hardly have failed to feel this pressure to enlist.

2.3 "Your country needs you!" The front cover of the magazine *London Opinion*, published on 5 September 1914, shortly after Britain's declaration of war. This image of Lord Kitchener, designed by the artist Alfred Leete (1882–1933), quickly achieved iconic significance, and featured prominently in British military recruitment campaigns from 1915 onwards.

While England lurched into a state of war for which it was not properly prepared, Lewis was settling in at Kirkpatrick's house, "Gastons," in Great Bookham. His relationship with Kirkpatrick would be of central importance, especially since his relationships with both his brother and father were by now somewhat strained and distant. Lewis travelled by steamer from Belfast to Liverpool, then by train to London. There he picked up a train from Waterloo Station to Great Bookham, where Kirkpatrick awaited him. As they walked together from the station to Kirkpatrick's house, Lewis remarked casually, as a way of breaking the conversational ice, that the scenery in Surrey was somewhat wilder than he had anticipated.

2.4   Station Road, Great Bookham, in 1924. C. S. Lewis and Kirkpatrick would have walked along this road on their way from the railway station to Kirkpatrick's home, Gastons.

Lewis had intended merely to begin a conversation; Kirkpatrick seized the opportunity to begin an aggressive, interactive discussion demonstrating the virtues of the Socratic method. Kirkpatrick demanded that he stop immediately. What did Lewis mean by "wildness," and what grounds had he for not expecting it? Had he studied some maps of the area? Had he read some books about it? Had he seen photographs of the landscape? Lewis conceded he had done none of these things. His views were not based on anything. Kirkpatrick duly informed him that he had no right to have any opinion on this matter.

Some would have found this approach intimidating; others might think it to lack good manners or pastoral concern. Yet Lewis quickly realised that he was being forced to develop his critical thinking, based on evidence and reason rather than his personal intuitions. This approach was, he remarked, like "red beef and strong beer."[35] Lewis thrived on this diet of critical thinking.

Kirkpatrick was a remarkable man, and must be given credit for much of Lewis's intellectual development, particularly in fostering a highly critical approach to ideas and sources.[36] Kirkpatrick had a distinguished academic career at Queen's College, Belfast, from which he graduated in July 1868 with First Class Honours in English, History, and Metaphysics.[37] In his final year at Queen's College, he had won the English Prize Essay under the nom de plume Tamerlaine. He was also awarded a Double Gold Medal by the Royal University of Ireland, the only student to gain this distinction that year. He applied unsuccessfully for the position of headmaster of Lurgan College when the college opened in 1873. There were twenty-two applications for the prestigious position. In the end, the school's governors had to choose between Kirkpatrick and E. Vaughan Boulger of Dublin. They chose Boulger.

Undeterred, Kirkpatrick looked elsewhere for employment. He was seriously considered for the Chair of English at University College, Cork. His opportunity came, however, late in 1875, when Boulger was appointed to the Chair of Greek at University College, Cork. Kirkpatrick applied again for headmaster of Lurgan College, and was appointed to the position effective 1 January 1876. His ability to encourage and inspire his students became the substance of legend. Albert Lewis may have made many mistakes in arranging for his younger son's education in England. But his biggest decision—based on his own judgement, rather than the flawed professional advice of Gabbitas & Thring—turned out to be his best.

Lewis's highly condensed summary of his most significant tutors merits consideration: "Smewgy taught me Grammar and Rhetoric and Kirk taught me Dialectic."[38] For Lewis, he was gradually learning how to use words and develop arguments. Yet Kirkpatrick's influence was not limited to Lewis's dialectical skills. The old headmaster forced Lewis to learn languages, living and dead, by the simple expedient of making him use them. Two days after Lewis's arrival, Kirkpatrick sat down with him and opened a copy of Homer's *Iliad* in the original Greek. He read aloud the first twenty lines in a Belfast accent (which might have puzzled Homer), offered a translation, and invited Lewis to continue. Before long, Lewis was confident enough to read fluently in the original language. Kirkpatrick extended the approach, first to Latin, and then to living languages, including German and Italian.

To some, such educational methods will seem archaic, even ridiculous. For many students, they would have resulted in humiliating failure and loss of confidence. Lewis, however, saw them as a challenge, causing him to set his sights higher and raise his game. It was precisely the educational method that was best adapted to his abilities and his needs. In one of his most famous sermons, "The Weight of Glory" (1941), Lewis asks us to imagine a young boy who learned Greek in order to experience the joy of studying Sophocles. Lewis was that young boy, and Kirkpatrick was his teacher. In February 1917, Lewis wrote with great excitement to his father, telling him that he had been able to read the first two hundred lines of Dante's *Inferno* in the original Italian "with much success."[39]

Yet there were other outcomes of Kirkpatrick's rationalism that Lewis was less keen to share with his father. One of them was his increasing commitment to atheism. Lewis was clear that his atheism was "fully formed" before he went to Bookham; Kirkpatrick's contribution was to provide him with additional arguments for his position. In December 1914, Lewis was confirmed at St. Mark's, Dundela, the church where he had been baptised in January 1899. His relationship with his father was so poor that he felt unable to tell him that he did not wish to go through with the service, having ceased to believe in God. Lewis later used Kirkpatrick as the model for the character of MacPhee, who appears in *That Hideous Strength*—an articulate, intelligent, and highly opinionated Scots-Irishman, with distinctly skeptical views on matters of religious belief.

Was Lewis inclined to agree with Kirkpatrick on this matter? The only person to whom Lewis appears to have felt able to open his heart regarding his religious beliefs was Arthur Greeves, who had by now completely displaced Warnie as Lewis's soul mate and confidant. In October 1916, Lewis provided Greeves with a full statement of his (lack of) religious beliefs. "I believe in no religion." All religions, he wrote, are simply mythologies invented by human beings, usually in response to natural events or emotional needs. This, he declared, "is the recognised scientific account of the growth of religions." Religion was irrelevant to questions of morality.[40]

This letter stimulated an intense debate with Greeves, who was then both a committed and reflective Christian. They exchanged at least six letters on the topic in a period of less than a month, before declaring that their views were so far apart that there was little point in continuing the discussion. Lewis later recalled that he "bombarded [Greeves] with all the thin artillery of a seventeen year old rationalist"[41]—but to little effect. For Lewis, there was simply no good reason to believe in God. No intelligent person would want to believe in "a bogey who is prepared to torture me for ever and ever."[42] The rational case for religion was, in Lewis's view, totally bankrupt.

Yet Lewis found his imagination and reason pulling him in totally different directions. He continued to find himself experiencing deep feelings of desire, to which he had attached the name "Joy." The most important of these took place early in March 1916, when he happened to pick up a copy of George MacDonald's fantasy novel *Phantastes*.[43] As he read, without realising it, Lewis was led across a frontier of the imagination. Everything was changed for him as a result of reading the book. He had discovered a "new quality," a "bright shadow," which seemed to him like a voice calling him from the ends of the earth. "That night my imagination was, in a certain sense, baptized."[44] A new dimension to his life began to emerge. "I had not the faintest notion what I had let myself in for by buying *Phantastes*." It would be some time before Lewis made a connection between MacDonald's Christianity and his works of imagination. Yet a seed had been planted, and it was only a matter of time before it began to germinate.

THE THREAT OF CONSCRIPTION

A somewhat darker shadow was falling on Lewis's life, as it was on so many others. The ravages of the first year of war meant that the British army required more recruits—more than could be secured by voluntary enlistment. In May 1915, Lewis wrote to his father, outlining how he then saw his situation. He would just have to hope that the war would come to an end before he was eighteen, or that he would be able to volunteer before he was forcibly conscripted.[45] As time passed, Lewis came to realise that he probably would be going to war. It was just a matter of time. The war showed no sign of an early victory, and Lewis's eighteenth birthday was fast approaching.

On 27 January 1916, the Military Service Act came into force, ending voluntary enlistment. All men aged between eighteen and forty-one were deemed to have enlisted with effect from 2 March 1916, and would be called up as needed. However, the provisions of the Act did not apply to Ireland, and it included an important exemption: all men of this age who were "resident in Britain only for the purpose of their education" were exempt from its provisions. Yet Lewis was aware that this exemption might only be temporary. His correspondence suggests he came to the conclusion that his military service was inevitable.

Shortly after the March deadline, Lewis wrote to Greeves, borrowing Shakespeare's imagery from the prologue to *Henry V*: "In November comes my 18th birthday, military age, and the 'vasty fields' of France, which I have no ambition to face."[46] In July, Lewis received a letter from Donald Hardman, who had shared a study with him at Malvern College. Hardman informed Lewis that he was to be conscripted at Christmas.

What, he asked, was happening to Lewis? Lewis replied that he didn't yet know. Yet in a letter to Kirkpatrick dated May 1916, Albert Lewis declared that Lewis had already made the decision to serve voluntarily—but wanted to try to get into Oxford first.[47]

But events in Ireland opened up another possibility for Lewis. In April 1916, Ireland was convulsed with the news of the Easter Rising—an uprising in Dublin organised by the Military Council of the Irish Republican Brotherhood, aimed at ending British rule in Ireland and establishing an independent Irish Republic. The Easter Rising lasted from 24 to 30 April 1916. It was suppressed by the British army after seven days of fighting, and its leaders were court-martialled and executed. It was now clear that more troops would need to be sent to Ireland to maintain order. Might Lewis be sent to Ireland, rather than France, if he enlisted?

Meanwhile, Kirkpatrick had been pondering Lewis's future. Taking his role as Lewis's mentor very seriously, Kirkpatrick reflected on what he had discovered about his charge's character and ability. He wrote to Albert Lewis expressing his view that Lewis had been born with a "literary temperament," and showed a remarkable maturity in his literary judgements. He was clearly destined for a significant career. However, lacking any serious competency in science or mathematics, he might have difficulty in getting into Sandhurst. Kirkpatrick's personal opinion was that Lewis should take up a legal career. Yet Lewis had no interest in following his father's footsteps. He had set his sights on Oxford. He would try for a place at New College, Oxford University, to study classics.

LEWIS'S APPLICATION TO OXFORD UNIVERSITY

It is not clear why Lewis chose Oxford University in general, or New College in particular. Neither Kirkpatrick nor any of Lewis's family had connections with either the university or the college. Lewis's concerns about conscription had eased by this stage, and no longer preoccupied him as they once had. At Kirkpatrick's suggestion, Lewis had consulted a solicitor about the complexities of the Military Service Act. The solicitor had advised him to write to the chief recruiting officer for the local area, based in Guildford. On 1 December, he wrote to his father to tell him that he was formally exempt from the Act, provided he register immediately. Lewis wasted no time in complying with this requirement.

On 4 December 1916, the matter of conscription having been resolved, Lewis travelled to Oxford to sit for the college entrance examinations. Confused by the directions he had been given, he took the wrong exit on leaving the railway station and ended up in the Oxford suburb of Botley. Only when he saw the open countryside ahead of him did he turn back and finally catch a glimpse of "the fabled cluster of spires and towers."[48] (The image of taking a wrong turn in life would remain with him.) He returned to the railway station and took a hansom cab to a guest house run by a Mrs. Etheridge at 1 Mansfield Road, just across the street from New College. There, he shared a sitting room with another hopeful candidate.

The next morning, it snowed. The entrance examinations took place in the Hall of Oriel College. Even during daylight hours, Oriel Hall was so cold that Lewis and his fellow candidates wrapped up in greatcoats and scarves, some even wearing gloves as they wrote their answers to the exam questions. Lewis had been so engrossed in his preparations that he had forgotten to tell his father exactly when they were taking place. He found time to write to him halfway through the exams, telling him of his delight in Oxford: it "has surpassed my wildest dreams: I never saw anything so beautiful, especially on these frosty moonlight nights."[49] After completing the examinations, Lewis returned to Belfast on 11 December, telling his father that he believed he had failed to gain a place.

He was right—but only partially so. He had failed to gain a place at New College. But his examination papers had impressed the dons at another college. Two days later, Lewis received a letter from Reginald Macan (1848–1941), the master of University College, informing him that, since New College had decided not to offer him a place, he had been elected to a scholarship at University College instead. Would he get in touch to confirm the arrangements? Lewis's joy knew no bounds.

Yet there was a cloud in the sky. Shortly afterwards, Macan wrote again to Lewis, making it clear that the changing situation concerning conscription would now make it a "moral impossibility" for any fit man over the age of eighteen to pursue studies at Oxford. Everyone in that category was now expected to enlist in the forces. Albert Lewis was anxious. If his younger son did not voluntarily enlist, he might be conscripted—and that would mean becoming a private soldier, rather than being an officer. What should they do?

In January 1917, Lewis returned to Oxford to discuss the situation further with Macan. Afterwards, he wrote to his father. A solution to their difficulty seemed to have been found. Lewis's best chance of securing an officer's commission in the British army was to join the Oxford University Officers' Training Corps and apply for a commission on the basis of this training.[50] Officers' Training Corps had been established at Oxford and other leading British universities in 1908 as a means of providing "a standardized degree of elementary military training with a view to providing candidates for commissions" in the British army. By joining the Officers' Training Corps immediately on his arrival at Oxford, Lewis would be fast-tracked towards an officer's commission.

Yet only members of Oxford University could join the university's Officers' Training Corps. The admission process to Oxford University at this time involved two stages. First, a candidate had to secure a place at one of Oxford's colleges. Lewis, having failed to gain a position at New College, had been awarded a scholarship to University College. This element of the process was thus completed. Yet admission to an Oxford college did not automatically mean acceptance by Oxford University. In order to ensure uniformly high standards across the colleges, the university authorities required new students to pass an additional examination—known as "Responsions"—in order to ensure they met its fundamental requirements.[51] Unfortunately for Lewis, Responsions included a paper in basic mathematics—a subject in which he had virtually no talent.

Once more, Albert Lewis decided to draw on Kirkpatrick's experience. If Kirkpatrick could help Lewis learn ancient Greek, surely he could teach him elementary mathematics. So Lewis returned to Great Bookham to complete his education. On 20 March, Lewis went back to Oxford to sit for this additional examination in the expectation that his military career would begin shortly afterwards. He then received a letter from University College informing him he could begin his studies on 26 April. The door to Oxford had been opened. But only partially.

Before Lewis would be able to complete his studies at Oxford, he would first have to go to war.

THE VASTY
FIELDS OF FRANCE: WAR

The French emperor Napoleon Bonaparte (1769–1821) once quipped that the best way of making sense of people is to find out what was happening in the world when they were twenty years old. A few weeks before 29 November 1918—the day that Lewis turned twenty—the Great War finally came to an end. Many felt guilty for surviving while their comrades had fallen. Those who served in trench warfare were permanently marked by the violence, destruction, and horrors they had experienced. Lewis's twentieth year was shaped by his firsthand experience of armed conflict. He arrived in the trenches near Arras in northwestern France on his nineteenth birthday, and on his twentieth was still recuperating from the war wounds he had suffered.

THE CURIOUS CASE OF THE UNIMPORTANT WAR

If Napoleon was right, Lewis's world of thought and experience would have been irreparably and irreversibly shaped by war, trauma, and loss. We might therefore expect Lewis's inner being to be deeply moulded by the impact of conflict and close brushes with death. Yet Lewis himself tells us otherwise. His experience of war was, he informs us, "in a way unimportant." He seemed to view his experience at English boarding schools as much more unpleasant than the time he spent in the trenches of France.[1]

While Lewis served on the battlefields of France in 1917 and 1918, experiencing the horrors of modern warfare, *Surprised by Joy* makes only scant reference to it. Lewis clearly believed that his woes during his year at Malvern College were of greater importance than his entire wartime experience—and, even then, seems to prefer to concentrate his narrative on the books he read and people he met. The unspeakable suffering and devastation around him had been filtered out. It had, Lewis tells us, been more than adequately written about by other people; he had nothing to add to it.[2] His voluminous later writings make little mention of the war.

Some readers will feel there is a certain sense of imbalance and disproportion here. Why did Lewis spend three chapters of *Surprised by Joy* detailing his relatively minor woes at Malvern College and pay so little attention to the vastly more significant violence, trauma, and horror of the Great War? This sense of imbalance is only reinforced by a reading of Lewis's works as a whole, in which the Great War is largely passed over—or, when mentioned, is treated as something that happened to someone else. It is as if Lewis was seeking to distance or dissociate himself from his memories of conflict. Why?

The simplest explanation is also the most plausible: Lewis could not bear to remember the trauma of his wartime experiences, whose irrationality called into question whether there was any meaning in the universe at large or in Lewis's personal existence in particular. The literature concerning the Great War and its aftermath emphasises the physical and psychological damage it wreaked on soldiers at the time, and on their return home. Many students returning to study at Oxford University after the war experienced considerable difficulty adjusting to normal life, leading to frequent nervous breakdowns. Lewis appears to have "partitioned" or "compartmentalised" his life as a means of retaining his sanity. The potentially devastating memories of his trau-matic experiences were carefully controlled so that they had a minimal impact on other areas of his life. Literature—above all, poetry—was Lewis's firewall, keeping the chaotic and meaningless external world at a safe distance, and shielding him from the existential devastation it wreaked on others.

We can see this process in *Surprised by Joy*, where we find Lewis dis-tancing himself from the *prospect* of war. His thoughts about the future possibility of the horrors of conflict seem to mirror his later attitudes towards the past actuality.

> I put the war on one side to a degree which some people will
> think shameful and some incredible. Others will call it a flight
> from reality. I maintain that it was rather a treaty with reality, the
> fixing of a frontier. [3]

Lewis was prepared to allow his country to have his body—but not his mind. A border was fixed and patrolled in his mental world, which certain intrusive and disturbing thoughts were not permitted to cross. Lewis would not run away from reality. Instead, he would negotiate a "treaty" by which reality could be tamed, adapted, and constrained. It would be a "frontier" that certain thoughts would not be allowed to penetrate.

This "treaty with reality" would play a critical role in Lewis's develop-ment, and we shall have cause to consider it further in later chapters. Lewis's mental map of reality had difficulty accommodating the trauma of the Great War. Like so many, he found the settled way of looking at the world, taken for granted by many in the Edwardian age, to have been shattered by the most brutal and devastating war yet known. Lewis's immediate postwar years were dominated by a search for meaning—not simply in terms of finding personal fulfilment and stability, but in terms of making sense of both his inner and outer worlds in a way that satisfied his restless and probing mind.

ARRIVAL AT OXFORD: APRIL 1917

To make sense of Lewis's attitude towards the Great War, we must first explore how he went into battle. Having spent the first few months of 1917 at Great Bookham, trying (somewhat unsuccessfully, as it turned out) to master mathematics, Lewis went up to University College, Oxford, on 29 April. For the first time since the English Civil War, when Charles I had made his military headquarters in the city in 1643, Oxford had become a military camp. The University Parks were turned into a parade ground and training area for new recruits. Many of the younger dons and college servants had gone to war. Lectures, if given at all, were sparsely attended. The *Oxford University Gazette*, normally given over to announcements of lectures and University appointments, published depressingly long lists of the fallen. These black-bordered lists spoke ominously of the carnage of the conflict.

Having virtually no students by 1917, Oxford's colleges had to find ways of coping with a drastic reduction in their income. University College, normally bustling, had only a handful of students in residence.[4] In 1914, the college boasted 148 undergraduates in residence; this plummeted to seven in 1917. A rare group photograph of college members taken in Trinity Term 1917 shows only ten people. Under the emergency statutes introduced in May 1915, University College relieved seven of its nine tutorial fellows of their duties; there was little for them to do.

Faced with a collapse in student numbers, University College needed funds urgently. Its internal sources of income slumped from £8,755 in 1913 to £925 in 1918.[5] Like many other colleges, it came to depend on the War Office as a source of income. University College rented out college rooms and facilities for use as troop barracks and military hospitals. Other colleges provided accommodation for refugees from war-torn Europe, especially Belgium and Serbia.

At this stage, much of University College was given over to use as a military hospital. Lewis was allocated room 5 on staircase XII in Radcliffe Quad. While Lewis may have been physically present in an Oxford college, he cannot really be said to have begun his Oxford education at this time. There was hardly anyone available to tutor him, and few lectures were being given anywhere in the university. Lewis's early impressions of the college were dominated by its "vast solitude."[6] One evening in July 1917, he wandered through silent staircases and empty passages, marvelling at its "strange poetry."[7]

3.1 The undergraduates of University College, Trinity Term 1917. Lewis is standing on the right-hand side of the back row. The college don in the centre of the photograph is John Behan, Stowell Law Fellow from 1909–1918, whose contract of employment was "continued for the emergency period."

Lewis's main object in coming into residence in the summer term of 1917 was to join the Oxford University Officers' Training Corps.[8] He submitted his application on 25 April, before arriving in Oxford.[9] His application was accepted without difficulty five days later, this positive response partly reflecting the fact that Lewis had already served in the Combined Cadet Force at Malvern School.[10] The college dean refused to arrange any academic tuition for him, on the grounds that his courses with the Oxford University Officers' Training Corps would take up all his time. Undeterred, Lewis made a private arrangement to be taught algebra under John Edward Campbell (1862–1924) of Hertford College, who refused to accept any fee for his services.[11]

Why this sudden concern to become proficient at mathematics, not normally seen as relevant to the study of the life and thought of the classical world? The answer lies partly in Lewis's desire to pass Responsions, but mainly in Albert Lewis's essentially correct perception that his son would stand a much better chance of surviving the war if he were to become an artillery officer.[12] Much better to be bombarding the Germans from well behind the front lines than to engage in the lethal trench warfare that had already claimed so many lives. However, the Royal Artillery required a knowledge of mathematics on the part of its officers, especially trigonometry, that Lewis simply did not have at this stage. It soon became painfully clear to Lewis that he would never master this field. He gloomily informed his father that his "chances of getting into the gunners" were low, as they recruited only officers "who can be shown to have some special knowledge of mathematics."[13]

Lewis's brief time at University College made a deep impression on him. He shared some of his feelings and experiences with Arthur Greeves, and rather fewer of them with his father and brother. He wrote to Greeves about the delights of bathing "without the tiresome convention of bathing things," and the wonderfully atmospheric library of the Oxford Union Society. "I never was happier in my life."[14] He seems to have invented other experiences for his father's benefit, being particularly anxious to conceal his increasingly trenchant atheism. He wrote to Albert Lewis about church and churches, but did not actually attend them.

Lewis was left in no doubt that he was being trained for trench warfare. His letters to his father towards the end of his time with the Officers' Training Corps deal with the preparations for war in France, including his description of model trenches, complete with "dug outs, shell holes and—graves."[15] After appraising Lewis's record, Lieutenant G. H. Claypole, the adjutant of the Oxford University Officers' Training Corps, reported that Lewis was "likely to make a useful officer, but will not have had sufficient training for admission to an O[fficer] T[raining] U[unit] before the end of *June*. INFANTRY." Lewis's fate was sealed. He would be sent to an infantry unit—almost certainly to fight in the trenches of France.

THE OFFICER CADET AT KEBLE COLLEGE

The Great War ruined lives and shattered dreams, forcing many to abandon their hopes for the future in order to serve their country. Lewis is a classic example of the reluctant soldier—a young man with literary and scholarly ideals and ambitions, who found his life redirected and reshaped by forces over which he had no control, and which he ultimately could not resist. University College saw 770 students serve in the Great War; 175 of these were killed in battle. Even in his short time at University College in the summer of 1917, Lewis would have been aware of how many of the College's undergraduates had gone to war, never to return. The fate of so many is captured in the sombre lines of the 1916 poem "The Spires of Oxford," by Winifred Mary Letts (1882–1972):[16]

> *I saw the spires of Oxford*
> *As I was passing by,*
> *The grey spires of Oxford*
> *Against a pearl-grey sky;*
> *My heart was with the Oxford men*
> *Who went abroad to die.*

Lewis would train alongside other young men of ideals and ambition, many seeing their enforced wartime service as "doing their bit" for their country, hoping to pick up their lives and start all over again once the war was over. Space allows us to note only one such example—the adjutant of the Oxford University Officers' Training Corps, who fatefully recommended that Lewis serve in the infantry.

Gerald Henry Claypole (1894–1961) served as lieutenant in the 5th King's Royal Rifle Corps.[17] He resigned his commission on 8 February

1919 due to ill health. Jerry Claypole had a love of English literature, which eventually led him to become Senior English Master at King Edward VII School in Sheffield in 1941. He retired in 1958, and died in January 1961. His obituary in the school magazine commented on his strong belief "that literature was to be experienced and enjoyed, not to be made the subject of theorising and argument"—precisely the views that Lewis himself would later develop and champion.[18] It is highly likely that Claypole would have read some of Lewis's writings, not least his introduction to *Paradise Lost*. Would Claypole have realised that he had played such a significant role in the subsequent twistings and turnings of Lewis's life? We shall never know.

What we do know is that on 7 May 1917, Lewis began training as a potential infantry officer in the British army. He was now irreversibly committed to active military service. By a welcome quirk of fate, this did not mean leaving Oxford and transferring to one of the many training camps then scattered throughout Britain. Lewis was transferred from the Oxford University Officers' Training Corps and posted to E Company, No. 4 Officer Cadet Battalion, stationed at Keble College, Oxford.[19]

A "School of Instruction" for Oxford students who were potential officers was established in January 1915. Some three thousand officer cadets passed through the school.[20] In February 1916, with the needs of the war effort in mind, the British army altered its regulations concerning officer cadets. Potential officers would have to be trained at an Officer Cadet Battalion. Only those aged over eighteen years and six months, and who were already serving in the ranks or had attended an Officers' Training Corps, were eligible to apply. Even though Lewis had been a member of the Officers' Training Corps for only a few weeks, this was enough to allow him to train as a future officer at one of the Officer Cadet Battalions.

Two such units were based at Oxford: No. 4 Officer Cadet Battalion and No. 6 Officer Cadet Battalion. Each of these maintained a nominal strength of 750, and were billeted in otherwise empty Oxford colleges. No. 4 Officer Cadet Battalion consisted of five companies of cadets, from A through E. Lewis was assigned to E Company, and billeted in

Keble College. Lewis was relieved to remain in Oxford. Having to live at Keble College was, however, another matter.

3.2 Keble College, Oxford, as photographed by Henry W. Taunt (1860–1922) in 1907. The characteristic brickwork of the college, which contrasted sharply with the stone of other Oxford colleges of this period, is clearly visible.

Keble was one of Oxford's more recent collegiate foundations,[21] with a grim reputation for its High Church Anglicanism and its somewhat Spartan living conditions. In founding Keble College in 1870, its sponsors had aimed to create an institution where an Oxford education could be made available for "gentlemen wishing to live economically." As a result, living conditions in the college were frugal and austere at the best of times. The additional privations caused by the war meant that the college offered only the most basic of comforts to its unfortunate occupants.

Lewis had to leave a rather comfortable set of rooms at University College for "a carpetless little cell with two beds (minus sheets or pillows) at Keble."[22] Lewis shared this miserable room with Edward Francis

Courtenay ("Paddy") Moore, an officer cadet of almost exactly his own age,[23] who had also been assigned to E Company of No. 4 Officer Cadet Battalion, joining the same day as Lewis himself: 7 May 1917. The majority of cadets who passed through Oxford on this course were not members of Oxford University. Some came from Cambridge; others—such as Moore—had little or no background in higher education. Although Moore had come to Oxford from Bristol, he had been born in Kingstown (now Dún Laoghaire), County Dublin. We see here an early example of Lewis's tendency to become close to people of Irish extraction—such as Theobold Butler and Nevill Coghill—while in England.

Along with Moore, Lewis formed friendships with four other young men in E Company: Thomas Kerrison Dawey, Denis Howard de Pass, Martin Ashworth Somerville, and Alexander Gordon Sutton. Lewis could not have known it, but eighteen months later he would mourn his colleagues. "I remember five of us at Keble, and I am the only survivor."[24]

From his correspondence of this period, it seems that Lewis was initially drawn to Somerville, rather than to his roommate, Moore. Somerville, he tells his father in a letter written a few days after joining the battalion, is his "chief friend," who, though quiet, is "very booky and interesting"; Moore, however, was a "little too childish for real companionship."[25] Yet Lewis had little time for reading now; days of trench digging and forced marches put an end to that. Only his weekends were free; these he spent back in his rooms at University College, catching up on his correspondence.

Yet as time passed, Lewis seems to have formed an increasingly close friendship with Moore. Lewis and his small group of friends went frequently to the nearby lodgings of Paddy's mother, Mrs. Jane King Moore. Mrs. Moore, originally from County Louth in Ireland, had separated from her husband, a civil engineer in Dublin, and had temporarily moved to Oxford from Bristol with her twelve-year-old daughter, Maureen, to be close to Paddy. At that time, she had taken rooms in Wellington Square, not far from Keble College. When Lewis first met Mrs. Moore, she was forty-five years old—almost exactly the same age as Lewis's mother, Flora, when she had died in 1908.

3.3 C. S. Lewis (left) and Paddy Moore (right) in Oxford during the summer of 1917. The identity of the figure to the back of the photograph is unknown.

It is clear from correspondence that Lewis and Mrs. Moore found each other attractive and engaging. Lewis first mentioned this "Irish lady" in a letter to his father of 18 June.[26] Mrs. Moore later wrote to Albert Lewis in October of that year, remarking that his son, who was her son's roommate, was "very charming and most likeable and won golden opinions from everyone he met."[27]

The wartime Battalion Orders for No. 4 Officer Cadet Battalion, commanded by Lieutenant-Colonel J. G. Stenning, have survived in the form of a yellowing set of duplicated foolscap sheets.[28] These documents, covering the years 1916–1918, are clearly incomplete and do not give a full picture of the identity or activities of this training unit. Not all of the officer cadets are mentioned specifically by name, and some names are incorrectly entered. For example, Paddy Moore was initially registered as "E. M. C. Moore"—an error corrected a week later to "E. F. C. Moore."[29] Nevertheless, despite their incompleteness and errors, these records give us a good picture of the training Lewis would have received—courses in the use of the "Lewis gun" (as the Lewis Automatic Machine Gun was popularly known) and how to survive a gas attack, compulsory church parades on Sunday, rules about discussing military matters with civilians, arrangements for intercollegiate cricket matches, and physical training exercises. Other records give us a good idea of the sort of training Lewis would have had in using weapons, especially rifles.[30]

The records also reveal the surprising fact that there were two C. S. Lewises in training at Keble College in the summer of 1917. The C. S. Lewis on which our narrative focusses joined E Company on 7 May 1917.[31] On 5 July 1917, another C. S. Lewis, assigned to the Oxford and Buckinghamshire Light Infantry, joined C Company.[32] Three months later, this Lewis was "discharged to commission" in the 6th Middlesex Regiment.[33]

It is clear from his correspondence of July 1917 that Lewis himself had become aware that another C. S. Lewis was also in training at Keble College at that time. He emphasised the importance of including "E Company" on any letters addressed to him, in order to keep correspondence intended for him from being delivered to the other C. S. Lewis, attached to C Company.[34] So who was this second C. S. Lewis? Happily, the records are good enough to allow an answer to this question.

Shortly after the end of the war, a complete list of every cadet who trained in C Company of No. 4 Officer Cadet Battalion was drawn up by their company commander, Captain F. W. Matheson, and checked against the official British army list of December 1918. Matheson then wrote to every known member of the company, and—where he received a reply— published their most recent address. This rare document, published privately by Keble College in 1920, includes the following reference:[35]

Lewis, C. S. 2nd Lt., 6th Middlesex Regt.
Brynawel, Pentala, Aberavon.

The annotation clearly indicates that Matheson was able to establish contact with this Lewis from C Company after the war and confirm his address—in South Wales. It is possible that confusion over these two C. S. Lewises may account for the War Office's failure to pay Lewis some salary he was owed around this time.[36]

LEWIS'S WARTIME EXPERIENCES AT OXFORD

On 24 October 1922, Lewis returned to University College for a meeting of the Martlets, a college literary society that he had been instrumental in reestablishing after the Great War. The group, Lewis discovered, were meeting on this occasion in the set of rooms that he himself had occupied in 1917. His diary entry for that day in 1922 is of interest, as it relates three memories of significance to him dating from five years earlier:

> Here I first was brought home drunk: here I wrote some of the poems in *Spirits in Bondage*. D had been in this room.[37]

Each of these memories alerts us to key aspects of Lewis's personal development during his time at Oxford in the summer of 1917. Only one of them was literary in character.

The first such memory concerns a dinner party in June 1917, when Lewis became "royally drunk." Lewis recalls the dinner as being at Exeter College; the evidence suggests it may actually have been at nearby Brasenose College, which itself points to Lewis's state of drunkenness on the evening in question. Disinhibited under the influence of what were clearly substantial quantities of alcohol, Lewis unwisely let slip his growing interest in sadomasochism, which he had already confided a little shamefully to Arthur Greeves.[38] Lewis recalls that he went around imploring everyone to let him "whip them for the sum of 1s. a lash."[39] Lewis had no other memory of that debauched evening, other than waking up on the floor of his own room in University College the next morning.

This intriguing streak in the young Lewis's character seems to have emerged earlier that year, and led him to investigate the erotic writings of the Marquis de Sade (1740–1814). Lewis also took pleasure around this time in reading the sections of Jean-Jacques Rousseau's *Confessions* (1770) dealing with the pleasures of beating, and compared himself to William Morris (1834–1896) as "a special devotee of the rod." He apologised to Greeves at one point for writing a letter "across his knee," only to find that this phrase triggered distracting erotic associations in his mind:

> "Across my knee" of course makes one think of positions for Whipping: or rather not for whipping (you couldn't get any swing) but for that torture with brushes. This position, with its childish, nursery associations wd. have something beautifully intimate and also very humiliating for the victim.[40]

Although Lewis's flagellant fantasies generally concerned beautiful women (possibly including Greeves's sister Lily),[41] his Oxford letters suggest he was also prepared to extend these to young men.

Three of his letters to Arthur Greeves of early 1917 are signed "Philomastix" (Greek, "lover of the whip").[42] In these letters, Lewis tries to explain something of his growing fascination with the "sensuality of cruelty," in the knowledge that Greeves did not share it and would not condone it. "Very, very few," Lewis conceded, were "affected in this strange way"[43]—and Greeves was certainly not one of them. Indeed, Lewis used a nickname for Greeves from about the spring of 1915 to the summer of 1918—"Galahad," a reference to his confidant's purity and ability to withstand the temptations to which Lewis himself clearly felt drawn.

Lewis's teasing of Greeves on this point is clearly grounded in fact. Greeves's personal diary around this time does indeed show a marked concern for his personal purity, especially after his confirmation into the Church of Ireland on 10 June 1917. This church service marked Greeves's religious "coming of age," which Greeves clearly regarded as a spiritual landmark. Perhaps unknown to Lewis, his friend seems to have been passing through some kind of crisis around this time. His diary mingles prayer that he may "keep pure minded"[44] with darker concerns about the meaninglessness of life. "What a terrible life! What is it all for? Trust in Him."[45]

The diaries reveal a lonely young man, who saw his friendship with Lewis and his faith in God as fixed stars in a gloomy and unstable firmament.

The second memory relates to Lewis's growing aspiration to be remembered as a poet. By this stage, there was increasing recognition of the category of the "war poet," which included writers such as Siegfried Sassoon (1886–1967), Robert Graves (1895–1985), and Rupert Brooke (1887–1915), the last of which achieved particular fame for three lines from "The Soldier":

If I should die, think only this of me:
   That there's some corner of a foreign field
That is for ever England.

Brooke died of sepsis from an infected mosquito bite on 23 April 1915, on his way to fight in the Gallipoli campaign. He was buried in a "corner of a foreign field" in an olive grove on the Greek island of Skyros.

Inspired by such examples, Lewis began to write his own war poetry during his time at Oxford, while preparing for conflict. These poems, published in March 1919 under the pseudonym "Clive Hamilton" (Hamilton was his mother's maiden name), have never been well regarded, and are rarely reprinted. Lewis initially titled the poems *Spirits in Prison: A Cycle of Lyrical Poems*. Albert Lewis, who was more widely read than many appreciated, pointed out that a novel by this name had been published by Robert Hitchens in 1908. Lewis took the point, and changed the title to *Spirits in Bondage*.[46]

Yet it is questionable whether *Spirits in Bondage* can properly be classified as war poetry. By my reckoning, over half of the poems in this collection were written before Lewis actually went to France and saw active service. These earlier poems are somewhat intellectualised reflections on war from a safe distance, untainted by the passions, despair, and brutality of the killing fields of France. The poems are often intellectually interesting, yet fail to sustain the poetic vision of a Sassoon or a Brooke.

So what do these poems tell us about Lewis? They are, after all, the first significant published works from his pen.[47] Stylistically, they perhaps show that Lewis's voice had some way to go before it would achieve its mature authority. At this stage in his career, however, the poems are of particular interest on account of their witness to his trenchant atheism. The most interesting parts of the cycle are its protests against a silent, uncaring heaven. The "Ode for New Year's Day," written when under fire near the French town of Arras in January 1918, declares the final death of a God who was in any case a human fabrication. Any idea that the "red God" might "lend an ear" to human cries of misery lay discredited and abandoned in the mud, a disgraced "Power who slays and puts aside the beauty that has been."[48]

These lines are important, as they express two themes that were clearly deeply impressed upon Lewis's mind at this time: his contempt for a God he did not believe to exist, yet wished to blame for the carnage and destruction that lay around him; and his deep longing for the safety and security of the past—a past he clearly believed to have been destroyed forever. This note of wistfulness over the irretrievability of a loved past is a recurrent theme in Lewis's later writings.

Perhaps the most important thing that *Spirits in Bondage* tells us about Lewis is aspirational—namely, that Lewis wanted to be remembered as a poet, and believed that he had the talent necessary to achieve this calling. Although Lewis is today remembered as a literary critic, apologist, and novelist, none of these corresponds to his own youthful dreams and hopes of his future. Lewis is a failed poet who found greatness in other spheres of writing. Yet some would say that, having failed as a writer of poetry, Lewis succeeded as a writer of prose—a prose saturated with the powerful rhythms and melodious phrasing of a natural poet.

But what of the third memory? Who is "D"?[49] And why does Lewis attach such importance to D's visit to his room in 1917? As the later diary makes clear, the reference is to Mrs. Moore, with whom Lewis was then living. This complex relationship, of which we shall have much more to say in due course, began during Lewis's time as an officer cadet at Keble College. Paddy Moore may have been the original occasion for Lewis's intimacy with Moore's mother, but the relationship rapidly developed independently of him.

There is no doubt that Lewis was close to Paddy Moore. Indeed, the relationship may have been closer than most biographers realise. A personal bond appears to have developed between Lewis and Moore during the time they shared a room together at Keble College. To explore this point, let us reflect on the question of the regiment of the British army in which Lewis would serve. On 26 September 1917, Lewis received a temporary commission as second lieutenant in the 3rd Somerset Light Infantry and was given a month's leave before being sent for further training in South Devon.[50] Paddy Moore was given a commission in the Rifle Brigade and was posted to the Somme.

But why did Lewis join the Somerset Light Infantry, when he had no family connections whatsoever with the county of Somerset? Most biographies fail to appreciate the importance of this question. There were certainly alternatives open to Lewis. One of the most obvious was the Oxford-based Oxford and Buckinghamshire Light Infantry, to which many of the cadets of No. 4 Officer Cadet Battalion were assigned. His Belfast origins meant that Lewis would also have had the option of being posted to one of the Irish regiments. So why did he end up with a commission in the Somerset Light Infantry?

Perhaps the Battalion Orders of No. 4 Officer Cadet Battalion contain a vital clue allowing us to answer this question. When an officer cadet is referred to in these documents, he is identified by the regiment to which he was provisionally assigned at the time of his recruitment, in which he would serve unless posted elsewhere—for example, as a result of technical skills he might demonstrate in training. The Battalion Orders indicate that the "other" C. S. Lewis, for example, was initially assigned to the Oxford and Buckinghamshire Light Infantry, but ended up being commissioned into the 6th Middlesex Regiment. Those same Battalion Orders record Paddy Moore's date of arrival at the course on 7 May 1917 in the following manner:[51]

| 37072 | Moore, E. M. C. | Som L. I. | 7.5.17 |

The vital clue to Lewis's choice of regiment lies here: Moore's assigned regiment was the Somerset Light Infantry. This makes perfect sense, since the Moores' home was in Redland, a suburb of the city of Bristol, which was treated as lying within the county of Somerset for military recruitment purposes. The corresponding entry in the Battalion Orders for Lewis makes it clear that he was initially assigned to the King's Own Scottish Borderers.

We therefore must take very seriously the possibility that Lewis *requested* a commission in the Somerset Light Infantry in the belief that this would allow him to serve alongside his close friend Paddy Moore. Was there some kind of pact between the two men, by which they would look after each other in the war? This possibility is strongly supported by Jane Moore's letter to Albert Lewis of 17 October 1917, in which she expresses Paddy's deep sorrow that he and Lewis would not be serving alongside each other in the Somersets.[52] The tone of this letter makes perfect sense if there had been an expectation that the two men would both be posted to the Somerset Light Infantry, allowing them to face the challenges of conflict together.

As it turned out, Moore was notified that he had been given a temporary commission in the Rifle Brigade a few days after Lewis received his commission in the Somerset Light Infantry. If our speculative line of exploration is correct, Lewis would have been devastated when he learned that he would not be serving alongside his new friend. He would have to go to war alone, without any close friends to support him.

It was during this visit to Bristol that Maureen Moore overheard Lewis and her brother enter into a pact. If either of them should die during conflict, the other would look after the deceased's remaining parent. It is not clear whether this pact was devised before or after Moore learned that he had been posted to the Rifle Brigade. Yet this development can easily be seen as an expression of a deeper bond between the two men, which developed at Oxford.

Lewis's relationship with his own family went into tailspin around this time. Albert Lewis expected that Lewis would spend his leave with him at Little Lea in Belfast. In fact, Lewis went to stay with the Moores in Bristol for three weeks, paying only a somewhat reluctant and perfunctory visit to his father (12–18 October) before joining his regiment at Crownhill, a "village of wooden huts" near Plymouth.[53] A slightly furtive letter to his father, written from Bristol, told Albert Lewis only part of the story.[54] Lewis had developed "a cold," and Mrs. Moore had sent him to bed.

For things had clearly moved on. On his return to Crownhill, Lewis wrote a hasty letter to Arthur Greeves, asking him to disregard certain things he had unwisely said about "a certain person."[55] Although the circumstantial evidence is strong that this is a reference to his growing intimacy with Mrs. Moore, it is not absolutely conclusive. Still, it fits a growing picture of deception and intrigue, by which Lewis sought to conceal this problematic yet special relationship from his father. Lewis was perfectly aware that if Albert Lewis were ever to learn the truth, their own relationship—already strained—could be totally ruptured. What if his father were to see Lewis's letter to Greeves of 14 December 1917, in which he explicitly referred to Greeves and Mrs. Moore as "the two people who matter most . . . in the world"?[56]

DEPLOYMENT TO FRANCE: NOVEMBER 1917

Paddy Moore was sent to France with the Rifle Brigade in October. Both Lewis and his father feared that Lewis would also be deployed to fight in France. Yet suddenly, everything changed. Lewis wrote to his father in "great excitement" on 5 November: he had just heard that his battalion was to be deployed to Ireland![57] Political tensions in Ireland were high, partly on account of the simmering aftermath of the Easter Rising. While this posting would not be without its dangers, Albert Lewis could hardly have failed to recognise that an Irish posting would be far less hazardous than the front line in France. In the end, the 3rd Somerset moved to the Irish city of Londonderry in November 1917, and then to Belfast in April 1918.

But Lewis did not move with them after all. He had been transferred to the 1st Somerset,[58] a combat regiment which had been stationed in France since August 1914.[59] The expectation was that the new recruits would be undergoing extensive further training before going into action. But again, things began to move very quickly. In the early evening of Thursday, 15 November, Lewis urgently telegraphed his father. He had been given forty-eight hours' leave before he had to report to Southampton for disembarkation to France. He was now in Bristol, staying with Mrs. Moore. Could his father come and visit him?[60] Albert Lewis wired back: he didn't understand what Lewis meant. Could he write and explain?

Lewis frantically wired his father again on the morning of Friday, 16 November. He had been ordered to France and was due to sail the following afternoon. He needed to know if his father could visit him before he left. Yet like the silent heaven against which Lewis protested in his poetry, Albert Lewis failed to reply. In the end, Lewis sailed for France without being able to say farewell to his father. The casualty rates among inexperienced junior officers were appallingly high. Lewis might never return. Albert Lewis's failure to appreciate the importance of that critical moment did nothing to mend his troubled relationship with his son. Some would say it ruptured it completely.

On 17 November, Lewis sailed from Southampton to Le Havre in Normandy to join his regiment. On his nineteenth birthday, Lewis was transferred, friendless, to the trenches near Monchy-le-Preux, east of the French town of Arras, close to the border with Belgium. Albert Lewis, meanwhile, tried yet again to get Lewis transferred to an artillery regiment. However, he was advised that only Lewis himself could request such a transfer, and this would require Lewis's commanding officer's permission in writing.[61] In a letter written from what Lewis describes as "a certain rather battered town somewhere behind the line," he rejected this possibility.[62] He would rather stay with his infantry regiment.

Although Lewis's letter of 13 December suggests that he was safely behind the front line, this was not the case. In fact, Lewis was already in the trenches, although he withheld this information in his correspondence with his father until 4 January 1918, presumably to shield him from anxiety. Even then, Lewis played down the danger of his situation. He reported that he was in danger only once —a shell had fallen near him, and that was when he was using the latrines.[63]

Lewis's scant references to the horrors of trench warfare confirm both its objective realities ("the horribly smashed men still moving like half-crushed beetles, the sitting or standing corpses, the landscape of sheer earth without a blade of grass") and his own subjective distancing of himself from this experience (it "shows rarely and faintly in memory" and is "cut off from the rest of my experience").[64] This is perhaps the most distinctive feature of Lewis's "treaty with reality"—the construction of a frontier, a barrier, which protected Lewis from such shocking images as "horribly smashed men," and allowed him to continue his life as if these horrors had been experienced by someone else. Lewis spun a cocoon around himself, insulating his thoughts from rotting corpses and the technology of destruction. The world could be kept at bay—and this was best done by reading, and allowing the words and thoughts of others to shield him from what was going on around him.

Lewis's experience of this most technological and impersonal of wars was filtered and tempered through a literary prism. For Lewis, books were both a link to the remembered—if sentimentally exaggerated—bliss of a lost past and a balm for the trauma and hopelessness of the present. As he wrote to Arthur Greeves several months later, he looked back wistfully to happier days, in which he sat surrounded by his "little library and browsed from book to book."[65] Those days, he reflected with obvious sadness, were gone.

Clement Attlee, a University College undergraduate who later became British prime minister, calmed his nerves under shell fire in the Great War by imagining himself taking a walk through Oxford.[66] Lewis preferred to read books to achieve the same outcome. Yet Lewis did more than read—though he read voraciously—while on active service in France. He also wrote poems. His cycle *Spirits in Bondage* includes a group of poems that clearly are a response to the directly experienced realities of war—such as "French Nocturne (Monchy-Le-Preux)." Lewis had discovered the calming and coping impact, not merely of reading literature, but of putting his feelings into his own words. It was as if the mental process of forging sentences tempered and tamed the emotions that originally inspired them. As he once advised his confidant Arthur Greeves, "Whenever you are fed up with life, start writing: ink is the great cure for all human ills, as I have found out long ago."[67]

For most of February 1918, Lewis was hospitalised in No. 10 British Red Cross Hospital at Le Tréport, not far from Dieppe on the French coast. Like so many others, he was suffering from "trench fever," often referred to as P. O. U. ("pyrexia origin unknown"), a condition widely believed to be spread by lice. Lewis wrote home to his father, recalling a happier time spent with his mother and brother at Berneval-le-Grand near Dieppe, only eighteen miles (29 kilometres) away, in 1907.[68] His letters to Greeves from around this time are packed with news of books he had been reading, or intended to read—such as Benvenuto Cellini's autobiography. If the gods were kind to him, he remarked, he might have a relapse and have to stay in the hospital longer. But, he wryly remarked, the gods hated him. And who could blame them, given the way he felt about them?[69] A week later, Lewis was out of the hospital. His company was moved out of the battle zone for further training at Wanquetin, practising the technique of "section rushes" in preparation for a major assault that was being planned, before moving back to the front line at Fampoux near Arras on 19 March.

WOUNDED IN BATTLE: THE ASSAULT ON RIEZ DU VINAGE, APRIL 1918

Arthur Greeves's diary for the months of March and April makes frequent reference to his own loneliness and his anxieties for Lewis. "I pray God to preserve my boy. I don't know what I should do without him."[70] On 11 April 1918, Greeves recorded the contents of a letter he had just received from Mrs. Moore: her "dear son" had been "killed."[71] Greeves was distraught with grief over Paddy Moore and growing fears for the safety of his closest friend. Two days later, he confided his hope for Lewis: "If only Jack could get wounded. He is in God's hands and I trust in Him to keep him safe."[72] Greeves's deepest hope was that Lewis would be wounded severely enough to be taken out of the front lines, or possibly even brought home to England. In the end, that was precisely what happened.

The Somerset Light Infantry began their assault on the small, German-held village of Riez du Vinage at 6.30 p.m. on 14 April. The British heavy artillery laid down a creeping barrage, behind which the infantry advanced.[73] The barrage was not sufficiently intense to suppress German resistance, and the advancing infantry came under heavy machine-gun fire. One of those wounded was Second Lieutenant Laurence Johnson, who died the following morning. Johnson, a scholar of Queen's College, Oxford, had joined up on 17 April 1917 and had become one of Lewis's few friends in the army.[74]

Lewis, however, reached Riez du Vinage safely with his company. "I 'took' about sixty prisoners—that is, discovered to my great relief that the crowd of field-gray figures who suddenly appeared from nowhere, all had their hands up."[75] By 7.15 p.m., the action was over. Riez du Vinage was in the hands of the Somerset Light Infantry.

The Germans immediately mounted a counterattack, initially by shelling the village, and then by launching an infantry assault, which was repelled. A German shell exploded close to Lewis, wounding him and killing Sergeant Harry Ayres, who was standing next to him at the time.[76] Lewis was taken to No. 6 British Red Cross Hospital near Etaples. A letter, presumably written by a nurse, was sent immediately to Albert Lewis, informing him that his son was "slightly wounded." This was followed by a similar telegram from the War Office: "2nd Lt. C. S. Lewis Somerset Light Infantry wounded April fifteenth."[77]

Albert Lewis, however, seems to have persuaded himself that his son was *severely* wounded, and wrote to Warnie—by then promoted to the rank of captain[78]—expressing his distress. Warnie, alarmed that his seriously wounded brother might not survive for long, set out to visit him immediately. But how was he to get there? His brother was fifty miles (80 kilometres) away.

Warnie's military record helps us understand what happened next. An examining officer responsible for assessing Warnie's promotion prospects around this time declared that he was "NOT a good horseman," but he was nevertheless "a keen motor-cyclist." In a move that was at one and the same time predictable and imaginative, Warnie borrowed a motor-bike and drove nonstop over rough terrain to see his brother in the field hospital. He was reassured to find that his brother was not in danger.[79]

In fact, Lewis had suffered a shrapnel wound that was sufficiently serious to merit his being sent back to England, but not life threatening—what many in the army then termed a "Blighty wound." Lewis had suffered lightly in comparison with others; shortly afterwards, he finally learned that his friend Paddy Moore was missing, believed dead.

It was at this time that Greeves wrote to Lewis, confiding that he realised he was probably homosexual, something Lewis had most likely already guessed.[80] Lewis's response to Greeves's confession shows a surprising tolerance towards this development, linked with a suspicion of traditional moral values: "Congratulations old man. I am delighted that you have had the moral courage to form your own opinions <independently,> in defiance of the old taboos."[81] While probably relieved that his friendship with Lewis had survived this disclosure, Greeves nevertheless confided to his diary that he felt "rather sad" on receiving Lewis's letter.[82] It is possible that a close reading of this letter led Greeves to realise that Lewis had subtly indicated that he did not share this sexuality.

So did Greeves have hopes that Lewis might share his sexual orientation? It is important to realise that Greeves's diary around this time indicates a deep emotional attachment to Lewis, which is without parallel elsewhere in Greeves's life. To judge by his diary entries, no other figure—male or female—plays such a significant role in his life, even though Lewis is physically absent for most of the time. When Lewis fails to write to him, Greeves sinks into despair. "Feel so unhappy regarding Jack, is he sick of me? Never a word from him."[83] His final entry for 1918 is particularly revealing: "What would I do without J[ack]?"[84] The evidence clearly suggests—but does not prove—that the chief object of Greeves's affections was Lewis himself.

This could easily have become a serious problem for the two young men. In the end, Greeves appears to have accepted the realities of the situation. Any awkwardness between the two on this point appears to have evaporated with relative ease, and did not become an issue of contention between them.[85] Lewis continued to regard Greeves as his confidant and closest friend at this time, and remained in touch with him until weeks before his death in 1963. Yet Lewis's complex relationship with Greeves clearly had an impact on Lewis's reflections on the focus and limits of friendship. It is important for readers of *The Four Loves* (1960) to appreciate that Lewis is here exploring, among other matters, the boundaries of intimacy, affection, and respect within *male* relationships.

Meanwhile, Lewis returned to England and became a patient at the Endsleigh Palace Hospital for Officers on 25 May 1918. This building was originally a London hotel, which had been requisitioned by the War Office to cope with the stream of wounded officers returning home from France. Lewis was well enough to be able to go to the opera (he tells Arthur Greeves of his delight at a performance of Wagner's *Valkyrie*), and to travel to Great Bookham to visit the "Great Knock." Lewis penned a long and affectionate letter to his father, describing this "pilgrimage," and inviting him to come and visit him in London.[86] Albert Lewis, however, never visited his son during his convalescence.[87] But Mrs. Moore did. In fact, she moved out of Bristol to be with him.

LEWIS AND MRS. MOORE: AN EMERGING RELATIONSHIP

So what was going on between Lewis and Mrs. Moore? Several factors must be taken into account in trying to reach some kind of understanding about the situation. First, we have no documents, including records of personal testimony, which allow us to reach reliable conclusions. Late in life Mrs. Moore destroyed her letters from Lewis. The only other person Lewis would have confided in about his relationship would have been Arthur Greeves. Again, we have no evidence from this source casting unambiguous light on this question.

We do, however, understand something of the context against which this relationship developed. We know that Lewis had lost his mother, and thus needed maternal affection and understanding at a difficult time in his life, when he was away from home and friends. Furthermore, he was preparing to go to war, facing possible death. Studies of the Great War emphasise its subversive impact on British social and moral conventions around this time. Young men about to go to the Front were the object of sympathy for women, old and young, which often led to passionate— yet generally ephemeral—affairs. Lewis, as his letters to Arthur Greeves indicate, was a sexually inquisitive young man. We are perfectly entitled to wonder what Mrs. Moore was doing in Lewis's rooms in University College in 1917—a memory that Lewis so clearly cherished, to judge by his diary entry of 1922.

It is possible that Mrs. Moore fused Lewis's idealised notions of women as the caring, supportive, empathetic mother on the one hand, and the exciting lover on the other. I have often been struck by what many regard as the most haunting of C. S. Lewis's poems—the sonnet titled "Reason," probably written in the early 1920s. Lewis here contrasts the clarity and strength of reason (symbolised by Athene, the "maid" of the poem) with the warm darkness and creativity of the imagination (Demeter, the earth-mother). For Lewis, the big question is this: Is there anyone who can be "both maid and mother" to him?[88]

Who indeed could achieve such a fusion, reconciling what many would see as polar opposites? At the intellectual level, Lewis was searching for a true marriage of reason and imagination—something that eluded him totally as a young man. It seemed to him then that his life of the mind was split into two disconnected hemispheres. "On the one side a many-islanded sea of poetry and myth; on the other a glib and shallow 'rationalism.'"[89] Lewis's later discovery of the Christian faith offered him a synthesis of reason and imagination which he found persuasive and authentic till the end of his life.

Might there be a deeper meaning to Lewis's imagery and words here, whether Lewis intended them or not? Might there be a hint at Lewis's desire for a woman who would nourish both his mind and his body? Was Mrs. Moore both the "mother" that Lewis had lost and the "maid" for whom he yearned?

What can be said with some confidence is that the circumstantial evidence suggests that Lewis developed a complex relationship with Mrs. Moore in the summer of 1917. George Sayer (1914–2005), a close friend of Lewis's who is widely regarded as one of his most insightful biographers, initially regarded their relationship as ambivalent but ultimately platonic. Older studies sympathetic to Lewis—including Sayer's important and relatively recent study *Jack* (1988)—considered and rejected the possibility that Lewis and Mrs. Moore were lovers. Yet the tide of opinion has changed. Sayer himself illustrates this shifting consensus. In a revised introduction to later editions of this work, written in 1996, Sayer stated that he was now "quite certain" that Lewis and Mrs. Moore had been lovers, and furthermore argued that this development was "not surprising," given Lewis's deep and unresolved emotional needs and conflicts at this time.[90] Yet their relationship cannot really be described as merely "sexual," if this is understood to define its focus and limits. Rather, it appears to have been strongly shaped by both maternal and romantic factors.

What is difficult to understand is perhaps not why such a relationship developed immediately before Lewis went to the Front, possibly never to return, but why this relationship continued for so long afterwards. Most wartime affairs of this kind were short lived (often because of the death of the departing soldier in battle), and were generally based on sympathy and expediency, rather than being more deeply rooted in personal affection and trust. It seems likely that the "pact" between Lewis and Paddy Moore is important in understanding the nature of this relationship. This established a context within which this relationship could be rationalised to outsiders, and likely gave some form of moral justification to Lewis himself. Lewis had no Christian beliefs at this stage, and clearly regarded himself as free to establish such values and practices as he saw fit. We shall return to this matter in the following chapter.

On 25 June 1918, Lewis was moved to Ashton Court, a convalescent hospital in Clifton, Bristol, close to Mrs. Moore's home. Lewis wrote to his father, explaining that he had tried to find a suitable hospital in Ireland, but none had been available.[91] It was here that he initially learned that his *Spirits in Prison* (as it was then titled) had been refused for publication by Macmillan, and subsequently that it had been accepted by Heinemann. At this stage, Lewis proposed to publish under the pen name "Clive Staples." On 18 November, he changed this to "Clive Hamilton," drawing on his mother's maiden name to conceal his identity.[92] The book would be published in March 1919.

In the meantime, Lewis was transferred to Perham Downs Camp on Salisbury Plain on 4 October. Mrs. Moore duly followed him, renting rooms in a nearby cottage. Lewis here enjoyed the unusual luxury of having a room to himself. On 11 November, the Great War finally came to an end. Lewis was transferred again—this time to an Officers Command Depot in Eastbourne, in Sussex. Again, Mrs. Moore followed him. Lewis informed his father of this arrangement—it was no longer a matter he regarded as secret—and announced that he was due some leave from 10 to 22 January, when he would come over to Belfast. Warnie, who was also due some leave from soldiering in France, arrived in Belfast on 23 December 1918, in time to celebrate Christmas with his father.

Then things moved with unexpected pace. Lewis was discharged from the hospital and demobilised on 24 December. Unable to alert his family in advance to his changed circumstances, he made his way home to Belfast unannounced. Warnie's diary entry for 27 December takes up the story:[93]

A red letter day today. We were sitting in the study about 11 o'clock this morning when we saw a cab coming up the avenue. It was Jacks! He has been demobilized. . . . We had lunch and then all three went for a walk. It was as if the evil dream of four years had passed away and we were still in 1915.

On 13 January 1919, Lewis returned to Oxford to resume his studies at Oxford University, so cruelly interrupted by the Great War. He would remain there for the next thirty-five years.

PART TWO

OXFORD

DECEPTIONS AND DISCOVERIES: THE MAKING OF AN OXFORD DON

With the ending of the Great War, Oxford was flooded with new students. More than 1,800 ex-servicemen either began or resumed their studies in the first year after the war ended. One of them was C. S. Lewis, who returned to Oxford to take up his scholarship at University College on 13 January 1919. To his surprise, the college porter—almost certainly the legendary Fred Bickerton[1]—recognised him immediately, and took him straight back to his old rooms in Radcliffe Quadrangle from the summer of 1917. Oxford University made a significant concession to their admission requirements in response to the postwar influx of students with military or naval service. Having served as a commissioned officer in the British army, Lewis found that he was now exempt from the prewar requirement to pass Responsions.[2] His lack of basic mathematical skills would no longer stand in his way to an Oxford degree.

Lewis had already fallen in love with Oxford, on account of both its stunning architecture and its rich intellectual heritage. It was a city based on culture and learning, not on Britain's imperial exploitation of its colonies nor industrial desecration of the local landscape. As Lewis put it in *Spirits in Bondage*, Oxford was one of the few great cities

That was not built for gross, material gains,
Sharp, wolfish power or empire's glutted feast.

For Lewis the undergraduate, as for the later Lewis, Oxford was a beautiful city that encouraged and affirmed the empires of the mind. It was

A clean, sweet city lulled by ancient streams,
A place of visions and of loosening chains,
A refuge of the elect, a tower of dreams.[3]

For Lewis, those visions and dreams were best fostered and nourished by returning to the fountainhead of Western civilization—the culture of ancient Greece and Rome. As part of the process of the "expansion of his mind," Lewis would immerse himself in the languages and literature of the classical age.

THE STUDENT OF CLASSICS: UNIVERSITY COLLEGE, 1919

Lewis had already made the all-important decision that he wanted to pursue an academic career at Oxford.[4] There really was no plan B. Lewis knew what he wanted to be, and the demands that this career choice would make of him. He had chosen to study classical languages and literature, referred to in Oxford as *Literae Humaniores*. This was the diamond in Victorian Oxford's academic crown, and was still seen as the intellectual flagship of Oxford's undergraduate academic degrees up to about 1920.

4.1 Radcliffe Quadrangle, University College, as photographed by Henry W. Taunt (1860–1922) in the summer of 1917. Lewis was given a set of rooms in this quadrangle on his arrival at University College in April 1917, and returned to those same rooms in January 1919.

In 1912, William Archibald Spooner (1844–1930), the celebrity classical scholar and Warden of New College, Oxford—whose fame may have led Lewis to apply originally to New College—summed up the purpose of *Literae Humaniores* as an "immersion in the civilization and thought of the ancient world." Often abbreviated as *Lit. Hum.*, this Latin term is not easily rendered into English. Literally translated as "more humane letters," it alludes to the Renaissance humanist vision of an enlarging and civilizing education, brought about through a direct engagement with the riches of the intellectual and cultural past.

Although the origins of *Literae Humaniores* at Oxford can be traced back to 1800, its social roots lie firmly in the concerns of the earlier eighteenth century. England had emerged, badly bruised yet not destroyed, from the civil war and revolution of the seventeenth century. Every effort was made to reconstitute a stable social order within the nation by emphasising the virtues of reason, nature, and order. The classical age was seen as a rich source of wisdom to enable the English to consolidate political and social stability, and encourage the emergence of shared cultural standards and norms.

Oxford undergraduates studying *Literae Humaniores* were required to engage directly with the literary, philosophical, and historical riches of the classical age in the original languages—not simply as a subject of academic interest, but as a means of ensuring England's survival and prosperity. *Lit. Hum.* was seen as a gateway to wisdom, rather than the mere accumulation of knowledge. It was about moral and cultural preparation for life, not simply the acquisition of factual information. Where other courses of study might aim merely to *fill* undergraduate minds, this one set out to *shape* them.

Because of the considerable linguistic demands that it made of students, *Lit. Hum.* required four years (i.e., twelve terms) of study, whereas other courses needed a mere three. The course was divided into two parts. After five terms, students would take the examination known as "Honours Moderations" (usually abbreviated to "Mods"); if they passed this, they were then permitted to continue with the remainder of the course, universally referred to by students as "Greats," eventually sitting for the final examination seven terms later. Each of these two examinations was "classified," in that students would be placed in the first, second, third, or fourth class.[5] Outstanding students might thus be said to have achieved a "Double First in *Literae Humaniores*," meaning that they were placed in the First Class in both Moderations and Greats. It does not mean that they obtained two degrees, simply that they achieved the highest possible classification at both assessment points of this single-degree course.

Oxford's academic year 1918–1919 was already under way when Lewis arrived. He had missed the first term of study. Oxford divided its academic year into three eight-week teaching terms: Michaelmas (usually October to early December), Hilary (January through March), and Trinity (April through June). However, having already been registered as a student at University College for the Trinity Term of 1917, Lewis was treated as a normal second-term student. He would have been behind with his Homer, but soon caught up with everyone else.

Full Term formally started on Sunday, 19 January 1919,[6] with the opening lectures of the term beginning the next day. Lewis set to work on his studies with obvious enthusiasm. After a week of studies, Lewis set out his daily routine in a letter to Arthur Greeves:

> Called at 7.30, bath, chapel and breakfast. . . . After breakfast I work (in the library or a lecture-room which are both warm) or attend lectures until 1 o'clock when I bycycle out to Mrs. Moore's. . . . After lunch I work until tea, then work again till dinner. After that a little more work, talk and laziness & sometimes bridge then bycycle back to College at 11. I then light my fire and work or read till 12 o'clock when I retire to sleep the sleep of the just.[7]

Lewis was obliged to live in college to meet Oxford University's residence requirements; absence from breakfast would be regarded as suspicious, and would prompt inquiries with potentially awkward outcomes.

But who "called" Lewis at 7.30? At this point, we need to mention the "scouts" of Oxford University. Lewis refers to these as "servants" in his correspondence, presumably to avoid having to translate Oxford jargon for his father or Arthur Greeves. At University College, scouts—who were invariably male—served long working days.[8] Each was assigned to a staircase or group of staircases, and was responsible for the care of both the rooms and their occupants. The scouts would typically begin work at 6.00 a.m., wake up students (who were always referred to as "gentlemen") from about 6.45, serve them breakfast in Hall or in their rooms, clean up their rooms, and finally serve dinner in Hall. Outside university terms, most scouts would find employment at English seaside hotels. While Lewis himself makes little reference to scouts in his correspondence or diaries, other students formed close relationships with their scouts and kept in touch with them.

Lewis's days as a student at Oxford thus revolved around his studies and—rather more surreptitiously—Mrs. Moore. After his morning's study, Lewis cycled over Magdalen Bridge, up Headington Hill, and into the village of Headington.[9] Mrs. Moore had found lodgings at 28 Warneford Road, a house owned by Miss Annie Alma Featherstone. Lewis would spend the afternoon and evening with Mrs. Moore before returning to spend the night at college. This arrangement was far from regular for Oxford undergraduates, and Lewis appears to have told nobody about it other than his confidant Arthur Greeves. (When Lewis spoke of "the family" to Greeves, he meant Mrs. Moore and Maureen.)[10] From July 1919, Lewis used the term "the Minto" (note the definite article) to refer to Mrs. Moore in his correspondence with Greeves, never offering an explanation of the origin of this curious nickname.[11] It is possible that this nickname is a variant of Maureen's pet name for her mother, "Minnie"; however, there may also be some connection with "the Minto," a boiled sweet that was hugely popular at the time, invented in 1912 by the Doncaster confectioner William Nuttall.[12]

Lewis tried to keep his father in the dark about his double life through an elaborate campaign of deception. For example, Mrs. Moore wrote daily to Lewis during his rare visits to his father. These letters were addressed to Arthur Greeves, who lived nearby, giving Lewis an additional reason to visit his old friend on these trips to Belfast.

ALBERT LEWIS'S CONCERNS ABOUT HIS SON

While Lewis lived out this double life in Oxford, Albert Lewis was campaigning on his behalf with the War Office. His son, he insisted, was entitled to compensation for his war wounds. Worn down both by Albert's persistence and his force of argument—one suspects primarily the former—the War Office eventually gave in. Grudgingly, they finally awarded Lewis a "wound gratuity" of £145 16s 8d. Delighted and encouraged by this victory, Lewis's father pressed the War Office still further; they eventually, and still more grudgingly, gave him a "further wound gratuity" of £104 3s 4d.

Yet relations between father and son were not good, and were becoming worse. Albert was increasingly worried about his son's cultural alienation from his native Ireland, the atheism he saw expressed in *Spirits in Bondage*, and perhaps most significantly his son's apparent lack of affection for him. Lewis wrote his father relatively few letters, was disinclined to spend any of his vacations with him, and showed virtually no interest in his well-being. Indeed, Lewis ended one of his letters to Greeves in June 1919 by remarking that he had not heard from his "esteemed parent for some time," and wondered whether he had "committed suicide yet."[13]

But beyond these worries, it is clear that Albert Lewis's chief concern about his younger son around this time was his perplexing relationship with Mrs. Moore. Initially inclined to put his suspicions down to an overactive imagination, Albert Lewis gradually (and reluctantly) came to the view that something serious was afoot. What were the financial implications of "Jack's affair"?[14] Albert was maintaining Lewis financially at this time, and was beginning to realise that it was not merely his son whom he was supporting. Mrs. Moore's absent husband (whom she referred to as "The Beast") provided her with an erratic income. It was not difficult to work out her main source of income. The direct source was, of course, Lewis. Yet the indirect source was Albert Lewis himself.

A showdown was inevitable. Lewis returned to Belfast on 28 July 1919, having spent the previous week on holiday in England with his brother, Warnie. In a tense meeting, Albert Lewis asked Lewis to explain his financial situation. Lewis replied that he had about £15 to his credit. Like many former army officers, Lewis banked with Cox & Co, of Charing Cross Road, London. The bank had been formed during the Napoleonic wars to pay soldiers' wages and act as regimental agents. Albert Lewis then found an opened letter from Cox & Co addressed to his son, informing him that he owed them £12. He challenged Lewis, who admitted that he had lied to his father about his financial situation.

In what appears to have been a forceful and unpleasant exchange, Lewis informed his father that he had no respect or concern for him. As Albert Lewis confided to his diary, Lewis "deceived me and said terrible, insulting, and despising things to me." It was "one of the most miserable periods of my life."[15] Perhaps it was just as well that Albert Lewis never saw his son's earlier letter to Arthur Greeves, wherein Lewis described himself as a "habitual liar," and gently chided Greeves for being so naive as to "swallow" his "lies with avidity."[16]

Yet however much Lewis might react with revulsion to his father, he still had no means of supporting himself, and was not in any position to assert his financial independence. To Lewis's relief, his father did not cancel his allowance. Despite their deep personal estrangement, Albert Lewis continued to support his son, knowing full well the purposes to which Lewis would put most of this allowance. Lewis's letters to his father around this time were polite. Yet it would be some time before their relationship returned to the way it was.

Lewis spent the academic year 1919–1920 living out of college, on Windmill Road, Headington, where Mrs. Moore had found new lodgings. It was normal for some undergraduates to choose to live in "digs" after their first year in college, and Lewis could now easily maintain the fiction that Mrs. Moore was his landlady. His second year was dominated by the prospect of examinations—Honours Moderations—which were due to take place in March and would be the first indication of Lewis's academic prowess. In the end, Lewis was one of thirty-one students to be placed in the First Class. Lewis wrote to tell his father the good news, casually mentioning that he was vacationing "with a man" who had been asking him "for some time to go and 'walk' with him."[17] In fact, Lewis was continuing to deceive his father. He spent the vacation with Mrs. Moore and Maureen.

ACADEMIC DISTINCTION: THE CHANCELLOR'S ESSAY PRIZE, 1921

In Trinity Term 1920, Lewis began the study of Greats, being taught ancient history by George H. Stevenson (1880–1952) and philosophy by Edgar F. Carritt (1876–1964). His letters home grumble about the high cost of books. However, it soon became clear that Lewis had set his sights on a new project. He had been "recommended to try for the Chancellor's Essay Prize" in April 1921. This was to be awarded for the best English essay by an undergraduate on a topic set for discussion—in this case, "Optimism." It would, Lewis told his father, be a "splendid advertisement" if he could win it, but he recognised that the competition would be "very keen."[18]

In the end, Lewis produced a manuscript of about eleven thousand words, and complained bitterly to his father about both the cost of having it typed and the many typing errors that resulted. The declaration of the result was delayed until Lewis's nerves were close to breaking. Finally, on 24 May, it was announced that Lewis had won the prize. He was invited to read an extract chosen by the Professor of Poetry and the Public Orator at the annual Encaenia—the honorary degree ceremony at the Sheldonian Theatre. At this ceremony, the guests of honour included Georges Clemenceau, prime minister of France from 1917 to 1920. Lewis spoke for all of two minutes, and wrote to his brother of his delight in being able to make himself heard in the large building.[19]

4.2 The Sheldonian Theatre, the site of Oxford University degree ceremonies, in 1922. The Sheldonian was completed in 1668 to a design by Sir Christopher Wren.

The Oxford publisher and bookseller Basil Blackwell immediately got in touch, offering to meet Lewis to discuss publishing the essay. Yet the essay was never published, and the manuscript has now been lost. In any case, Lewis seemed to have little faith in the literary merits of the work. It would, he suggested to his father, "soon be forgotten." It was the fact of winning the prize, rather than the essay itself, that really mattered.[20] We can only hope that Lewis is right. No copy remains in the Lewis family papers, nor in the archives of Oxford University.[21] We do not know what Lewis had to say on "Optimism," nor how he said it. All that we know is that it impressed the panel of judges, and helped shape the perception that Lewis was a rising star in Oxford's firmament.

Lewis's academic career might now be showing distinct signs of promise; his relationship with his father, however, remained distant and tense. Their simmering differences over Mrs. Moore threatened to come to the fore in July 1921, when Albert Lewis wrote to let his son know that he would be travelling to England, and intended to visit Oxford to see Lewis and his college rooms. Alarmed at the prospect of his father meeting Mrs. Moore, Lewis invented a "friend" who would make such a visit impossible. Lewis claimed that he had been "moved out of College," and that he was now sharing a room with a man who was "up to his eyes in work" and would resent visitors interrupting him.[22]

In a magnificent act of theatrical deception, Lewis hastily transformed the back room of Mrs. Moore's house to look like "an undergraduate's digs." He managed to persuade his fellow student Rodney Pasley to move in with him for the duration of this unwelcome paternal visit, pretending to be his overworked and unsociable roommate. However, in the end his father contented himself with a substantial lunch at the Clarendon Hotel in Oxford's Cornmarket, and showed no interest in seeing either Lewis's rooms or his college.[23]

SUCCESS AND FAILURE: ACADEMIC DISTINCTION AND UNEMPLOYMENT

Lewis's final academic year (1921–1922), studying Greats at University College, saw him focussing on two goals: excelling in the final examinations in June, and finding employment afterwards. His diary for this period presents an extraordinary record of books read, household chores accomplished, Mrs. Moore's friends and family engaged in conversation, job possibilities explored, and unsuccessful attempts to check his growing anxieties about his future academic employment prospects.

4.3 Cornmarket Street, one of Oxford's busiest shopping areas, in 1922. The Clarendon Hotel is clearly visible on the left-hand side of the street.

Those doubts crystallised into near certainty in May 1922, less than a month before he was due to sit for his final examinations. Edgar Carritt, his college philosophy tutor, made it clear that there were no academic jobs for him in the near future. He suggested to Lewis that there was only one realistic option if he was set on an academic career: he must spend a further year in Oxford and "take another school."[24] What Carritt meant by this was that Lewis ought to make himself as employable as possible by studying for a second Final Honour School. Lewis should expand his fields of competency by going beyond Greats and studying English literature.

Reginald Macan (1848–1941), the master of University College, gave him similar advice when they met later that month. Macan had just been asked by an American colleague to recommend a promising young scholar for a one-year studentship at Cornell University in New York. Lewis was his first choice for the position. However, the somewhat modest stipend would not have covered even Lewis's travelling expenses, and would have had a devastating impact on Lewis's private life. Lewis chose to draw the former point, but not the latter, to the master's notice.

Macan asked Lewis what he proposed to do next. After Lewis had set out his hopes of securing a fellowship at Oxford, Macan tried to explain to him how times had changed. The old, prewar days, in which brilliant students were offered a college fellowship immediately after their final examinations, were long gone. The Royal Commission on Oxford and Cambridge Universities, often known as the "Asquith Commission," set up in November 1919, had made a number of recommendations on how Oxford should modernise to meet the needs of the postwar age. University College would have no option other than to implement these reforms, which would include the abolition of certain types of college fellowships.[25] Lewis would have to adapt to the new realities of academic life. He would need to prove himself by studying for another Honour School and try to pick up another university prize. Macan hinted that the college would renew his scholarship if he chose to do this; he would not need to worry about paying tuition fees.

Lewis wrote to his father, explaining the advice he had been given and its possible implications. In his sober letter, Lewis tried to explain how the postwar world was changing, so that there might no longer be a place for someone who was an expert in the increasingly arcane world of classical languages and literature, or even philosophy. If he could not find an academic position at Oxford, his only realistic future occupation was "schoolmastering"—a desperate strategy of last resort, which Lewis regarded with a total lack of enthusiasm. In any case, Lewis knew that he would not be seen as an especially attractive prospect by English public schools. His "inability to play games"—which had made his time at Malvern College so miserable—would count decisively against him. His only serious option was to become an Oxford don. Nobody expected them to be any good at sport. Yet it was becoming increasingly clear that, to make himself employable in the university world, Lewis would need to supplement the general excellence of Greats with the specialist knowledge of a distinct field. Lewis had no doubt what this additional subject ought to be. There was one "'rising' subject" at Oxford, and it was English literature.[26]

Further reflection on this matter was postponed, as Lewis had to spend every available moment studying for his final examinations, which took place from 8–14 June. Lewis faced papers including Roman history, logic, an unseen Greek translation from Philostratus, and an unseen Latin translation from Cicero. Lewis was unsure of how he had performed, although he was at least clear in his own mind that he had not failed.

The exams over, Lewis tried to calm himself while he waited for the results by penning some cantos for his poem *Dymer*. This was conceived as an epic poem in the tradition of Homer, Milton, and Tennyson. Although Lewis began sketching this work while at Great Bookham, its proper inception dates from 1922. Lewis's diary from 1922 to 1924 contains frequent short statements along the lines "worked on *Dymer* this afternoon." We shall return to this work, published in 1926, later.

While he waited, Lewis also tried to remedy his somewhat precarious financial situation. To raise more funds, he took out an advertisement in the local newspaper, *The Oxford Times*, offering to tutor schoolboys or undergraduates in classics during the months of August and September. He explored an opening as a lecturer in classics at Reading University, a thirty-minute train journey from Oxford. Yet it was made clear to him at the interview that he would have to move to Reading if he secured the position. This was out of the question, given Lewis's domestic situation. Maureen was happy at Headington School, and Lewis had no desire to disrupt either her education or her social life. He withdrew his application. As might be expected, he offered a quite different explanation of the situation to his father. He was not really the "pure" classicist that Reading was looking for.[27]

Then another possibility emerged: a fellowship in classics was being offered at Magdalen College. Lewis put in an application for this position out of a sense of duty rather than with any real hope of securing the position, having been forewarned that his application would probably come to nothing. The outcome would be settled by a competitive examination in September. There was nothing Lewis could do to improve his chances before then.

In any case, Lewis had other things to worry about. On 28 July, he presented himself at the Examination Schools in Oxford's High Street for the viva voce examination. He recalled it taking no more than five minutes. He was called upon to defend some statements he had made in his examination papers, including a possibly unwise reference to "poor old Plato," before the examiners. A few days later, Mrs. Moore moved again, having found a new home ("Hillsboro") for the summer at 2 Western Road, Headington,[28] which they could enjoy rent-free. Mrs. Moore was just as anxious about their financial situation as Lewis himself, and had arranged to sublet Warneford Road to Rodney Pasley and his wife, while also taking in a paying guest at Western Road. They needed every shilling they could save. She also took in sewing work to raise money. By November of that year, Lewis confided to his diary that she was taking on too much.[29] The strain caused by their faltering financial situation was becoming increasingly difficult to bear.

On 4 August, Lewis took a bus into Oxford, and went to the Examination Schools to find out when the results of the final examinations would be posted. To his surprise, he discovered that they were already displayed. He was relieved to discover that he was one of the nineteen students who had secured First Class Honours. But what was he to do next?

In the end, Lewis threw all his hopes and efforts into winning the fellowship in classics offered by Magdalen College.[30] The fellowship would be one of three offered by the college that year which would be awarded by open competition through an extended written examination. On 29 September, Lewis turned up with ten other hopefuls at Magdalen for the first examination.[31] He was discouraged when he realised the calibre of the other candidates, including future academic stars such as A. C. Ewing (1899–1973) and E. R. Dodds (1893–1979). (Dodds went on to become Regius Professor of Greek at the University of Oxford in 1936.) Aware of how slim his chances were, Lewis confided to his diary that he would "act as though" he had "not got the fellowship," and prepare to study for the School of English.[32] It was not until 12 October that Lewis finally learned that the Magdalen fellowship had been awarded to another candidate.[33] But by then, Lewis had already followed his tutors' advice and thrown himself fully into the study of English.

Sir Herbert Warren (1853–1930), president of Magdalen College, wrote personally to Lewis in November, confirming that he had not been elected to the fellowship in classics and offering some feedback. Magdalen had elected three new fellows around that time, and Warren explained that Lewis had come close to being one of them. The fact remained, however, that the college had offered the fellowship in classics to another candidate:

> I am afraid you cannot have done yourself full justice, whatever may have been the reason, although you came well up, and were one of six especially mentioned to the College as having reached the Fellowship standard, and worthy of election, you were not one of the three finally recommended.[34]

Warren's letter mingled affirmation and criticism in about equal measure. Yet the shrewd reader of that letter quickly realises that its covert message was ultimately encouraging. The talent was there, but the moment was not right. There might be another opportunity.

Lewis's diaries and correspondence of 1920–1922 bear witness to his personal anxieties and plans for the future, not least concerning his employment prospects. If he could not secure an academic position in classics, might he find one in philosophy instead? His undergraduate studies had given him a firm grasp of the subject. Yet Lewis's preoccupation with his own future seems to have blinded him to other matters, most notably the serious tensions in his native Ireland. Lewis makes curiously little reference to the momentous events of 1920–1923, in which Ireland was convulsed by political turmoil. The political struggle for Irish independence, given new energy by the Great War, had erupted into violence in 1919. The British began to lose control of rural areas of Ireland to the Irish Republican Army (IRA). On "Bloody Sunday" (21 November 1920), the IRA shot dead fourteen British intelligence operatives and informers in Dublin. Later that day the British authorities retaliated at Croke Park, also killing fourteen people. Violence spread to the northern cities of Londonderry and Belfast. The Protestant community felt under threat from Republican gunmen.

In 1920, the British government offered limited home rule to Ireland. It was not enough. The Irish wanted political and national independence, not some form of devolved government. The violence continued. On 11 July 1921, a truce was declared. Yet it did not stop the violence in Belfast. Finally, the British government agreed to the creation of the Irish Free State on 6 December 1922. The six predominantly Protestant northern counties were given a month from that date to decide whether they wished to remain part of the Irish Free State or rejoin the United Kingdom. A day later, the parliament of Northern Ireland requested that it be allowed to become part of the United Kingdom again. Ireland was now partitioned.

Lewis seems to have been curiously indifferent to and disengaged from these developments, despite their momentous implications for his family and friends in Ireland. According to Lewis's diary entry for the critical date of 6 December 1922, the big question on his mind was not Irish independence, nor the political future of Belfast, nor the safety of his father, but whether the word *breakfast* was to be understood as "a cup of tea at eight or a roast of beef at eleven."[35] So why this astonishing lack of interest in the biggest political and social upheaval in Ireland during his lifetime? Perhaps the most obvious answer is also the most persuasive: Lewis did not see himself as belonging there anymore. His home, his real family, and his heart were in Oxford. Mrs. Moore, not Albert Lewis, was the lodestar of his family life.

MRS. MOORE: THE CORNERSTONE OF LEWIS'S LIFE

At this point, we need to explore Lewis's relationship with Mrs. Moore in a little more detail. Lewis's unusual domestic arrangements were not well known at Oxford. During the 1930s, most of his acquaintances had the impression that Lewis was a typical bachelor don, who lived with his "old mother" in Headington. Few knew that his mother had died in his childhood, and that the so-called "mother" in question played a rather more complex role in Lewis's life.

Many accounts of Lewis's personal life take their cue from Warnie's frequently expressed dislike of Mrs. Moore, leading them to characterise this relationship in quite negative terms. She is portrayed as a domineering, selfish, and demanding woman, who often treated Lewis like a servant or errand-boy, and offered him little in the way of intellectual stimulation.

There are good reasons for accepting some such evaluation of the situation in the late 1940s, when Mrs. Moore's health began to fail and she became increasingly difficult as dementia set in. Yet Lewis's difficulties at this later stage were probably caused as much by Warnie's alcoholism as by the ailing Mrs. Moore's petulant demands. But we must not read the situation of two decades later back into these early days. A younger Mrs. Moore was there for him when Lewis needed the emotional support and comfort which no other member of his family seemed able or willing to provide—at the time of his departure to war in France (his father's absence being especially hurtful to Lewis), during his convalescence from his war wounds, and as he sought to secure an academic position at Oxford. It is arguable that Mrs. Moore created an environment of relative structure and stability for him on his return from combat, easing his transition into academic life.

Lewis, it must be remembered, was separated from his mother by death, and from his family through his father's ill-considered (if well-intentioned) decision to send him away to boarding school in England. In 1951, the British psychologist John Bowlby (1907–1990) produced a study for the World Health Organization dealing with the mental health problems of children displaced by war. His main conclusion was that childhood experiences of interpersonal relationships were crucial to their psychological development.[36] Bowlby went on to develop the notion of a "secure base," from which the child could learn to cope with challenges, develop independence, and mature emotionally. But Bowlby's research came too late to influence Albert Lewis's decisions. Lewis clearly possessed such a "secure base" as a young boy; it was, however, shattered by the death of his mother and his enforced attendance at boarding school.

Lewis's comments in *Surprised by Joy* about the impact of his mother's death deserve close attention: "It was all sea and islands now; the great continent had sunk like Atlantis."[37] Lewis's rich language uses geographical imagery to describe his emotional loss of stability and security, inevitably leading to a longing for their future restoration. He was like someone doomed to sail the seas, unable to find a safe and permanent harbour. Lewis's writings of the 1920s provide strong evidence that Mrs. Moore's extended family came to provide that secure base for him. She offered him emotional support and encouragement as he explored career options, and coped with his early failure to secure them. However, she was no intellectual, and was unable to function as his academic soul mate—a point which helps us understand Lewis's later attraction to intelligent women, capable of writing serious books. Yet Mrs. Moore arguably provided Lewis with vital elements of the context he needed at this formative stage of his scholarly career.

Perhaps most obviously, Mrs. Moore provided Lewis with a ready-made family. His diaries from 1922 to 1925 show him to have developed a settled and secure family life—something he thought he had lost after the death of his mother at Little Lea. Maureen became a sister to him, and he became a brother to her. Maureen is too easily neglected in accounts of Lewis's development; his diaries make more appreciative reference to her than many realise.

4.4 "The Family": Lewis, Maureen, and Mrs. Moore on the balcony of a tea shop in St. Agnes Cove, Cornwall, in 1927.

There is no doubt that Lewis ended up doing all kinds of menial household chores—running to get margarine from a corner store, retrieving Mrs. Moore's purse from the bus station, or responding immediately to the sudden collapse of Mrs. Moore's bedroom curtain rails. But he was the only man in the household, and appears to have willingly pulled his weight to ensure its smooth running. These things had to be done, and Lewis did them. In any case, Lewis came to see such tasks as examples of the tradition of "courtly love," which he declared to be a noble and honourable code of conduct by which a young man might "leap up on errands" or "go through heat or cold, at the bidding of one's lady."[38] Lewis might have been able to invest such household chores with dignity and significance by conceiving them as ennobling expressions of "courtly love."

Mrs. Moore also extended Lewis's social circle. She was hospitable to a fault, regularly inviting family and friends to supper. Lewis found himself developing the relational skills and emotional intelligence that he might never have acquired had he remained cloistered within the walls of University College. As he himself was the first to admit, his own circle of

97

friends was somewhat restricted. "I am apt to regard my own set, which consists mainly of literary gents," he told his father, as being "central, normal and representative."[39] Lewis made relatively few friends while studying Greats; indeed, he seems to have earned the nickname "Heavy Lewis,"[40] in that he was perceived to be "heavy going" by other students. (The unflattering name was probably a play on the Lewis Light Machine Gun of the Great War.) Lewis's ability to relate to people may have been late in developing, but it was encouraged more by Mrs. Moore's circle than by his own.

The Moore household was also visited regularly by Maureen's friends from Headington School. One of these—Mary Wiblin—features prominently in Lewis's diary entries of the early 1920s. Wiblin (affectionately known as "Smudge") was Maureen's music teacher; by way of payment, Lewis taught her Latin. There are hints here of a possible romantic relationship with Lewis. Yet nothing ever developed, possibly due to Lewis's complex relationship with Mrs. Moore.

THE STUDENT OF ENGLISH LANGUAGE AND LITERATURE, 1922–1923

Oxford was late in recognising the importance of English literature as a subject worthy of serious academic study. Both University College London and King's College London offered undergraduate courses in the subject from the 1830s. The growing importance of the subject was catalysed by a number of factors. The long reign of Queen Victoria had helped create a strong sense of English national identity. Just as important, many shrewd politicians realised the importance of emphasising how the English shared a rich literary tradition. A landmark in this development was the establishment of a Chair in English Language and Literature at Oxford in 1882. Yet no School of English existed until 1894, despite growing demand for such a development.[41]

The simple truth is that Oxford resisted any such development. Indeed, the establishment of the School of English in 1894 was mired in controversy and bitterness. Some derided its introduction as a way of giving weaker students something easy and pointless to study. Others were alarmed at the danger of creating a new degree that would be seen as second-rate. Greats were meaty and substantial; how could English be anything other than subjective reflections on novels and poems? How could "mere chatter about Shelley"[42] be taken with academic seriousness? It was impressionistic and superficial—not the sort of thing that Oxford University would wish to encourage.

Nevertheless, the pressure for the academic study of English literature mounted.[43] It was still seen by many traditionalists at Oxford as an undemanding subject, suitable for less able male students destined for the ranks of schoolmasters in England's public schools—and, of course, for women. Many women, excluded from the study of the sciences and humanities at Oxford, saw the study of English literature as one of the few means of entering an educational career open to them. From 1892, the Association for Promoting the Higher Education of Women in Oxford organised a series of lectures and classes for their students, in which English literature featured prominently.

A second group for whom the study of English literature became important in the later Victorian period was civil servants. The Indian Civil Service, anxious to ensure it recruited and promoted the best people, introduced examinations in English from 1855 onwards. Prospective imperial civil servants among Oxford's undergraduates noted the way the wind was blowing and began to study English literature with their future career prospects in mind. Yet the emphasis at Oxford was clearly more on *English* than on *literature*. As British imperialism flourished in the later Victorian and Edwardian periods, the study of English literature came to be seen as a means of affirming and asserting English cultural superiority over the upstart Americans and the rebellious colonials.

England's final victory over Germany in the Great War of 1914–1918 provoked a minor surge of nationalism, which gave added patriotic motivation to the study of English literature. Yet the study of English literature at Oxford was augmented by factors other than a renewed nationalism.

For many more thoughtful souls, literature offered a way of dealing with the trauma and destruction of the war, allowing them to frame their questions in new ways and find deeper spiritual solutions that went beyond the mere jingoism of the Establishment.

The rise of the "war poets" is perhaps the most important of these developments. Many found comfort in their writings, allowing them to see the nightmare of the war in new and helpful ways. Others saw these poets as expressing a legitimate anger about the violence and futility of war, and sought to channel this anger in politically and socially constructive ways. The motivations for the study of English literature in the immediate postwar era may have been complex. They were, however, real, and led to a new interest in a field once regarded as culturally and intellectually inferior to the study of classics.

By the 1920s, Oxford's School of English Language and Literature was expanding, benefitting from a resurgence of interest in the subject after the war. For the historical reasons just noted, it was still initially dominated by women students and those with an interest in serving in the Indian Civil Service. As the Oxford school expanded, colleges began to take note of this trend. Tutorial fellowships in English Language and Literature began to be established. Lewis could hardly have failed to have been aware of this development. If he could not secure a position in classics or philosophy, there was now an alternative possibility.

Lewis began his studies in English Language and Literature on 13 October 1922, when he met with A. S. L. Farquharson at University College to discuss his programme of study. Farquharson advised him to go to Germany and learn the language; the future, in his view, lay in European literature, and that was where the jobs would be. For obvious reasons, Lewis decided not to follow this advice. Neither Mrs. Moore nor Maureen would have had any enthusiasm for a visit to his former enemy, or for his extended absence when there was so much that needed to be done around the house.

Lewis found the study of English exhausting. It demanded not merely a total immersion in a vast literature, but the acquisition of the linguistic skills needed to read some of its classic texts. But the real problem was that Lewis was doing a course in less than nine months that was designed to be studied over three years. Normally an undergraduate would spend the first year studying the basic literature and then move on to a more detailed study for the final two years of the course. Lewis was exempted from the first year of the course through having "senior status"—he already had an Oxford degree. But he would still need to cram the work of the final two years of the course into one; otherwise, he would have been "overstanding for Honours," and could have been awarded only a pass degree. He desperately needed to win First Class Honours to make his scholarly mark and secure an academic job.

A major gulf began to open up between the approaches to English literature at England's two ancient universities at this time. Where the Oxford school focussed on historical, textual, and philological questions throughout the 1920s and 1930s, the Cambridge school—shaped by scholars such as I. A. Richards (1893–1979) and F. R. Leavis (1895–1978)—adopted a more theoretical approach, treating works of literature as "texts" or "objects" that could be subjected to scientific literary criticism. Lewis felt perfectly at home in the Oxford context. His focus was on texts and authors, and he developed an aversion to literary theory—a characteristic of his scholarly writings for the remainder of his career.

Lewis's study of English pressed him to his limits. He wrote relatively few letters during the academic year 1922–1923; many of these refer to his growing interest in Old English (Anglo-Saxon) and the demands that mastering this language made on him. He also became aware that there was a clear sociological distinction between his fellow students in Greats and those in English literature: the latter, he confided to his diary, consisted mainly of "women, Indians, and Americans" and possessed "a certain amateurishness" in comparison with Greats students.[44] His diary for Michaelmas Term 1922 exudes a tangible sense of intellectual loneliness, occasionally alleviated by interesting lectures and stimulating conversations. But for the most part, Lewis derived his mental pleasures from books, often working to midnight to get through his reading list.

Yet friendships began to emerge, to complement (though never displace) his long-standing relationship with Arthur Greeves. Two are of especial importance. Lewis originally met Owen Barfield (1898–1997) in 1919. Barfield was then studying English at Wadham College. Lewis quickly recognised him as someone who was both intelligent and well read, even though he disagreed with him on virtually everything. "Barfield has probably forgotten more than I ever knew," he ruefully confided to his diary.[45]

Lewis dubbed Barfield the "wisest and best of my unofficial teachers,"[46] and was willing to be corrected by him. As an example of this, Lewis notes his early error of referring to philosophy as "a subject." "It wasn't a *subject* to Plato," retorted Barfield, "it was a way."[47] Barfield's interest in Rudolf Steiner's philosophy of "anthroposophy," which aimed to extend the scientific method to human spiritual experiences, began to develop after he heard Steiner lecture in 1924, and became a particular matter of contention with Lewis, then an atheist. Lewis jokingly referred to the "Great War" that developed between them on this and other matters. "Everything that I had labored so hard to expel from my own life seemed to have flared up and met me in my best friends."[48] Lewis began to feel embattled and threatened by questions that Barfield was posing, which he seemed unable to answer entirely to his own satisfaction.[49]

Yet despite his differences with Barfield, Lewis credits him with bringing about two fundamental changes in his own thinking. The first of these was the demolition of Lewis's "chronological snobbery," which Lewis defined as "the uncritical acceptance of the intellectual climate common to our own age and the assumption that whatever has gone out of date is on that account discredited."[50]

The second change related to Lewis's way of thinking about reality. Lewis, like most of that age, tended to assume that "the universe revealed by the senses" constituted "rock-bottom reality." For Lewis, this was the most economical and commonsense way of thinking about things, which he took to be thoroughly scientific. "I wanted Nature to be quite independent of our observation; something other, indifferent, self-existing."[51] But what of human moral judgements? Or feelings of joy? Or the experience of beauty? How did such subjective ways of thinking and experiencing fit into this?

It was no idle thought. As an undergraduate at Oxford, Lewis had been influenced by what he styled the "New Look," a rationalist way of thinking which led him to believe that he must abandon any notion that his fleeting experiences of "Joy" were clues to the deeper meaning of life.[52] Lewis went with the flow, immersing himself in this then-fashionable way of thinking. He came to believe that his boyhood desires, longings, and experience had been exposed as meaningless. Lewis decided that he was "done with all that." He had "'seen through' them." He was "never going to be taken in again."[53]

Yet Barfield persuaded Lewis that these lines of argument were inconsistent. Lewis was relying on precisely the same inner patterns of thought that he had dismissed in order to secure his knowledge of an allegedly "objective" world. The consistent outcome of believing only in "the universe revealed by the senses" was to adopt "a Behaviouristic theory of logic, ethics, and aesthetics." Yet Lewis regarded such a theory as unbelievable. There was an alternative, which gave full weight to the importance of human moral and aesthetic intuitions and did not discount or dismiss them. For Lewis, this led to only one conclusion: "Our logic was participation in a cosmic *Logos*."[54] And where might that line of thought take him?

This theme is explored in a short story titled "The Man Born Blind,"[55] which has particular significance since it is thought to be the earliest piece of prose fiction that survives from the adult Lewis. It is not well written, and has little sign of Lewis's mature style or powerful imaginative vision. It is a parable, told in less than two thousand words, from before his conversion to Christianity. Its basic theme is that of a man born blind who regains his sight. He expects to see light, but he fails to appreciate that light is not something seen, but something that makes seeing possible. It is not something we see, but something *by which* we see.

For Lewis, human thought depends upon a "cosmic *Logos*," which is not itself seen or understood, or even *capable* of being seen or understood, but is nevertheless the condition necessary for human sight and understanding. This idea can be interpreted in a Platonic way. However, early

Christian writers steeped in the Platonic tradition—such as Augustine of Hippo (354–430)—were able to show that this was easily adapted to a Christian way of thinking, which understood God as the one who illuminates reality and enables humanity to discern its features.

Lewis's second friendship to develop during his study of English literature was with Nevill Coghill (1899–1980), an Irish student who had served in the Great War. After taking a first degree in history at Exeter College, Coghill had chosen to study English. Like Lewis, he was attempting to manage the course in a single year. They first met at a discussion presided over by Professor George Gordon, and rapidly came to appreciate each other's insights into the texts they were engaging. This reading of texts, Coghill recalled, was "a continuous intoxication of discovery,"[56] leading into discussion and debate which extended over long walks in the Oxfordshire countryside. Coghill would play an important role in shaping Lewis's later ideas.

The long year of intense study came to an end in June 1923, when Lewis sat for the final examinations. His diary entries for these days reveal his frustration; he had not performed as well as he had hoped. He calmed himself down by mowing the lawn. The viva voce examinations were set for 10 July. Lewis duly dressed himself in *sub fusc*—a black gown, dark suit, and white bow tie—and presented himself with the other candidates. The examiners dismissed all but six of them, whom they wished to press further on some of their answers. Lewis was among those who had to stay behind for the potential ordeal of an oral examination.

More than two hours later, Lewis finally faced his examiners. They raised some concerns about his examination papers. He had used the word *little-est* in an answer to one question. How could he possibly justify using such a strange word? Without batting an eyelid, Lewis gave his reply. It could be found in the correspondence between Samuel Taylor Coleridge and Thomas Poole.[57] And surely he had been too severe on Dryden? Lewis thought not, and told them why. After less than three minutes, Lewis was dismissed. The viva was over. Lewis left the Examination Schools and returned home. He had other things to worry about—such as earning some money. For the remainder of that summer, he had agreed to act as an examiner for the Higher School Certificate, marking hundreds of generally dull schoolboy essays, while Mrs. Moore took in paying guests to help cover the bills.

On 16 July, the examination results were published. Only six of the ninety students entered for the examinations had gained First Class Honours, including

Coghill, N. J. A. (Exeter); and
Lewis, C. S. (University).

Lewis had now secured a "Triple First," a rare distinction at Oxford. Yet Lewis still had no job prospects. He was highly qualified and highly learned, but he was, as he later told his father, "adrift and unemployed"[58]— at a time when economic recession was stalking much of the Western world. Things looked bleak. Lewis scrabbled around, desperately looking for students he could coach or articles he could write for newspapers or journals. He needed the money.

So why did University College itself not establish a tutorial fellowship in English at this time? After all, the college had appointed Ernest de Sélincourt as a lecturer in English in 1896, the first such college appointment in the university.[59] Yet Sélincourt was never appointed as a tutorial fellow of the college, and eventually moved to the University of Birmingham in 1908 to take up its newly established Chair of English. After the end of the Great War, more and more students wished to study the subject. Perhaps more important, the college had, in Lewis, an outstanding talent who would be more than capable of doing the job.

The answer lies in a bequest given to the college by one of its former members, Robert Mynors (1817–1895).[60] Mynors, a successful barrister, left the college funds to endow a college fellowship "for the study and teaching of the Social Sciences." The funds were finally released to the college in 1920, and a decision was made in 1924 to create a Fellowship in Economics and Politics. This modest expansion of its fellowship was all that the college felt able to cope with. There would be no Fellowship in English until Peter Bayley was appointed to such a position in 1949.

Lewis's hopes of securing a job anywhere else in Oxford regularly rose, and just as regularly fell. St. John's College wanted a tutor in philosophy. Lewis was hopeful, but it came to nothing. By May 1924, Lewis was still unemployed, living on piecemeal, part-time earnings. His letters to his father spoke of cutting back to the bare essentials. He had hopes of securing a fellowship at Trinity College. But that might well crumble, like all his hopes to date.

Then fate stepped in. Reginald Macan had resigned as master of University College in April 1923, and was succeeded by Sir Michael Sadler.[61] Sadler had read Lewis's work with approval in the summer of 1923, and had recommended him to various literary colleagues as a potential reviewer. On 11 May 1924, Lewis wrote to his father in some excitement. Edgar Carritt, his old philosophy tutor at University College, was going to teach in Ann Arbor, Michigan, for a year. The college needed a temporary replacement. Sadler had offered him the job for a salary of £200. It wasn't much, he conceded, but it was better than nothing. He would have to work under the supervision of his old tutor Farquharson. But it might lead to better things in due course. And if he got the fellowship at Trinity, he would be allowed to withdraw his acceptance of the position at University.[62]

Trinity liked Lewis. The fellows had invited him to dinner—a traditional Oxford way of allowing serious potential candidates to be evaluated by all the fellows. But they decided they didn't like him as much as another candidate. Lewis had lost out again. This time, however, he had something to fall back on.

Lewis now had a job, even if it failed to satisfy his deepest longings. Lewis was obliged to teach philosophy, when he really wanted to be a poet. *Dymer* was the passion of his life, and the basis of his potential reputation. As things had worked out, Lewis was a frustrated poet who was obliged to teach philosophy to earn a living. He was not the only poet in such a situation. T. S. Eliot (1888–1965), whose poetry Lewis detested, had written his poetry while working in the Colonial and Foreign Department of Lloyds Bank in London.

Lewis's dislike of Eliot led to his later attempting to perpetrate a hoax on the older poet, who edited the *New Criterion*. In June 1926, Lewis hit on the idea of sending a series of spoof poems, mimicking Eliot's style, to the journal, hoping that the parody would be accepted for publication. Henry Yorke, one of Lewis's coconspirators, came up with a superb opening line: "My soul is a windowless façade."[63] Unfortunately, the only line Lewis could construct to follow it made a revealing mention of the Marquis de Sade. In the end, nothing came of the hoax.

Writing poetry eased Lewis's tensions, even if it did little to further his employment prospects. Lewis's poem *Dymer*, published in 1926, was a poetic rendering of an earlier prose work. It achieved neither significant commercial success nor critical acclaim. Indeed, it seems fair to suggest that its failure marked the end of Lewis's dreams to be a recognised poet, whether English or Irish. There was always a possibility that Lewis might come to represent an Irish voice in poetry. Yet his early Oxford experience led him to realise that the appeal of Irish poetry was not universal. Why, he wondered, was W. B. Yeats not more admired in Oxford literary circles? "Perhaps," Lewis remarked, "his appeal is purely Irish."[64] Yet Lewis also came to understand that his own voice would not count as "Irish." He was an atheist—more accurately, an Ulster Protestant atheist. This did not fit in with the strongly Catholic associations of being "Irish." And he had in any case left Ireland for England as a young boy, selling his birthright (so his critics would say) for an English education. And finally, Lewis did not write on specifically Irish themes. Lewis's inclination was clearly towards classical and universal themes, not those traditionally embraced by confessedly Irish poets. Lewis's authorial voice might have been shaped by his Irish homeland; it did not, however, speak explicitly of those roots.

On reading *Dymer*, I found myself from time to time delighted by the verbal elegance and philosophical acumen of some of its individual phrases or lines. Yet those moments of pleasure are rare and infrequent. The whole is somehow not equal to its parts. Its few shards of brilliance are not sustained and are overwhelmed by expanses of lacklustre and flat lines. *Dymer*, considered as a poem, simply does not work. As one of Owen Barfield's friends remarked, "The metrical level is good, the vocabulary is large: but Poetry—not a line."[65]

It is not clear when Lewis finally accepted that he would never achieve recognition as a poet. He would continue to write poems for his private enjoyment, as a way of clearing his mind. Yet the failure of *Dymer* on its appearance in 1926 does not seem to have precipitated any crisis of identity or loss of confidence. Lewis simply reinvented himself as a writer of prose. Paradoxically, *Dymer* points to the reason why Lewis has achieved such recognition and fame—his ability to write prose tinged with a poetic vision, its carefully crafted phrases lingering in the memory because they have captivated the imagination. The qualities we associate with good poetry—such as an appreciation of the sound of words, rich and suggestive analogies and images, vivid description, and lyrical sense—are found in Lewis's prose.

THE FELLOWSHIP AT MAGDALEN COLLEGE

Lewis spent the academic year 1924–1925 teaching University College's undergraduate students philosophy, while giving lectures on philosophical themes. He was overwhelmed with work. His diary contains no entries between 3 August 1924 and 5 February 1925. He gave sixteen undergraduate lectures on "The Good, its position among the values." His maiden lecture, given on Tuesday, 14 October at University College, was attended by a mere four people. (He faced stiff competition from H. A. Pritchard, and the university lecture list mistakenly informed its trusting readers that Lewis's lecture would take place at a totally different location—Pembroke College).[66]

Alongside this, Lewis tutored college students in philosophy, and took on additional work to supplement his income—mostly correcting school examination papers. Yet Lewis's busyness could not shield him from his own looming unemployment. His post was temporary and would expire at the end of the academic year. He would have no job beginning in the summer of 1925. Then Lewis heard the news that would prove to be a turning point in his life.

In April 1925, Magdalen College announced that it wished to elect a tutorial fellow in English. The announcement of the "Official Fellowship and Tutorship in English" specified that the successful candidate would be required to

> act as Tutor, and give instruction, to all the undergraduate
> members of the College reading for the Honour School of English
> Language and Literature, to give Inter-Collegiate Lectures as the
> College representative for the Honour School of English, and also
> to supervise the work of any undergraduates who may read for the
> Pass School of English Literature.[67]

Lewis was already known to Magdalen, and was clearly seen by them as meeting the intellectual standards they required of their fellows. He lost no time in applying. However, as he informed his father in a somewhat dejected frame of mind, he had few hopes.[68] His own English tutor—Frank Wilson—was rumoured to be one of the candidates, reflecting the fact that Magdalen was far better endowed than most Oxford colleges. Lewis would not stand a chance against Wilson's superior experience. However, Lewis could see a faint silver lining to this cloud: if Wilson got the job, he would have to give up teaching his students from University and Exeter Colleges. Someone would have to teach these students—and why should it not be Lewis?

Then his hopes were raised by an unexpected development. Wilson would not be a candidate! Encouraged and emboldened, Lewis wrote to Wilson and George Gordon, Professor of English Literature, asking if they would write in his support for the Magdalen fellowship. Both declined. They had already agreed to lend their support to Nevill Coghill. Neither of them, they informed him, had been aware that Lewis was interested in English literature, and had assumed that he was looking for positions in philosophy. They were both very apologetic, but they were now committed to supporting Coghill.

Lewis was devastated. Wilson's and Gordon's support was of vital importance in getting Magdalen to take him seriously. Without that backing, he would not stand a chance. It was "enough to make anyone despair," he told his father. Then, in a second unexpected development, Nevill Coghill was offered a fellowship by his own college, Exeter. Coghill withdrew immediately from the Magdalen competition, allowing both Wilson and Gordon to pledge their full support to Lewis. Gordon, as Professor of English Literature, was consulted by Magdalen about the list of candidates, and made it clear that he regarded Lewis as the best.

Following a long tradition, Magdalen invited the preferred candidates to dinner in order that the fellowship as a whole could assess them. Lewis asked his colleague Farquharson about the dress code at Magdalen. Farquharson confidently and erroneously assured him that Magdalen was severely formal on this occasion. Lewis should wear a white tie and coat tails.

4.5 The tower of Magdalen College, Oxford, in the snow during the winter of 1910.

Lewis duly turned up wearing this excessively formal attire. To his embarrassment, everyone else turned out to be wearing the much less formal dinner jacket and black tie. But Lewis made a good impression, despite his unorthodox garb. A rumour reached him that there were only two serious candidates in the race: he was one of them; the other was another Irishman, John Bryson.

On the following Saturday, Lewis happened to meet the president of Magdalen, Sir Herbert Warren, in the street, and exchanged a few words with him. On Monday, Warren wrote to Lewis, asking to see him the next morning. It was, Warren declared, "most important." Lewis was worried: had something gone wrong? Had they discovered something about him that had sunk his chances?

Apprehensive, Lewis arrived at the president's lodgings at Magdalen. Warren informed him that they would be making the election the following morning. Lewis was their preferred candidate, and he wished to check that Lewis fully understood what the duties and responsibilities of a fellow were. Most important, he wanted to ensure that Lewis would be willing to teach philosophy as well as English. Hugely relieved, Lewis assured him that this would indeed be the case. That was it. Warren indicated that the meeting was over, and asked Lewis to be sure he was available to be contacted by telephone at University College the following afternoon.

The call came through. Lewis made the short walk to Magdalen, where Warren informed him that he had been elected. He would receive a salary of £500, rooms in college, a dining allowance, and a pension. The appointment was for five years initially, and if things worked out well, it would be renewed.[69] Lewis rushed to the post office and sent a telegram to his father: "Elected Fellow Magdalen. Jack." A somewhat fuller announcement appeared on 22 May in the London *Times*:

> The President and Fellows of Magdalen College have elected to an official Fellowship in the College as Tutor in English Language and Literature, for five years as from next June 15, Mr Clive Staples Lewis, M.A. (University College).

Mr Lewis was educated first at Malvern College. He won a scholarship in classics at University College in 1915, and (after war service) a first class in Classical Moderations in 1920, the Chancellor's Prize for an English essay in 1921, a first class in *Literae Humaniores* in 1922, and a first class in the Honour School of English Language and Literature in 1923.[70]

Lewis would no longer be reliant on his father for support. His life suddenly seemed much more stable and settled. He thanked his father for his "generous support" over six long years, without complaint and always with encouragement. Lewis had arrived. He was finally an Oxford don.

FELLOWSHIP, FAMILY, AND FRIENDSHIP: THE EARLY YEARS AT MAGDALEN COLLEGE

M agdalen College, Oxford, was founded in 1458 by William Waynflete (ca. 1398–1486), Bishop of Winchester and Lord Chancellor of England. As the bishop of a wealthy diocese, and without any close family, Waynflete saw the endowment of Magdalen College as his personal project. Over a period of twenty years, Waynflete showered his new college with buildings and assets. When Waynflete drew up Magdalen's first statutes in 1480, the college was wealthy enough to support forty fellows, thirty scholars, and a chapel choir. Few Oxford or Cambridge colleges could hope to be so well endowed. When Lewis took up his fellowship, Magdalen was still—along with St. John's—widely regarded as the richest of the Oxford colleges.

FELLOWSHIP: MAGDALEN COLLEGE

Lewis was formally admitted to his fellowship at Magdalen in a ceremony in August 1925. The entire fellowship of the college assembled to witness his admission, following the ancient tradition. Lewis was required to kneel before the president as a long Latin formula was read out. The president then lifted Lewis to his feet, addressing him with the words, "I wish you joy." The dignity of the occasion was somewhat spoiled when Lewis clumsily tripped over his gown. Happily, he recovered from this disaster, and slowly worked his way around the room so that everyone present might personally wish him "joy," while clearly wishing they were somewhere else.[1] The reader might linger over that repeated word *joy*, given its significance for Lewis.

Lewis actually took up his fellowship on 1 October. After spending more than two weeks with his father in Belfast, Lewis returned to Oxford to move into a set of rooms in Magdalen's New Building (1733), a magnificent eighteenth-century Palladian structure which was originally intended to be the north side of a new quadrangle, but in the end remained standing alone in splendid isolation. Lewis was allocated room 3 on staircase III, a set of rooms consisting of a bedroom and two sitting rooms. The larger of the sitting rooms looked north over Magdalen Grove, home to the college's herd of deer. The bedroom and smaller sitting room faced southwards, giving Lewis a magnificent view over a lawn to the main college's buildings and famous tower. It is no exaggeration to say that Lewis had managed to secure one of the most beautiful views in Oxford.

The character of Magdalen College at this time had been shaped by Sir Herbert Warren—affectionately known as "Sambo" to the fellows—who had been elected president of the college in 1885 at the age of thirty-two. Warren would not retire until 1928, and over the forty-three years of his presidency, he moulded the college in his own likeness. Perhaps one of the most striking features of the academic culture established by Warren was Magdalen's "almost exaggerated collegiality and communal living."[2] Fellows were strongly encouraged to lunch and dine together. Bachelor fellows living in college—such as Lewis—would also breakfast together.[3] Lewis had become part of a community of scholars.

5.1 The president and fellows of Magdalen College, July 1928. This photograph was taken to mark the retirement of Sir Herbert Warren (centre front) as president of the college. Lewis is standing to the right of Warren in the back row.

Where some colleges allowed their fellows to lunch or dine privately in their rooms, Warren insisted on fellows sharing meals, seeing this as a way of developing the corporate identity of the college and reinforcing its social hierarchy. At college dinner, fellows were required to process in gowns into Hall from the Senior Common Room in order of seniority. Their seats at High Table were likewise allocated according to seniority, and the familiar use of forenames was avoided. Fellows would refer to each other by surname or by office—"Mr. Vice-President," "Senior Fellow," or "Science Tutor."[4]

The complex social and intellectual machinery of Oxford University at this time was lubricated by vast quantities of alcohol. Magdalen was perhaps one of the most bibulous of Oxford's colleges, with its resident fellows being particularly prone to overindulgence. During 1924 and 1925, the Senior Common Room paid off a debt by selling twenty-four thousand bottles of port, raising the sum of £4,000.[5] Fellows who wagered against each other would calculate their winnings in terms of cases of claret or port, rather than cash. The Senior Common Room butler was once observed carrying a silver tray laden with brandy and cigars through the college cloisters at eleven o'clock one morning. On being asked what he was doing, the butler replied that he was bringing one of the fellows his breakfast. Lewis kept a barrel of beer in his rooms to entertain colleagues and students, but otherwise seems to have avoided the alcoholic excesses of the prewar years.

President Warren's trenchant views on collegiality shaped Lewis's weekly routines. By January 1927, Lewis had perfected his regular working pattern. Outside university Full Term, he would reside at Hillsboro, and take a bus into college, where he remained during working hours, lunching in college. During university Full Term, Lewis slept in college, and bussed home to be with "the family" for the afternoons when he had no teaching or administrative responsibilities. He would return to Magdalen in the late afternoon, and dine with his colleagues.

Lewis was paid a salary of £500 a year as an official tutorial fellow. It was a generous stipend, at the top of the range for fellows of the college. Had Lewis been elected a fellow by examination, he would have enjoyed only half that amount.[6] However, it soon became clear that college life at Magdalen would turn out to be rather more expensive than Lewis had anticipated. For a start, his rooms were devoid of any furniture or carpets. Lewis found two, and only two, items already present in his rooms: a washstand in his bedroom, and some linoleum in his smaller sitting room. He would have to furnish his rooms completely at his own expense. In the end, Lewis had to spend £90—a substantial sum in those days—buying carpets, tables, chairs, a bed, curtains, coal boxes, and fire irons. It was a massive and unexpected expense, even though Lewis economised wherever possible by buying secondhand goods.[7]

Furthermore, Lewis regularly received demands from the college bursary for "Battels"—Oxford's arcane term for college expenses incurred, such as meals and drink. Lewis confided to his diary that Mrs. Moore was far from happy when she discovered that he was receiving rather less income than he had led her to expect. After some rather awkward conversations with James Thompson, the college's home bursar, Lewis began to realise that, after deductions, he would actually be taking home about £360 annually.[8] And then there was still income tax to pay.

5.2 The New Building, Magdalen College, around 1925.

Lewis broke off his diary after a long entry for 5 September 1925 and did not resume until 27 April 1926. It is not difficult to work out why. Lewis was settling into a new way of life, with new colleagues to meet and a new institution whose workings he needed to understand. He had new lecture courses to prepare and tutorials to give. His tutorial work in philosophy was undemanding and uninteresting. Harry Weldon, Magdalen's philosophy don, was inclined to dump the less interesting and less able pupils on Lewis, keeping the best students for himself. Yet the bulk of Lewis's work consisted in giving lectures and tutorials in English literature, as well as teaching textual criticism to research students. There were few students reading English (and thus requiring tuition) at Magdalen at this time. But Lewis was still required to work up a new course of intercollegiate lectures in English literature, which he found very demanding.

Lewis taught undergraduates at Magdalen (and other colleges by arrangement) in tutorials. This teaching method, characteristic of both of England's "ancient universities" of Oxford and Cambridge, typically involved a single student reading an essay to a tutor, followed by discussion and criticism. Lewis quickly developed a reputation as a harsh and demanding tutor, although this mellowed over time. The 1930s are generally regarded as Lewis's golden period of teaching at Oxford, by which time he had perfected his lecturing and tutorial techniques.[9]

His early years, however, were marked chiefly by his impatience at the laziness and lack of perceptiveness on the part of his students, such as John Betjeman (1906–1984). Many of them seemed to regard their time at Oxford as an inebriated extension of their bawdy, lazy schooldays. It was no coincidence that the author P. G. Wodehouse (1881–1975) placed his immensely likable (yet equally lazy and slow-witted) character Bertie Wooster (author of "What the Well-Dressed Man Is Wearing" in *Milady's Boudoir*) as an undergraduate at Magdalen just before the time of Lewis's arrival.

FAMILY RUPTURE: THE DEATH OF ALBERT LEWIS

The death of Lewis's mother in 1908 had marked a turning point in Lewis's life. Lewis adored his mother, who was the anchor and foundation of his life. As we have seen, he came to despise and deceive his father. An X-ray of 26 July 1929 gave Albert Lewis's doctors cause for concern, and led Lewis's father to enter a comment in his pocket book: "results rather disquieting."[10] Early in September 1929, Albert Lewis was admitted to a nursing home at 7 Upper Crescent, Belfast. An exploratory operation revealed that he had cancer, although it was considered not to be sufficiently advanced to warrant immediate concern.

5.3 The last known photograph of Albert Lewis, 1928.

Lewis had travelled to Belfast to be with his father, arriving on 11 August. He found it to be a tedious business. He wrote to his close friend Owen Barfield, making his negative feelings towards his father disturbingly clear: "I am attending at the almost painless sickbed of one for whom I have little affection and whose society has for many years given me much discomfort and no pleasure."[11] Even though he had no affection for his father, he was finding his father's deteriorated condition unbearable. What, he wondered, would it be like to attend the deathbed of someone you really loved?

Lewis decided that his father's condition was stable enough to permit him to return to Oxford on 21 September.[12] He had no desire to stay with his father, and there seemed no point in doing so. He had work to do in Oxford to prepare for the beginning of the new academic year. This understandable decision turned out to be a misjudgement. Two days later, his father lost consciousness and then died from an apparent brain haemorrhage, possibly a complication arising from the operation, rather than from the cancer itself. Lewis, having been notified of his father's turn for the worse, hurried back to Belfast from Oxford, but failed to arrive in time. In the end, Albert Lewis died on Wednesday, 25 September 1929, alone in the nursing home, unaccompanied by either of his sons.[13]

The two leading city newspapers—the *Belfast Telegraph* and the *Belfast Newsletter*—published extensive obituaries of Albert Lewis, recalling his outstanding professional reputation and deep love for literature. It was easy to understand Warnie's absence at his father's death; after all, he was serving in the army, stationed far away in Shanghai. There was no way he would have been able to return from the Far East in time.

Where most would see Lewis's attitude towards his father as strained but dutiful, others believed that the esteemed solicitor had been let down by his younger son, who had compounded his lamentable decision to leave Ireland by not being with his father in his final hours.

Albert Lewis had supported his younger son financially for six long years, and some in Belfast seem to have felt that he deserved better at Lewis's hands. Canon John Barry (1915–2006), a former curate of

St. Mark's, Dundela—where Albert Lewis's funeral took place on 27 September 1929—recalls a "sort of chill" later occasioned in certain Belfast circles by the mention of C. S. Lewis's name, apparently on account of lingering resentment over the way he had treated his father.[14] People have long memories in Belfast.

Lewis unquestionably felt both pain and guilt at his father's death for much of the remainder of his life. There are hints of this at numerous points in his letters, especially in the dramatic opening sentence of a letter of March 1954: "I treated my own father abominably and no sin in my whole life now seems to be so serious."[15] Some agree with this criticism; others, however, feel that it is overstated.

It is important to see this episode against the cultural background of the time in Belfast, particularly concern over sons who had left their parents to seek their fortunes in England. Yet Lewis did not choose to be educated in England; his father made that decision for him, thus laying the foundation for his younger son's career at Oxford. A sympathetic reading of Lewis's correspondence around this period indicates that his sense of duty towards his father took precedence over any absence of affection. Lewis spent six long weeks with his father in the summer of 1929, away from "the family," and was unable to get work done to prepare for the new academic year at Oxford University. He needed to get home, and he justifiably believed his father was out of danger. Lewis returned to Ireland the moment he knew things had turned out badly.

During his brief stay in Belfast around the time of his father's funeral, Lewis came to certain decisions. Although his father's will had appointed both sons as executors and sole beneficiaries, Warnie's enforced absence in China meant that Lewis would have to act on their joint behalf in making certain legal decisions. Most important, Little Lea would have to be sold, though Lewis delayed on this. He sacked the gardener and housemaid, while retaining Mary Cullen—whom Lewis affectionately dubbed the "Witch of Endor"—as housekeeper until the house was sold. The decision to postpone selling the house was an uneconomic one, not least because the house would deteriorate over the winter, reducing its potential sale value.

Yet Lewis felt he had to wait for the return of his brother before making any final decisions about the disposal of the contents of the house.[16]

Warnie finally returned on leave from Shanghai on 16 April 1930 and stayed with Lewis and Mrs. Moore in Oxford. Little Lea had not yet found a buyer. Lewis and Warnie travelled to Belfast to visit their father's grave, and make their final joint visit to the memory-laden house. Both brothers found their visit to their former home depressing, partly on account of its state of decay, and partly on account of the irretrievable memories linked to it. Overwhelmed by the "intense stillness" and "utter lifelessness" of the rooms,[17] the brothers solemnly buried their toys in the vegetable patch. It was a sad and forlorn farewell to their childhood, and the imaginary worlds they had once constructed and inhabited. In the end, Little Lea sold for £2,300—substantially less than they had anticipated—in January 1931. It was the end of an era.

THE LINGERING INFLUENCE OF ALBERT LEWIS

Lewis might have secured closure on his father in a legal and financial sense. Yet there is every reason to think that in Lewis's own later years, he came to see his attitude towards his father in his declining years as reprehensible. Lewis secured emotional closure on the issue in his own characteristic way—by writing a book. Although *Surprised by Joy* can be read as a spiritual autobiography, rich in Lewis's memories of his own past and the shaping of his inner world, it clearly played another role: it allowed Lewis to come to peace with his past behaviour.

In a letter written to Dom Bede Griffiths in 1956, shortly after the publication of *Surprised by Joy*, Lewis reflected on the importance of being able to discern patterns in an individual's life. "The gradual *reading* of one's own life, seeing the pattern emerge, is a great illumination at our age."[18] It is difficult to read Lewis's autobiographical reflections without bearing this point in mind. For Lewis, the narration of his own story was about the identification of a pattern of meaning. This enabled him to grasp the "big picture" and discern the "grand story" of all things, so that the snapshots and stories of his own life could assume a deeper meaning.

Yet the next sentence in this letter to Griffiths discloses a deeper concern that Lewis clearly saw as significant: "getting *freed from* the past as past by apprehending it as structure." The close reader of *Surprised by Joy* will note the omission or marginalization of three extended issues that clearly caused Lewis emotional difficulty for much of his later life.

First, and perhaps most famously, he makes it clear that he is honour bound not to mention Mrs. Moore, despite the enormous role she played in his personal history. "Even were I free to tell the story," he writes, "I doubt if it has much to do with the subject of the book."[19]

The second notable feature is the relative absence of reference to the suffering and devastation of the Great War, which created intellectual havoc in the minds and souls of so many. We have drawn attention to this point earlier in this narrative, and it is important to understanding Lewis's development, both as a scholar and as a Christian apologist. Where some have argued that Lewis's rediscovery of religious faith can be seen within a broadly psychoanalytic narrative thread that gives unity to Lewis's development, the evidence does not warrant such a conclusion. The real issue lies in the destruction of the fixed certainties, values, and aspirations of an earlier generation by the haunting memories of the horrors of the mass carnage of modern warfare—a theme that pervades much English literature of the 1920s.

The third understatement concerns the death of Albert Lewis in 1929. This, Lewis declares, "does not really come into the story" he wants to tell.[20] Perhaps Lewis deemed it irrelevant. Perhaps it was also too painful to discuss. How much are we to read into a section of Lewis's later essay "On Forgiveness" (1941), in which he emphasises the need to accept that we have been forgiven, even though we believe ourselves to be unforgivable? In inviting his audience to reflect on the need to acknowledge human failings, Lewis gives some examples of persistent behaviours that need constant forgiveness. One stands out to all who know Lewis's personal history: the "deceitful son." "To be a Christian means to forgive the inexcusable, because God has forgiven the inexcusable in you."[21]

One of the major themes of *Till We Have Faces* (1956)—arguably the most profound piece of fiction written by Lewis—is the difficulty of coming to know ourselves as we really are, and the deep pain that such knowledge ultimately involves. Perhaps we ought to read *Surprised by Joy* with this point in mind. The suppression of certain themes in Lewis's account of his own development is not a mark of dishonesty, but of the pain their memory engendered.

There is one particular point that puzzles the reader of Lewis's correspondence around the time of his father's death. In *Surprised by Joy*, Lewis tells us he began to actively believe in God at some point during Oxford's "Trinity Term of 1929"[22]—at least three months, and possibly five, before his father's death. Yet at no point in his correspondence around the time of his father's death—or, indeed, for the six months following—does Lewis mention this belief, or speak of deriving any consolation from it.

Lewis did not regard his father with great affection, and seems to have found his passing a relief rather than a trauma. Yet this absence of reference to God around this time is as conspicuous as it is curious. It does not fit well into Lewis's own chronology of his conversion. Might it be that the death of Albert Lewis actually caused Lewis to *explore* the question of God, instead of being something that Lewis interpreted in the light of such a belief? Might his father's death have prompted Lewis to ask deeper—and as yet unanswered—questions about life, and search for more satisfying answers? We shall return to this question in the following chapter, where we shall raise further concerns about the traditional understanding of Lewis's journey from atheism to Christianity.

FAMILY RECONNECTION: WARNIE MOVES TO OXFORD

In 1930, Lewis's domestic arrangements changed significantly. As we have seen, following the death of their father in September 1929, the two Lewis brothers were left as sole heirs to Little Lea. Lewis had corresponded with his brother, Warnie, in Shanghai in January 1930 about the difficult and painful matter of placing their childhood home on the market.

Warnie wanted to visit the house for one last time before it was sold; Lewis wanted to get it sold as soon as possible, while realising that an early sale would prevent his brother from making such a sentimental visit.[23]

It is clear that another possibility was beginning to emerge in Lewis's mind: the re-creation of the brothers' shared childhood "Little End Room" of "Little Lea" *in Oxford*. What if Warnie were to move in with Lewis when he left the army—perhaps by using one of Lewis's set of rooms at Magdalen? Or perhaps by joining with Mrs. Moore and getting a larger house than Hillsboro? Mrs. Moore, it must be emphasised, appears to have been actively supportive of this latter, more ambitious possibility. It was a natural outcome of her intrinsically hospitable nature. Warnie would not be their guest, but an integral part of their household—their *family*.

In raising this possibility with his brother, Lewis emphasised that this would have drawbacks. Would he be able to abide by their indifferent "cuisine"? With Maureen's frequent "sulks"? With "Minto's mare's nests"? Yet there was no concealing that Lewis wanted Warnie to be part of his family life. "I have definitely chosen and don't regret the choice. What I hope—very much hope—is that you, after consideration, may make the same choice, and not regret it."[24]

In May 1930, Warnie made two decisions. First, he would edit the papers of the Lewis family, as a way of paying homage to his parents; second, he would move into Hillsboro with his brother and his brother's family as soon as it was possible. Another possibility was developing even as Warnie made his decision—the purchase of a new and larger house. Up to this point, Lewis and Mrs. Moore had rented properties together. But Lewis's fellowship had been renewed after its initial five years. He was now in a financially stable situation, with the assurance of a regular income for the rest of his working life. He and Warnie could expect to receive a reasonable sum when Little Lea finally sold. Warnie had savings. And Mrs. Moore had inherited a trust fund as a result of the death of her brother, Dr. John Askins. If they pooled their resources, they could purchase a property big enough for them all.

5.4 Lewis, Mrs. Moore, and Warnie at The Kilns during the summer of 1930.

On 6 July 1930, Lewis, Warnie, and "the family" saw "The Kilns" for the first time. It was a somewhat unimpressive, low-lying building in Headington Quarry, close to the foot of Shotover Hill, where Lewis enjoyed walking. Set in eight acres of grounds, the property would need expansion to accommodate four people. Yet all three partners in the enterprise pronounced themselves satisfied with the property, even with all the work that needed to be done. The asking price was £3,500, which was negotiated down to £3,300. Warnie paid the cash deposit of £300, and contributed £500 towards the mortgage. Mrs. Moore's trustees advanced her £1,500, and Lewis himself added £1,000.[25] Two additional rooms were added on shortly afterwards, ready for Warnie's final return from military service.

The property was held in Mrs. Moore's name, with each brother having permanent right of occupation during his lifetime. The Kilns was not, strictly speaking, Lewis's home. He lived there, but did not own it. He had all that he needed—a "Right of Life" tenancy which allowed him and Warnie permanent right of abode until their deaths. On Mrs. Moore's death in January 1951, title to the property passed to her daughter, Maureen, with both Lewis brothers continuing to have right of abode until their deaths.[26] (In the end, free-and-clear title to the house and estates passed to Maureen on the death of Warnie in 1973.)

The Kilns would play a significant role in consolidating Lewis's life, not least because it provided a stable home for his brother. Warnie embarked from Shanghai on 22 October 1932 on the SS *Automedon*. He arrived in the port city of Liverpool on 15 December, and then travelled south to Oxford. "It all seems too good to be true!" Lewis wrote to him. "I can hardly believe that when you take your shoes off a week or so hence, please God, you will be able to say 'This will do for me—for life.'"[27] Warnie finally retired from the army on 20 December, although he remained on the reserve list.[28] This renewed relationship with his brother, for better or worse (and it was mostly better), would be of critical importance for the remainder of Lewis's life.[29]

Yet we must mention another relationship to emerge around this time, which would also be of importance to Lewis: his deepening friendship with John Ronald Reuel Tolkien (1892–1973).

FRIENDSHIP: J. R. R. TOLKIEN

Lewis's teaching responsibilities extended beyond Magdalen. He was a member of Oxford University's Faculty of English Language and Literature, and delivered intercollegiate lectures on aspects of English literature—such as "Some Eighteenth-Century Precursors of the Romantic Movement." He also attended meetings of the faculty, which largely consisted of discussing teaching and administrative arrangements. These meetings were held at 4.00 p.m., following afternoon tea at Merton College, the home base of Oxford's two Merton Professors of English, and were often referred to as the "English Tea."[30]

5.5 J. R. R. Tolkien, photographed in his rooms at Merton College in the 1970s.
© Billett Potter, Oxford.

It was at an English Tea on 11 May 1926 that Lewis first met J. R. R. Tolkien—a "smooth, pale, fluent little chap,"[31] who had joined Oxford's English faculty as Rawlinson and Bosworth Professor of Anglo-Saxon the previous year. Lewis and Tolkien would quickly find themselves embattled over the shape of the Oxford English curriculum. Tolkien argued for a curriculum closely focussed on ancient and medieval English texts, requiring the mastery of Old and Middle English; Lewis believed English was best taught by focussing on English literature after Geoffrey Chaucer (ca. 1343–1400).

Tolkien was prepared to defend his corner, and worked hard to promote the study of forgotten languages. To advance his agenda, he founded a study group he named the *Kolbítar*, aimed at fostering an appreciation of Old Norse and its associated literature. Lewis became a member.[32] The curious term *Kolbítar* was adopted from Icelandic; it literally means "coal-biters," and was a derisive term for Norsemen who refused to join in the hunt or fight battles, preferring instead to stay indoors and enjoy the protective warmth of the fire. As Lewis put it, the term (which he insisted is to be pronounced "Coal-béet-are")[33] refers to "old cronies who sit round the fire so close that they look as if they were biting the coals." Lewis found this "little Icelandic club" a massive stimulus to his imagination, throwing him back into "a wild dream of northern skies and Valkyrie music."[34]

The relationship between Lewis and Tolkien is one of the most important of his personal and professional life. They had much in common, in terms of both literary interests and shared experiences of the battlefields of the Great War. Yet Lewis's correspondence and diary make little save incidental reference to Tolkien until late in 1929. Then evidence of a deepening relationship begins to emerge. "One week I was up till 2.30 on Monday (talking to the Anglo Saxon Professor Tolkien)," Lewis wrote to Arthur Greeves, "(who came back with me to College from a society and sat discoursing of the gods & giants & Asgard for three hours)."[35]

Something that Lewis said that evening must have persuaded Tolkien to take the younger man into his confidence. Tolkien asked Lewis to read a long narrative poem he had been composing since his arrival in Oxford, titled *The Lay of Leithian*.[36] Tolkien was a senior Oxford academic with a public reputation in the field of philology, but with a personal and intensely private passion for mythology. Tolkien had drawn the curtains aside from his private inner self and invited Lewis into his sanctum. It was a personal and professional risk for the older man.

Lewis could not have known it, but at this point Tolkien needed a "critical friend," a mentor who would encourage and criticise, affirm and improve, his writing—above all, someone who would force him to bring it to completion. He had had such "critical friends" in the past, in the form of two of his old school friends—Geoffrey Bache Smith (1894–1916) and Christopher Luke Wiseman (1893–1987).[37] However, Smith had joined the Lancashire Fusiliers, and died of wounds inflicted in the Battle of the Somme; and Wiseman had drifted from Tolkien after his appointment in 1926 as headmaster of the Queen's College, Taunton, in England's West

Country. Tolkien was a niggling perfectionist, and he knew it. Indeed, his late story "Leaf by Niggle"—which deals with a painter who can never finish his painting of a tree because of his constant desire to expand and improve it—can be seen as a self-parodying critique of Tolkien's own difficulties in writing. Someone had to help him conquer his perfectionism. And what Tolkien needed he found in Lewis.

We may safely assume that Tolkien breathed a deep sigh of relief when Lewis responded enthusiastically to the poem. "I can quite honestly say," he wrote to Tolkien, "that it is ages since I have had an evening of such delight."[38] While we must pause the telling of this particular story as we move on to focus on other matters, it is no exaggeration to say that Lewis would become the chief midwife to one of the great works of twentieth-century literature—Tolkien's *Lord of the Rings*.

Yet in a sense, Tolkien would also be a midwife for Lewis. It is arguable that Tolkien removed the final obstacle that stood in Lewis's path to his rediscovery of the Christian faith—a complex and important story, which demands a chapter in its own right.

THE MOST RELUCTANT CONVERT: THE MAKING OF A MERE CHRISTIAN

Lewis is today remembered as a Christian writer. Yet the tone of his writings of the early 1920s is unquestionably atheistic, severely critical if not totally dismissive of religion in general and Christianity in particular. So how and why did he change his mind? In this chapter, we shall consider the slow conversion of Lewis from his early atheism, initially to a firm intellectual belief in God by the summer of 1930, and finally to an explicit and informed commitment to Christianity by the summer of 1932. It is a complex story, worth telling in detail both on account of its intrinsic interest and as a means of allowing us to understand Lewis's rise to fame as a Christian voice in the quite different worlds of literary scholarship and popular culture.

THE ENGLISH LITERARY RELIGIOUS RENAISSANCE OF THE 1920S

In 1930, the celebrity author Evelyn Waugh (1903–1966)—whose novel *Vile Bodies* had been hailed earlier that year as "*the* ultramodern novel"—dropped a bombshell in literary circles. He announced that he had become a Catholic. This development was so unexpected and significant that it immediately made the front pages of one of Britain's leading newspapers, the *Daily Express*. How, its editor wondered, could an author best known for his "almost passionate adherence to the ultramodern" have embraced the Catholic faith? For the next week, the paper's columns were filled with comment and reflection on this unexpected and baffling development.

Yet the cultural attention given to Waugh's conversion was only partly due to his celebrity status as a fashionable young author of bestselling satirical novels. Waugh was the latest in a long line of literary figures to embrace Catholicism—such as G. K. Chesterton (1874–1936), who converted in 1922, and Graham Greene (1904–1991), who converted in 1926.[1] Some began to wonder if a Christian literary renaissance was under way.

Not all of the literary figures to convert to Christianity in this brief yet intense period of Christian revival adopted Catholicism. In 1927, T. S. Eliot (1888–1965)—then best known for his poem "The Waste Land" (1922), still widely acknowledged as one of the finest and most-discussed poems of the twentieth century—converted to Anglicanism. Although Eliot's conversion did not make quite the same newspaper headlines as Waugh's, Eliot's huge reputation as a poet and literary critic ensured that his conversion was widely discussed and debated. Eliot found in Christianity a principle of order and stability located outside the human self, which allowed him a secure vantage point from which to engage with the world.

Some four or five years later, Lewis became a Christian. Like Eliot, he chose to become a member of the Church of England. Yet nobody had ever heard of Lewis, and nobody paid any attention to this development—if they noticed it at all. Lewis, it must be appreciated, was almost totally unknown in 1931. He had published two cycles of poems under the pseudonym Clive Hamilton. Neither had been a critical or commercial success. Lewis's rise to popular fame would not begin until 1940, with the publication of *The Problem of Pain*, which can now be seen to have set in motion a series of developments leading to his celebrity status as a wartime apologist. Where Evelyn Waugh drew attention to his religious faith on account of his fame as a novelist, Lewis's faith would be the basis for the works that would eventually secure him popular acclaim.

Nevertheless, Lewis fits into a broader pattern at this time—the conversion of literary scholars and writers *through and because of their literary interests*. Lewis's love of literature is not a backdrop to his conversion; it is integral to his discovery of the rational and imaginative appeal of Christianity. Lewis hints at this throughout *Surprised by Joy*. "A young man who wishes to remain a sound Atheist cannot be too careful of his reading. There are traps everywhere."[2] Lewis's reading of the classics of English literature forced him to encounter and evaluate the ideas and attitudes that they embodied and expressed. And to his chagrin, Lewis began to realise that those who were grounded on a Christian outlook seemed to offer the most resilient and persuasive "treaty with reality."

Many leading writers came to faith around the same time through reflecting on literary issues. For example, Graham Greene criticised modernist writers such as Virginia Woolf (1882–1941) and E. M. Forster (1879–1970) for creating characters who "wandered like cardboard symbols through a world that was paper-thin." There was, Greene argued, no sense of *reality* in their writings. To lose sight of "the religious sense," as they had so clearly done, was also to lose any "sense of the importance of the human act."[3] Great literature depends upon a passionate commitment to a real world—which, for Greene, demanded a foundation in a deeper order of things, grounded in the nature and will of God.

Evelyn Waugh made much the same point. Without God, an author could not give his characters reality and depth. "You can only leave God out by making your characters pure abstractions."[4] Good novels rested on a plausible account of human nature, which, for Waugh, in turn rested on the remarkable capacity of the Christian faith to make sense of the world in general and human nature in particular. It provided a lens which brought the distorted world around him into sharp focus, allowing him to understand it properly for the first time. Waugh spoke of his delight in discovering this new way of engaging reality in a letter of 1949:

> Conversion is like stepping across the chimney piece out of a
> Looking-Glass world, where everything is an absurd caricature,
> into the real world God made; and then begins the delicious
> process of exploring it limitlessly.[5]

Similar concerns seem to have played a role in catalysing Lewis's growing interest in the Christian faith. In *Surprised by Joy*, Lewis comments on his discovery in the early 1920s of the surprising depth of the literature shaped by and grounded in the Christian faith. Modernist writers such as George Bernard Shaw (1856–1950) and H. G. Wells (1866–1946) "seemed a little thin"; there was "no depth in them"; they were "too simple." "The roughness and density of life" was not adequately represented in their works.[6]

The Christian poet George Herbert (1593–1633), in marked contrast, seemed to Lewis to "excel . . . in conveying the very quality of life as we actually live it"; yet instead of "doing it all directly," he "insisted on mediating it" through what Lewis then termed "the Christian mythology."[7] By the early 1920s, Lewis had yet to conclude that Christianity was true; he was, however, gradually coming to grasp its potential impact for an understanding of the world and the self. But he failed at that stage to appreciate the implications of "the ludicrous contradiction between my theory of life and my actual experiences as a reader."[8]

Are we to see here a classic approach to the discovery of the divine, so memorably described by Blaise Pascal (1623–1662) in the seventeenth century? For Pascal, there was little point in trying to *persuade* anyone of the truth of religious belief. The important thing, he argued, was to make people *wish* that it were true, having caught sight of the rich and satisfying vision of reality it offered. Once such a desire was implanted within the human heart, the human mind would eventually catch up with its deeper intuitions. The poets George Herbert and Thomas Traherne (1636–1674) did not persuade Lewis to believe in God; rather, they led him to think that such a belief offered a rich and robust vision of human life, making him wonder whether there might, after all, be something to be said for their way of thinking.

To piece together the story of Lewis's conversion is primarily to explore the development of an internal world, which is unfortunately not available for public inspection. Clues to these developments abound, but they need to be woven together into a coherent whole. In what follows, we shall try to make sense of this complex yet fascinating story.

THE REALISING IMAGINATION: LEWIS'S REDISCOVERY OF GOD

Lewis's writings of the early 1930s show him to have been searching for a fundamental principle of order in life—what ancient Greek philosophers might have termed an *archē*—that was not a human invention but was grounded in a deeper order of things. Where could such a unifying vision of reality be found?

One of the reasons Lewis was drawn to study the literature of the Middle Ages was his sense that it witnessed to an understanding of the greater scheme of things that had been lost in the West through the trauma of the recent Great War. For Lewis, medieval culture offered an imaginative vision of a unified cosmic and world order, expressed in poems such as Dante's *Divine Comedy*. There was a "big picture" of reality which was able to embrace its fine detail. Works such as the *Divine Comedy*, Lewis argued, demonstrate that "medieval art attains a unity of the highest order, because it embraces the greatest diversity of subordinated detail."[9] We see here the literary expression of a fundamentally theological idea—namely, that there is a certain way of seeing reality that brings it into the sharpest focus, illuminating the shadows and allowing its inner unity to be seen. This, for Lewis, is a "realising imagination"— a way of seeing or "picturing" reality that is faithful to the way things actually are.[10]

Lewis's literary reflections here resonate with his own inner personal quest for truth and meaning. In part, Lewis's deep love for the best literature of the Middle Ages reflects his belief that it had found something that modernity had lost—and that he himself yearned to recover. Could the disruption of unity and continuity revealed by the Great War be healed?

Might there be a way of bringing things back together again? Was there a way of reconciling his reason and imagination?

Gradually, the pieces of this jigsaw puzzle began to fall into place, eventually to come into sharp focus in a devastating moment of illumination. In *Surprised by Joy*, Lewis sets out the series of moves which led him to faith in God, using a chessboard analogy.[11] None of these is logically or philosophically decisive; all are at best suggestive. Yet their force lies not in their individual importance, but in their cumulative weight. Lewis portrays these, not as moves which *he* made, but moves which were made *against him*. The narrative of *Surprised by Joy* is not that of Lewis's discovery of God, but of God's patient approach to Lewis.

What Lewis describes in *Surprised by Joy* is not a process of logical deduction: *A*, therefore *B*, therefore *C*. It is much more like a process of crystallisation, by which things that were hitherto disconnected and unrelated are suddenly seen to fit into a greater scheme of things, which both affirms their validity and indicates their interconnectedness. Things fall into place. A fundamental harmony between theory and observation emerges, once things are seen in the right way.

It is like a scientist who, confronted with many seemingly unconnected observations, wakes up in the middle of the night having discovered a theory which accounts for them. (The great French physicist Henri Poincaré once remarked, "It is by logic that we prove, but by intuition that we discover."[12]) It is like a literary detective, confronted with a series of clues, who realises how things must have happened, allowing every clue to be positioned within a greater narrative. In every case, we find the same pattern—a realisation that, if *this* was true, everything else falls into place naturally, without being forced or strained. And by its nature, it demands assent from the lover of truth. Lewis found himself compelled to accept a vision of reality that he did not really wish to be true, and certainly did not *cause* to be true.

Any attempt to tell the story of Lewis's conversion has to try and relate the events of his outer and inner worlds. Lewis presents himself as doing this in *Surprised by Joy*, telling the story of two quite different—

yet interconnected—worlds: his external worlds of English schools and Oxford University, and his internal world of yearning for "Joy," racked for so long by a tension between the rational and the imaginative.

> On the one side a many-islanded sea of poetry and myth; on the other a glib and shallow "rationalism." Nearly all that I loved I believed to be imaginary; nearly all that I believed to be real I thought grim and meaningless.[13]

It is not, however, always easy to correlate events in Lewis's inner world with the historical events in the world outside. For example, in the external world, Lewis travelled on a bus up Headington Hill, on his way from Magdalen College to his home in the former village of Headington (recently incorporated into the city of Oxford); in his internal world, he experienced the collapse of his mental defences against the approach of a God whom he never wanted to acknowledge, let alone meet.[14] Two quite different journeys thus converged on that single bus trip.

One of the chief difficulties in reading *Surprised by Joy* lies in attempting to construct a map of Lewis's development which adequately and accurately links the events in his inner and outer worlds. Lewis's own account of the relationship between these worlds, to the extent that it can be verified, is not always accurate. As we shall argue in this chapter, his rediscovery of God is almost certainly not to be dated from the summer of 1929, as Lewis himself suggests in *Surprised by Joy*, but from the late spring or early summer of 1930. Yet the subjective reality of Lewis's memories is not to be doubted. Lewis is quite clear about the rearrangement of the furniture of his mind, and the factors which led to this; the difficulty lies in the historical timing of that rearrangement.[15]

The process of crystallisation around belief in God appears to have taken place over an extended period of time, culminating in a dramatic moment of decision. His resistance to what he increasingly realised to be true could not be sustained. This was not something he sought, but something that seemed to seek him.

Lewis's prose here recalls Blaise Pascal's famous distinction between the anodyne, disinterested "God of the philosophers," and the fiery, living "God of Abraham, Isaac, and Jacob." What Lewis had thought to be at best an abstract philosophical idea proved to have a life and will of its own:

> As the dry bones shook and came together in that dreadful valley of Ezekiel's, so now a philosophical theorem, cerebrally entertained, began to stir and heave and throw off its gravecloths, and stood upright and became a living presence. I was to be allowed to play at philosophy no longer.[16]

A close reading of Lewis's correspondence confirms what this passage in *Surprised by Joy* suggests—a previous dabbling with divinity that has not been fully acknowledged. In a 1920 letter to his Oxford friend Leo Baker, Lewis remarked that, while reflecting on the philosophical question of the existence of matter, he had come to the conclusion that the "least objectionable theory" was to "postulate some sort of God." Perhaps, he mused, this was a "sign of grace." He had "stopped defying heaven."[17] Was this the "playing at philosophy" that Lewis had in mind?

The key point about this passage in *Surprised by Joy* is that Lewis now describes an assertive, active, and *questing* God, not simply a mental construct or philosophical game. God was pounding on the door of Lewis's mind and life. Reality was imposing itself upon him, vigorously and aggressively demanding a response. "Amiable agnostics will talk cheerfully about 'man's search for God.' To me, as I then was, they might as well have talked about the mouse's search for the cat."[18]

One of the most powerful visual images in *The Lion, the Witch and the Wardrobe* is the melting of snow, signifying the breaking of the Witch's power and the imminent return of Aslan. Lewis applied this potent image to describe his own diminishing resistance to the divine advent in *Surprised by Joy*, as he reflected on his own conversion: "I felt as if I were a man of snow at long last beginning to melt. The melting was starting in my back— drip-drip and presently trickle-trickle. I rather disliked the feeling."[19]

Lewis's 1916 "treaty with reality" was now in the process of collapsing around him, as he realised he could no longer maintain his old mental frontiers in the light of the superior forces mustered against him. "The reality with which no treaty can be made was upon me."[20] The point that Lewis is making here is too easily overlooked. The image of a "treaty with reality" conveys a radical and comprehensive compartmentalisation of thought that enables troubling and disturbing thoughts to be locked away so that they do not disturb everyday life. We saw Lewis using precisely this strategy to deal with the horror of the Great War. Reality was subjugated to thought, which was like a net thrown over reality, taming it and robbing it of its ability to take by surprise and overcome. What Lewis discovered was that he could no longer domesticate reality. Like a tiger, it refused to be constrained by its artificial cage. It broke free, and overwhelmed its former captor.

Lewis finally bowed to what he now recognised as inevitable. "In the Trinity Term of 1929 I gave in, and admitted that God was God, and knelt and prayed: perhaps, that night, the most dejected and reluctant convert in all England."[21] Lewis now believed in God; he was not yet a Christian. Nevertheless, Lewis tells us that as a public manifestation of this theistic belief, he then began to attend college chapel, and became a regular worshiper at his local parish church of Holy Trinity, Headington Quarry, not far from his home.[22]

This change in behaviour, which Lewis dates to Oxford's Trinity Term of 1929 (that is, between 28 April and 22 June 1929), is of enormous importance, as it allows the correlation of Lewis's inner and outer worlds. A change in the way Lewis thought led to a change in his public behaviour—something which marked a change in his habits and could be seen by others.

Lewis's new and unexpected interest in chapel was the subject of much discussion and intrigue among other Magdalen dons in the early 1930s. The American philosopher Paul Elmer More, who visited Magdalen in 1933, later wrote of intense college gossip about Lewis's new habit of attending chapel.[23] Yet Lewis insists that, at this stage, this was "a merely symbolical and provisional practice," which neither indicated nor enabled a specific commitment to Christianity.[24] Yet it is a marker for the date of his conversion to theism. If we can identify when Lewis began to attend chapel, we have a clue to when he started to believe in God.

More important, Lewis began to see himself in a new way. "One of the first results of my Theistic conversion was a marked decrease . . . in the fussy attentiveness which I had so long paid to the progress of my own opinions and the states of my own mind."[25] One practical outcome of this decision to break with this narcissistic introspection was inevitable: having failed to keep up his diary since March 1927, Lewis abandoned any thought of taking it up again. "If Theism had done nothing else for me, I should still be thankful that it cured me of the time-wasting and foolish practice of keeping a diary."[26]

Having ceased to keep a diary since 1927, Lewis's recollection of events after that date turns out to be somewhat unreliable. As he himself remarked in 1957, he could now "never remember dates."[27] His brother was more emphatic: Lewis had a "life-long inability to keep track of dates."[28] *Surprised by Joy* is primarily an account of changes in Lewis's internal world, which are correlated—at times a little loosely and uncertainly—with events in the external world. It is "suffocatingly subjective,"[29] an introspective piece of writing dealing primarily with the rearrangement of Lewis's interior world of thought and experience.

The traditional dating of Lewis's transition to belief in God, set out by Lewis himself, locates this shift in the early summer of 1929. Yet this dating raises some puzzling questions. For example, if Lewis really came to faith in God around then, why did his correspondence around the time of the death of his father, several months later, contain no hint whatsoever of a belief in God, however emergent, on his part? Might his father's death *instead* have acted as a stimulus for Lewis to reflect more deeply on the question of God in the midst of the emotional turmoil that he experienced around this time?

In preparing for this biography, I read all of Lewis's published works in their order of composition. At no point in Lewis's writings of 1929 did I discern any signs of the dramatic developments that he describes as having taken place in his inner life that year. There is no hint of a change in tone or tempo in any works written up to January 1930. Furthermore, Lewis makes it clear that, as a result of his conversion, he began to attend church and college chapel. There is no trace of such a significant—and publicly observable—change of habit, either as a topic of observation or discussion, in his correspondence of 1929. Even allowing for Lewis's reluctance to self-disclose, his writings of this period do not point to any kind of conversion experience in 1929. As we shall see, however, his writings of 1930 tell a very different story.

So is Lewis right about the date of his own conversion as stated in *Surprised by Joy*? Might Lewis's memory be faulty at this point? There is no doubt that Lewis recalled a conversion experience in his inner world, and describes its shape with some care. But how does this relate to the events of his outer world of years and months? Might Lewis have made a mistake? After all, there are other historical errors in the narrative of *Surprised by Joy*. (For example, Lewis recalls his first reading of George MacDonald's *Phantastes* as taking place in August 1915, but this should actually be dated to March 1916.)

Given the importance of this question, it needs to be considered in greater depth.

THE DATE OF LEWIS'S CONVERSION: A RECONSIDERATION

In *Surprised by Joy*, as we have just seen, Lewis dates the moment of his conversion to the Trinity Term of 1929. Lewis here refers to Oxford's eight-week teaching term, which is to be dated from 28 April to 22 June 1929.[30] This date is accepted and repeated in every major biography of Lewis to date. The traditional chronology of Lewis's conversion to Christianity is usually stated in terms of five landmarks:

1. 28 April–22 June 1929: Lewis comes to believe in God.
2. 19 September 1931: A conversation with Tolkien leads Lewis to realise that Christianity is a "true myth."
3. 28 September 1931: Lewis comes to believe in the divinity of Christ while being driven to Whipsnade Zoo.
4. 1 October 1931: Lewis tells Arthur Greeves that he has "passed over" from belief in God to belief in Christ.
5. 15–29 August 1932: Lewis describes his intellectual journey to God in *The Pilgrim's Regress*, written at this time in Belfast.

I do not believe that this chronology is the best explanation of the evidence contained in the primary sources, and propose a significant revision. Lewis's spiritual journey, by my account, is a year shorter than has traditionally been believed. The chronology which I propose, based on a close reading of the primary sources, is as follows:

1. March–June 1930: Lewis comes to believe in God.
2. 19 September 1931: A conversation with Tolkien leads Lewis to realise that Christianity is a "true myth."
3. 28 September 1931: Lewis comes to believe in the divinity of Christ while being driven to Whipsnade Zoo.
4. 1 October 1931: Lewis tells Arthur Greeves that he has "passed over" from belief in God to belief in Christ.
5. 15–29 August 1932: Lewis describes his intellectual journey to God in *The Pilgrim's Regress*, written at this time in Belfast.

What is the evidence for this proposed revision of the traditional view of the development of Lewis's religious beliefs and commitments? To begin with, let us consider the date of Lewis's conversion to theism—that is to say, when he began to believe in God. There is no evidence for any change of heart on this matter in any of Lewis's writings dating from 1929, the time of his father's death. But then things change in 1930. And only two people are allowed to know about it.

In a 1931 letter to Arthur Greeves, Lewis remarked on how he divided his acquaintances into "first class" and "second class" friends. In the former category, he placed Owen Barfield and Greeves himself; in the latter, J. R. R. Tolkien.[31] If Lewis was to tell any of his circle about this new development in his life, it would have been his "first class" friends, Barfield and Greeves. Yet there is nothing in Lewis's correspondence of 1929 with these two individuals which suggests that something significant had happened to him at any point during that year.

Yet things look very different in 1930. Lewis's correspondence with Barfield and Greeves now points to a significant development, corresponding to the transition Lewis describes in *Surprised by Joy*, having taken place in (or perhaps slightly before) Trinity Term 1930—about a year later than Lewis's own account. In what follows, we shall examine one crucial letter from Lewis to each of these two "first class" friends. Both date from *1930*, not *1929*.

First, consider his very short, deeply introspective letter to Owen Barfield, dated 3 February 1930. In this letter, following a brief introduction, Lewis writes as follows:

> Terrible things are happening to me. The "Spirit" or "Real I" is showing an alarming tendency to become much more personal and is taking the offensive, and behaving just like God. You'd better come on Monday at the latest or I may have entered a monastery.[32]

At this point, Professor Henry Wyld came to visit Lewis and interrupted his flow of thought. Like Samuel Taylor Coleridge's "person from Porlock," who disrupted the composition of his great poem "Kubla Khan" in 1797, Wyld prevented Lewis from saying anything more on this matter to Barfield. But what he says is enough. This is precisely the development that Lewis later described in *Surprised by Joy*, though he located it in Trinity Term *1929*. God was becoming real to him, and taking the offensive. Lewis felt he was about to be overwhelmed by a greater force. As he put it in *Surprised by Joy*, he was being "dragged through the doorway."[33]

Lewis's comments to Barfield must prefigure his conversion; they make no sense if they took place a year later, referring to an experience Lewis had already undergone. Barfield himself was clear about the importance of this letter in a 1998 interview regarding its significance for Lewis: it marked "the beginning of his conversion."[34] Yet Barfield's interviewer at this point (Kim Gilnett) mistakenly assigned this letter to 1929, thus accommodating it within the framework proposed by Lewis in *Surprised by Joy*—despite the fact that the letter dates from the following year. This letter anticipates exactly the themes that Lewis described as converging on the devastating, imminent moment of conversion, which clearly lay *ahead of*, not *behind*, him.

The second significant letter was written to Arthur Greeves on 29 October 1930. As we noted earlier, Lewis explicitly states that he began to attend chapel at Magdalen College following his conversion. There is no hint of Lewis's attending college chapel on a regular basis in his correspondence with anyone in 1929, or in the first half of 1930. Yet in a highly significant section of this 1930 letter to Greeves, Lewis mentions that he has now "started going to morning Chapel at 8,"[35] which meant that he had to go to bed much earlier than he had used to. This is clearly presented as a *new development*, a significant change in his routine, affecting his personal working habits, dating from the beginning of the academic year 1930–1931.

If Lewis's own chronology for his conversion is correct, he would have begun attending college chapel in October 1929. There is no reference in his correspondence of that period to any such change of habit. Furthermore, the reference to attending college chapel in the letter of October 1930 clearly implies that Lewis was now doing something *that was not part of his regular routine up to this point*. If Lewis really was converted during the Trinity Term of 1929, why did he wait over a year before starting to attend college chapel? It makes little sense.

6.1 The interior of Magdalen College chapel, around 1927. Lewis began to attend chapel regularly in October 1930.

The traditional date of Lewis's conversion would seem to require review. The evidence is best understood if Lewis's subjective location of the event in his inner world is accepted, but his chronological location of the event is seen to have been misplaced. The nature or reality of Lewis's conversion experience is not being called into question. The problem is that Lewis's location of this event in the external world of space and time appears to be inaccurate. Lewis's conversion is best understood as having taken place in the Trinity Term of 1930, not 1929. In 1930, Trinity Term fell between 27 April and 21 June.

Yet in rediscovering God in this way, Lewis had reached only a resting place, not his final destination. There was another milestone which had to be passed, which Lewis regarded as significant—a shift from a generic belief in God (often referred to as "theism") to a specific commitment to Christianity. This appears to have been an extended and complex process, to which others were midwives. Some—such as George Herbert—spoke to Lewis as living voices from the past. Yet one person in particular spoke to Lewis in the present. In what follows, we shall tell the story of a nighttime conversation between Lewis and J. R. R. Tolkien, which totally changed Lewis's outlook on Christianity.

A NIGHTTIME CONVERSATION WITH TOLKIEN: SEPTEMBER 1931

The final chapter of *Surprised by Joy* speaks briefly and tantalizingly of Lewis's transition from "pure and simple" theism to Christianity. Lewis takes pains to make it clear that this conversion had nothing to do with desire or longing. The God to whom he surrendered in Trinity Term 1930 was "sheerly nonhuman." He had no idea that "there ever had been or ever would be any connection between God and Joy."[36] Lewis's conversion was essentially rational, unrelated to his long-standing fascination with "Joy." "No kind of desire was present at all."[37] His conversion to theism was, in one way, a purely rational matter.

Lewis's rhetoric at this point can be understood as preempting a long-standing atheist caricature of faith as "wish-fulfilment." This idea, given classic expression in the writings of Sigmund Freud (1856–1939), has an intellectual pedigree going back into the mists of time. In this view, God is a consoling dream for life's losers, a spiritual crutch for the inadequate and needy.[38] Lewis distances himself from any such idea. The existence of God, Lewis insists, was not something that he wished to be true; he valued his independence far too much for that. "I had always wanted, above all things, not to be 'interfered with.'"[39] In effect, Lewis was confronted with something that he did not *wish* to be true, but was forced to concede *was* true.

This rational God bore little, if any, relation to Lewis's world of imagination and longing on the one hand, and to the person of Jesus of Nazareth on the other. So how and when did Lewis make these deeper connections, so characteristic of his mature writing? The simple answer is that *Surprised by Joy* does not really tell us. Lewis pleads that he is now "the least informed" on this final stage of his spiritual journey from "mere Theism to Christianity,"[40] and that he may not fully be relied upon to provide a complete or accurate account.

What we find instead is a paper trail of disconnected ideas and memories, leaving the reader with the task of trying to link these thoughts and episodes into a coherent whole. Yet it is clear from Lewis's correspondence that one extended conversation was of critical importance in enabling him to transition from belief in God to acceptance of Christianity. In view of its importance, we shall consider it in detail.

On Saturday, 19 September 1931, Lewis hosted Hugo Dyson (1896–1975), a lecturer in English at nearby Reading University, and J. R. R. Tolkien for dinner at Magdalen College.[41] Dyson and Tolkien already knew each other, having been exact contemporaries at Exeter College, where they studied English together. It was a still, warm evening. After dinner, they went for an extended stroll along Addison's Walk, a circular footpath following the River Cherwell within the college grounds, discussing the nature of metaphor and myth.

6.2 Addison's Walk, named after Joseph Addison (1672–1719), a former fellow of Magdalen College, photographed in 1937.

After a wind came up, causing leaves to fall to the ground with a noise like pattering rain, the three men retired to Lewis's rooms and continued the discussion, which had now shifted to Christianity. Tolkien eventually made his excuses at 3.00 a.m., and headed home. Lewis and Dyson kept going for another hour. This evening of conversation with these two colleagues played a critical role in Lewis's development. The imagery of the wind seemed to him to hint at the mysterious presence and action of God.[42]

Although Lewis now kept no diary, he wrote two letters to Greeves shortly afterwards, explaining the events of that night and their significance for his reflections on religious faith.[43] In his first letter, dated 1 October, Lewis informed Greeves of the outcome of the evening's discussion, but not its substance:

> I have just passed on from believing in God to definitely believing in Christ—in Christianity. I will try to explain this another time. My long night talk with Dyson and Tolkien had a good deal to do with it.[44]

Greeves naturally wanted to know more about this intriguing development. Lewis provided a more extended account of the evening's events in his next letter, dated 18 October. Lewis explained that his difficulty had been that he could not see "how the life and death of Someone Else (whoever he was) 2000 years ago could help us here and now." An inability to make sense of this had been holding Lewis back "for the last year or so." He could admit that Christ might provide us with a good example, but that was about as far as it went. Lewis realised that the New Testament took a very different view, using terms such as *propitiation* or *sacrifice* to refer to the true meaning of this event. But these expressions, Lewis declared, seemed to him to be "either silly or shocking."[45]

Although Lewis's "long night talk" involved both Dyson and Tolkien, it is Tolkien's approach that seems to have opened a door for Lewis to a wholly new way of looking at the Christian faith. To understand how Lewis passed from theism to Christianity, we need to reflect further on the ideas of J. R. R. Tolkien. For it was he, more than anyone else, who helped Lewis along in the final stage of what the medieval writer Bonaventure of Bagnoregio (1221–1274) describes as the "journey of the mind to God." Tolkien helped Lewis to realise that the problem lay not in Lewis's *rational* failure to understand the theory, but in his *imaginative* failure to grasp its significance. The issue was not primarily about *truth*, but about *meaning*. When engaging the Christian narrative, Lewis was limiting himself to his reason when he ought to be opening himself to the deepest intuitions of his imagination.

Tolkien argued that Lewis ought to approach the New Testament with the same sense of imaginative openness and expectation that he brought to the reading of pagan myths in his professional studies. But, as Tolkien emphasised, there was a decisive difference. As Lewis expressed in his second letter to Greeves, "The story of Christ is simply a true myth: a myth working on us in the same way as the others, but with this tremendous difference that *it really happened*."[46]

The reader must appreciate that the word *myth* is not being used here in the loose sense of a "fairy tale" or the pejorative sense of a "deliberate lie told in order to deceive." This is certainly how Lewis once understood myths—as "lies breathed through silver." As used in the conversation between Lewis and Tolkien, the term *myth* must be understood in its technical literary sense if the significance of this exchange is to be appreciated.

For Tolkien, a myth is a story that conveys "fundamental things"—in other words, that tries to tell us about the deeper structure of things. The best myths, he argues, are not deliberately constructed falsehoods, but are rather tales woven by people to capture the echoes of deeper truths. Myths offer a fragment of that truth, not its totality. They are like splintered fragments of the true light. Yet when the full and true story is told, it is able to bring to fulfilment all that was right and wise in those fragmentary visions of things. For Tolkien, grasping Christianity's *meaningfulness* took precedence over its *truth*. It provided the total picture, unifying and transcending these fragmentary and imperfect insights.

It is not difficult to see how Tolkien's way of thinking brought clarity and coherence to the jumble of thoughts that so excited Lewis's mind at this time. For Tolkien, a myth awakens in its readers a longing for something that lies beyond their grasp. Myths possess an innate capacity to expand the consciousness of their readers, allowing them to transcend themselves. At their best, myths offer what Lewis later termed "a real though unfocused gleam of divine truth falling on human imagination."[47] Christianity, rather than being one myth alongside many others, is thus the fulfilment of all previous mythological religions. Christianity tells a true story about humanity, which makes sense of all the stories that humanity tells about itself.

Tolkien's way of thinking clearly spoke deeply to Lewis. It answered a question that had troubled Lewis since his teenage years: how could Christianity alone be true, and everything else be false? Lewis now realised that he did not have to declare that the great myths of the pagan age were *totally false*; they were echoes or anticipations of the full truth, which was made known only in and through the Christian faith. Christianity brings to fulfilment and completion imperfect and partial insights about reality, scattered abroad in human culture. Tolkien gave Lewis a lens, a way of seeing things, which allowed him to see Christianity as bringing to fulfil-ment such echoes and shadows of the truth that arose from human quest-ing and yearning. If Tolkien was right, similarities between Christianity and pagan religions "*ought*" to be there."[48] There would be a problem only if such similarities did *not* exist.

Perhaps more important, Tolkien allowed Lewis to reconnect the worlds of reason and imagination. No longer was the realm of long-ing to be sidelined or suppressed, as the "New Look" demanded, and as Lewis feared belief in God might imply. It could be woven—naturally and convincingly—into the greater narrative of reality that Tolkien had presented. As Tolkien later put it, God had willed that "the hearts of Men should seek beyond the world and should find no rest therein."[49]

Christianity, Lewis realised, allowed him to affirm the importance of longing and yearning within a reasonable account of reality. God was the true "source from which those arrows of Joy had been shot . . . ever since childhood."[50] Reason and imagination alike were thus affirmed and reconciled by the Christian vision of reality. Tolkien thus helped Lewis to realise that a "rational" faith was not necessarily imaginatively and emotionally barren. When rightly understood, the Christian faith could integrate reason, longing, and imagination.

LEWIS'S BELIEF IN THE DIVINITY OF CHRIST

As a result of his conversation with Tolkien and Dyson, Lewis was able to grasp the imaginative appeal of Christianity. Yet this did not take the form of an understanding of its individual elements—such as the core doc-trines of the creeds. Rather, Lewis came to appreciate the comprehensive view of reality that he found in the Christian faith. Yet Lewis's description of his journey of discovery specifically makes reference to wrestling with core doctrines, including the identity of Jesus of Nazareth. So when did this process of intellectual exploration take place?

Lewis recalled experiencing a process of intellectual clarification and crystallisation, during which the more theological aspects of his faith finally fell into place. His account of this development in *Surprised by Joy* makes clear that it happened during a journey to Whipsnade Park Zoo, yet makes no reference to any specific dates:

> I know very well when, but hardly how, the final step was taken. I was driven to Whipsnade one sunny morning. When we set out I did not believe that Jesus Christ is the Son of God, and when we reached the zoo I did. Yet I had not exactly spent the journey in thought.[51]

We see here the repeated pattern of Lewis's using a journey to mull over things in his mind, the pieces naturally falling into place without undue mental effort on his part. But when did this "final step" take place?

Lewis biographers have traditionally dated this "final step" to 28 September 1931, when Warnie drove Lewis to Whipsnade Park Zoo in Bedfordshire on a misty morning in the sidecar of his motorbike. It is now the received wisdom of Lewis biographers that this date marks Lewis's conversion to Christianity.[52] This is supported by Warnie's remark that it was during this "outing" in 1931 that Lewis decided to rejoin the church.[53]

If this interpretation is correct, the final stages of Lewis's conversion from believing in God to commitment to Christianity might be pieced together as follows:

1. 19 September 1931: A conversation with Tolkien and Dyson leads Lewis to realise that Christianity is a "true myth."
2. 28 September 1931: Lewis comes to believe in the divinity of Christ while being driven to Whipsnade Zoo in a motorbike by his brother, Warnie.
3. 1 October 1931: Lewis tells Arthur Greeves that he has "passed over" from belief in God to belief in Christ.

Following this scenario, Lewis's process of conversion to Christianity is quite rapid, its critical elements having taken place over a period of ten days (19–28 September 1931). This is the traditional understanding of Lewis's gradual rediscovery of Christianity, and it fits in well with the evidence of his writings.

Lewis's conversation with Tolkien and Dyson allowed him to catch a glimpse of the imaginative potential of the Christian story, illuminating questions that had troubled him for some time. Having experienced the "imaginative embrace" of Christianity, Lewis began the rational exploration of its landscape. This rational exploration, expressed in terms of Christianity's doctrines, follows on from the captivation of the imagination through its images and stories.

As has often been observed, Lewis sees theory as secondary to reality[54]—in effect, as intellectual reflection that arises after something has been apprehended or appreciated, primarily through the imagination. Lewis grasped the reality of Christianity through his imagination, and then began to try and make rational sense of what his imagination had captured and embraced. The traditional account of Lewis's conversion suggests that this process was essentially complete within ten days. Yet Lewis's correspondence suggests that it may have been a more extended and complex process, taking months rather than days.[55] So how confident can we be that Lewis's Christological insight took place on the way to Whipsnade Zoo in September 1931?

Lewis's account of the significant visit to Whipsnade Zoo in *Surprised by Joy* is traditionally held to refer to 28 September 1931, when he was driven to Whipsnade Zoo by Warnie in the sidecar of his motorbike. There is no doubt that Lewis visited Whipsnade on this occasion. But is this the occasion on which Lewis's views on Christ were resolved? It is important to note that the narrative of *Surprised by Joy* makes no reference to Warnie, nor to a motorbike, nor to September, nor to 1931. Furthermore, Lewis wrote a long letter to his brother shortly after that visit, briefly recalling their day at Whipsnade—but making no reference to any religious transformation or significant theological adjustment on his part.[56]

A closer examination of Warnie's recollections of that day in September 1931 also raises some doubts about the traditional interpretation.[57]

Warnie's reflections on that day are clearly not based on any personal and privileged disclosures from his brother, but from his own correlation of that journey with the narrative in *Surprised by Joy*. What some have interpreted as Warnie's memory of a conversation with Lewis is clearly Warnie's later interpretation of an event. And, as we shall see, this interpretation of that event is open to question. What if Lewis had been driven to Whipsnade on *another* occasion, when Warnie was *not* present? What if *that* was the occasion for his theological clarification?

Lewis's memory of that critical day at Whipsnade Zoo, as set out in *Surprised by Joy*, includes a lyrical passage recalling "the birds singing overhead and the bluebells underfoot," commenting that this scene at "Wallaby Wood" had been quite ruined by more recent construction work at the zoo.[58] Yet the English bluebell (*Hyacinthoides non-scripta*) blooms from late April into late May (depending on the weather), and its leaves wither and disappear by the late summer.[59] Bluebells flower later than usual at Whipsnade, due to the slightly colder climate on the elevated downs on which the zoo is located.[60] There would have been no sign of "bluebells underfoot" at Whipsnade in September. But they would have been blooming in profusion there in May and early June.

Perhaps the significance of this fact has been overlooked by some, or the English bluebell has been confused with its Scottish counterpart (*Campanula rotundifolia*, known as the "harebell" in England), which continues to flower into September. Lewis's "Edenic" recollection of the birds and bluebells at Whipsnade Zoo recorded in *Surprised by Joy* is clearly a memory of a late spring or early summer day, not a day in early autumn.

Lewis's heightened attention to the bluebells may well reflect their symbolic association with this moment of insight—after all, Lewis tells us that he had long been a self-confessed "votary of the Blue Flower" (page 16).[61] The "Blue Flower" motif in German Romanticism has complex historical roots. It was first stated in Novalis's posthumously published fragment of a novel *Heinrich von Ofterdingen* (1802), and came to symbolise a longing for the elusive reconciliation of reason and imagination, the observed world outside the mind and the subjective world within. The bright blue European cornflower is often cited as the inspiration for this symbol.[62] It is easily extended to bluebells.

Upon reflection, it is quite clear that this "Blue Flower" passage in *Surprised by Joy* refers not to the autumn of 1931, but to a *second* visit to Whipsnade, made in the first week of June 1932, when Lewis was again driven to the zoo—but this time in a car on a "fine day" by Edward Foord-Kelcey (1859–1934). On 14 June, shortly after this trip, Lewis wrote to his brother, specifically noting the "masses of bluebells" he had seen during this visit to Whipsnade, and commenting on the state of "Wallaby Wood."[63] The phrasing of this section of the letter is very similar to that of the critical passage in *Surprised by Joy*. Might this later date mark the occasion when Lewis finally came to believe in the Incarnation, perhaps as the apex of his exploration of the Christian faith? If so, it would clearly represent a deepened understanding of his faith from within, as Lewis had clearly identified himself as a Christian by this time. This would require a revision of the traditional chronology of events, as follows:

1. 19 September 1931: A conversation with Tolkien and Dyson leads Lewis to realise that Christianity is a "true myth."
2. 1 October 1931: Lewis tells Arthur Greeves that he has "passed over" from belief in God to belief in Christ.
3. 7(?) June 1932: Lewis comes to believe in the divinity of Christ while being driven to Whipsnade Zoo in a car by Edward Foord-Kelcey.

So did Lewis's restless, questing mind finally bring everything together in a journey to Whipsnade Zoo in September 1931, a week or so after his conversation with Tolkien? Or was the process of reflection and crystallisation more extended, only being completed during a later journey to Whipsnade in June 1932? Lewis's letter of 1 October 1931 to Greeves, in which he speaks of now "definitely believing in Christ," could certainly be interpreted as an embryonic realisation of the significance of Christ that needed extended exploration and formulation, culminating in June 1932. Yet his correspondence of this later period—including a letter of 14 June

1932 to Warnie—makes no explicit reference to such a development. Nor can we eliminate the possibility that Lewis may have confused individual aspects of these two visits to Whipsnade in writing *Surprised by Joy*. He may even have *fused* them in his memory, bringing together the imagery and themes of two different visits, and telescoping them into one. So which of these two visits marks the true moment of illumination? We noted earlier how Lewis was not totally reliable concerning dates, and it is possible that the narrative in *Surprised by Joy* involves blurring of the boundaries between similar events.

We are left here, as so often in relation to this most tantalising of Lewis's works, wishing for more, yet forced to work with what we have. The best solution at present is to allow the traditional date of Lewis's conversion to Christianity—September 1931—to stand, while noting the ambiguities and uncertainties that surround it. Lewis's letter to Greeves of 1 October 1931 makes most sense if a decisive Christological step has already been taken, even if the full unfolding and exploration of this insight continued into the following year.

Yet whenever Lewis's insight is to be dated, it is to be seen as bringing to a conclusion an extended process of reflection and commitment, which proceeded in a series of stages. We cannot seize on a single moment—such as this one—as defining or dating Lewis's "conversion" to Christianity; instead, we can trace an ascending arc of reflection, of which the conversation with Tolkien represents a critical imaginative transition, and the trip to Whipsnade Zoo its logical outworking.

One point on this ascending arc of Christian commitment merits special comment. Lewis attended a service of Holy Communion for the first time since his childhood at Holy Trinity Church, Headington Quarry, on Christmas Day 1931. In a long letter to his brother, Lewis briefly yet explicitly mentions attending the "early celebration"[64] on that day at Holy Trinity, Headington Quarry—in other words, a service of Holy Communion. Lewis would have no doubt that his brother would have understood the significance of this development, given the traditions of the Church of England at this time.

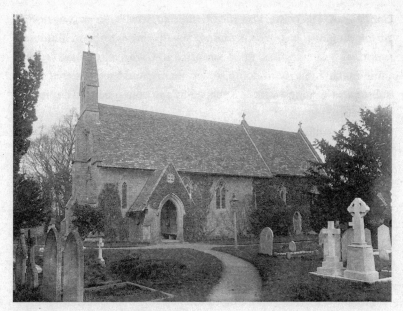

6.3 Holy Trinity Church, Headington Quarry, Oxford, seen from the south, showing the entrance porch, as photographed by Henry W. Taunt (1842-1922) in 1901.

Up to this point, Lewis had attended Matins, a "service of the word," often leaving—to the irritation of the vicar, Wilfrid Thomas—during the last hymn, before the service had ended properly. But Lewis was clear that, while anyone could attend Matins, Holy Communion was only for the committed. By informing his brother of his decision to attend such a communion service, Lewis wanted to let his brother know that he had moved on significantly in his journey of faith.

What Lewis did not know was that Warnie had made a similar journey of faith, and had received communion for the first time since his childhood at the Bubbling Well Chapel in Shanghai[65]—also on Christmas Day 1931. The two brothers, unknown to each other, had made a public profession of commitment to Christianity on exactly the same day.

In the end, it is not so much the precise date of Lewis's conversion to Christianity as its implications for his future writings that is of ultimate importance. His conversion might, after all, have been an inner event, of importance to Lewis, but without any obvious impact on his literary work. For example, T. S. Eliot converted to Christianity in 1927, generating much publicity in doing so. Yet many would suggest that Eliot's subsequent writings were less shaped by this conversion than might be expected.

Lewis is different. From the outset, Lewis seems to have realised that if Christianity was true, it resolved the intellectual and imaginative riddles that had puzzled him since his youth. His youthful "treaty with reality" had been his own attempt to *impose* an arbitrary (yet convenient) order on a chaotic world. Now he began to realise that there was a deeper order, grounded in the nature of God, which could be discerned—and which, once grasped, made sense of culture, history, science, and above all the acts of literary creation that he valued so highly and made his life's study. Lewis's coming to faith brought not simply understanding to his reading of literature; it brought both motivation and theoretical underpinning to his own literary creations—best seen in his late work *Till We Have Faces* (1956), but also evident in the Chronicles of Narnia.

It is simply not possible to make sense of Lewis's work as a scholar and author without grasping the ordering principles of his inner world, which—after a period of incubation and reflection—finally began to fall into place in the early autumn of 1931, and reached their final synthesis by the summer of 1932. When Lewis went to spend a holiday with Arthur Greeves between 15 and 29 August 1932, he was ready to map out his new and essentially complete vision of the Christian faith in the work that became *The Pilgrim's Regress* (discussed on pages 169–174). Although Lewis would continue to explore the relation of reason and imagination in the domain of faith, the fundamental features of his settled understanding of Christianity were now in place.

In this chapter, we have explored the trajectory of Lewis's complex and extended conversion to Christianity, raising concerns about some traditional datings and interpretations of this development. We must, however, avoid portraying Lewis's as a representative or typical conversion.

As Lewis later remarked, his specific way of coming to faith was "a road very rarely trodden,"[66] and could not in any way be regarded as normative. His account of his conversion represents it as an essentially private affair, marked by understatement and a studied evasion of any dramatic gestures or declarations. Yet gradually, Lewis's faith would become both public and prominent, as we shall see when we consider his wartime role as an apologist.

But there is much more that needs to be said about Lewis as an Oxford don, above all about his approach to literature—the topic of the next chapter.

A MAN OF LETTERS: LITERARY SCHOLARSHIP AND CRITICISM

By 1933, Lewis's Oxford world seemed to be a stable place. He had been reelected to his tutorial fellowship in English, a position he retained until December 1954, when he moved to Cambridge. His family life was settled. The Kilns had been extended, and its grounds were being tamed and replanted. Warnie, now retired from the British army, had settled in with Lewis and Mrs. Moore at The Kilns for good. To Lewis, it seemed as if the "old days" had been restored. After the arrival of Warnie, Lewis increasingly came to see The Kilns as a re-creation or extension of Little Lea. It was as if everything that had happened between 1914 and 1932 had been reversed.[1]

That sense of continuity with bygone days was reinforced by Warnie's decision to edit the Lewis family letters, papers, and diaries, cataloguing them and finally typing them up on his old Royal typewriter. The result of Warnie's efforts, originally intended simply as a record of "ordinary, undistinguished" people, became the eleven volumes of *The Lewis Papers: Memoirs of the Lewis Family, 1850–1930*. They have since become an essential research tool for Lewis scholars.

Lewis thus reestablished the "secure base" that had been taken away from him by the death of his mother and the scattering of his family. As Lewis remarked to Greeves late in 1933, "stability" was now his strong point.[2] Having realised that he would never achieve fame as a poet, Lewis was now focussing on the world of literary scholarship, seeing this as the field in which he could achieve distinction, perhaps even eminence.

LEWIS THE TEACHER: OXFORD TUTORIALS

Lewis's primary responsibility from 1927–1954 was tutorial teaching and university lecturing. He was a member of the Faculty of English by virtue of his teaching appointment at Magdalen. Membership in this faculty permitted him to give lectures open to all Oxford University students. Unlike his colleague J. R. R. Tolkien, Lewis was never a "professor" at Oxford University. He was always—as the painted college nameplate on his staircase in the Magdalen New Building attested—simply "Mr. C. S. Lewis." Given the importance of tutorials and lectures for Lewis's academic life, it is appropriate to reflect on what we know of these.

During the nineteenth century, Oxford University developed the weekly tutorial as the foundation of its pedagogy. Colleges established "tutorial fellowships" with the object of raising academic standards, particularly in *Literae Humaniores*. Typically, a tutorial was an hour long. To begin with, a student would read aloud an essay of his own composition. The remainder of the time was taken up with close discussion of the student's ideas and arguments.

Lewis's account of a typical working day during the eight teaching weeks of Oxford's full term indicates how his faith was now woven into his life, along with his heavy teaching load. Apart from Mondays and Saturdays, his working days from 1931 onwards looked like this:

7.15 a.m. Woken by scout with cup of tea
8.00 a.m. Chapel
8.15 a.m. Breakfast with Dean of Chapel and others

9.00 a.m. Tutorials begin, continuing until 1.00 p.m.

1.00 p.m. Driven home to Headington (Lewis did not drive)

Afternoon: working in garden, walking the dog, time with "the family"

4.45 p.m. Driven back to college

5.00 p.m. Tutorials recommence, ending at 7.00 p.m.

7.15 p.m. Dinner[3]

While at Great Bookham, Lewis had fallen into a set routine that continued, with appropriate adaptations to his circumstances, for the rest of his working life. The morning was set aside for working, the early afternoon was set aside for solitary walking, the late afternoon for more work, and the evening for talking. Lewis's walks at The Kilns were often not strictly solitary; he was generally accompanied on these by whatever dog Mrs. Moore happened to own at the time. Yet the routine seemed to work, and Lewis saw little reason to change it.

Students having tutorials with Lewis at Magdalen in the early 1930s often commented on the "clacking" of the typewriter from behind a door, as Warnie worked on *The Lewis Family Papers* in the smaller sitting room, while their tutorial proceeded in the larger. Lewis himself never learned to type, always depending on pens. One reason for this was that the same "native clumsiness" arising from Lewis's having only one joint in his thumbs prevented him from using a typewriter properly.

Yet there is more to it than this. Lewis actively *chose* not to type. This mechanical mode of writing, he believed, interfered with the creative process in that the incessant clacking of the typewriter keys dulled the writer's appreciation of the rhythms and cadences of the English language. When reading Milton or other poets, or composing a work of one's own, Lewis argued, it was essential to appreciate how the writing *sounded*. As he later advised anyone thinking about writing seriously, "Don't use a typewriter. The noise will destroy your sense of rhythm, which still needs years of training."[4]

By the mid-1930s, Lewis's tutorial load was heavy. We possess a number of accounts of Lewis's approach to tutorials during the 1930s, all of which emphasise his acutely critical questioning, his desire not to waste time, and a certain degree of impatience with weaker or lazier students. Lewis did not see it as his responsibility to impart information to his students. He resented and resisted what some then called the "gramophone" model of tuition, in which the tutor simply imparted the knowledge that the student had so signally failed to discover for himself.

Lewis saw himself as enabling the student to develop the skills necessary to uncover and evaluate such knowledge for himself. For example, George Sayer (1914–2005) recalls Lewis using a strongly Socratic method in their tutorials of the mid-1930s, perhaps modelled on his experience when studying at Great Bookham under Kirkpatrick. "What exactly do you mean by the word *sentimental*, Mr. Sayer? . . . If you are not sure what the word means or what you mean by it, wouldn't it be very much better if you ceased to use it at all?"[5]

The most perceptive account of Lewis as a tutor at this time is generally thought to be by John Lawlor (1918–1999), who became one of only two students to study English at Magdalen College in October 1936. Lawlor's finely observed account of tutorials with Lewis captures something significant about both the man and his pedagogic method. He recalls the jovial and resonant bellow, "Come in," when the student, wearing a black gown and nervously clutching his flimsy essay, clambered up the stairway and knocked on the doors of Lewis's rooms; the red-faced bald man, dressed in baggy jacket and trousers, who would sit smoking in his shabbily comfortable armchair, doodling and occasionally taking notes, while the student read his essay for about twenty minutes; and the inevitable scrupulous examination of the essay that followed. Lewis had no hesitation in finding fault with what was said, and perhaps more important, with what had also been left unsaid.[6]

For Lawlor, it was not difficult to work out that Lewis did not really enjoy tutorials; students who made the experience more engaging and interesting were therefore especially welcome to Lewis. For at its best, as Lawlor rightly notes, the Oxford tutorial provides an "unmatched experience in intellectual exhilaration—a sight of wide horizons and a growing sense of . . . the mastery of the thing."[7] The tutorial was not simply about the accumulation of knowledge; it was also about developing critical thinking—fostering a spirit of analysing and evaluating important ideas or beliefs in an effort to calibrate their quality and to improve them, and to discover unexamined assumptions and challenge them.

Lawlor's feelings towards Lewis changed as the term progressed. He gradually "passed from dislike and hostility to stubborn affection, and then to gratitude for the weekly bout in which no quarter was asked or given." Yet for all the argumentativeness and rhetorical force of Lewis's interaction with his students, Lawlor recalls a point of no small significance: "One thing Lewis never did, in any recollection I have of him. He never imposed his Christianity on the argument."

By the 1940s, Lewis was famous. John Wain (1925–1994) recalls that students of that period would approach Lewis's room through an "echoing antechamber of reputation," to experience "dense clouds of smoke from a rapidly puffed cigarette or pipe," a "brisk argumentative manner," and above all "a love of debate."[8] Yet perhaps the most characteristic memory of Lewis's tutorials concerns his personal appearance. Terms such as "shabby," "untidy," or "unkempt" occur frequently in accounts of Lewis the tutor from his students. Warnie once remarked on his brother's "complete indifference" to the clothes he wore—such as his old tweed sports jacket, or a pair of slightly tattered carpet slippers. Lewis was a heavy smoker, usually puffing a pipe during tutorials, with clouds of smoke enveloping the room. Lewis's habit of using his carpet as an ashtray added further to the general impression of grand decrepitude usually then associated with confirmed bachelors living on their own.

Yet Lewis's untidiness was seen with affection by his students—a sign of his indifference to external matters, arising from his love and knowledge of deeper and more significant matters. Furthermore, it fitted perfectly with an Oxford stereotype of that period—the bachelor don, whose only female company was an ageing mother. It suited Lewis perfectly to be characterised in this way, in that it deflected attention from the true nature of his unusual domestic arrangements.

One of Lewis's abilities must be noted here, for it is of obvious relevance to his gifts as a writer: his formidable memory. Lewis's mastery of the Renaissance skill of the *ars memorativa* unquestionably contributed to the success of his Oxford lectures, enabling him to recite quotes from memory. Kenneth Tynan (1927–1980), an "angry young man" of the 1960s, whom Lewis tutored in the 1940s, recalls Lewis playing a memory game with him. Tynan would read aloud a line he had arbitrarily chosen from a book he had selected from Lewis's library. Lewis would then identify the work in question, and set the line in its proper context.[9]

Lewis, it seems, could remember texts primarily because he had absorbed their deep inner logic. His diaries bear witness to his habit of reading an astonishing number of texts; his personal library contains annotations indicating when a book was first read, and then read again. He was good at explaining complex ideas to others, because he had first explained them to himself: "I'm a professional teacher and explanation happens to be one of the things I've learned to do."[10] Lewis achieved this feat partly by neglecting other sources of reading—such as daily newspapers. As a result, even his friends sometimes found him worryingly ignorant of current affairs.

William Empson (1906–1984), a leading literary critic who had little time for Lewis's views on Milton, nevertheless declared that "he was the best read man of his generation, one who read everything and remembered everything he read."[11] It showed. Students attending his lectures were impressed by his grasp not simply of the texts of leading works of literature—above all, Milton's *Paradise Lost*—but his deeper grasp of their internal structure. Rarely did university lectures both inform and inspire; yet these quickly became the hallmarks of Lewis's academic lecturing style.

LEWIS THE TEACHER: OXFORD LECTURES

With such a capacity for memorization, it was perhaps inevitable that Lewis would deliver his lectures without notes. Lewis gave his first lectures at Oxford in October 1924. Even then, he had decided that he would not speak from a full text. Lectures that were simply read out to their audiences, he explained to his father, tend to "send people to sleep." He would have to learn to talk to his audiences, not to recite his lectures to them.[12] He had to engage their attention, not merely discharge information.

By the end of the 1930s, Lewis had established a reputation as one of Oxford's finest lecturers, drawing crowds that others could only dream of attracting. His robust, resonant, clear tone—described by one hearer as a "port wine and plum pudding voice"—was ideal for lecture podiums. Lewis spoke only from brief notes, which typically identified quotes that were to be used, and points that were to be made. The fluent performance which followed dazzled most of the audience. Perhaps this was just as well, as Lewis did not allow time for questions at the end of his lectures. His lectures were a rhetorical event, a theatrical performance, complete in their own terms. Like a Renaissance artist, Lewis threw open a window on a larger landscape,[13] extending his audience's vision.

It was inevitable that Oxford University would formally recognise Lewis's abilities. Although Lewis held only a college appointment as tutorial fellow in English at Magdalen, the university bestowed additional titles upon him in recognition of his widening academic role. From 1935, he appears in official Oxford University publications as a "faculty lecturer in English literature";[14] from 1936, as "University lecturer in English literature."[15] While remaining based at Magdalen College, Lewis was gaining wider recognition within the university as a whole. The publication of his *Allegory of Love* in 1936 would enhance the esteem in which he was held still further.

Lewis's most famous Oxford lecture courses were two sets of sixteen lectures, entitled "Prolegomena to Medieval Studies" and "Prolegomena to Renaissance Studies." These lectures displayed a vast range of reading in the primary sources, arranged and explained in terms that were both accessible and interesting. The substance of these lectures, developed over many years, would eventually appear in his *The Discarded Image* (1964). Lewis made no secret of the fact that he found deep satisfaction in these older ways of thinking. "The old Model delights me as I believe it delighted our ancestors."[16]

7.1 The Examination Schools, close to Magdalen College, where Lewis delivered many of his lectures during his career at Oxford University. Completed in 1892, when this photograph was taken, these buildings acted as both examination rooms and lecture theatres for the university.

Yet it would be unfair to dismiss Lewis as antiquarian and backward looking. His point, as we shall see, is that the study of the past helps us to appreciate that the ideas and values of our own age are just as provisional and transient as those of bygone ages. The intelligent and reflective engagement with the thought of a bygone era ultimately subverts any notion of "chronological snobbery." Reading texts from the past makes it clear that what we now term "the past" was once "the present," which proudly yet falsely regarded itself as having found the right intellectual answers or moral values that had eluded its predecessors. As Lewis later put it, "All that is not eternal is eternally out of date."[17] The quest for a *philosophia perennis*—a deeper view of reality that underlies all things at all times—was unquestionably one of the factors in leading Lewis to rediscover the Christian faith.

Yet some at Oxford around this time formed the impression that Lewis saw his obligatory tutoring and lecturing as getting in the way of the thing he really wanted to do—write books. Tutorials and lectures might inform those books; nevertheless, Lewis preferred reading books and discussing them with informed colleagues—the Inklings being a case in point—to listening to somewhat amateurish and uninformed evaluations of their significance from his students. In what follows, we shall look at Lewis's first prose work, and explore how it both illuminates his past and foreshadows his future.

THE PILGRIM'S REGRESS (1933): MAPPING THE LANDSCAPE OF FAITH

In January 1933, Lewis wrote to Guy Pocock, an editor at the London publishing firm of J. M. Dent. Would they be interested in publishing a book he had just completed? It would be "a kind of Bunyan up to date"[18]—a reference to John Bunyan's classic *Pilgrim's Progress* (1678–1684). Lewis's hesitant tone in this letter clearly reflects some embarrassment about the poor sales figures of his earlier work *Dymer*. He hastens to assure Pocock that this new book would be published under his own name. Within three weeks, Pocock had made the decision to publish *The Pilgrim's Regress*.

Lewis wrote *The Pilgrim's Regress*, his first novel, in a burst of sustained literary activity between 15 and 29 August 1932, while visiting his close friend and confidant Arthur Greeves at his Belfast home, Bernagh. (This was just across the road from Lewis's own recently sold childhood home, Little Lea.) Lewis's first prose book is best understood as an imaginative mapping of the landscape of faith. As both its title and the correspondence with Pocock suggest, this book can be thought of as taking its inspiration from Bunyan's *Pilgrim's Progress*. Yet it is important to approach this work on its own terms, and not to expect it to be either a simple retelling of Bunyan's allegory for the modern age or a narrative account of Lewis's own conversion. For Lewis, the key issue he wanted to explore was not the personal story "Lewis meets God," but the intellectual issue of how reason and imagination may be both affirmed and integrated within a Christian vision of reality.

The Pilgrim's Regress can be read at several levels. It is most plausibly read as Lewis's attempt to clear his mind—to put into words and images the processes of thought that had shattered his settled intellectual world during the previous three years. Lewis's conversion had forced him to redraw his intellectual maps, renegotiating his "treaty with reality." The new "treaty with reality," set out in this early work, creates space for reason and imagination within an ordered world. It offers meaningful norms and criteria of evaluation without degenerating into either the anti-intellectualism of more extreme forms of Romanticism, or the emotionally impoverished forms of rationalism that eliminate the transcendent as a matter of principle.

Lewis was a strongly visual thinker, often using images to make important philosophical and theological points—for example, his famous image of the beam of light in a dark toolshed to make a distinction between "looking along" and "looking at." *The Pilgrim's Regress* is not a philosophical defence of faith, but the construction of an almost medieval *mappa mundi*—a cosmographical account of the situation in which humanity finds itself and its struggle to find its way to its true goal and destiny. Lewis treats the ability of the map to make sense of human experience as an indication of its reliability.

To many readers today, this work seems opaque and complex, peppered with a needlessly large number of difficult quotations. This sense of an impenetrable text (Lewis himself later admitted the book's "needless obscurity"[19]) is perhaps heightened by the book's original title, *Pseudo-Bunyan's Periplus: An Allegorical Apology for Christianity, Reason, and Romanticism*, wisely shortened when Lewis corrected the proofs. Lewis himself seems to have belatedly realised the difficulties that many readers experienced in engaging with his first book, and appears to have learned from this in his later writings.

Most modern readers find *The Pilgrim's Regress* to be like a cryptic crossword puzzle. It provides baffling clues about people and movements in English intellectual and cultural life in the 1920s and early 1930s that need to be decoded and disentangled. Whom did Lewis have in mind when he wrote about "Mr. Neo-Angular"? In fact, Lewis had T. S. Eliot in his gunsights here. Yet most readers will wonder what all the fuss is about. By making his book so focussed on intellectual and cultural movements of his own time, Lewis made himself less intelligible to later readers, who don't know these people or movements, or why they might be important.

Lewis himself realised there was a problem. By 1943, a decade after the work's original publication, Lewis conceded that there had been a "profound change" in patterns of thought,[20] so that the movements he described were no longer familiar to many readers. The world had moved on; old threats had passed into history, and new ones arisen. In one sense, *The Pilgrim's Regress* is likely to be of interest mostly to intellectual historians. It is now one of the least read of Lewis's works.

Yet the work can be read without the need to make such connections. Indeed, Lewis himself condemned "the pernicious habit of reading allegory as if it were a cryptogram to be translated."[21] The best way to understand this book is to see it as a quest for the true origins, objects, and goals of human desire. Inevitably, this involves identifying and critiquing "false turns," which Lewis often engages in such detail that he loses his readers' attention. In what follows, we shall explore the main themes of the work, without becoming trapped in the fine details of Lewis's analysis.

The central character of *The Pilgrim's Regress* is the pilgrim— "John"—who has visions of an Island that evokes a sense of intense yet transitory longing. At times, John is overwhelmed by this yearning as he struggles to understand it. Where does it come from? What is he yearning *for*? A subsidiary, yet important, theme concerns a sense of moral obligation. Why do we long to do right? Where does this sense of obligation come from? And what does it signify—if anything? For Lewis, human experience—moral and aesthetic—is littered with false attempts to *understand* this sense of longing, and equally false understandings of this longing's true object. *The Pilgrim's Regress* is basically an exploration of these false turns along the road of life.

Like many before him, Lewis chose to describe this philosophical quest in terms of a journey. He uses the image of a road leading to the mysterious Island, with badlands on either side. To the north lie objective ways of thinking based on reason; to the south, subjective ways based on emotion. The farther John departs from the central road, the more extreme these positions become.

It is clear that the relationship between reason and imagination is of critical importance to Lewis. *The Pilgrim's Regress* defends rational thought against arguments based purely on feeling, yet refuses to accept an exclusively rational approach to faith. For Lewis, there has to be a position which reconciles reason and imagination, as indicated in his sonnet "Reason," probably written in the 1920s. This poem contrasts the clarity of reason (symbolised by the "maid" Athene) with the creativity of the imagination (symbolised by Demeter, the earth-mother). How, Lewis wondered, might these seemingly opposed forces be reconciled?[22]

As the narrative of *The Pilgrim's Regress* proceeds, it becomes clear that such a reconciliation can be provided only by "Mother Kirk"—an allegorical figure which some have interpreted specifically as Catholicism, but which Lewis clearly intended to be an image of nondenominational Christianity. This was the "mere Christianity" of which the Puritan writer Richard Baxter (1615–1691) wrote, and which Lewis increasingly came to expound in the 1940s.

As John travels north of the road, he encounters ways of thinking which are deeply suspicious of feeling, intuition, and imagination. The coldly and clinically "rational" northern region is the realm of "rigid systems," wooden orthodoxies characterised by "an arrogant and hasty selectiveness on some narrow *a priori* basis," which leads to the incorrect conclusion that "every feeling . . . is suspect." To the south of the road, however, he encounters "boneless souls whose doors stand open day and night" to anyone, especially those who offer some kind of emotional or mystical "intoxication." "Every feeling is justified by the mere fact that it is felt."[23] The rationalist philosophy of the Enlightenment, romantic art, modern art, Freudianism, asceticism, nihilism, hedonism, classical humanism, and religious liberalism are all located on this map, only to be tried and found wanting.

This dialectic between "northernness" and "southernness" provides Lewis with a framework to explore the proper relation of reason and imagination, focussing especially on the theme of longing. Some try to explain "Desire" away; others attach it to false objects. Lewis remarks that he has made all these mistakes himself: "I have myself been deluded by every one of these false answers in turn, and have contemplated each of them earnestly enough to discover the cheat."[24]

So what is the ultimate object of Desire—this "intense longing"? Lewis here anticipates his "argument from desire," which is central to the Christian apologetic he would develop further in his wartime radio broadcasts a decade later, and subsequently collect together in *Mere Christianity*. Lewis opens up a line of thought originally employed by the French philosopher Blaise Pascal (1623–1662)—namely, that there is an "abyss" within the human soul, which is so great that only God can fill it. Or, to change the imagery, there is a "chair" in the human soul, awaiting some guest who has yet to arrive. "If nature makes nothing in vain, the One who can sit in this chair must exist."[25]

Our experience of this Desire both discloses our true identity and intimates our true goal. We initially understand this Desire as a yearning for something tangible within the world; then we realise that nothing within the world is able to satisfy our Desire. John, the pilgrim, initially desires the Island. Yet he gradually comes to realise that his true longing is actually for the "Landlord"—Lewis's way of referring to God. All other explanations and proposed goals for this sense of yearning fail to satisfy, intellectually or existentially. They are "false objects" of Desire, whose falsity is ultimately exposed by their failure to satisfy the deepest yearnings of humanity.[26] There is indeed a chair in the human soul, and its intended occupant is God.

> If a man diligently followed this desire, pursuing the false
> objects until their falsity appeared and then resolutely
> abandoning them, he must come out at last into the clear
> knowledge that the human soul was made to enjoy some

object that is never fully given—nay, cannot even be imagined as given—in our present mode of subjective and spatio-temporal experience.[27]

In the light of Lewis's more mature ways of thinking, one further point stands out as being particularly interesting. *The Pilgrim's Regress* actually describes *two* journeys—there, and back again. Having realised the true significance of the Island, the pilgrim now retraces his steps. Yet when the pilgrim walks back through the same landscape *after* coming to faith—the "regress" of the book's title—he discovers that its appearance has changed. He sees it in a new way. His Guide explains that he is "seeing the land as it really is." His discovery of the true state of affairs changes the way he sees things. "Your eyes are altered. You see nothing now but realities."[28] Lewis here anticipates one of the leading themes of his later writings: that the Christian faith allows us to see things as they really are. There are strong hints here of some images in the New Testament, such as eyes being opened and veils being removed.[29]

It is important not to treat *The Pilgrim's Regress* as embodying Lewis's definitive understanding of the relationship of faith, reason, and imagination. Although some writers have suggested that Lewis's mature thought appears almost full blown in his earlier writings, it is not quite as straightforward as this. Throughout the 1930s and 1940s, Lewis was exploring the relationship between reason and the imagination, between "the true" and "the real"—in particular, the relationship between rational argument and the use of imaginative narratives. At this stage, Lewis tends to see the imagination as the primary means by which an individual is brought to a point of giving serious rational attention to the Christian faith; yet he does not see it as the means by which that faith may be entered.

In part, Lewis's development of these points was due to his interaction with colleagues, who helped him to sharpen and refine his thinking. One of the most significant groups to help him improve and develop his ideas, and their literary expressions, was the small literary group known as the "Inklings," to which we now turn.

THE INKLINGS: FRIENDSHIP, COMMUNITY, AND DEBATE

Lewis's regular meetings with Tolkien, which date back to 1929, reflected an increasingly close professional and personal bond between the two men. Tolkien developed a habit (not in any way discouraged by Lewis) of dropping in on his friend on Monday mornings for a drink, some gossip (usually about faculty politics), and a swapping of news about each other's literary works. It was, Lewis declared, "one of the pleasantest spots in the week."[30] As their personal friendship deepened, they even began to dream about occupying the two Merton Chairs of English and redirecting the course of Oxford's Faculty of English together.[31] At this stage, Tolkien was Professor of Anglo-Saxon and a fellow of Pembroke College; Lewis was simply a fellow of Magdalen College. But both dreamed of a better and brighter future. And already there were hints of blossoming literary projects. In February 1933, Lewis told Greeves that he had just had a "delightful time reading a children's story" by Tolkien.[32] This, of course, was *The Hobbit*, which would eventually be published in 1937.

This personal friendship between Lewis and Tolkien was supplemented by the many literary clubs, societies, and circles which existed in Oxford around this time. Sometimes these focussed on a specific college (for example, Nevill Coghill and Hugo Dyson both belonged to the Exeter College Essay Club while they were undergraduates in the 1920s). Sometimes they focussed on literary or linguistic themes (such as the *Kolbítar*, founded by Tolkien to enhance appreciation of the Old Norse language and its literature). Yet while Lewis and Tolkien were both active members of various literary networks within Oxford, their own friendship transcended these, deepening when Lewis converted to Christianity by the end of 1931. Tolkien read parts of *The Hobbit* to Lewis; Lewis read parts of *The Pilgrim's Regress* to Tolkien.

This small nucleus would expand into a group which has since acquired almost legendary status—the Inklings. There was never any intention that this would become an elite discussion group for matters of faith and literature. Like Topsy, it just "growed"—largely by accident and happenstance. Yet the invention of the Inklings in 1933 was as inevitable as the rising of the sun. That was how Lewis and Tolkien expanded their horizons: through books, through friends, and through friends discussing books.

The first addition to the Lewis-Tolkien axis was Lewis's brother, Warnie, who was then developing a passion for the history of seventeenth-century France.[33] Like both Lewis and Tolkien, Warnie had served in the British army during the Great War. Tolkien seems to have acquiesced with gradually diminishing reluctance to the inclusion of Warnie in their discussions. Over a period of time, others were drawn in. Most of the early members were already part of Lewis and Tolkien's circle—such as Owen Barfield, Hugo Dyson, and Nevill Coghill. Others gradually attached themselves by invitation and mutual consent. There was no formal membership, and no agreed-upon means of electing new members.

There was no solemn initiation of the group, as in Tolkien's legendary founding of the "Fellowship of the Ring." There were no oaths, no pledges of allegiance; in fact, there was no name for the group until well after it had been formed. It was, as Tolkien put it, an "undetermined and unelected circle of friends."[34] The Inklings were basically a group of friends with shared interests. The "gate-crashers" who came unbidden were not encouraged to return. The group's collective identity was slow to emerge, and shifted over time. Its identity, to the extent that this can be pinpointed, lay in its focus on Christianity and literature—both terms being interpreted generously.

It is not clear at what point (or by whom) the group came to be called the Inklings. For Tolkien, it was always a "literary club." Charles Williams, a member of the group from 1939 to 1945, does not use the term *Inklings* to refer to this group in his correspondence with his wife: it is simply the "Tolkien-Lewis group."[35] The title *Inklings*—which Tolkien attributes to Lewis—suggested "people with vague or half-formed intimations and ideas plus those who dabble in ink."[36] This name was not original. It seems that Lewis borrowed the name of an earlier literary discussion group with which he had been associated, once it ceased to meet.

The original Inklings were a group of undergraduates who met in the rooms of Edward Tangye Lean (1911–1974)—the younger brother of David Lean, the future film director—at University College to read unpublished papers for discussion and criticism. Lean, who initiated and organised the group, chose the term *Inklings* to suggest the idea of dabbling with writing. Lewis and Tolkien were both invited to attend these predominantly undergraduate meetings. When Lean left Oxford in June 1933, the group ceased to function. Perhaps for that reason, Lewis felt it was permissible to appropriate the same name for the new group then coalescing around him and Tolkien.

One of the earliest references to the Inklings is found in a letter Lewis wrote to Charles Williams on 11 March 1936. Lewis had just read Williams's novel *The Place of the Lion* (1931), and was delighted by it. It was clearly the sort of book he would have liked to have written himself—a philosophical novel, in which Platonic archetypes descend to earth in the form of animals. Oxford University Press then based its more commercial operations—such as the printing of Bibles and educational material—at Amen House in London, not far from St. Paul's Cathedral, while retaining its academic publications base in Oxford. Lewis extended an invitation to Williams, who was working at Amen House, to visit him in Oxford and meet others who had read the book—himself, his brother, Tolkien, and Coghill, "all buzzing with excited admiration." Together, they made up "a sort of informal club called the Inklings,"[37] focussing on issues having to do with writing and the Christian faith.

In effect, the group that gathered around Lewis and Tolkien acted as "critical friends" for the discussion and development of works in progress. The Inklings were not strictly a "collaborative group." Its function was to hear works in progress read aloud and to offer criticism—not to *plan* such work. The only apparent exception here lies in the collection of essays gathered together to honour Charles Williams. This, however, was clearly a project initiated and driven by Lewis himself. It is important to note that only four other Inklings were involved, and that it included one author from outside the group: Dorothy L. Sayers (1893–1957). (The high profile of this collection of essays may have fostered the belief that Sayers was herself a member of the Inklings, but she was not.)

There are two cardinal errors that the student of Lewis could make concerning the Inklings: first, in giving them a retrospective significance and internal unity they did not really possess at the time; and second, in assuming that Lewis's literary contacts and influences were limited to them.

Lewis was part of an extended writing community that went far beyond the Inklings, and expanded further after 1947, during which time the group continued to meet, but shed its more explicit literary functions. The importance of this wider community made up for an obvious short-coming of the Inklings: there were no female members. In its historical context, this is not surprising; during the 1930s, Oxford University was still a firmly male institution, with its emerging women scholars restricted to a small group of all-women colleges, such as St. Hilda's College, Somerville College, and Lady Margaret Hall. (Dorothy L. Sayers's 1935 novel *Gaudy Night* is set in a fictional all-women college, and brings out well the pre-vailing university attitudes towards women of that time.)

Nevertheless, there are deeper issues here, reflecting Lewis's views about women that many now find problematic. Lewis's later writings—especially *The Four Loves* (1960)—give expression to the idea that mas-culine forms of friendship are essentially different from their feminine equivalents, suggesting that the exclusively male membership of the Inklings may have been deliberate, rather than happenstance.

Nevertheless, Lewis's literary friendships included significant women authors such as Katharine Farrer, Ruth Pitter, Sister Penelope, and Dorothy L. Sayers. His letter to Janet Spens—tutor in English at Lady Margaret Hall—offering a detailed appreciation of her *Spenser's Faerie Queene* (1934), punctuated with a few fine scholarly quibbles, is one of many indications that, in matters of scholarship, Lewis was alert to erudi-tion and blind to gender.[38]

There was a clear distinction—which at times became a source of tension—between those members of the Inklings who actually wrote, and those who merely commented. Nor did all members attend the meetings. Although nineteen names (all male) are linked with the Inklings throughout their history,[39] serious literary discussion often seems to have been limited to around half a dozen people in Lewis's rooms at Magdalen College after dinner on Thursday evenings.

We possess a number of accounts of these meetings during the 1930s, all emphasising their joviality and informality. When half a dozen people were gathered in Lewis's room, Warnie would make a pot of strong tea, pipes would be lit, and Lewis would ask whether anyone had brought something to read. There was no question of distributing a text for discussion; in fact, there appears to be little question of advance planning. The Inklings read texts aloud to each other for comment and criticism as and when they were ready. This did cause a certain degree of gentlemanly awkwardness, as Tolkien did not read particularly well—perhaps explaining why his university lectures were poorly attended. This problem eventually resolved itself when his son Christopher began to attend, and read his father's works with a clear and attractive voice.

These Thursday evening sessions were supplemented by Tuesday lunchtime drinking sessions in the "Rabbit Room"—a private lounge at the back of the Eagle and Child (a public house known as the "Bird and Baby" to many Inklings) in St. Giles, made available to them by the pub's landlord, Charles Blagrove. The Tuesday meetings were clearly understood to have a primarily social, rather than literary, function. These were supplemented from time to time during the summer months by outings to other public houses, such as The Trout, a riverside pub at Godstow, just north of Oxford.

There was never any doubt throughout the 1930s about the identity of the central figures of the group. The Inklings were a system of male planets orbiting its two suns, Lewis and Tolkien (the latter regularly nicknamed "Tollers"). Neither can be said to have dominated or directed the group, as if they had some proprietorial rights over its functions and fortunes. There was a tacit and unchallenged assumption, which was reinforced as their literary reputations grew, that these were the natural focus of the group.

7.2 A group of Inklings at The Trout, Godstow, near Oxford. From left to right: James Dundas-Grant, Colin Hardie, Dr. Robert. E. Havard, Lewis, and Peter Havard (not a member of the Inklings).

As Lewis pointed out in his 1944 essay "The Inner Ring," every group runs the risk of becoming an "Inner Ring," or seeing itself as the "Important People" or the "People in the Know." Did the Inklings fall into this trap? Some suspected so. And one event in particular suggests that there might be some substance to this suspicion.

Every five years, Oxford University elects a "Professor of Poetry." Although sometimes poets of real substance were appointed—such as Matthew Arnold—the position was then usually determined by university politics, rather than poetic ability. The establishment weighed down in favour of Sir Edmund Chambers. One of the Inklings regarded this as an absurd choice. Adam Fox (1883–1977) suggested over breakfast one morning at Magdalen College that even he would make a better candidate. It was more a rhetorical gesture than a definite proposal; Fox was no poet, and had intended merely to criticise Chambers, not to promote himself. But for reasons that remain unclear, Lewis took this outlandish suggestion seriously. Fox's name duly appeared on the list of three candidates, sponsored by Lewis and Tolkien. Lewis launched an aggressive campaign to get Fox elected over the heads of two other candidates, mobilising Inklings and their circle on Fox's behalf. In the end, Lewis and his circle succeeded in getting Fox elected. Tolkien saw this as a famous victory for the Inklings. "Our literary club of *practising poets*," he wrote, had triumphed over the power of establishment and privilege![40]

Yet it was an unwise move. Fox had indeed written a poem—the "long and childlike" "Old King Cole." On subsequently hearing Fox lecture, Lewis seems to have realised that he and his colleagues had made something of a blunder. He mistakenly assumed it was simply a literary error, when it was in reality a political mistake. Lewis had alienated the Oxford establishment. And Oxford has a long memory.

The Inklings would finally begin to decline in 1947—not in a blaze of argument, nor in an agreed act of noble dissolution because their artistic mission had been successful. It simply petered out as a literary discussion group, even though its members continued to socialise and discuss issues of university politics and literature. But while it lasted, it was a crucible of literary creativity and energy. As John Wain observed, "In a very dead period of Oxford's history, Lewis and his friends provided a stir of life."[41] Whatever their faults, the Inklings arguably gave rise to one canonical classic of English literature, as well as other lesser works. The classic? Tolkien's *Lord of the Rings*.

Despite many statements to the contrary in popular works about Lewis, the Narnia Chronicles were never presented to the group for discussion. On 22 June 1950, Lewis passed around proofs of *The Lion, the Witch and the Wardrobe* to those who had turned up to drink and chat at the Eagle and Child. Yet this was not an occasion for formal discussion or debate. It was more a case of "show and tell" for a work in proof, not serious criticism of a work in draft.

Yet this is to run ahead of our narrative. We must now consider the work which established Lewis's reputation as a serious literary scholar—and which remains widely read to this day—the 1936 classic *The Allegory of Love*.

THE ALLEGORY OF LOVE (1936)

Writing to an old friend in 1935, Lewis summarised his present situation in three short statements: "I am going bald. I am a Christian. Professionally I am chiefly a medievalist."[42] There is little of interest to be said about the first point, except to note that photographs of Lewis from this period confirm his own diagnosis. We have already devoted a chapter to the second point. But what of the third? Lewis's *Allegory of Love* is his first major work to deal with his professional field of activity. It fully deserves discussion, not least because it develops literary themes that find religious transposition in so many of Lewis's subsequent writings.

7.3 Duke Humfrey's Library, the oldest part of Oxford's Bodleian Library, in 1902. This reading room, reserved for manuscripts and early printed works, has changed little since Lewis's time.

Lewis had been planning *The Allegory of Love* for some time, but had been held back in completing it by his duties as an examiner. He had begun to draft the first chapter of his study of "mediaeval love poetry and the mediaeval idea of love" by July 1928.[43] He spent hours in Duke Humfrey's Library, the oldest part of the Bodleian Library, wishing he were allowed to smoke, which would have helped his faltering concentration. Yet Lewis, like all readers in the Bodleian Library, had been required to promise "not to bring into the Library, or kindle therein, any fire or flame, and not to smoke in the Library." The project stalled.

By February 1933, however, things were clearly moving apace once more. Lewis wrote to Guy Pocock, asking for a change to his contract with Dent for *The Pilgrim's Regress*. He wanted the "option clause" to be revised, so that he could offer his next book to the Clarendon Press, Oxford.[44] This, he explained, would be an academic work, dealing with the subject of allegory, which he thought would be of little interest to Pocock or his readership. He suggested that the option clause should refer to his "next work of a popular character," rather than his "next book."[45]

Pocock appears to have agreed to this suggestion. Lewis submitted the typescript of *The Allegory of Love* to Kenneth Sisam, an English scholar who served as assistant secretary to Oxford University Press. The work was duly accepted by the press, who later sent a proof copy to their Amen House office in London so that one of their editors could develop promotional material for it. The editor entrusted with it—unknown to Lewis—was Charles Williams. Indeed, on the very same day in March 1936 that Lewis decided to write to Williams to tell him how much he liked his novel *The Place of the Lion*, Williams had resolved to write to Lewis to tell him how much he admired *The Allegory of Love*. "I regard your book as practically the only one that I have ever come across, since Dante, that shows the slightest understanding of what this very peculiar identity of love and religion means."[46]

The Allegory of Love was dedicated to Owen Barfield, who Lewis declares taught him "not to patronise the past" and "to see the present as itself a 'period.'" Even on the first page of the work, Lewis sets out a theme that recurs throughout his writings:

> Humanity does not pass through phases as a train passes through stations: being alive, it has the privilege of always moving yet never leaving anything behind.[47]

Where some argue that humanity must embrace a synthesis of contemporary science and social attitudes as "the truth"—to be contrasted with the "superstitions" of the past—Lewis declares that this simply leads to humanity becoming a by-product of its age, shaped by its predominant cultural moods and intellectual conventions. We must, Lewis argues, break free from the shallow complacency of "chronological snobbery," and realise that we can learn from the past precisely because it liberates us from the tyranny of the contemporaneous.

The focus of *The Allegory of Love* is the idea of "courtly love," which Lewis defines as "love of a highly specialised sort, whose characteristics may be enumerated as Humility, Courtesy, Adultery, and the Religion of Love."[48] The emergence of "courtly love" reflects a change in attitude towards women that began in the late eleventh century, and was shaped by the ideals of chivalry emerging around this time. Courtly love is the expression of the noble, knightly worship of a refining ideal, which is embodied in the person of the woman who is loved.

This act of loving was seen as ennobling and refining, allowing expression of some of the deepest values and virtues of human nature. It is possible that the prevalence of arranged marriages in the twelfth century necessitated some means of expressing romantic love. Such a love expressed itself in terms that were simultaneously feudal and religious. Just as a vassal was expected to honour and serve his lord, so a lover was expected to serve his lady with absolute obedience, obeying her commands. Courtly love affirmed the ennobling potential of human love, the elevation of the beloved above the lover, and depicted love as an ever-increasing desire which could never be satisfied.

Yet what Lewis depicted as a historical actuality has come to be seen by others as a literary fiction. During the 1970s, many scholars began to interpret "courtly love" as an essentially nineteenth-century invention, reflecting the aspirations of that later age, which were then read back into the earlier Middle Ages. Lewis, who luxuriated in the writings of Victorian medieval revivalists, such as William Morris (1834–1896), might therefore be seen as reading the works of the Middle Ages through Victorian spectacles.[49] However, as more recent studies have made clear, the situation is not quite as straightforward as these critics have suggested.[50] In any case, Lewis's concern is actually with the poetic conventions developed to express "courtly love," rather than the historical notion itself. Lewis's book is really about texts, not about history.

The crowning glory of *The Allegory of Love* is its chapter on the Elizabethan poet Edmund Spenser (ca. 1522–1599). Lewis's book radically altered critical perceptions of Spenser's *Faerie Queene*, while also reinvigorating discussion and debate about the role and meaning of both "courtly love" and the genre of allegory in the medieval tradition. Lewis shows how the use of allegory is a matter of philosophical necessity, reflecting the nature and limits of human language, rather than representing some conceited desire for stylistic ornamentation or sentimental attachment to the literary conventions of earlier ages. Allegory, Lewis argues, is far better placed to represent such complex notions as "pride" and "sin" than abstract concepts. It provides a handle on such realities, without which discussion of some of the most fundamental themes of life becomes difficult.

From today's perspective, Lewis's achievement in *The Allegory of Love* actually rests more on his highly perceptive discussion of Spenser than his account of courtly love. His analysis of the 34,695 lines of Spenser's vast poem *The Faerie Queene*—particularly the nature and status of its imagery—remains both winsome and plausible. As a recent definitive work on the reception of Spenser in the twentieth century remarked, "Lewis's chapter makes more original observations about the *Faerie Queene*—sources, prosody, philosophy and design—than all of nineteenth-century criticism laid end to end."[51]

Some Lewis biographies suggest that *The Allegory of Love* won the Hawthornden Prize, the oldest major British literary prize awarded annually to an English writer for "the best work of imaginative literature." This is not correct; it did, however, win the Sir Israel Gollancz Memorial Prize in 1937.[52] This prestigious prize, administered by the British Academy, was awarded for outstanding published work either "on subjects connected with Anglo-Saxon, Early English Language and Literature, English Philology, or the History of English Language," or for original "investigations connected with the history of English Literature or the works of English writers, with preference for the earlier period." This was a considerable accolade for Lewis, marking out *The Allegory of Love* as a work of distinction from a highly promising younger scholar. What stands out in this work is its remarkable ability to summarise, to explain, to synthesise, and to engage. As Lewis's Oxford colleague Helen Gardner later observed, it is clearly "written by a man who loved literature and had an extraordinary power of stimulating his readers to curiosity and enthusiasm."[53]

Perhaps it is this, when taken along with his obvious gifts as a lecturer—his ability to communicate, to enthuse, and to excite—which explains the reason for Lewis's drawing such large audiences in Oxford lecture rooms in the 1930s and 1940s. Lewis draws his readers along with him as he offers informed and enthusiastic readings of texts (whether familiar or obscure), and attempts to "rehabilitate" authors, texts, and themes which have been ignored through ignorance or marginalised through prejudice.[54] Lewis was, quite simply, a champion of literature and its place in human culture and learning.

LEWIS ON THE PLACE AND PURPOSE OF LITERATURE

Throughout his career, Lewis devoted much thought and ink to the place and purpose of literature, whether in relation to the enriching of human culture, the cultivation of religious sensibilities, or the forging of personal wisdom and character. Although some of Lewis's ideas about literature developed further during the 1940s and 1950s, most of them were firmly in place by 1939.

Lewis's understanding of how literature is to be approached and understood differs significantly from the dominant viewpoints of contemporary literary theory. For Lewis, the reading of literature—above all, the reading of *older* literature—is an important challenge to some premature judgements based on "chronological snobbery." Owen Barfield had taught Lewis to be suspicious of those who declaimed the inevitable superiority of the present over the past.

Lewis makes this point with particular force in his essay "On the Reading of Old Books" (1944). Here Lewis argues that a familiarity with the literature of the past provides readers with a standpoint which gives them critical distance from their own era. Thus, it allows them to see "the controversies of the moment in their proper perspective."[55] The reading of old books enables us to avoid becoming passive captives of the Spirit of the Age by keeping "the clean sea breeze of the centuries blowing through our minds."[56]

Lewis here clearly has Christian theological debates in mind; he is writing in particular about the importance of past theological resources to enrich and stimulate the present. Yet his argument has a broader significance. "A new book is still on its trial and the amateur is not in a position to judge it."[57] Since we cannot read the literature of the future, we can at least read the literature of the past, and realise the powerful implicit challenge that this makes to the ultimate authority of the present. For sooner or later, the present will become the past, and the self-evident authority of its ideas will be eroded—unless that authority is grounded in the intrinsic excellence of those ideas, rather than their mere chronological location.

As Lewis pointed out, with the rise of the ideologies of the twentieth century in mind, someone who "has lived in many places" is not likely to be taken in by the "local errors of his native village." The scholar, Lewis declares, has "lived in many times" and can thus challenge the automatic presumption of finality inherent in present judgements and trends:

> We need intimate knowledge of the past. Not that the past has any magic about it, but because we cannot study the future, and yet need something to set against the present, to remind us that the basic assumptions have been quite different in different periods and that much which seems certain to the uneducated is merely temporary fashion.[58]

Lewis insists that to understand the literature of the classical or Renaissance periods, it is necessary to "suspend most of the responses and unlearn most of the habits" that result from "reading modern literature"[59]—such as an unquestioning assumption of the innate superiority of our own situation. Lewis uses a familiar cultural stereotype to help make his point—the English tourist abroad, so heavily pilloried in works such as E. M. Forster's *Room with a View* (1908). Lewis asks us to imagine an Englishman travelling abroad, fully persuaded of the superiority of English cultural values to those of the savages of Western Europe. Instead of seeking out the local culture, enjoying the local food, and allowing his own presuppositions to be challenged, he mixes only with other English tourists, insists on seeking out English food, and sees his "Englishness" as something to be preserved at all costs. He thus takes his "Englishness" that he brought with him, and "brings it home unchanged."[60]

There is another way of visiting a foreign country, and a correspondingly different way of reading an older text. Here, the tourist eats the local food and drinks the local wine, seeing "the foreign country as it looks, not to the tourist, but to its inhabitants." As a result, Lewis argues, the English tourist comes home "modified, thinking and feeling" in different ways. His travel has enlarged his vision of things.

The point Lewis is making here is that literature offers us a different way of seeing things. It opens our eyes, offering new perspectives for evaluation and reflection:

> My own eyes are not enough for me, I will see through those of
> others. . . . In reading great literature I become a thousand men
> and yet remain myself. Like the night sky in the Greek poem,
> I see with a myriad eyes, but it is still I who see.[61]

Literature, for Lewis, enables us "to see with other eyes, to imagine with other imaginations, to feel with other hearts, as well as with our own."[62] It offers us an imaginative representation of reality which challenges our own.

To read literature is thus potentially to make ourselves open to change: to open ourselves up to new ideas, or force us to revisit those we once believed we were right to reject. As Ralph Waldo Emerson remarked, "In every work of genius, we recognize our own rejected thoughts: they come back to us with a certain alienated majesty."[63] Lewis thus insists that texts challenge us as much as they inform us. Insisting that the text conform to our presuppositions, to our way of thinking, is to force it into a mould of our own making, and deny it any opportunity to transform, enrich, or change us. Reading works of literature is about "entering fully into the opinions, and therefore also the attitudes, feelings and total experience" of other people.[64] It is about what Plato termed *psychagogia*—an "enlargement of the soul."

For Lewis, it is more important to note *what* has been said than to become preoccupied with *who* said it. For Lewis, literary "criticism" consisted in understanding the intentions of the writer, receiving the work, and thus experiencing an inner enlargement. We see this best expressed in his *Preface to "Paradise Lost"* (1942), which sets out superbly the background to Milton's epic poem, and considers its meaning. Lewis argued forcefully that what mattered in poetry was not the poet but the poem. A totally opposing view was set out by the Cambridge scholar E. M. W. Tillyard (1889–1962). For Tillyard, *Paradise Lost* was "really about the true state of Milton's mind when he wrote it."

This led to the famous debate of the 1930s, usually dubbed "The Personal Heresy." To simplify a complex debate, Lewis argued for an objective, or impersonal, point of view, that poetry is about something "out there"; whereas Tillyard defended a subjective, or personal, point of view, that poetry is about something that is inside the poet. Lewis would later term this view "the poison of subjectivism." For Lewis, poetry works not by directing attention to the *poet*, but to *what the poet sees*: "The poet is not a man who asks me to look at *him*; he is a man who says 'look at that' and points." The poet is thus not a "spectacle" to be viewed, but a "set of spectacles" through which things are to be seen.[65] The poet is someone who enables us to see things in a different way, who points out things we otherwise might not notice. Or again, the poet is not someone who is to be looked *at*, but someone who is to be looked *through*.

We could summarise all this by saying that Lewis understands reading literature as a process of imagining and entering an alternative world, which has the ability to illuminate the empirical world in which we really live. Lewis regularly offers himself as a travel guide to others engaged on such a pilgrimage. For many, he is at his best when he introduces Spenser and Milton to those encountering them for the first time.

Yet Lewis was not merely the recorder of other writers' imaginary worlds. He himself became a creator of such worlds—worlds that are clearly influenced by the ideas and images of those who went before him. We must never forget that one possible outcome of engaging with great literature is not merely a desire to write such works oneself, but to incorporate the wisdom, wit, and elegance of the past into forms that can engage the present. Lewis turned out to be rather good at that, as we shall see when we explore the creation of Narnia and consider how Lewis uses an imaginary world to illuminate our own.

But Narnia lay in the future. Events in the real world at this point began to take a disturbing turn. On 1 September 1939, German forces invaded Poland. The British prime minister, Neville Chamberlain, initially tried to negotiate peace terms between Germany and Poland. After a parliamentary revolt against this move, Chamberlain presented Hitler with an ultimatum: Adolf Hitler must withdraw his forces from Poland. On 3 September, having failed to secure any response from Adolf Hitler, Britain declared war on Germany. The Second World War had begun.

NATIONAL ACCLAIM: THE WARTIME APOLOGIST

On Sunday, 22 October 1939, the University Church of St. Mary the Virgin, Oxford, was packed with students and dons. The audience was large and attentive; the mood was subdued and sombre; the preacher's topic was "None Other Gods: Culture in War Time"; the preacher was C. S. Lewis. By all accounts, it was a powerful defence of the academic life in the face of conflict, uncertainty, and confusion, which made a deep impression on its audience. The outbreak of war made clear the way things really were, Lewis argued, forcing us to abandon optimistic illusions about ourselves and the world. Realism had returned to its throne. "We see unmistakably the sort of universe in which we have all along been living, and must come to terms with it."[1]

No one who had been at Oxford during the Great War of 1914–1918 could fail to recall the devastating impact of the conflict on the university. Student numbers collapsed; academics went to war; college and university buildings were put to wartime use. The same pattern was repeated, though not on the same scale, at the outbreak of the Second World

War. Yet new challenges emerged. The threat of bombing raids by the Luftwaffe could not be ignored. The wartime blackout plunged the entire city into a stygian darkness it had not known since the Middle Ages. Paper shortages meant that students could no longer get copies of the books they needed for tutorials.

There were immediate changes at The Kilns, as well. On 2 September, the day after the German invasion of Poland, Warnie was recalled to active military service. (Warnie had remained a member of the Regular Army Reserve of Officers since retiring from military service on 21 December 1932). He was instructed to leave immediately for Catterick in Yorkshire. Two weeks later, he was sent to France to organise troop transport and military supplies for the British Expeditionary Force with the rank of acting major.

Within hours of Warnie's departure, The Kilns had four new occupants—schoolgirls evacuated from London. The threat of bombing raids on London led to a constant stream of "evacuees" at The Kilns, who often stayed there for several months. Lewis's correspondence during this time notes with amusement their constant complaints that they had nothing to do. Couldn't they *read* something? Lewis wondered.

But Lewis had other, more weighty matters on his mind during the first weeks of the war. The National Service (Armed Forces) Act, which came into force on 3 September 1939, enforced full conscription on all males between eighteen and forty-one residing in the United Kingdom. Lewis, then aged forty, was clearly alarmed. Would he be called up? Surely he would not have to fight in a second war? On the day after the invasion of Poland, he arranged to see George Gordon, the president of Magdalen College, who dismissed his fears. Lewis would be forty-one on 29 November—in just over two months. He had nothing to worry about.[2]

As things turned out, Lewis would be a spectator to the conflict, not an active participant. He became a member of the Local Defence Volunteers—later renamed the "Home Guard"—in the summer of 1940, spending one night in nine "mooching about the most depressing and malodorous parts of Oxford."[3] He felt somewhat ridiculous making his rounds from 1.30 to 4.30 in the morning with a rifle on his shoulder, comparing himself to constable Dogberry in Shakespeare's *Much Ado about Nothing*.[4] However, he came to value the peace and seclusion of patrolling Oxford's cool and deserted streets in the early summer mornings.

8.1 The Oxford Home Guard on parade in 1940. The parade is crossing The Plain, from which it would pass over Magdalen Bridge on its way to the centre of Oxford.

Lewis's correspondence of the early 1940s paints a picture familiar to all students of wartime Britain—the need for economy, shortages of food and essential goods, taking in displaced people, and deep anxiety about the future. Lewis's own ways of dealing with these issues were occasionally comical—for example, his "war-time economy" of drinking tea rather than Madeira when discussing Dante with friends. With

Warnie away, Lewis now worked in the smaller of his two sitting rooms at Magdalen College, as it was cheaper to heat, using up less coal.[5]

LEWIS'S FRIENDSHIP WITH CHARLES WILLIAMS

One result of the war was the flowering of what would be one of Lewis's most significant friendships. On 7 September 1939, Oxford University Press evacuated its London offices for the duration of the war, and relocated its staff to Oxford. Charles Williams thus moved to Oxford, leaving his wife and son behind in Hampstead. With Lewis's encouragement and support, Williams now became a part of the Oxford scene, and a regular member of the Inklings. The Faculty of English was short of lecturers, and was easily persuaded by Lewis that Williams was the answer to their prayers. In the end, Williams's lectures were regarded as something of a sensation, attracting large audiences and high praise in about equal measure.

The Inklings were changed irreversibly within a year of Williams's arrival. Up to that point, the dominant figures had been Lewis and Tolkien. Perhaps it was inevitable that Williams—already with a string of novels, poems, plays, and biographies to his credit—would come to play a role of no small prominence within the group, disturbing its slightly precarious equilibrium. Tolkien, who had counted Lewis as his closest friend from 1925–1940, realised that Williams had now come between them, and interpreted this as a sign of alienation between himself and Lewis.[6] Yet on balance, there is little doubt that Williams was good for the Inklings, and the Inklings good for Williams.

Things were also changing at The Kilns. Maureen married Leonard Blake, a music teacher at Worksop College, Nottinghamshire, in August 1940. Lewis disliked Blake, dismissing him as "a very small, dark, ugly, silent man who hardly ever utters a word."[7] Yet Leonard and Maureen Blake would subsequently show considerable kindness to Lewis at critical points in his life, particularly during the final years of Mrs. Moore's life, and in helping care for Joy Davidman's two sons in the late 1950s.

8.2 The novelist and poet Charles Williams (1886–1945).

On 16 August 1940, Warnie—then based at the Supply Technical Training and Mobilization Centre, Wenvoe Camp, Cardiff—was taken off the active service list, and returned to the Regular Army Reserve of Officers. It is not clear precisely what happened to Warnie's military career, which appears to have imploded at a time when the British army was trying to recover from the near catastrophe of Dunkirk, and needed experienced officers to help with its reconstruction. Warnie's military record offers no explicit reason for his discharge, while leaving its readers wondering what is to be read into its terse statements. Inevitably, given his subsequent history, many will suspect that alcohol addiction played a part in it. Warnie returned to Oxford, where he joined the Oxford Home Guard, with the rank of private soldier. The two Lewis brothers were together again.

Other changes were taking place around Lewis. Oxford University terminated all arrangements for paying those who gave intercollegiate lectures "for the duration." To his irritation, Lewis found that he would be £200 a year worse off. He would still give his usual lectures, of course, despite not being paid for them.

Magdalen College moved to a wartime economy, making savings wherever possible. The herd of deer in Magdalen Grove was culled. Fellows were offered haunches of venison for their private use. Mrs. Moore's attempts to cook it "filled the whole house with the most intolerable stench"; yet Lewis pronounced the end product to be "excellent."[8]

A letter to Warnie (at that point still in France) of November 1939 makes it clear that the Inklings were continuing to meet and discuss one another's works. After dining together at the Eastgate Hotel (just across the street from Magdalen), they enjoyed "a really first-rate evening's talk" about three works in progress from members:

> The bill of fare afterwards consisted of a section of the new
> Hobbit book from Tolkien, a nativity play from Williams
> (unusually intelligible for him, and approved by all), and
> a chapter out of the book on the Problem of Pain from me.[9]

The first work mentioned is an early draft of a section of *The Lord of the Rings*; the second is Charles Williams's play *The House by the Stable*; the third is Lewis's work *The Problem of Pain*, which he had begun to draft around this time.

Lewis's role in the writing of Tolkien's "new Hobbit book" cannot be overlooked. Too often, Lewis is seen simply as an author in his own right. The story of the completion of this classic work of English literature allows us to see him in quite a different light—as a literary midwife, who encouraged others to produce their masterpieces. In this case, some critics suggest, Lewis helped bring about a classic that would be greater than anything he himself would write.

LEWIS THE LITERARY MIDWIFE: TOLKIEN'S *LORD OF THE RINGS*

Every writer needs encouragement to write, both in terms of discernment of possibilities and getting the job done. Charles Williams, for example, relied on his wife, Florence, to keep him focussed on his writing tasks. His evacuation to Oxford during the war removed this stimulus to write. In April 1945, Williams wrote to Florence, lamenting her absence from his Oxford exile: "Why are you not here to give me a cup of tea, & then make me do some work? An infinite distaste of writing is upon me."[10] Like so many before and after him, Williams needed a mentor to help him write.

Tolkien had the same problem. He was a man of immense creativity who nevertheless needed someone to affirm him in what he was writing—and, more important, persuade him to finish it. Tolkien was inundated with responsibilities as an examiner, and found these intruded on his writing time. The early sections of Tolkien's first novel, *The Hobbit*, were drafted quickly between 1930 and 1931, until he reached the section dealing with the death of Smaug the dragon. Then he ran out of creative steam—like Richard Wagner writing his *Ring of the Nibelungs*, who left his Siegfried under his Linden Tree, unable to work out where to take things next. Tolkien produced a rough draft of the ending, and left it there. As his relationship with Lewis developed, Tolkien finally plucked up the courage to ask Lewis to read it, and give him his opinion of it. Lewis declared that he liked it, while having some misgivings about its ending.

The eventual publication of *The Hobbit* was the result of a series of fortunate accidents. Tolkien had lent the typescript of *The Hobbit* to one of his students, Elaine Griffiths (1909–1996). Griffiths in turn drew the text to the attention of Susan Dagnall, a former Oxford student now working for the London publisher George Allen & Unwin. After securing a copy of the typescript, Dagnall passed it on to publisher Stanley Unwin for his evaluation. Unwin in turn asked his ten-year-old son, Rayner, to read it. Rayner gave it such an enthusiastic review that Unwin decided to publish it. The contract's deadline for submission gave Tolkien the motivation he so badly needed to complete the writing. On 3 October 1936, the work was complete.

The Hobbit appeared on 21 September 1937. Its initial print run of 1,500 copies sold out quickly. Realising the potential of this new and unexpected market for hobbits, Allen & Unwin pressed Tolkien to write another "Hobbit-Book"—quickly. As Tolkien had no intention whatsoever of writing a sequel to his book, this demand proved to be something of a challenge.

After writing an opening chapter—"A Long-Expected Party"—with relative ease, Tolkien began to lose momentum and enthusiasm. The plot became more complex, and its tone darker. His ambition to write a more sophisticated mythological work kept intruding. In the end, the writing process stalled. Like his self-referential character Niggle, Tolkien found that he was better at painting leaves than trees. Fine detail delighted him, especially where it concerned the minting of new myths and strange words; broad narrative structure began not so much to weary him as to *overwhelm* him.

Tolkien simply could not sustain his enthusiasm for the project in the midst of a busy academic life. His perfectionism, the burden of family life and academic responsibilities, and his own preference for working on his invented languages rather than writing prose, all combined to delay and defer his new "Hobbit-Book." Discouraged, he turned to other matters.

Only one other person seemed to be interested in the work: Lewis. After Lewis's death, Tolkien emphasised the critical role that Lewis had played in keeping him working on *The Lord of the Rings*:

> The unpayable debt that I owe to [Lewis] was not "influence" as it is ordinarily understood, but sheer encouragement. He was for long my only audience. Only from him did I ever get the idea that my "stuff" could be more than a private hobby. But for his interest and unceasing eagerness for more I should never have brought *The L. of the R.* to a conclusion.[11]

Lewis showed considerable personal commitment to encouraging Tolkien in his literary endeavours around this time. He made a nighttime visit in December 1939 to Tolkien's home in North Oxford while Tolkien's wife, Edith, was recovering from an operation in the Acland nursing home. The wartime blackout made this journey hazardous. Lewis walked north along Longwall Street and Holywell Street "almost as one does in a dark room," struggling to find his bearings. When he passed Keble College, things got easier, and he eventually arrived at Tolkien's home at 20 Northmoor Road. They spent the evening "drinking gin and lime juice," discussing Tolkien's "new Hobbit" and Lewis's "Problem of Pain."[12] By the time Lewis headed back to Magdalen at midnight, the moon had risen, making his homeward journey much easier than the outward.

By the beginning of 1944, Tolkien's writing had stalled again. Like Niggle, he had become bogged down in details. He had lost confidence both in the project and in his own ability to complete it. The contrast with Lewis at this point is striking. Lewis was primarily a storyteller, who conceived images of Narnia which guided his pen. A fluent writer, Lewis did not unduly worry about resolving the inconsistencies that abound in the Chronicles of Narnia. Although Tolkien was also a storyteller, he took his role as a "subcreator" with great seriousness, devising complex histories and languages, and populating his novels with characters whose roots went deep into the story of Middle-earth.

Inevitably, Tolkien found himself overwhelmed with the need to maintain consistency, ensuring the proper correlation of his complicated and detailed backstory and the written narrative. Each leaf on the "tree of stories" had to be just right—a process which inevitably made the achievement of consistency triumph over imaginative subcreation. Tolkien became trapped in his own complex world, unable to complete it because of his anxieties about the coherence and consistency of what he had already written. His fussiness threatened to overwhelm his creativity.

A turning point was reached when Tolkien lunched with Lewis on 29 March 1944. Although Lewis does not mention or give any details of this meeting in his correspondence, it clearly gave Tolkien a new injection of energy and enthusiasm. Tolkien began to read chapters to Lewis at their private meetings on Monday mornings, and was encouraged by Lewis's reactions—indeed, at points, Lewis was reduced to tears.[13] Sections of the work began to feature regularly at Inklings meetings, often generating high praise from some. But not all. Hugo Dyson took an intense dislike to the book, and regularly attempted to prevent its being read at the meetings. In the end, Lewis often had to intervene. "Shut up, Hugo! Come on, Tollers!"

If this book were mainly about Tolkien, there would be much more to be said about the genesis and development of the text of *The Lord of the Rings*. But it is not. The point to be made is that Lewis was a willing and dedicated supporter and encourager of others—just as others encouraged him. We have already noted how the Inklings discussed Lewis's ideas about the "Problem of Pain." This book is widely seen as marking the beginning of Lewis's rise to fame as a Christian apologist. So what is this book, and how did it come to be written?

THE PROBLEM OF PAIN (1940)

The Problem of Pain was Lewis's first published work of "Christian apologetics"—the business of identifying, understanding, and answering concerns and difficulties that ordinary people have about the Christian faith, and also demonstrating its power to explain things and satisfy the deepest longings of the human heart. The book's best-known sentence perhaps fails to do justice to the overall argument: "God whispers to us in our pleasures, speaks in our conscience, but shouts in our pains: it is His megaphone to rouse a deaf world."[14] Although this is a subsidiary point, it is often incorrectly presented as if it were the total sum of Lewis's approach.

Lewis opens the book by recalling the period of his life when he was an atheist. As he later commented, if you are to "warn others against something," you must "have loved it once" yourself.[15] There are hints everywhere in this opening chapter of the themes raised, but not answered, in *Spirits in Bondage* and *Dymer*—human suffering in the face of a seemingly deaf heaven and a silent God. Lewis sketches the universe he once believed in himself—a futile place of darkness and cold, of misery and suffering. He invokes the spectacle of civilizations pointlessly rising and passing away, of a human race that science condemns to a final extinction, and of a universe that is bound to die. Speaking as he once spoke twenty years earlier, he concludes that "either there is no spirit behind the universe, or else a spirit indifferent to good and evil, or else an evil spirit."[16]

But is it really that straightforward, he muses? "If the universe is so bad, or even half so bad, how on earth did human beings ever come to attribute it to the activity of a wise and good Creator?" Having argued for the intrinsic reasonableness of faith, Lewis then turns to the problem that is posed by pain: "If God were good, He would wish to make His creatures perfectly happy, and if God were almighty He would be able to do what He wished. But the creatures are not happy. Therefore God lacks either goodness, or power, or both."[17] Yet with his characteristic Socratic approach, Lewis then observes that the terms being used—such as *good*, *almighty*, and *happy*—need careful examination. If these words bear the meanings of everyday language, there is indeed a serious problem. But what if they do not? What if we have to learn their special meanings, and see things in their light?

For Lewis, people too easily confuse *goodness* with *kindness*, and so approach the problem of pain from a false perspective. The "goodness" of

God means that we must see ourselves as true objects of his love, not as objects of an indifferent divine welfare project. There are, Lewis suggests, four ways of thinking about this love of God for us: the love of an artist for what has been created, the love of a human being for an animal, a father's love for a son, and a man's love for a woman. After exploring the notion of God's love for humanity, Lewis expresses his wonder at "why any creatures, not to say creatures such as we, should have a value so prodigious in their Creator's eyes." Our problem is that we want to be left alone, not loved as passionately as this. "You asked for a loving God: you have one."[18]

Lewis insists that these notions must be understood in terms of the Christian way of thinking—which for Lewis (as for Augustine and Milton before him) involves the recognition of human sinfulness and rebellion. Lewis's own spiritual journey, in which the conquest of his fixation on independence is prominent, spills over into his analysis. Indeed, there are points at which everything fits together so well for Lewis that he does not quite see the need to explain them in more detail to his readers. This perhaps helps us understand the occasional stalling of the argument, its change of mood and pace, the logical shortcuts, and the imaginative leaps which are not fully bridged by argument.

Lewis then makes an essentially Christological move, hinted at in the epigram he chose to place at the beginning of his work: George MacDonald's remark that "the Son of God suffered unto the death, not that men might not suffer, but that their sufferings might be like His." The incarnation of God in Christ, for Lewis, must be the focus of a Christian answer to the problem of pain:

> The world is a dance in which good, descending from God, is
> disturbed by evil arising from the creatures, and the resulting
> conflict is resolved by God's own assumption of the suffering
> nature which evil produces. The doctrine of the free Fall
> asserts that the evil which thus makes the fuel or raw material
> for the second and more complex kind of good is not God's
> contribution but man's.[19]

In a later section of the book, Lewis considers what may be learned from suffering. This is not understood to be a defence of God in the face of suffering, but an attempt to ask how we can work with suffering. Suffering can show us when we take wrong turns, or do bad things. It can bring home to us the frailty and transience of our existence, and challenge our belief that we can get by on our own. Pain thus helps to shatter the illusion that "all is well," allowing God to plant "the flag of truth within the fortress of a rebel soul." And it can help us make good choices. This might be taken to imply that Lewis sees pain as some kind of "moral instrument" to make us better people (a slightly puzzling criticism later levelled against him by his Oxford colleague Austin Farrer). But the context suggests otherwise.

The book has many strengths, not least its elegant style, clear exposition, and Socratic analysis of the concepts that lead to the formulation of the "problem of pain." Yet the reader is left wondering if there is a disconnection between the intellect and the emotions. In a letter to his brother, Warnie, written while working on the book, Lewis seems to suggest that the experience of pain in "actual life" has no bearing on the essentially intellectual issue under discussion:

> N.B. If you are writing a book about pain and then get some
> actual pain . . . it does *not* either, as the cynic wd. expect, blow the
> doctrine to bits, nor, as a Christian wd. hope, turn into practice,
> but remains quite unconnected and irrelevant, just as any other
> bit of actual life does when you are reading or writing.[20]

Lewis here seems to suggest that the experience of pain is irrelevant to any discussion about its significance. Intellectual thought is presented as detached from the world of experience. It is a curious statement, reflecting an equally curious thought. Lewis's highly intellectual approach to the problem of pain seems to be totally disconnected from the experience of pain. So what if Lewis were to experience suffering, either himself or in someone whom he loved, whose pain he felt as his own? There is a sense in which *The Problem of Pain* laid the groundwork for the emotional maelstrom of *A Grief Observed*. But we shall have more to say of this later in our narrative.

Dedicated to the Inklings, *The Problem of Pain* gradually became accepted as a classic Christian response to the problem of pain. Its faults are well known—its overstatements, simplifications, and omissions. Yet many of its readers found a voice that was sympathetic to their concerns, and reassuring in its responses. It won Lewis many admirers, but did not make Lewis famous. Yet it proved to be a critical link in the chain that soon led to the emergence of that fame. And Lewis was wise enough to know that fame could be destructive.

Did Lewis anticipate this development? More important, did he *fear* it? Would he be able to cope with his looming celebrity status—or would it destroy him in an "orgy of egoism"? An important development in Lewis's personal life around this time is probably linked to this concern. In 1941, Lewis wrote to Father Walter Adams (1869–1952), an Anglican High Churchman with a reputation as an outstanding spiritual director and confessor, asking if he would be open to offering him some spiritual guidance and direction. Adams was based at the Society of St. John the Evangelist (often referred to as the "Cowley Fathers"), a ten-minute walk from Magdalen College.

In early 1930, Lewis had declared that Greeves was his "only real Father Confessor."[21] This comment, possibly written before Lewis's conversion, refers to Lewis's long habit of disclosing personal confidences to Greeves, which he felt he could share with no one else. Yet as Christianity came to play a larger role in Lewis's life, he may well have felt the need to have a more spiritually discerning confidant. Greeves, as far as I can see, never learned about Adams.[22]

Lewis made his first confession to Adams in the final week of October 1941, anxious about an "orgy of egoism."[23] The two would meet every Friday thereafter. We know virtually nothing of their conversations, other than of Adams's persistent emphasis on the "three patiences"—"patience with God, patience with my neighbour, with oneself."[24]

Adams was a subtle and important influence in moving Lewis away from the Low Churchmanship he had inherited from the Church of Ireland, and helping him discover the importance of liturgy and the regular reading of the Psalter as an aid to personal devotion.[25] Lewis made it clear from the outset that he felt Adams was "much too close to Rome," and that he "couldn't follow him in certain directions."[26] Yet Adams became a critical spiritual friend to Lewis, playing a low-profile role in helping Lewis cope, initially with fame, and then with its aftermath.

LEWIS'S WARTIME BROADCAST TALKS

The war brought changes to many British institutions, including the state broadcaster, the British Broadcasting Corporation (BBC). It became clear by the middle of 1940 that the BBC would play a key role in maintaining national morale. A shortage of newsprint led to an increasing number of people relying on BBC radio transmissions for information and entertainment. On 1 September 1939, the BBC had ceased regional radio broadcasts,[27] and concentrated all its resources on a single domestic radio broadcasting service, now known as the "Home Service." Religion was widely recognised to be an integral and important aspect of the national fabric, and the BBC saw itself as having a duty to offer both religious instruction and inspiration in the darker moments of the war.

The rise of radio led to certain "voices" becoming popular and highly recognisable during the war. C. H. Middleton (1886–1945) became the BBC's "voice of gardening," and authored the wartime bestseller *Digging for Victory*. Dr. Charles Hill (1904–1989), the "radio doctor," became the "voice of medicine." But there was no "voice of faith"—a sensible, engaging, and authoritative voice that commanded confidence and elicited affection.

And such a voice was sorely needed. Partly to solve a scheduling problem, the BBC Religious Programmes Department was launching a new series of "broadcast talks" on religious themes. But who could deliver them? Early in 1941, Dr. James Welch, a commissioning editor at the BBC, began to search for a voice that could speak to the spiritual anxieties and concerns of the British people during the war. It proved a difficult task.

One particular difficulty was the tensions that were then beginning to emerge between the BBC and the leadership of the various Christian churches.[28] The BBC saw itself as a national broadcaster, speaking to the people of Great Britain. It did not see itself as the voice of the established Church of England. The churches tended to be concerned with safeguarding their own interests, being preoccupied with congregational attendances and questions of their respective social status. While national church leaders—such as William Temple (1881–1944), Archbishop of Canterbury—were welcomed as speakers on the BBC, it became clear that the BBC began to prefer speakers who would not speak from any denominational agenda or platform, but would simply present a trans-denominational vision of Christianity to the nation as a whole. But who could do this?

Then Welch came across a book by an Oxford don—reassuringly, a layman. He liked what he read. The book was *The Problem of Pain*. Lewis could not have known it, but the "mere Christianity" that he was increasingly advocating—though not then by that name—was precisely what the BBC was looking for.[29] Lewis was a layman, and would thus be seen as being outside the power structures (and power struggles) of the denominations. Welch noted that Lewis wrote well. But could he speak? What would he be like in front of a microphone? Would he end up being yet another ponderous and pretentious "churchy" voice, whose tone would disincline people to listen to its content?

There was only one way to find out. Welch had never met Lewis, but decided to take a risk. He wrote to Lewis, complimenting him on *The Problem of Pain*, and inviting him to speak for the BBC. Would Lewis consider speaking on a topic such as "The Christian Faith As I See It—by a Layman"? Lewis could be sure of a "fairly intelligent audience of more than a million."[30]

Lewis replied cautiously. He would like to give such a series of talks, but would have to wait until the university vacation.[31] Welch then passed

Lewis over to his colleague Eric Fenn (1899–1995), who would handle the arrangements from that point onwards.[32]

In the meantime, Lewis found himself becoming involved in another area of war work—speaking at Royal Air Force (RAF) stations. This suggestion came from W. R. Matthews, dean of St. Paul's Cathedral, London, who had a fund at his disposal which he proposed to use to establish a visiting lectureship. The RAF was at this point attracting some of the finest of the country's young men, and Matthews wanted to make sure that they had access to Christian teaching and encouragement. He had no doubt about whom he wanted to fill this role. He proposed that Lewis should be offered the position.

Maurice Edwards, chaplain in chief of the RAF, agreed to put this proposal to Lewis, and travelled to Oxford to discuss it with him. Edwards was not entirely sure that Lewis was the right person for this job. Lewis was used to teaching the best university students in Britain. How would he cope with "plodders"—young men who had left school at sixteen, and who had no intention of doing anything even remotely academic? Lewis probably had similar misgivings. Nevertheless, he accepted the offer. It would, he believed, be good for him, forcing him to translate his ideas into "uneducated language."

Lewis's first speaking engagement was at No. 10 Operational Training Unit, a Royal Air Force training base for the bomber command based at Abingdon, about a fifteen minute's drive south of Oxford. Afterwards, Lewis took a gloomy view about his talks. "As far as I can judge they were a complete failure."[33] But they weren't, and the RAF asked for more. Gradually, Lewis learned how to adapt his style and vocabulary to meet the needs of an audience he had never encountered before.

Lewis's reflections on how a speaker should "learn the language of the audience" are contained in an important lecture given to clergy and youth leaders in Wales in 1945. The lecture bristles with insights and wisdom, clearly learned the hard way—through experience. Lewis seemed to regard two points as especially important: discovering how ordinary people speak, and translating your ideas into their way of speaking.

> We must learn the language of our audience. And let me say at
> the outset that it is no use at all laying down *a priori* what the
> "plain man" does or does not understand. You have to find out
> by experience.[34]

It is not hard to imagine Lewis engaged in discussion and debate with a hard-nosed, no-nonsense, tough-talking aircrew, learning how his academic style did not connect with them—and resolving to do something about it.

> You must translate every bit of your Theology into the
> vernacular. This is very troublesome, and it means you can
> say very little in half an hour, but it is essential. It is also of
> the greatest service to your own thought. I have come to the
> conviction that if you cannot translate your thoughts into
> uneducated language, then your thoughts were confused.
> Power to translate is the test of having really understood
> one's own meaning.[35]

Lewis would put into practice in his broadcast talks precisely the ideas he learned the hard way through lecturing for the RAF.

In the meantime, the arrangements for the broadcast talks were going ahead smoothly. As Lewis had requested, these would take place in August 1941, deep in the university vacation, when he could fully devote his thoughts and time to them.[36]

By the middle of May, Lewis had more or less worked out his approach. The talks would be apologetic, not evangelistic, preparing the ground for the gospel, rather than explicitly presenting it. Lewis decided he would offer a *"praeparatio evangelica* rather than *evangelium"* which would "attempt to convince people that there is a moral law, that we disobey it, and that the existence of a Lawgiver is at least very probable."[37] But Lewis still had to face the ordeal of a microphone test. Would his voice come over well on the air?

In May 1941, Lewis sat down in front of a microphone to undertake a "voice test" at the BBC. It was, he remarked, a surprise to hear himself speak. "I was unprepared for the total unfamiliarity of the voice."[38] But the BBC was satisfied. There would be no difficulty in understanding Lewis on air. In the end, some complained about his "Oxford accent," and asked him to change it. Lewis retorted that he wasn't aware of having *any* accent. Anyway, if he changed it, it would just end up being a *different* accent. Why make such a fuss about "simply accidental phenomena"?[39]

Yet changes continued to be made. Eric Fenn remarked that Lewis's proposed title for the series of talks was "a little dull."[40] An alternative title was eventually agreed upon: "Inside Information." The dates and titles of the four talks were to be:

6 August: "Common Decency"
13 August: "Scientific Law and Moral Law"
20 August: "Materialism or Religion"
27 August: "What Can We Do about It?"[41]

However, two further changes had to be made. First, Leslie Stannard Hunter, bishop of Sheffield, who was due to give the next series of four talks following Lewis, asked if he could delay the series by a week, due to previous commitments. This left the BBC with a week without its regular religion talk. Fenn asked Lewis if he would fill this vacant slot by doing a fifth session. Realising that it was too late for Lewis to write an additional talk, Fenn suggested he might like to respond to questions raised by listeners.[42] Lewis agreed to this proposal.

The final change concerned the title of the talks. "Inside Information" was criticised in an internal BBC memorandum in July as "rather unseemly."[43] After some hasty consultations, the title was revised to "Right and Wrong: A Clue to the Meaning of the Universe?"[44] In the view of many, this revised title was far better than any of its predecessors.

Although Lewis scripted all these talks himself, the final versions were developed in dialogue with his producer, Eric Fenn. At times, this seems to have led to a certain coolness between the two, particularly when Lewis felt that Fenn's proposed changes were intrusive. However, Lewis eventually seems to have realised the value of Fenn's experienced ear. What Lewis had not appreciated was that, unlike a book, a radio talk has to be understood the first time around.

The first talk was transmitted live from Broadcasting House in London at 7.45 on the evening of Wednesday, 6 August 1941, immediately following a fifteen-minute news broadcast at 7.30. Every broadcaster knows that the "slots" most likely to attract large audiences are those following popular items—and during wartime, news broadcasts attracted a considerable following. If Lewis had any hopes that his programme might benefit from the large audiences that news broadcasts traditionally attracted, he would have been disappointed. This particular news broadcast was aimed at listeners in Nazi-occupied Norway, who could pick up the BBC on 200 kHz long wave. It was in Norwegian.

Yet despite this far-from-ideal beginning, Lewis secured and retained a large audience. The rest, as they say, is history. Lewis became the "voice of faith" for the nation, and his broadcast talks achieved classic status. Fenn was delighted with their success. Although he commented that the second talk was somewhat "turgid," Fenn wisely sugared this pill by inviting Lewis to contribute a second series, to be broadcast for the Home Service on Sundays in January and February 1942.[45]

Once more, these talks proved enormously successful. After reading the draft scripts in December 1941, Fenn declared them to be "first class," especially praising the "clarity" of their expression and the "inexorableness" of their argument.[46] Lewis developed these talks in dialogue with four clergy colleagues, wishing to ensure that he spoke for Christianity as a whole, rather than simply from his own perspective. The clergy were Eric Fenn (Presbyterian); Dom Bede Griffiths (Roman Catholic); Joseph Dowell (Methodist); and an unknown clergyman of the Church of England, who may possibly have been Austin Farrer, by then an Oxford colleague of Lewis's.

8.3 Broadcasting House, London, around 1950, from which Lewis's wartime talks were transmitted. The church to the right of the picture is All Souls Church, Langham Place, which rose to fame through the ministry of John Stott (1921–2011).

We can see Lewis's idea of "mere Christianity" being put into practice—a consensual, nonclerical, transdenominational vision of the Christian faith.[47] Yet even at this stage, it was clear that Lewis's conception of the Christian faith was rather individualist, even solitary. There was little here about the church, the community of faith, or Christianity in relation to society. Lewis depicted Christianity as something that shapes the individual's way of thinking, and hence, way of behaving. Yet there is little sense of Christianity being embedded in the life of communities. Lewis felt completely at home talking about sin, the natural law, or the Incarnation. But he had little to say about the institution of the church—a point noted with particular concern by some Roman Catholic listeners.[48]

In these talks, Lewis moved from a tentative exploration of the reasonableness of faith to a more committed statement of "What Christians Believe." These generated a considerable correspondence from listeners, which Lewis found difficult to manage, not least because so many of his most gushing admirers and trenchant critics alike seemed to expect immediate and enormously detailed personal responses to their letters.

On 13 July 1942, Geoffrey Bles published the first two series of talks with the title *Broadcast Talks*. Lewis contributed a short preface, which is a shortened form of the introduction to the broadcast talk on 11 January 1942, in which Lewis reintroduces himself to his listeners.

> I gave these talks, not because I am anyone in particular, but because I was asked to do so. I think they asked me chiefly for two reasons: firstly, because I am a layman, not a clergyman; and secondly, because I had been a non-Christian for many years. It was thought that both these facts might enable me to understand the difficulties that ordinary people feel about the subject.[49]

Lewis followed this with a further series of eight talks, this time to be broadcast over the BBC Forces' Network.[50] Thanks to his experience with the RAF, Lewis was by now much more comfortable with pitching his talks at a suitable level for such an audience. Indeed, Lewis spent the week before the first talk speaking at an RAF station in Cornwall. These talks were delivered on the theme of "Christian Behaviour" on eight consecutive Sunday afternoons, from 20 September to 8 November 1942. But there was a problem. Lewis had assumed that each of the eight talks would last fifteen minutes, as in the previous series. After having drafted his talks accordingly, he then discovered that in fact he was only to be allowed ten minutes for each.[51] Drastic cuts proved necessary: 1,800 words got pared down to 1,200.

Finally, after frequent requests to broadcast again, Lewis agreed to give a fourth series of seven talks on the BBC Home Service from 22 February to 4 April 1944. On this occasion, Lewis was permitted to prerecord three of the talks, each of which was published two days later in the BBC's weekly magazine, *The Listener*. Lewis had pleaded to be allowed to record some talks in advance, since the talks were scheduled for transmission at 10.20 p.m., which would not allow Lewis to get back to Oxford that same evening.

By the end of the series, Lewis was a national celebrity. It was clear that the reactions of listeners varied considerably, from near-adulation to total contempt. But as Lewis pointed out to Fenn, this was a reaction to his subject matter, not him as a speaker. "It is an old story, isn't it. They love, or hate."[52]

Lewis's four series of broadcast talks would later be reworked into the classic *Mere Christianity* (1952), which retains much of the structure, content, and tone of the original radio scripts. *Mere Christianity* is now regarded as Lewis's finest work of Christian apologetics. In view of its importance, we shall consider it in more detail in the next chapter. But first we must consider another popular work which gained Lewis an even wider readership in Great Britain, and which triumphantly introduced him to a North American audience—the satanic parody known as *The Screwtape Letters*.

INTERNATIONAL FAME: THE MERE CHRISTIAN

L ewis soared to national fame through his wartime broadcast talks, which made him one of the most recognised voices in Great Britain. Yet even while Lewis was writing his radio scripts, he was already working on another idea—one that would eventually win him international fame. The inspiration seems to have come to him during an especially dull sermon at Holy Trinity, Headington Quarry, in July 1940:

Before the service was over—one cd. wish these things came more seasonably—I was struck by an idea for a book wh. I think might be both useful and entertaining. It wd. be called *As One Devil to Another* and would consist of letters from an elderly retired devil to a young devil who has just started work on his first "patient."[1]

He wrote with enthusiasm to his brother—who was now back in England, having been safely evacuated from Dunkirk—about the idea, savouring the points he reckoned he could make. The "elderly retired devil" would be called "Screwtape."

THE SCREWTAPE LETTERS (1942)

As Lewis later recalled, he "had never written anything more easily."[2] The thirty-one "Screwtape Letters"—one for each day of the month— began to appear in a weekly church magazine called *The Guardian* (not to be confused with the major British newspaper of the same name) on 2 May 1941.

The letters portray Hell as a bureaucracy (possibly the kind of thing that Lewis felt Oxford University was in danger of becoming). It seemed entirely natural to Lewis to depict the diabolical in terms of "the bureaucracy of a police state or the offices of a thoroughly nasty business concern." Lewis took great pleasure in working out the kind of advice that the shrewd Screwtape might give to the novice Wormwood about how to keep his "patient" safely out of the Enemy's hands. The letters are packed with witty observations (particularly about wartime conditions), occasionally cruel caricatures of certain kinds of people Lewis clearly disliked, and a developing sense of religious wisdom about how to cope with life's mysteries and enigmas.

How much are we to read into *Screwtape*? Does Lewis express feelings about the increasingly despotic Mrs. Moore in this work—feelings he would never have dared to express openly? For example, one of Wormwood's "patients" is an elderly lady who is described as "a positive terror to hostesses and servants." One of her many weaknesses is "the gluttony of Delicacy." Whatever is offered to her never seems to be quite to her taste. Her requests may be very modest; yet they are never met, and she is never satisfied. "*All* she wants is a cup of tea properly made, or an egg properly boiled, or a slice of bread properly toasted."[3] Yet neither maid nor family ever seems able to get it right. Something is always wrong, always lacking—and retribution on those who fail her is never far away. We know that Lewis was increasingly concerned about Mrs. Moore's fussiness and fixations around this time. Might we see these concerns reflected here?

One of Lewis's distinctive emphases is that literature allows us to see things in a new way. *The Screwtape Letters* can be seen as offering a new way of seeing traditional, sound spiritual advice, by re-presenting it within a highly original framework. Where more pedestrian preachers would encourage their congregations not to rely on their experience, Lewis inverts this perspective. Screwtape tells his apprentice to get to work on his patient's experiences, and make him *feel* that Christianity "can't really be true." It is the perspective Lewis adopts, not the advice given, that is so innovative. Both Lewis's spiritual wisdom and the novel manner of its presentation secured a grateful and enthusiastic readership for *Screwtape*.

Ashley Sampson noticed the letters in *The Guardian*, and drew them to the attention of the publisher Geoffrey Bles, who offered to publish the collected letters in the form of a book. *The Screwtape Letters* was published in February 1942. Dedicated to J. R. R. Tolkien, it became a wartime bestseller. (Tolkien, by the way, did not appreciate this dedication of such a lightweight work to him, particularly when he later learned that Lewis "was never very fond of it."[4])

Screwtape consolidated Lewis's reputation as a popular Christian theologian—someone who was able to communicate the themes of the Christian faith in an intelligent and accessible way. In July 1943, Oliver Chase Quick (1885–1944), Regius Professor of Divinity at Oxford University, wrote to William Temple, Archbishop of Canterbury, expressing his view that Lewis deserved to be awarded an Oxford doctorate of divinity—the highest degree Oxford could offer—in recognition of the importance of his theological writings. Quick remarked that Lewis, along with Dorothy L. Sayers (1893–1957), was one of the few British writers who then seemed able to "put across to ordinary people a reasonably orthodox form of Christianity."[5] This correspondence between Oxford University's most senior theologian and the Church of England's most senior cleric is an important testimony to Lewis's high esteem in influential British academic and ecclesiastical circles.

When *Screwtape* was published in the United States a year later, Lewis was propelled to an international fame for which he was ill prepared. Here was an urbane, witty, imaginative, and thoroughly orthodox book that was—as one American reviewer put it—a "spectacular and satisfactory nova in the bleak sky." America wanted to find out more about this new star in their religious heavens. His earlier books were quickly brought out in American editions. The BBC's New York office contacted Broadcasting House in London, suggesting devoting more American airtime to Lewis, noting the "considerable interest" resulting from his "new approach to religious subjects."[6]

Perhaps it is not surprising that the first serious academic studies of Lewis were written by American scholars. The first PhD thesis to study Lewis's work was completed in 1948 by Edgar W. Boss, a student at Northern Baptist Theological Seminary in Chicago. A year later, Chad Walsh's pioneering study *C. S. Lewis: Apostle to the Skeptics* was published in New York.

Yet Lewis's academic reputation at Oxford was not well served in this way. He had unwisely declared himself to be a "Fellow of Magdalen College, Oxford" on the book's title page. There was much grumbling and sniping in Magdalen's Senior Common Room about the devaluation of the academic currency by such a rampantly populist book. Lewis won the hearts and minds of many through this book; yet he also alienated many whose support he might need if he were to secure an Oxford chair in the future.

MERE CHRISTIANITY (1952)

Although Lewis had published a lightly edited version of his broadcast talks during the war, he was not entirely happy with them. These appeared as three separate pamphlets: *The Case for Christianity* (1942), *Christian Behaviour* (1943), and *Beyond Personality* (1944). It seemed to him that they needed to be given still greater clarity of expression and focus. They were seen by readers as being independent works, rather than the stages of an interconnected argument. Furthermore, the text of one set of talks was omitted altogether. Lewis gradually came to see how he could create a single book that developed a coherent case for Christianity, linking the material he had developed for his four sets of broadcast talks. *Mere Christianity*—the final version of these wartime talks—is now regarded as one of Lewis's most significant Christian writings. Although published in 1952, the work is clearly an edited version of his wartime material, making discussion of its themes appropriate at this point in our narrative.

Lewis is often—and rightly—criticised for coming up with some strange titles for his works. His 1956 masterpiece *Till We Have Faces*, for example, was originally titled *Bareface*. Yet Lewis chose a brilliant title for his synthesis of his four sets of broadcast talks. He avoided any reference to their origin, and chose to focus instead on their subject matter. The title *Mere Christianity* intrigued its readers. So what did Lewis mean by this title? And why did he choose it?

Lewis found the phrase in the writings of Richard Baxter (1615–1691), a Puritan writer whom Lewis had encountered in the course of his wide reading in English literature. Writing in 1944, Lewis argued that the best remedy against the theological errors encountered in recently published books "is to have a standard of plain, central Christianity ('mere Christianity' as Baxter called it) which puts the controversies of the moment in their proper perspective."[7]

So what did Baxter mean by this curious phrase? Living through a period of tumultuous religious controversy and violence during the seventeeth century—including the English Civil War and the execution of Charles I—Baxter came to the conclusion that theological or religious labels distorted and damaged the Christian faith. In his late work *Church History of the Government of Bishops and Their Councils* (1681), Baxter protested against the divisiveness of religious controversy. He believed in "meer Christianity, Creed, and Scripture."[8] He wished to be known as a "meer Christian," equating "meer Christianity" with "Catholick

Christianity," in the sense of a universal vision of the Christian faith, untainted by controversies and theological partisanship.

It is not clear how Lewis came to discover this phrase from Baxter; I have not encountered any other reference to this work of Baxter's in Lewis's writings from before the Second World War. Nevertheless, it clearly expresses Lewis's own vision of a basic Christian orthodoxy, shorn of any denominational agendas or interest in ecclesiastical tribalism. It is what Lewis believed the Church of England to represent at its best— not a narrowly denominational "Anglicanism" (a notion for which Lewis had little sympathy), but the historic orthodox Christian faith as it found expression in England (for which Lewis had great admiration). As Lewis rightly pointed out, Richard Hooker (1554–1600)—often regarded as one of the best apologists for the Church of England—"had never heard of a religion called Anglicanism."[9]

Lewis had no difficulty in accepting and respecting the existence of individual Christian denominations, including his own Church of England; he insisted, however, that each of these was to be seen as distinct embodiments or manifestations of something more fundamental—"mere Christianity." This "mere Christianity" is an ideal, which *requires* denominational embodiment if it is to work. He illustrated this idea with an analogy that has stood the test of time remarkably well:

> [Mere Christianity is] like a hall out of which doors open into several rooms. If I can bring anyone into that hall I shall have done what I attempted. But it is in the rooms, not in the hall, that there are fires and chairs and meals. The hall is a place to wait in, a place from which to try the various doors, not a place to live in.[10]

This analogy enables us to appreciate the essential point that Lewis wished to make: that there is a notional, transdenominational form of Christianity, which is to be cherished and used as the basis of Christian apologetics; yet the business of becoming or being a Christian requires commitment to a *specific form* of this basic Christianity. "Mere Christianity" might take primacy over individual denominations; yet those denominations are essential to the business of Christian living. Lewis was not advocating "mere Christianity" as the only authentic form of Christianity. His argument was rather that it underlies and nourishes all those forms.

It is this "mere Christianity" that Lewis wished to explain and defend in this work of apologetics. In his 1945 lecture "Christian Apologetics," Lewis had emphasised that the task of apologists was not to defend the denomination to which they belonged, nor their own specific theological perspective, but the Christian faith itself. Indeed, it is Lewis's explicit commitment to this form of Christianity that has made him a figure of such universal appeal within the global Christian community.

Lewis presents himself to his readers simply as a "mere Christian," whom they can adapt to their own denominational agendas and concerns, or can defend and proclaim as a gateway into their own specific "room," in which there are "fires and chairs and meals." Lewis is an apologist for Christianity; he would have been appalled to be cited as an apologist for "Anglicanism"—partly because he disliked denominational squabbles, but chiefly because he did not believe in the conceptual extension of the "Church of England" into a global notion of "Anglicanism."

Lewis's works—especially *Mere Christianity*—generally show little inclination to become involved in denominational squabbles about baptism, bishops, or the Bible. For Lewis, such debates must never be allowed to trump or overshadow the big picture—the grand Christian vision of reality, which transcends denominational differences. It is the breadth and depth of his vision of Christianity that achieved such resonance with Catholics and Protestants alike in North America.

There is evidence that Lewis's interest in this kind of approach developed during the early 1940s. In September 1942, while visiting Newquay in Cornwall, Lewis purchased a copy of W. R. Inge's study of Protestantism. One phrase in that book—heavily underlined in Lewis's copy—clearly attracted his attention: "the scaffolding of a simple and genuinely

Christian faith."[11] This phrase encapsulates the essence of Lewis's notion of "mere Christianity."

Yet Lewis was not alone at this time in wanting to defend a form of Christianity that avoided the fussiness and pedanticism of denomination-alism. In 1941, Dorothy L. Sayers—like Lewis, a lay Anglican—set out a similar vision. In the end, this foundered, having become mired in the complexities of denominational politics.[12] Lewis, however, succeeded by ignoring them, speaking directly to ordinary Christians over the heads of denominational leaders. And ordinary Christians listened to him, as they listened to no other.

So how did Lewis go about defending this "mere Christianity"? His apologetic strategy in *Mere Christianity* is complex, perhaps reflecting the fact that four quite distinct sets of talks have been merged into a single book. What is particularly striking is that *Mere Christianity* does not start out with any Christian presuppositions at all. Lewis does not even list some Christian doctrines that cause people problems, and then try to defend them. He begins from human experience, and shows how every-thing seems to fit around core ideas, such as the idea of a divine Lawgiver, which can then be connected with the Christian faith.

Mere Christianity does not set out to provide deductive arguments for the existence of God. As Austin Farrer perceptively remarked of *The Problem of Pain*, Lewis makes us "think we are listening to an argument," when in reality "we are presented with a vision; and it is the vision that carries conviction."[13] This vision appeals to the human longing for truth, beauty, and goodness. Lewis's achievement is to show that what we observe and experience "fits in" with the idea of God. His approach is inferential, not deductive.

For Lewis, Christianity is the "big picture" which weaves together the strands of experience and observation into a compelling pattern. The first part of *Mere Christianity* is entitled "Right and Wrong as a Clue to the Meaning of the Universe." It is important to note this carefully chosen term *clue*. Lewis is noting that the world is emblazoned with such "clues," none of which individually proves anything, but which taken together give a cumulative case for believing in God. These "clues" are the threads that make up the great pattern of the universe.

Mere Christianity opens—as did the original broadcast talks—with an invitation to reflect on two people having an argument. Any attempt to determine who is right and who is wrong depends, Lewis argues, on recognition of a norm—of some standard which both parties to a dispute recognise as binding and authoritative. In a series of argumentative moves, Lewis first contends that we are all aware of something "higher" than us—an objective norm to which people appeal, and which they expect others to observe; a "real law which we did not invent and which we know we ought to obey."[14]

If there is a God, this would provide a firmer foundation for the deep human instinct and intuition that objective moral values exist, and a defence of morality against more irresponsible statements of ethical relativism. God, for Lewis, is made known through our deep moral and aesthetic intuitions:

If there was a controlling power outside the universe, it could not show itself to us as one of the facts inside the universe—no more than the architect of a house could actually be a wall or staircase or fireplace in that house. The only way in which we could expect it to show itself would be inside ourselves as an influence or a command trying to get us to behave in a certain way. And that is just what we do find inside ourselves.[15]

Although everyone knows about this law, everyone still fails to live up to it. Lewis thus suggests that "the foundation of all clear thinking about ourselves and the universe we live in" consists in our knowledge of a moral law, and an awareness of our failure to observe it.[16] This awareness ought to "arouse our suspicions" that there "is a Something which is directing the universe, and which appears in me as a law urging me to do right and making me feel responsible and uncomfortable when I do wrong."[17] Lewis suggests that this points to an ordering mind governing the universe.

The second line of argument concerns our experience of longing. It is an approach that Lewis had earlier developed in his university sermon "The Weight of Glory," preached at Oxford on 8 June 1941. Lewis reworked this argument for the purposes of his broadcast talks, making it much easier to understand. The argument can be summarised like this. We all long for something, only to find our hopes dashed and frustrated when we actually achieve or attain it. "There was something we grasped at, in that first moment of longing, which just fades away in the reality."[18] So how is this common human experience to be interpreted?

Lewis initially notes two possibilities that he clearly regards as inadequate: to assume that this frustration arises from looking in the wrong places, or to conclude that further searching will only result in repeated disappointment, so that there is no point in bothering to try and find something better than the world. Yet there is, Lewis argues, a third approach—to recognise that these earthly longings are "only a kind of copy, or echo, or mirage" of our true homeland.[19]

Lewis then develops an "argument from desire," suggesting that every natural desire has a corresponding object, and is satisfied only when this is attained or experienced. This natural desire for transcendent fulfillment cannot be met through anything in the present world, leading to the suggestion that it could be satisfied beyond the present world, in a world towards which the present order of things points.

Lewis argues that the Christian faith interprets this longing as a clue to the true goal of human nature. God is the ultimate end of the human soul, the only source of human happiness and joy. Just as physical hunger points to a real human need which can be met through food, so this spiritual hunger corresponds to a real need which can be met through God. "If I find in myself a desire which no experience in this world can satisfy, the most probable explanation is that I was made for another world."[20] Most people, Lewis argues, are aware of a deep sense of longing within them, which cannot be satisfied by anything transient or created. Like right and wrong, this sense of longing is thus a "clue" to the meaning of the universe.

This might seem to suggest that Lewis is portraying Christianity in terms of "rules" or "laws," losing sight of such central Christian themes as a love for God or personal transformation. This is not the case. As Lewis pointed out in his study of Milton's *Paradise Lost*, an understanding of virtue is shaped by a vision of reality. We must never think that Milton "was inculcating a rule when in fact he was enamoured of a perfection."[21] For Lewis, a love of God leads to behavioural adaptation, in the light of (and in response to) the greater vision of God that is grasped and enacted through faith.

In his arguments from both morality and desire, Lewis appeals to the capacity of Christianity to "fit in" what we observe and experience. This approach is integral to Lewis's method of apologetics, precisely because Lewis himself found it so persuasive and helpful a tool for making sense of things. The Christian faith provides a map that is found to "fit in" well with what we observe around us and experience within us.

For Lewis, the kind of "sense-making" offered by the Christian vision of reality is about discerning a resonance between the theory and the way the world seems to be. This is one of the reasons why Lewis was so impressed by the Christian view of history as set out in G. K. Chesterton's *Everlasting Man* (1925): it seemed to make sense of what actually happened. Though Lewis used surprisingly few musical analogies in his published writings, his approach could be described as enabling the believer to hear the harmonics of the cosmos, and realise that it fits together *aesthetically*—even if there are a few logical loose ends that still need to be tied up.

Lewis often emphasised that his own conversion was essentially "intellectual" or "philosophical," stressing the capacity of Christianity to make rational and imaginative sense of reality. We find perhaps the fullest and most satisfactory statement of this "sense-making" approach at the end of his 1945 essay "Is Theology Poetry?" Here Lewis affirms God as both an *evidenced* and an *evidencing* explanation, using the analogy of the sun illuminating the landscape of reality. After noting the ability of Christian theology to "fit in" science, art, morality, and non-Christian religions, he declares, in a concluding statement, "I believe in Christianity as I believe that the Sun has risen, not only because I see it but because by it I see everything else."[22]

It is easy to criticise *Mere Christianity* on account of its simple ideas, which clearly need to be fleshed out and given a more rigorous philosophical and theological foundation. Yet Lewis wrote for multiple audiences, and it is quite clear whom Lewis envisaged here as his audience. *Mere Christianity* is a popular, not an academic, book, which is not directed towards a readership of academic theologians or philosophers. It is simply unfair to expect Lewis to engage here with detailed philosophical debates, when these would clearly turn his brisk, highly readable book into a quagmire of fine philosophical distinctions. *Mere Christianity* is an informal handshake to begin a more formal acquaintance and conversation. There is much more that needs to be said.

Yet there are many points in *Mere Christianity* at which Lewis is open to legitimate criticism, and it is important to note some of them. The most obvious concern is Lewis's notion of the "trilemma," which he deploys in his defence of the doctrine of the divinity of Christ. For Lewis, the notion that God was fully disclosed in Christ was of landmark significance. As he wrote to Arthur Greeves—a critic of this view—in 1944:

> The doctrine of Christ's divinity seems to me not something
> stuck on which you can unstick but something that peeps out
> at every point so that you'd have to unravel the whole web to
> get rid of it. . . . And if you take away the Godhead of Christ,
> what is Xtianity all *about*? How can the death of one *man* have
> this effect for all men which is proclaimed throughout the New
> Testament?[23]

Yet many feel that Lewis's defence of this doctrine in *Mere Christianity* lacks the vibrancy and conviction that are found elsewhere in his writings. The so-called "trilemma" is proposed by Lewis as a way of eliminating false trails in making sense of Jesus of Nazareth. Where is he to be located on a conceptual map? After reviewing some of the issues,

Lewis reduces the field to three possibilities: a lunatic, a diabolical figure, or the Son of God.

> A man who was merely a man and said the sort of things Jesus
> said would not be a great moral teacher. He would either be
> a lunatic—on a level with the man who says he is a poached
> egg—or else he would be the Devil of Hell. You must make your
> choice. Either this man was, and is, the Son of God: or else a
> madman or something worse.[24]

It's a weak argument. Lewis offered a considerably longer discussion of this point in the original broadcast talks, which he pruned down drastically as he revised it for publication. The original form included discussion of other options, and was much less trenchant than the abbreviated discussion in *Mere Christianity*. Many Christian theologians might argue that Lewis here failed to account for the concerns of more recent New Testament critical scholarship, and that his simplified argument could easily backfire under the light of a more critical reading of the Gospels.

Yet the main problem is that this argument does not work *apologetically*. It may well make sense to some Christian readers, who already know why they have come to this conclusion, and are glad to have Lewis reinforce their position. Yet the inner logic of this argument clearly presupposes a Christian framework of reasoning. It would not necessarily make sense to Lewis's intended audience of nonbelievers, who might—to give one obvious example—suggest the alternative possibility that Jesus was a well-loved religious leader and martyr whose followers later came to see him as divine. The option that Jesus was someone who was not mad or bad, but was nevertheless *wrong* about his identity, needs to be considered as a serious alternative. Lewis, normally so good at anticipating objections and meeting them carefully, seems to have misjudged his audience at this point. The whole section cries out for expansion, and more careful qualification.

Another problem concerns the "datedness" of the material in Lewis's broadcast talks, much of which is incorporated unchanged in *Mere Christianity*. Lewis's analogies, turns of phrase, envisaged concerns, and manner of engaging his audience are all located in a vanished world—to be precise, a southern English middle-class culture during the Second World War. Yet it is not unfair to point out that the modern reader's difficulties often reflect Lewis's success as a communicator in the 1940s. By embedding his "translation" of the Christian faith so well in this one specific world, now passed, Lewis has to some degree implicitly forfeited the ability to achieve a comparable degree of success with other worlds, present or future.

Yet the aspect of *Mere Christianity* perhaps most difficult for twenty-first-century readers is Lewis's code of social and personal ethics, particularly his assumptions about women. These are deeply embedded in the bedrock of a social order that has long since disappeared. Even when seen in the light of those standards, some of Lewis's statements seem somewhat peculiar. Consider, for example, the following ill-judged remarks.

What makes a pretty girl spread misery wherever she goes by collecting admirers? Certainly not her sexual instinct: that kind of girl is quite often sexually frigid.[25]

I recall a conversation with a colleague about these two sentences some years ago. We had a copy of *Mere Christianity* open at the appropriate page. "Why did he write *that*?" I asked, pointing to the first sentence. "How could he know *that*?" he replied, pointing to the final part of the second.

Lewis's assumption that his readers will agree with—or at least acknowledge the merits of—his views on such matters as marriage and sexual ethics may well have been justified in Britain during the 1940s and early 1950s. Yet the massive changes in social attitudes following the upheavals of the 1960s now make Lewis seem very dated to secular readers. If *Mere Christianity* is indeed a work of apologetics, intended to communicate the Christian faith to those outside the churches, it must be recognised that Lewis's social and moral assumptions now pose a significant barrier to the book's intended readership. This is not necessarily a criticism of Lewis as a writer, or of *Mere Christianity* as a book. It is simply an observation of the implications of rapid social change for the later reception of Lewis's ideas as they are expressed in this work.

Conservative though Lewis's views on marriage were, they seemed to be hopelessly liberal to Tolkien. Lewis drew a sharp distinction between "Christian marriage" and a "state marriage," holding that only the former made a demand for total commitment.[26] (It was a distinction that Lewis would later invoke when marrying Joy Davidman in a civil marriage at Oxford's Register Office in April 1956.) For Tolkien, this amounted to a betrayal of any Christian notion of marriage. He penned a scathing critique of Lewis at some point in 1943, but never sent it.[27] Yet the reader is left in no doubt that a wide gulf was opening between Tolkien and Lewis. Personal distance was being supplemented by a disagreement on a matter of deep personal importance for Tolkien.

OTHER WARTIME PROJECTS

By the time *Mere Christianity* was published in 1952, Lewis had established a significant following in Great Britain—and a growing reputation in the United States—as an apologist. His success in this field overshadowed his other significant achievements of the wartime era. Three lecture series are of particular importance: the Ballard Matthews Lectures in Bangor, Wales; the Riddell Memorial Lectures at the University of Durham; and the Clark Lectures at Trinity College, Cambridge. Each merits brief comment.

On the evening of Monday, 1 December 1941, Lewis delivered the first of his three Ballard Lectures on the themes of Milton's *Paradise Lost* at the University College of North Wales, on a hillside overlooking the Welsh coastal town of Bangor. He saw these three lectures, given over three successive evenings, as a "preliminary canter" to a more substantial book.[28] This larger (although still comparatively brief) work appeared in

October 1942 from Oxford University Press, titled *A Preface to "Paradise Lost,"* dedicated to Charles Williams. It remains a classic study, and still features prominently on reading lists for Milton's masterpiece.

Lewis clearly positions this book as an introduction to *Paradise Lost* (first published in 1667) for those who would otherwise find it forbidding, unapproachable, or simply incomprehensible. The first half of the book deals with general questions, before addressing specific themes in the work. The first question, Lewis declares, is to determine what sort of work this is: "The first qualification for judging any piece of workmanship from a corkscrew to a cathedral is to know *what* it is—what it was intended to do and how it is meant to be used."[29] For Lewis, *Paradise Lost* is an epic poem, which demands that we read it as such.

Yet Lewis's real concern soon becomes clear. Although focussed on Milton's classic work, Lewis engages a question that is of universal significance: Is there an "Unchanging Human Heart" beneath Milton's classic and all other works of literature? Lewis makes it clear that he wishes to challenge the idea that:

> . . . if we strip off from Virgil his Roman imperialism, from [Sir Philip] Sidney his code of honour, from Lucretius his Epicurean philosophy, and from all who have it their religion, we shall find the Unchanging Human Heart, and on this we are to concentrate.[30]

This means, Lewis argues, that the reader of a literary work tries to eliminate its specifics, "twisting" the work into a shape the poet never intended.

Lewis argues that this is unacceptable. It detaches a text from its historical and cultural roots; it gives a "false prominence" to elements of the text which are seen to offer "universal truth"; and it dismisses as irrelevant those portions of the text which are not seen to speak to our own day. Instead, Lewis argues, we must allow the text to interrogate and expand our experience. Rather than trying to get rid of a medieval knight's suit of armour so that he becomes just like us, we should try to find out what it is like to wear that armour. We should set out to explore what it would be like to adopt the beliefs of Lucretius or Virgil. Literature is meant to help us see the world through other spectacles, to offer alternative ways of understanding things. As we shall see, this theme becomes prominent in the Chronicles of Narnia.

Two years after giving the Ballard Matthews Lectures, Lewis delivered the Riddell Memorial Lectures at the Newcastle upon Tyne campus of the University of Durham on three consecutive evenings, 24–26 February 1943.[31] These remarkable lectures were published as *The Abolition of Man* in 1943 by Oxford University Press. Lewis here argues that contemporary moral reflection has been undermined by a radical subjectivity—a trend he discerns within contemporary school textbooks. In response to this development, Lewis calls for a renewal of the moral tradition based on "the doctrine of objective value, the belief that certain attitudes are really true, and others really false, to the kind of thing the universe is and the kind of things we are."[32]

Lewis here criticises those who argue that all statements of value (such as "this waterfall is pretty")[33] are merely subjective statements about the speaker's feelings, rather than objective statements concerning their object. Lewis argues that certain objects and actions *merit* positive or negative reactions—in other words, that a waterfall can be *objectively* pretty, just as someone's actions can be *objectively* good or evil. He argues there is a set of objective values (which he terms "the Tao")[34] that are common to all cultures, with only minor variations. Although *The Abolition of Man* is now considered a difficult book, its arguments remain highly significant.[35]

In 1944, Lewis was invited to deliver the Clark Lectures at Trinity College, Cambridge. In inviting him on behalf of the college council, George Macaulay Trevelyan, the master of Trinity College, expressed particular appreciation of Lewis's earlier works—especially *The Allegory of Love*.[36] These prestigious lectures, which Lewis delivered in May 1944, would become the basis of his classic volume in the Oxford History of English Literature series—which Lewis playfully abbreviated to his friends as "O HEL"—on English literature in the sixteenth century (excluding drama).

Finally, we must note *The Great Divorce*, a highly imaginative book which Lewis composed in 1944. Tolkien described this book as "a new moral allegory or 'vision' based on the medieval fancy of the Refrigerium, by which the lost souls have an occasional holiday in Paradise."[37] Lewis has been much criticised by Catholic theologians for his obviously faulty analysis of medieval theology at this point.[38] Indeed, *The Great Divorce* is clearly best regarded as a "supposal": if the inhabitants of hell were to visit heaven, what would happen?

Lewis initially titled this work *Who Goes Home?* but was happily persuaded to alter the title. The work is chiefly remarkable on account of its use of an innovative imaginative framework, similar in some ways to *The Screwtape Letters*, to explore a series of very traditional questions—such as the limits of human free will and the problem of pride.

Perhaps the most important feature of this work, however, is Lewis's demonstration—by art of narrative rather than by force of argument—that people easily become trapped in a way of thinking from which they cannot break free. Those in hell, on exploring heaven, turn out to be so comfortable with their distorted view of reality that they choose not to embrace truth on encountering it. Lewis deploys familiar cultural stereotypes of his day—such as the career artist who is obsessed with the avant-garde, or the theologically liberal bishop infatuated with his intellectual fame—to challenge the lazy and unevidenced Enlightenment assumption that humans recognise and accept truth when they see it. Human nature, Lewis suggests, is rather more complex than this trite, superficial rationalism allows.

Although Lewis's writings of the wartime period tend to employ evidence-based reasoning, which defends or explores fundamental Christian ideas, we also find a highly significant theme beginning to emerge—the capacity of imaginative narrative to embody and communicate truth. This idea is integral to understanding Lewis's Chronicles of Narnia. To comprehend the importance of this point, let us consider a series of three works to appear during the period of 1938–1945, generally known as the Space Trilogy, but which are more accurately designated the Ransom Trilogy.

THE SHIFT TO FICTION: THE RANSOM TRILOGY

Mere Christianity represents a highly important strand of the approach to apologetics that Lewis developed during the Second World War. In effect, Lewis argues that the "map" of reality offered by the Christian faith corresponds well to what is actually observed and experienced. Books of this type—including *The Problem of Pain* and the later *Miracles* (1947)—make a fundamental appeal to reason. Although Lewis is far too canny a thinker to believe that he can "prove" the existence of God—like Dante, he knows that reason has "short wings"—he nevertheless holds that the fundamental reasonableness of the Christian faith can be shown by argument and reflection.

Yet Lewis appears to have realised that argument was only one of a number of ways of engaging cultural anxieties about the Christian faith, or challenging its alternatives. From about 1937, Lewis seems to have appreciated that the imagination is the gatekeeper of the human soul. Having initially merely enjoyed reading works of fantasy—such as the novels of George MacDonald—Lewis began to realise how fiction might allow the intellectual and imaginative appeal of worldviews to be explored. Might he try his hand at writing such works himself?

As a child, Lewis read voraciously and widely, pillaging the amply stocked bookshelves of Little Lea to pass away the time. And so he came across writers such as Jules Verne (1828–1905) and H. G. Wells (1866–1946), whose novels spoke of travel in space and time, and explored how science was changing our understanding of the world. "The idea of other planets exercised upon me then a peculiar, heady attraction, which was quite different from any other of my literary interests."[39]

Such childhood memories were given a new sense of urgency and direction around 1935, when Lewis read David Lindsay's novel *A Voyage to Arcturus* (1920). Although Lindsay's book is poorly written, its imaginative appeal more than adequately compensates for its stylistic deficiencies. Lewis began to realise that the best forms of science fiction can be thought of as "simply an imaginative impulse as old as the human race working under the special conditions of our own time."[40] If they are done well—and Lewis is quite clear that this is often not the case—then they expand our mental and imaginative horizons. "They give, like certain rare dreams, sensations we never had before, and enlarge our conception of the range of possible experience."[41] For Lewis, writing the right kind of science fiction was thus a soul-expanding business, something that could potentially be compared to the best poetry of the past.

So why did Lewis get so excited about this narrative form? To understand his concerns, and appreciate the solution that he found, we need to understand more about the British cultural world of the late 1920s and early 1930s—above all, the rise of what we might now call "scientism" as a worldview. At this time, this view was advocated openly in the writings of J. B. S. Haldane (1892–1964), a disillusioned Marxist who transferred his crusading temperament and enthusiasm to advocating the merits of science as a cure for all of humanity's ills. Lewis was no critic of science; he was, however, worried about exaggerated accounts of its benefits and naive ideas concerning its application. Lewis was anxious that the triumphs of science might have run ahead of necessary ethical developments that could provide the knowledge, self-discipline, and virtue that science needed.

Yet Lewis was perhaps more concerned about the implicit advocation of such views in the science fiction novels of H. G. Wells, which used fictional narratives to argue that science is both prophet and saviour of humanity, telling us what is true and saving us from the human predicament. For Wells, science is a secularised religion. Such ideas remain deeply embedded in Western culture, although they are now associated with other voices. But Lewis encountered them through Wells. And if Wells used science fiction to advocate such views, why not use science fiction to argue against him? Lewis regarded "interplanetary ideas" as a new and exciting mythology, but was concerned that it was becoming dominated by a "desperately immoral outlook." Could the genre be redeemed? Might it become a vehicle for a profoundly moral view of the universe? Might it even become the medium for a theistic apologetic?

In December 1938, Lewis expressed his growing realisation that the forms of science fiction hitherto used to promote various forms of atheism and materialism could equally well be used to *critique* these viewpoints and advocate an alternative.[42] Why not use the same medium to advocate a quite different "mythology"? (Lewis here means by *mythology* something like a "metanarrative" or "worldview.") We see this technique put into action in *Out of the Silent Planet* (1938), *Perelandra* (1943), and *That Hideous Strength* (1945). The quality of these is somewhat uneven, with the third being particularly difficult in places. Yet the main thing to appreciate is not so much their plots and points, but the medium through which these are expressed—*stories*, which captivate the imagination and open the mind to an alternative way of thinking.

It is impossible to summarise the rich imaginative gambits and intellectual finesse that are so characteristic of this trilogy. What really needs to be appreciated is that a story is being told which subverts the more contestable themes of the "scientism" of Lewis's day. To illustrate this, we shall consider one of the themes that Lewis explicitly engages—the form of social Darwinism advocated by Haldane in his essay "Eugenics and Social Reform."[43] Like many progressives in the 1920s and 1930s, Haldane advocated the optimization of the human gene pool by preventing certain types of people from breeding. This socially illiberal attitude was seen as being rigorously grounded in the best science, with the best possible motivation—to ensure the survival of the human race. But at what cost, Lewis wondered?

Bertrand Russell followed Haldane in his *Marriage and Morals* (1929), advocating the compulsory sterilization of the mentally deficient. Russell advocated that the state should be empowered to forcibly sterilise all those regarded as "mentally deficient" by appropriate experts, and that this measure should be introduced *despite* the drawbacks to which it might be liable. He suggested that reducing the number of "idiots, imbeciles and feeble-minded" people would be of sufficient benefit to society to outweigh any dangers of its misuse.

These views are rarely encountered today, partly because they have become tainted by their subsequent association with Nazi eugenic theories, and partly because they are seen as incompatible with liberal democratic ideals. Yet they were widely held among the British and American intellectual elites in the period between the two world wars. Three World Eugenics Conferences (London 1912, New York 1921, New York 1932) argued for "birth selection" (as opposed to "birth control"), and for the genetic elimination of those who were deemed unfit.[44]

Lewis felt that these views had to be challenged. One element of Lewis's response was *That Hideous Strength*. Though Lewis was often conservative in his views, this work shows him to have been a prophetic voice, offering a radical challenge to the accepted social wisdom of his own generation.

In *That Hideous Strength*, Lewis introduces us to the National Institute for Coordinated Experiments (NICE), a hypermodern institution dedicated to the improvement of the human condition through scientific advance—for example, through forced sterilization of the unfit, the liquidation of backward races, and research by means of vivisection. Lewis has little difficulty in exposing the moral bankruptcy of this institute, and the deeply dysfunctional vision of the future of humanity it embodies. The conclusion of the work includes a dramatic scene in which all the caged animals intended for vivisection are set free.

As readers of the chapter on "Animal Pain" in *The Problem of Pain* will appreciate, Lewis—unlike Haldane—was an opponent of vivisection. George R. Farnum, President of the New England Anti-Vivisection Society, noted the importance of Lewis's comments, and invited him to write an essay on this theme. Lewis's essay "Vivisection" (1947) remains one of the most intellectually significant critiques of vivisection, and has not received the attention it deserves.[45] It makes clear that Lewis's outspoken opposition to vivisection was not grounded on sentimentality, but upon a rigorous theological foundation. If we are brutal towards animals, we are just as likely to be brutal to our fellow humans—especially those we regard as inferior to us:

> The victory of vivisection marks a great advance in the triumph of ruthless, non-moral utilitarianism over the old world of ethical law; a triumph in which we, as well as animals, are already the victims, and of which Dachau and Hiroshima mark the more recent achievements. In justifying cruelty to animals we put ourselves also on the animal level.[46]

Lewis's views on this matter lost him many friends at Oxford and elsewhere, as vivisection was then widely regarded as morally justified by its outcomes. Animal pain was the price paid for human progress. However, for Lewis there was a deep theological question here, which naturalism ignored. We "ought to prove ourselves better than the beasts precisely by the fact of acknowledging duties to them which they do not acknowledge to us."[47] As we shall see, such attitudes towards animals find their classic expression in the Chronicles of Narnia.

There is far more to the Ransom Trilogy than this brief account can hope to convey—especially its lyrical description of strange worlds, its development of imaginatively engaging scenarios, and its exploration of theologically fertile themes, such as the fate of the beautiful, newly created, and unfallen world of Perelandra. Yet in the end, it is the medium as much as the substance that really matters. Lewis demonstrates that stories can be told which subvert some established truths of the day, and expose them as shadows and smoke. The grand retreat of the British cultural elite from eugenics after the Second World War indicates that ideas and values that were once fashionable can be abandoned within a generation. The extent to which Lewis himself undermined them remains to be clarified. But the potential of his approach was clear.

The period of 1938–1945 saw Lewis emerge from the cloistered obscurity of academia to become a major religious, cultural, and literary figure. Without ceasing to publish works of academic merit, such as his *Preface* to "Paradise Lost," he had established himself as a public intellectual who commanded the media, and was on the road to international celebrity. What could go wrong?

Sadly, the answer soon became clear. Rather a lot could go wrong. And it did.

A PROPHET WITHOUT HONOUR?: POSTWAR TENSIONS AND PROBLEMS

By 1945, Lewis was famous. In the British academic world, a scholar's status is calibrated by several measures, including the number and perceived significance of publications. The ultimate mark of distinction for any scholar in the humanities is to be elected a fellow of the British Academy. Lewis achieved this honour in July 1955. Yet in the eyes of his biographers, this important mark of academic acknowledgement has been totally overshadowed by the recognition of a very different audience.

C. S. LEWIS—SUPERSTAR

On 8 September 1947, Lewis appeared on the front cover of *Time* magazine, which declared this "best-selling author," who was also "the most popular lecturer in [Oxford] University," to be "one of the most influential spokesmen for Christianity in the English-speaking world." *Screwtape* had taken England and America by storm. (America, it must be recalled, had not heard Lewis's broadcast talks on the BBC.) The opening paragraph helps capture the tone of the piece: a quirky and slightly weird Oxford academic— "a short, thickset man with a ruddy face and a big voice"—unexpectedly hits the big time.[1] Were there more bestsellers on the way? *Time* cautioned its excited readers that they would just have to wait: "He has no immediate plans for further 'popular' books, fantastic or theological."

The *Time* article of 1947 can be seen as a tipping point—both signaling Lewis's arrival on the broader cultural scene, and extending his reach by drawing wider attention to his works. Yet Lewis was ill equipped, organisationally and temperamentally, to deal with his rise to fame that began in 1942. His high profile led to both adulation and invective being poured on him, and his private life—which Lewis had hitherto protected—began to come into the public domain. He became the subject of discussion in British newspapers, which often portrayed him in unrecognisable terms. Tolkien was particularly amused by one media reference to an "Ascetic Mr. Lewis." This bore no relation to the Lewis he knew. That very morning, Tolkien had told his son that Lewis had "put away three pints in a very short session." Tolkien had cut down on his own drinking, as it was Lent—a time of self-denial for many Christians. But not, Tolkien grumbled, for Lewis.[2]

Lewis was now inundated with letters from devotees and critics, demanding his immediate and full answers to questions great, trivial, and downright improper. Like a gallant knight of old, Warnie came to his brother's rescue. From 1943, he typed replies to his brother's burgeoning correspondence with two fingers on his battered Royal typewriter, often without consulting Lewis about their content. Warnie later estimated that he typed twelve thousand such letters. Warnie also devised an imaginative technique for getting rid of the increasing number of self-important people who demanded to speak to Lewis at home personally by telephone.[3] As Tolkien recalled, Warnie's method was to "lift the receiver and say 'Oxford Sewage Disposal Unit,' and go on repeating it until they went away."[4] Yet Lewis's growing fame in the United States had one unexpected consequence of which Warnie thoroughly approved: food parcels, packed with long-forgotten luxuries, now arrived regularly from Lewis's growing army of wealthy American well-wishers.

The evidence suggests that Lewis's writings resonated at this time with many American Christians, both ordained and lay, reflecting a changed national cultural mood. Preoccupation with the economic woes of the 1920s and 1930s was passing; however, after America entered the Second World War in December 1941, a new interest in the deeper questions of life arose. God was being talked about again. Religious publishing began to experience a revival. And in the midst of this new openness towards religious questions, a new voice appeared—one that was perceived to be authoritative and interesting, and above all concerned with the religious questions of ordinary people.

The strongly apologetic tone of Lewis's works was welcomed by those ministering to people wrestling with the big questions raised by the war— such as college and university chaplains. Although Lewis was generally not well regarded by academic theologians in America, the evidence suggests that they nevertheless broadly welcomed the new quality of engagement that he brought to religious issues. Lewis offered provisional answers that could be further developed in the seminaries and universities.

Yet Lewis's popular fame did cause a certain degree of irritation for some academics. One line in the *Time* article particularly riled some professional theologians, who baulked at the suggestion that "a man who could talk theology without pulling a long face or being dull was just what a lot of people in war-beleaguered Britain wanted." The wise kept their counsel, hoping that people would soon forget about Lewis; the foolish let rip with theological broadsides, thereby raising both Lewis's profile and his appeal.

One such broadside came from the pen of an obscure American Episcopalian theologian, Norman Pittenger (1905–1997). Irritated that *Time* had incomprehensibly overlooked his own vastly superior claims to be the nation's top Christian apologist, Pittenger declared that Lewis was a theologically lightweight heretic—a total liability for the kind of intelligent Christianity that he himself so conspicuously represented. America took no notice of such self-promotion, and went back to reading Lewis.

Lewis, then, was famous by the time the Second World War ended in the summer of 1945. If the simple philosophy of life propounded by modern celebrity culture has any validity, Lewis at that point should have been a happy and fulfilled person. Yet Lewis's personal history for the next nine years tells a quite different story. Fame may have raised Lewis's profile, but in the first place, this just made him a more obvious target for those who disliked his religious beliefs. And in the second, many of his academic colleagues came to believe that he had sold out to popular culture to secure that fame. He had sold his academic birthright for a populist pottage. Though he does not appear to have realised this shift, Lewis was about to enter into a period of rejection, misfortune, and personal struggle.

THE DARKER SIDE OF FAME

The Second World War finally ended in Europe on 8 May 1945. Tolkien felt that things had been looking up for a while. "The Bird"—as he referred to the Eagle and Child—was now "gloriously empty," the beer "improved," and the landlord "wreathed in welcoming smiles." Their Tuesday meetings were once more a "feast of reason and flow of soul."[5] The first meeting of the Inklings after the ending of the war in Europe was scheduled for Tuesday, 15 May at the Eagle and Child.

Charles Williams would not be attending. He had been taken ill the previous week, and was recuperating in the Radcliffe Infirmary, only a few moments' walk north of the Eagle and Child. Lewis decided to visit Williams on the way to the first postwar Inklings gathering, so that he could convey his friend's best wishes to the group. Nothing could have prepared him for what happened next. To his shock, he was told that Williams had just died.

Although all the Inklings were stunned by this unexpected news, Lewis was by far the most affected. Williams had become his literary and spiritual lodestar throughout the period of the war, displacing Tolkien in his affections. A small volume of essays that the Inklings had planned as a tribute to Williams now became his memorial instead. It was a crushing personal blow for Lewis.

Others, however, soon put this sad event behind them. Tolkien's bibulous delight that the war had ended was soon enhanced further by the news that he had been elected to one of Oxford's two Merton Professorships of English in 1945. He had long dreamed to establish himself in one of these chairs, and Lewis in the other. One goal had now been achieved; the second soon seemed within their reach. There was no doubt in Tolkien's mind that Lewis needed a professorship, for the sake of his sanity.

Why so? Once the war was ended, student numbers at Oxford University began to rise. Although this was good news for the university as a whole, bringing much-needed financial revitalization to an institution that had been under-resourced during the war years, it placed the college tutorial systems under considerable strain. Lewis's personal workload increased substantially, leaving him less and less time for reading and writing. If Lewis became an Oxford professor, he would not have to give tutorials to undergraduates. Although he would be required to give lectures at undergraduate level for the faculty and undertake graduate supervision, these demands were modest in comparison with the crippling postwar tutorial workload that Lewis was beginning to experience. A promotion would be good news for Lewis.

Then the window of opportunity opened. In 1947, David Nichol Smith retired from the second Merton Chair of English. Lewis had expectations of filling the position, and Tolkien was clear that it ought to be his. As one of the electors to the chair, Tolkien was well placed to support Lewis's election. But Tolkien seems to have been unaware of the hostility that had been building up towards Lewis at Oxford. As he pressed Lewis's case, Tolkien was taken aback by the "extraordinary animosity"[6] directed against Lewis within the Faculty of English. His recent populist writings and negative attitude towards higher degrees were seen as potential liabilities for the faculty. Tolkien totally failed to persuade his fellow electors Helen Darbishire, H. W. Garrod, and C. H. Wilkinson to take Lewis seriously as a candidate. In the end, the second Merton Chair went to F. P. Wilson, a solid if slightly dull Shakespearean scholar, whose virtues included not being C. S. Lewis.

But more bad news was to come. In 1948, Oxford's Goldsmith's Chair of English Literature, linked to a fellowship at New College, fell vacant. In the end, it was offered to the noted literary biographer Lord David Cecil. Lewis was passed over.

The next rejection took place in 1951, as Oxford University prepared to elect a new Professor of Poetry. The ballot paper had only two names. They were confusingly similar, and voting errors were a real possibility. Lewis's single opponent was Cecil Day Lewis (1904–1972), later to become the British poet laureate. (A third candidate dropped out, to allow the anti–C. S. Lewis faction a clear run.) In the end, C. D. Lewis won the ballot by 194 votes to 173. Once more, Lewis faced rejection.

There were, however, consolations in the midst of this bleakness. On 17 March 1948, the Council of the Royal Society of Literature unanimously voted to elect Lewis as a fellow of the Society.[7] Yet Lewis had no doubt that he was regarded by many of his academic colleagues with suspicion or derision. He seemed to be a prophet without honour in his own city and university.

This prickly hostility towards Lewis, occasionally degenerating to an irrational hatred, was also evident within his own college. A. N. Wilson, in researching his 1990 biography of Lewis, recalled discussing him with an old man who had been a fellow of Magdalen around this time. Lewis, the former don declared, was "the most evil man he had ever met." Wilson naturally wanted to know the basis of this bizarre geriatric judgement. Lewis's degeneracy, it turned out, was that he believed in God, and used his "cleverness to corrupt the young." As Wilson rightly remarked, precisely that same charge had once been levelled against Socrates.[8]

While this ludicrous attitude is easily dismissed, even though it is still often repeated, the academic hostility towards Lewis within Oxford at this time was not totally irrational or vindictive. The winds of change were blowing, and Lewis was coming to be seen as a potential problem rather than a resource for the future of the Oxford Faculty of English. Graduate students were beginning to flock to Oxford, often to study for a BLitt (Bachelor of Letters) in English literature, bringing much-needed income to both individual colleges and the university. These students needed supervision—a task for which Lewis had no enthusiasm. He was regularly heard to remark that Oxford knew three kinds of literacy: the literate, the illiterate, and the B.Litterate—and that his personal sympathies lay entirely with the first two. As the Oxford Faculty of English began to reestablish its teaching and research programmes after the war, Lewis's negative attitude towards higher degrees and research was increasingly seen as unhelpful, and out of touch with the changing educational situation.

DEMENTIA AND ALCOHOLISM: LEWIS'S "MOTHER" AND BROTHER

Lewis's problems were not limited to his professional work; they extended to his personal life. Although the gloom of wartime economies and shortages gradually lifted, life was not easy for Lewis at The Kilns. His letters of the late 1940s show a concern about Mrs. Moore's health, and broad hints that things were becoming difficult within the household. Maureen had long since left home, leaving Lewis to deal with a fraught situation. Maids now had to be employed to keep the household running smoothly, and their relationships with Mrs. Moore (and each other) were often fractious. Lewis found it hard to cope. When the University of St. Andrews in Scotland awarded Lewis an honorary degree in July 1946, he gloomily remarked that he would much have preferred to receive a "case of Scotch whiskey."[9]

That suggestion would have delighted Lewis's brother, Warnie. At this time, Warnie was fighting what we now know to have been a losing battle with alcohol addiction. While on holiday in Ireland in the summer of 1947, Warnie engaged in binge drinking of such ferocity that he was taken unconscious to a hospital in Drogheda before he finally dried out and was allowed to go home. Sadly, this pattern was now to be repeated, its unpredictability making it all the more difficult to cope with.

The Kilns had become a dysfunctional household. Lewis's domestic life revolved around an increasingly irritable and confused Mrs. Moore, now showing the classic symptoms of dementia, and his increasingly irritated and alcoholic brother. It was hardly a happy environment, made worse by postwar austerity measures, including the continued rationing of many everyday items. In 1947, Lewis wrote to a colleague to apologise for having difficulty attending meetings: his time was "almost fully" and "unpredictably" taken up with his "duties as a nurse and a domestic servant."[10] His challenges, he remarked, were both material and psychological. Life at The Kilns was becoming unbearable, with Lewis acting as caregiver regularly for his "mother" and occasionally for his brother. It was all too much.

Maureen had noticed the pressure that the Lewis brothers were under in caring for her aging mother and her decrepit dog, Bruce, and did what she could to relieve them. She and her husband moved into The Kilns and allowed Lewis and Warnie to live in their house in Malvern for two weeks. It was, however, only a temporary respite. In April 1949, Lewis apologised to Owen Barfield for his tardiness in replying to letters; he was trying to cope with "Dog's stools and human vomits."[11]

On 13 June 1949, Lewis was hospitalised with symptoms of exhaustion, later diagnosed as a streptococcus infection requiring injections of penicillin every three hours. He was finally allowed to go home on 23 June. Warnie was outraged that his brother was so exhausted by the needs of Mrs. Moore, and demanded that she allow Lewis time to recover. Gratefully, Lewis planned to spend a month in Ireland to rest and recharge his batteries in the company of Arthur Greeves. Yet before he could go, Warnie succumbed to another extended bout of alcohol overdose. (Anxious to protect his brother's dignity, Lewis described his brother's problem as "nervous insomnia," only revealing its true nature—"Drink"—to his confidant Arthur Greeves.)[12] In the end, Lewis was left with no option but to cancel his proposed trip to Ireland, and look after Mrs. Moore on his own.

There were unquestionably moments of joy in this dark period in Lewis's life. Yet even his joy at reading the finally completed text of Tolkien's *Lord of the Rings* in October was tempered by his knowledge that the two men now rarely met. Few can miss the pathos in Lewis's letters to his old friend: "I miss you very much."[13] Though the two men lived and worked in the same city and university, they were no longer close. Lewis found at least some degree of intellectual consolation elsewhere, as is evident from the flurry of correspondence with the novelist Dorothy L. Sayers around this time. Yet the tectonic plates of Lewis's life were shifting. Old friendships were withering, and with them the intellectual stimulation and support they had once brought.

Throughout this troubled period, Mrs. Moore was becoming increasingly confused and disturbed, and eventually declined to the point that she had to be admitted to a nursing home. After she had fallen out of bed three times on 29 April 1950, the decision was made to admit her to Restholme, a specialist nursing home at 230 Woodstock Road, Oxford. Lewis, who visited her every day, was plunged into a new anxiety. The nursing fees were £500 per year. How could he afford this? What would happen when he retired and no longer had a college income on which to rely?

In the end, the issue was settled by an influenza pandemic which broke out in the northern English port city of Liverpool late in December 1950. It spread rapidly, and reached its peak in mid-January 1951. Official figures indicate that the death rate was about 40 percent greater than that of the 1918–1919 flu pandemic, which had caused Britain such misery during its recovery from the Great War. At its height, on 12 January 1951, the pandemic claimed the life of Mrs. Moore at the age of seventy-nine. She was laid to rest at Holy Trinity churchyard on 15 January, in the same grave as her old friend Alice Hamilton Moore, who had been buried there on 6 November 1939. (The parish burial records indicate that Alice Moore had lived at The Kilns before her death, suggesting that she had been part of the household around that time.) Warnie was unable to attend her funeral, being himself a victim of the same flu that had carried her off.

HOSTILITY TOWARDS LEWIS AT OXFORD

Meanwhile, Lewis's personal difficulties were compounded by persistent institutional hostility and rejection within Oxford University. A small part—but *only* a small part—of this hostility represented the predictable prejudice of those few who believed Christianity was a sign of mental illness or moral depravity. The real roots of the problem were Lewis's popular acclaim and his seeming disregard for the norms of traditional academic scholarship. His popular works, it was suggested, distracted him from academic research and writing, placing him on the margins of academic culture, rather than at its centre. Lewis, it was pointed out by his

247

critics, had not published anything of academic seriousness and weight since *A Preface to "Paradise Lost"* in 1942. Lewis would need to remedy this deficit as a matter of urgency if he was to regain his academic credibility.

Lewis was painfully aware of such criticisms, which were not without merit. Indeed, it is difficult not to read Lewis's correspondence of the postwar period without sensing unease, uncertainty, and unhappiness over his situation. Lewis had signed a contract in 1935 with Oxford University Press for a volume on sixteenth-century English literature, and was feeling under some pressure to complete it. Yet his home situation was so chaotic that he simply could not find the time to read the vast number of primary sources needed to produce this book. By the middle of 1949, he was exhausted and physically incapable of the intense concentration that the reading and writing for this landmark book would take. Popular books were less demanding, and flowed easily from Lewis's pen. But this one was different.

Nothing could be done while Mrs. Moore remained alive and required Lewis's constant ministrations. After her death in January 1951, Lewis was able to secure a year's sabbatical leave from his teaching responsibilities at Magdalen College to allow him to work flat out on this project during the academic year 1951–1952. By September 1951, Lewis felt able to inform his Italian correspondent Don Giovanni Calabria (1873–1954) of his change in health. *Iam valeo*—"I am now better."[14] His spirits would have further been lifted by a letter from the British prime minister, Winston Churchill, offering to recommend him for a C. B. E. (Commander of the Order of the British Empire, one level below a knighthood) in the 1952 King's New Year's Honours List. Lewis declined;[15] it was, however, clearly a boost for his morale.

He began work with a vengeance on his new project on English literature. Helen Gardner recalled regularly seeing Lewis hard at work in Duke Humfrey's Library, working his way resolutely through the Bodleian Library's holdings of the writers of this bygone age. Never one to trust secondary sources, Lewis devoured the originals, spitting out what was useless and digesting what was valuable.

If Lewis's academic reputation had been flagging, it was more than amply restored with the publication of this seven-hundred-page work in September 1954. His election as a fellow of the British Academy the following year was directly related to this massive piece of scholarship. But it was too late to change the way he was seen at Oxford. Perceptions had crystallised. Lewis was seen as a spent force by many in the late 1940s and early 1950s.

Other problems pressed in on him. The regular Thursday evening meetings of the Inklings continued after the war, often enlivened by the arrival of food parcels from Lewis's American admirers. Lewis insisted on sharing this bounty with his friends, all of whom were suffering from food shortages caused by the postwar austerity measures. Yet all was not well with the Inklings. Tensions rose between members. Tempers flared. Enthusiasm waned. Numbers fell. Finally, on 27 October 1949, Warnie's diary recorded the end of those meetings: "Nobody came." Although members of the group would continue to socialise at the Eagle and Child on Tuesdays, the Inklings had come to an end as a serious literary discussion group.

Things were unquestionably complicated by the growing estrangement between Tolkien and Lewis, which Tolkien put down in no small part to the influence of Charles Williams during the period of the war. Tolkien felt—not without reason—that he had been displaced by Williams in Lewis's affections. It was, in Tolkien's view, a lamentable development, which he deeply regretted. But it had happened. And it would get worse. Tolkien was irritated by what seemed to him to be Lewis's unacknowledged borrowing of Tolkien's mythological ideas at points in his science fiction trilogy. In 1948, Tolkien wrote Lewis a long letter, clearly in response to a significant falling out between them over a literary issue.[16] Yet despite the cooling in their friendship, Tolkien continued to do all he could to help Lewis secure academic preferment at Oxford. For Tolkien, this was a simple matter of justice.

To make things even worse, Tolkien and Lewis faced a significant challenge over the English curriculum at Oxford in the late 1940s. For Tolkien and Lewis, there was no need to study any English literature after 1832. Yet with the austerity of the war years behind them, the Faculty of English reopened the debate. It was becoming increasingly clear that the Victorian Age had produced a massive and significant literature. Why should Oxford students not engage with Alfred, Lord Tennyson, or William Makepeace Thackeray? Or with Charles Dickens or George Eliot? Younger dons began to press the case for curriculum reform, with Helen Gardner playing a significant role as advocate for change. It became clear that the future direction of the faculty was likely to be one with which Lewis would not feel comfortable.

Yet some biographers have argued that the most significant issue Lewis had to face around this time was a challenge to his intellectual authority, issued by a rising young philosophical star, Elizabeth Anscombe (1919–2001). This story also needs to be told, and its implications explored.

ELIZABETH ANSCOMBE AND THE SOCRATIC CLUB

In 1893, the Oxford Pastorate was founded by a group of evangelicals within the Church of England, with the intention of allowing Oxford undergraduates exposure to a more lively and intellectually engaging form of the Christian faith than was usually encountered in compulsory college chapel. From 1921, the Pastorate came to be based at St. Aldate's Church, just south of Oxford city centre, close to the heart of the university. Although the Oxford Pastorate was originally both pastoral and evangelistic in its orientation, its leadership increasingly became aware of the importance of apologetic issues. How could Christians engage positively as well as critically with the major intellectual issues of the day? How could Christian students find intellectual engagement and reassurance, rather than bland spiritual platitudes?

In 1941, Stella Aldwinckle (1907–1989), the Pastorate's chaplain for women students, decided the time had come to establish a student forum for the discussion of these issues. She came to this conclusion after a conversation with Monica Ruth Shorten (1923–1993), a student of zoology of Somerville College, who complained that churches and religious societies "just take the real difficulties as solved—things like the existence of God, the divinity of Christ and so on." Yet people clearly needed help to understand and defend these beliefs, which could not simply be assumed as true in Oxford's rigorously critical intellectual environment. Shorten—who went on to become an authority on the British grey squirrel—clearly saw the need for an apologetic ministry among Oxford's students.

After hosting a series of discussions for agnostics and atheists at Somerville College, Aldwinckle decided to establish such a forum across the university as a whole. The Socratic Club was founded as an Oxford University student society. Under the rules of the university, a student club or society requires a "Senior Member"—a don who would take responsibility for the organisation. Aldwinckle initially thought that the novelist Dorothy L. Sayers, a former scholar of Somerville College, might be appropriate. However, Sayers lived in London, and could not be counted on to attend regularly.[17] An Oxford academic was clearly called for. But who should it be?

In a stroke of genius, Aldwinckle bypassed all the safe choices (such as college chaplains) and went straight to the man she regarded as the rising star of apologetics at Oxford—C. S. Lewis. By the time the society met for the first time in January 1942, Lewis had soared to national fame. The Socratic Club rapidly became one of the most important university societies for discussion of issues relating to the Christian faith. It met on Monday evenings during full term. Lewis, usually present, was rarely the main attraction, on average speaking only once a term. Yet his presence was formidable. The list of speakers sparkled with Oxford philosophical luminaries. Though the club was explicitly Christian in orientation, it was generous in its range of speakers. Evidence and argument were the tools of its trade. As Lewis himself put it in the first edition of the *Socratic Digest*:

> It was the Christians who constructed the arena and issued the challenge. . . . We never claimed to be impartial. But argument is. It has a life of its own. No man can tell where it will go. We expose ourselves, and the weakest of our party, to your fire no less than you are exposed to ours.[18]

An interesting aspect of the Socratic Club has passed unnoticed. Its members were primarily women. Perhaps this reflects the personal influence of Aldwinckle, or its original links with Somerville College. The membership list for Michaelmas Term 1944 records 164 members, of whom 109 were from Oxford's five all-women colleges: Lady Margaret Hall (20), St. Anne's (19), St. Hilda's (18), St. Hugh's (39), and Somerville (13).[19]

Given Lewis's prominent role in the club, it was natural that visiting speakers would engage with his ideas, and provoke debate with him. So when Lewis published *Miracles: A Preliminary Study* in 1947, it was to be expected that the themes of this book would be up for discussion and debate. The most important of these was Lewis's assertion that naturalism is self-refuting. The basic lines of this argument are laid out in the third chapter of *Miracles*, titled "The Self-Contradiction of the Naturalist." On 2 February 1948, a young Catholic philosopher, Elizabeth Anscombe, called Lewis to task over his critique of naturalism.

So what form did Lewis's critique of naturalism take? Lewis's argument is foreshadowed in earlier works, and can be summed up in a sentence from his 1941 essay "Evil and God": "If thought is the undesigned and irrelevant product of cerebral motions, what reason have we to trust it?"[20] In response to those who asserted that Christian beliefs—such as belief in God—are simply the result of environmental factors or evolutionary pressures, Lewis insisted that such approaches ended up invalidating the thought processes on which they ultimately depended. Those who represent all human thought as an accident of the environment are simply subverting all their own thoughts—including the belief that thought is determined by the environment.

Lewis's line of thought is both suggestive and creative, and resonates with concerns expressed by "naturalist" thinkers of his day—such as J. B. S. Haldane, with whom Lewis crossed swords on several occasions. Haldane, a materialist, found himself discomfited by the following line of thought:

If my mental processes are determined wholly by the motions of atoms in my brain I have no reason to suppose that my beliefs are true. They may be sound chemically, but that does not make them sound logically. And hence I have no reason for supposing my brain to be composed of atoms. In order to escape from this necessity of sawing away the branch on which I am sitting, so to speak, I am compelled to believe that mind is not wholly conditioned by matter.[21]

Haldane here anticipates the argument that Lewis would use against this position. In *Miracles*, Lewis points out that if naturalism is the result of rational reflection, then the validity of that process of thought has to be assumed in order to reach this conclusion. Or, to put this another way, if all events are determined by "irrational causes," as Lewis holds naturalism to assume, then rational thought must itself be recognised as a product of such irrational causes—which contradicts the core assumptions of the process of reasoning which is involved in reaching this naturalist position. *"No thought is valid if it can be fully explained as the result of irrational causes."*[22]

There are some important lines of thought in this analysis. Yet a critical reader of this chapter of *Miracles* might (not unreasonably) draw the conclusion that it has been written in some haste. There are signs of logical shortcuts, perhaps because Lewis was so familiar with his argument that he assumed he had made it sufficiently clear to his readers. He hadn't. If Elizabeth Anscombe had not pulled Lewis up over these weaknesses, someone else would have.

The problem did not lie with Lewis's rejection of naturalism. Anscombe made it clear from the outset in her presentation of February 1948 that she agreed with Lewis that naturalism is untenable. Yet she did not regard his specific argument, as set out in the first edition of *Miracles*, as being sufficiently rigorous to justify this conclusion. Her main concern related to Lewis's insistence that naturalism was "irrational."[23] Anscombe made the entirely fair point—which will probably cross the mind of any informed reader of Lewis's original chapter—that not all natural causes are "irrational." Anscombe rightly pointed out that many (probably most) natural causes can legitimately be described simply as "non-rational." If rational thought is produced by natural "non-rational" causes, there is no need to doubt its "validity" *for that reason*—unless those causes can be shown to predispose it to false or unreasonable beliefs.

It was an uncomfortable encounter for Lewis. Yet it was clear that this chapter did require revision—not because the conclusion was wrong, but because the arguments used in reaching that conclusion were not as robust as they ought to have been. Lewis rose to Anscombe's criticism, as if she were a kind of philosophical Inkling, and rewrote his argument in the light of her criticisms. The revised version of this chapter, first published in 1960, was retitled "The Cardinal Difficulty of Naturalism." Apart from its first six paragraphs, the chapter was rewritten to take Anscombe's points into account. It is much stronger intellectually, and is to be seen as Lewis's definitive statement on this important theme.

The real significance of this slightly bruising encounter with Anscombe concerns its interpretation for the future direction of Lewis's writing projects. Some of Lewis's biographers, primarily A. N. Wilson, have seen this incident as signalling, perhaps even causing, a major shift in Lewis's outlook. Having been defeated in argument, they contend, Lewis lost confidence in the rational basis of his faith, and abandoned his role as a leading apologist. They claim that his shift to writing fictional works—such as the Chronicles of Narnia—reflects a growing realisation that rational argument cannot support the Christian faith.

However, the substantial body of written evidence concerning this exchange points to a quite different conclusion. A chastised Lewis recognised the weakness of one specific argument he had deployed (a little hastily, it must be said), and worked to improve it. Lewis was an academic writer, and academic books are tested against the criticisms and concerns of colleagues until the arguments and evidence are presented in the best possible way. Lewis was already used to giving and receiving literary criticism in this way, both through the Inklings and through personal discussions with colleagues such as Tolkien.

Anscombe would have seen herself as an agent of intellectual refinement, not contradiction, for Lewis's general position, with which she clearly felt sympathy. Lewis appears to have been taken aback at having the weakness of his argument demonstrated so publicly, and expressed unease about the incident to some of his closer friends. Yet Lewis's embarrassment concerned the somewhat public nature of this refinement, not the intellectual process itself. The positive and beneficial outcome of Anscombe's intervention is clearly evident in the revised version of Lewis's argument.

There is no evidence of Lewis retreating into some kind of nonrational fideism or reason-free fantasy as a result of this encounter. Lewis's subsequent writings continue to show a strong sense of the rational coherency of the Christian faith, and of the importance of apologetics in the contemporary cultural context. Later papers—such as "Is Theism Important?" (1952) and "On Obstinacy in Belief" (1955)—clearly show a continued recognition of the importance of reasoned argument in apologetics. Furthermore, when Lewis published *Mere Christianity* in 1952, he did not significantly modify the rational approach to apologetics he had developed in the broadcast talks of the 1940s, despite having the opportunity to do so.

Nor can Anscombe's critique be seen as constituting a "tipping point," leading Lewis to abandon rational argument in favour of imaginative and narrative approaches to apologetics. It must be recalled that Lewis had, by the time of this debate, written three substantial works of what might reasonably be called "imaginative narrative apologetics"—namely, the Ransom Trilogy (see pages 233–238). Lewis was thus already persuaded of the importance of the use of narrative and the appeal to the imagination in apologetics. As Lewis once remarked, the Ransom Trilogy, like Narnia, had its origins in images rather than ideas.

Narnia was not Lewis's escape route from a failed rational apologetic;

it was one of several strands to his approach, held together by his cele-brated reconciliation of reason and imagination in the Christian vision of reality. Sadly, A. N. Wilson does not offer any compelling evidence for his suggestion that "*The Lion, the Witch and the Wardrobe* grew out of Lewis's experience of being stung back into childhood by his defeat at the hands of Elizabeth Anscombe at the Socratic Club,"[24] or his amusing, but ultimately unevidenced, suggestion that Lewis based the White Witch of Narnia on Anscombe. The timing of Lewis's weaving together of the rich imaginative threads of Narnia, like the images in Spenser's Faerie Land, may conceivably owe something to Anscombe—but that is about as far as it goes. Lewis was writing about Narnia before Anscombe's 1948 presentation.

Anyway, it was not a "defeat"; it was a critical evaluation of a sound argument that had been imperfectly stated, leading to its improved pre-sentation in 1960. The Oxford philosopher J. R. Lucas presented Lewis's arguments again in a rerun of the debate with Anscombe at a meeting of the Socratic Club in the late 1960s. His assessment of the original debate remains important:

> Miss Anscombe's argument was based on a distinction between reasons and causes, which had been drawn by Wittgenstein, and was thought to be important by Wittgensteinians. It was a distinction unknown to, and unknowable by, Lewis at the time he was writing *Miracles*, and dubiously relevant to his thesis.[25]

Lucas had no doubt about what Lewis's problems were back in 1948, and why he succeeded against her in the later replay:

> Miss Anscombe was a bully, and Lewis a gentleman, which inhibited him from treating her as she had treated him. But I had come across her in previous encounters, and had no inhibitions. So the contest was determined by the actual cogency of the arguments adduced. That is to say, I won.

10.1 A rare moment of peace. Lewis and his brother, Warnie, on holiday at Annagassan, County Louth, Ireland, in the summer of 1949. Vera Henry, Mrs. Moore's goddaughter, owned a holiday home in the area, where Lewis and Warnie vacationed from time to time.

LEWIS'S DOUBTS ABOUT HIS ROLE AS AN APOLOGIST

While it is important to avoid exaggerations about the impact of Anscombe on Lewis in his later Oxford years, there are clear indications that she played a part in causing Lewis to rethink his role as an apologist around this time. Basil Mitchell, later Nolloth Professor of the Philosophy of Religion at Oxford, was a professional philosopher who succeeded Lewis as president of the Socratic Club after Lewis's move to Cambridge. Mitchell took the view that Lewis came to believe that he was not sufficiently informed about contemporary philosophical debates—Anscombe was an expert on Wittgenstein—and decided this was now best left to the experts. He would focus on what he knew best.

Lewis's wartime role as an apologist can be seen as a response to the needs of that era. Three straws in the wind suggest that Lewis wished to move away from a frontline apologetic role after the war. First, Lewis clearly found this draining. This point is made explicitly in his 1945 lecture "Christian Apologetics," in which he remarks that "nothing is more dangerous to one's own faith than the work of an apologist. No doctrine of that Faith seems to me so spectral, so unreal as one that I have just successfully defended in a public debate."[26] A decade later, after his move to Cambridge, Lewis again commented that apologetics is "very wearing."[27] Did Lewis see apologetics as an important episode in his career, rather than as its goal and zenith? His correspondence certainly suggests this. In fact, there are indications that he believed his writing lacked its former energy and vitality.

Lewis expresses these fears with particular clarity and force in his Latin correspondence with Don Giovanni Calabria, a remarkable Italian priest who was canonised by John Paul II on 18 April 1999. An Italian translation of *The Screwtape Letters* had appeared in 1947, and generated considerable interest.[28] Calabria read this book and wrote an appreciative note to its author. Not knowing English, he wrote to Lewis in Latin. They exchanged letters in Latin from 1947 until Calabria's death in December 1954.[29] In a letter of January 1949, Lewis reveals his growing despair about his ability to write, which seemed to be in a state of collapse: "I feel that my enthusiasm for writing, and whatever flair I once possessed, have decreased."[30] Perhaps believing that the use of Latin allowed him to express himself more frankly than he might have dared if the correspondence had been in English, Lewis even went so far as to suggest that it might actually be good for him if he lost his skills as a writer: it would put an end to any vain ambitions or quests for glory. In June 1949, Lewis suffered a breakdown in his health, and was hospitalised. Four months later, his mood was still darker. It was not until late 1951 that Lewis began to regain something of his confidence and motivation. Yet the death of Walter Adams, his confessor, in May 1952, clearly caused him further distress, robbing him of a wise critic and friend.

Another reason Lewis may have backed away from his role as an apologist was an acute awareness that he had failed as an apologist towards those who were closest to him—Arthur Greeves and Mrs. Moore. Mrs. Moore remained hostile towards Christianity throughout her later life, and Greeves moved away from his somewhat austere Ulster Protestantism to an equally austere Unitarianism. And even Warnie regarded *The Problem of Pain* as apologetically unconvincing. How could Lewis maintain a profile as a public apologist with any integrity in the light of such private failures?

Finally, and probably related to these two earlier points, there are strong indications in his correspondence that Lewis believed his moment as an apologist had passed, and it was time to make room for younger voices. Two slightly different themes can be discerned: first, Lewis's feeling that new issues had arisen, which he was not best placed to engage; and second, Lewis's growing conviction that he had peaked in his abilities as an apologist. Declining Robert Walton's invitation to take part in a BBC discussion on the evidence for religious faith, Lewis commented that "like the old fangless snake in *The Jungle Book*, I've largely lost my dialectical power."[31]

There is no doubt that Anscombe helped Lewis to reach this conclusion. On 12 June 1950, Stella Aldwinckle wrote to Lewis in her capacity as secretary of the Socratic Club, reminding him that they needed to plan the programme for Michaelmas Term 1950. Lewis made a list of rising stars as possible speakers: Austin Farrer on the historical value of the New Testament; Basil Mitchell on faith and experience; and Elizabeth

Anscombe on "Why I believe in God." Lewis made it clear that Anscombe was his top pick: "Having obliterated me as an Apologist, ought she not to *succeed* me?"[32]

Lewis seems to have seen his move to Cambridge in January 1955 as marking a fresh start. It is striking how few of his writings of this later period of his life deal specifically with apologetic themes, if understood in terms of the explicit rational defence of the Christian faith. In a letter of September 1955, declining the invitation of the American evangelical leader Carl F. H. Henry (1913–2003) to write some apologetic pieces, Lewis explained that while he had done what he could "in the way of frontal attacks," he now felt "quite sure" those days were over. He now preferred more indirect approaches to apologetics, such as those which appealed to "fiction and symbol."[33]

These remarks to Carl Henry—one of the most significant figures in the history of postwar American evangelicalism—are clearly relevant to the creation of Narnia. Many would see this comment about "fiction and symbol" as a reference to his Chronicles of Narnia, which can easily be categorised as works of narrative or imaginative apologetics, representing a move away from the more deductive or inductive argumentative approaches of his wartime broadcast talks. If Anscombe raised doubts in Lewis's mind about his apologetic approach, these concerned its medium, rather than its content. Lewis might have lost his "dialectical power"; but what about its imaginative counterpart?

We can rightly see Narnia as the imaginative outworking of the core philosophical and theological ideas Lewis had been developing since the mid-1930s, expressed in a narrative rather than a rational manner. The Narnia novels express in the form of a story the same philosophical and theological arguments advanced in *Miracles*. Fiction becomes the means of allowing readers to see—more than that, to *enjoy*—the vision of reality Lewis had already set out in his more apologetic works.

We must now tell the story of how Lewis wrote the Chronicles of Narnia, and try to understand why they have captivated the imagination of a generation.

PART THREE

NARNIA

CHAPTER 11

REARRANGING REALITY: THE CREATION OF NARNIA

I n 2008 the London publishers HarperCollins invited Diane Simpson, a professional graphologist, to examine some specimens of the handwriting of C. S. Lewis. Simpson had no idea whom she was investigating. She found the "small, neat script" suggestive of someone who was "guarded and careful," with sharp critical faculties. Simpson also noticed something else. "I wonder whether he has a garden shed of sorts (or some other sort of world) in which to disappear when he chooses."[1] Simpson was absolutely right. Lewis did indeed have "some other sort of world" into which he would disappear—an imagined world we now know as Narnia.

Let us pause at this point. Narnia is an *imaginative*, not an *imaginary*, world. Lewis was quite clear that a distinction had to be drawn between these ideas. The "imaginary" is something that has been falsely imagined, having no counterpart in reality. Lewis regards such an invented reality as opening the way to delusion. The "imaginative" is something produced by the human mind as it tries to respond to something greater than itself, struggling to find images adequate to the reality. The more imaginative a mythology, the greater its ability to "communicate more Reality to us."[2] For Lewis, the imaginative is to be seen as a legitimate and positive use of the human imagination, challenging the limits of reason and opening the door to a deeper apprehension of reality.

So how did Lewis invent this imaginative world? And why? Was it a retreat into the security of his childhood at a time of personal and professional stress? Was Lewis like Peter Pan, an emotionally retarded boy who never really grew up, and Narnia his version of "Never Never Land"? There may be a grain of truth in these suggestions. As we have already seen, Lewis turned to writing when he was stressed, finding relief in the exercise. Yet there is clearly another factor in play here: Lewis's growing realisation that children's stories offered him a marvellous way of exploring philosophical and theological questions—such as the origins of evil, the nature of faith, and the human desire for God. A good story could weave these themes together, using the imagination as the gateway to serious thinking.

The origins of the Narnia stories lay, Lewis tells us, in his imagination. It all began with an image of a faun carrying an umbrella and parcels through a snowy wood. Lewis's celebrated description of the creative process depicts it as unfolding from mental images, which were then consciously connected to form a consistent plot. There are obvious and important parallels with the origins of Tolkien's novel *The Hobbit*. In a letter to W. H. Auden (1907–1973), Tolkien recalled being bored to death during the early 1930s marking school certificate exam papers (he needed the extra money), when for some inexplicable reason, an idea came into his head. "On a blank leaf I scrawled: 'In a hole in the ground there lived a hobbit.' I did not and do not know why."[3]

Yet Lewis did not really see himself as "creating" Narnia. As he once commented, "creation" is "an entirely misleading term." Lewis preferred to think of human thought as "God-kindled,"[4] and the writing process as the rearrangement of elements that God has provided. The writer takes "things that lie to hand," and puts them to new use. Like someone who plants a garden, the author is only one aspect of a "causal stream."[5] As we shall see, Lewis drew extensively on "elements" he found in literature. His skill lay not in inventing these elements, but in the manner he wove them together to create the literary landmark that we know as the Chronicles of Narnia.

11.1 Mr. Tumnus, a faun, carrying an umbrella and parcels through a snowy wood, accompanied by Lucy. This is one of the best-known images provided by Pauline Baynes for *The Lion, the Witch and the Wardrobe*.

THE ORIGINS OF NARNIA

"I'm going to write a children's book!" Mrs. Moore and Maureen greeted Lewis's unexpected announcement one morning over breakfast, probably around the outbreak of the Second World War in September 1939,[6] with good-natured derision.[7] Not only did Lewis have no children of his own; he had virtually no contact with any children other than sporadic meetings with his godchildren. Their laughter soon died down, but Lewis's idea did not fade away. Narnia was taking shape in his mind, as ideas and images going back to his childhood began to crystallise.

The composition of the series was generally fluid and easy. Despite Lewis's mounting personal and professional problems, he was able to write five of the seven novels between the summer of 1948 and the spring of 1951. A fallow period then followed, before Lewis began writing *The Last Battle* in the autumn of 1952, finishing it the following spring. The final volume to be completed was *The Magician's Nephew*, which Lewis clearly found more problematic than other works in the series. Although Lewis began drafting this work shortly after he finished the text of *The Lion, the Witch and the Wardrobe*, he did not complete it until March 1954.

Some would see this ease of composition as a mark of Lewis's creative genius. Others—most notably, J. R. R. Tolkien—regarded the speed with which they were written as an indication of their shallowness. They lacked a strong and consistent backstory, and were mythological crossbreeds, lacking a sense of coherence. Why, Tolkien wondered, introduce Father Christmas into the story? He didn't really belong there. Harbouring darker thoughts, Tolkien also suspected that Lewis had borrowed some of his own ideas and had woven them into the Narnia Chronicles without due acknowledgement.

It is easy to understand Tolkien's concerns. Yet it must be pointed out that recent Lewis scholarship has identified a deeper coherence to the Narnia stories, linked with Lewis's subtle—indeed, one might say *cryptic*—use of medieval symbolism. We shall consider this point in the following chapter.

So where did the name *Narnia* come from? While studying classics under William Thompson Kirkpatrick at Great Bookham, between 1914 and 1917, Lewis acquired a copy of an atlas of the classical world, published in 1904. On one of its maps, Lewis underscored the name of an ancient Italian town because he liked the sound of its name.[8] The town was Narnia—now the modern Italian town of Narni in Umbria, located roughly in the centre of Italy. (Lewis never visited it.) One of the most famous inhabitants of Narni was Lucia Brocadelli (1476–1544), a renowned visionary and mystic who became its patron saint. Yet no particular significance can be attached to these facts as they relate to real history of Narnia, or its cultural role in the late classical or early medieval periods—or even the importance of this Lucy to this Narnia. It seems Lewis simply liked the sound of the Latin name, and it became fixed in his memory—despite the fact that it designated a city, not a region or land.

The discovery of Narnia has become one of the best-known scenes in children's literature. Four children—Peter, Susan, Edmund, and Lucy—are evacuated from London during the Second World War to escape the bombing of England's capital city.[9] Separated from their family, they are taken to an old house in the country, owned and occupied by a genial, well-meaning, yet slightly eccentric professor (whom many regard as a thinly disguised version of Lewis himself). Prevented from exploring the outside world by heavy rain, the children decide to explore the book-strewn corridors and rooms inside the house instead. (There is a clear parallel here with Lewis's long-term fascination with the distinction between the "exterior world" and the "interior world.") Finally, they stumble into a "room that was quite empty except for one big wardrobe."[10]

Lucy, entering the wardrobe, finds herself in a cold, snowy land—a world in which it is "always winter and never Christmas." In her encounters with its inhabitants—primarily with fauns and beavers—Lucy learns a story about Narnia: the true king of Narnia is a great lion named Aslan, who has been absent for many years but is now "on the move again." Her brother Edmund hears a very different story from the White Witch, who presents herself as the true and lawful ruler of Narnia.

At one level, *The Lion, the Witch and the Wardrobe* is about the testing of these characters and their stories about Narnia. Who is to be trusted? Which story about Narnia is to be believed? To make the right judgements about what they should do, the children need to discover and trust the true master narrative of the mysterious world into which they have stumbled, and within which they seem destined to play a significant role.

11.2 The four children discover the mysterious wardrobe in an empty room in the Professor's house. An illustration by Pauline Baynes from *The Lion, the Witch and the Wardrobe*.

The contrast with some earlier children's stories is quite striking. In *The Wonderful Wizard of Oz* (1900), for example, Dorothy is told which witches are wicked, and which are good. In Narnia, characters do not wear name tags declaring their moral character. The children (and readers) have to work these things out for themselves. The characters they encounter are complex and multifaceted. Their true moral character has to be discovered.

The Chronicles of Narnia illuminate how human beings understand themselves, face up to their weaknesses, and try to become the people they are meant to be. They are about a quest for meaning and virtue, not simply the quest for explanation and understanding. That is perhaps one reason why the Chronicles of Narnia have proved to have such a powerful appeal: they speak of choices to be made, of right and wrong, and of challenges that must be faced. Yet this vision of goodness and greatness is not set forth as a logical or reasoned argument, but is affirmed and explored through the telling of a story—a story that captures the imagination.

Through the influence of Charles Williams in the early 1940s, Lewis discovered the power of the imagination to make readers long for moral goodness. It was Williams, he declared, who taught him that "when the old poets made some virtue their theme they were not teaching but adoring, and that what we take for the didactic is often the enchanted."[11] The key to moral improvement is thus the captivation of the imagination through powerful stories telling of "brave knights and heroic courage."[12] Such stories inspire and ennoble, making us yearn to do the same in our own worlds.

THE THRESHOLD: A KEY NARNIAN THEME

A central theme in the Chronicles of Narnia is that of a door into another world—a threshold that can be crossed, allowing us to enter a wonderful new realm and explore it. There are obvious religious overtones to the idea, which Lewis discussed in earlier works, such as the 1941 sermon "The Weight of Glory." For Lewis, human experience suggests that there is another and more wonderful world, in which our true destiny lies—but that we are at present on the "wrong side" of the door that leads into this world.

The idea of a threshold to strange worlds is a familiar theme in children's literature, past and present. Today's readers are likely to think of J. K. Rowling's "Platform 9¾" at King's Cross Station in London. Readers of an earlier age—including Lewis himself—would think of the children's stories of E. Nesbit (1858–1924), now remembered for her classic Edwardian novels *The Railway Children* (1906) and *The Enchanted Castle* (1907).

Lewis had read several of Nesbit's works with great appreciation as a child, and recalled particularly being entranced by Nesbit's trilogy *Five Children and It* (1902), *The Phoenix and the Carpet* (1904), and *The Story of the Amulet* (1906). Lewis singled out the last of these as being of especial importance to him, and notes that he could still "reread it with delight."[13] All three stories centre on a family group of five children who have to leave home for various reasons, and discover exciting new things in the company of strange and wonderful people and creatures. It is through being distanced from their familiar context that the children encounter new and mysterious worlds and ideas—a theme that recurs in the Narnia novels.

One of Nesbit's central themes is that there is a link or bridge between two worlds, which the wise are able to find and traverse. Like George MacDonald (1824–1905) before her, Nesbit wrote about a mysterious threshold between the ordinary and the magical, between the everyday world and an enchanted realm. As she explained this idea in *The Enchanted Castle*:

> There is a curtain, thin as gossamer, clear as glass, strong as iron,
> that hangs for ever between the world of magic and the world
> that seems to us to be real. And when once people have found
> one of the little weak spots in that curtain which are marked
> by magic rings, and amulets, and the like, almost anything
> may happen.[14]

Lewis's debt to Nesbit goes beyond the idea of a general threshold to strange worlds. In her collection of stories *The Magic World* (1912), we find a series of plotlines which bear an uncanny resemblance to those found in Narnia. In "The Aunt and Amabel," we read of Amabel, a young girl who unintentionally wrecks her aunt's flowerbed, and is sent upstairs to a bedroom as punishment. There she finds a bed, a large wardrobe, and a railway timetable. The wardrobe turns out to contain a secret railway station, which can transport her to other worlds.[15]

The theme of crossing thresholds plays an important imaginative role in the Narnia series. It allows the reader to enter a strange world, which is explored through the actions and adventures of the chief characters. This process is significantly helped through the illustrations of Pauline Baynes (1922–2008), who had earlier provided the artwork for Tolkien's *Farmer Giles of Ham* (1949). Baynes produced a series of line illustrations that seemed to Tolkien to capture the essence of his text perfectly. He wrote with delight to his publishers, declaring that they were even better than he had dared to hope. "They are more than illustrations, they are a collateral theme." For

Tolkien, the illustrations were so good that his friends considered that they reduced his text "to a commentary on the drawings."[16] So began a long and mutually respectful relationship between author and illustrator. There is little wonder that Tolkien should recommend her to Lewis when his publisher insisted on illustrations for *The Lion, the Witch and the Wardrobe*.

In the end, Baynes's relationship with Lewis turned out to be rather formal and distant. They appear to have met only twice. One of these two meetings was a highly perfunctory and brief discussion at London's Waterloo Station, during which Lewis frequently consulted his watch, anxious not to miss his train. (Her diary entry for that day was rumoured to read: "Met C. S. Lewis. Came home. Made rock cakes.") It was not an easy relationship, particularly when Baynes learned that Lewis, having been very positive about her illustrations to her face, was somewhat more critical of her artistic gifts behind her back—especially her ability to draw lions.

Lewis seems to have made a significant misjudgement here, failing to realise how Baynes's illustrations would help his readers visualise Narnia, and especially the noble and magisterial Aslan. Wouldn't Lewis's childhood experience of coming to love Wagner through Arthur Rackham's illustrations (pages 28–29) have made him alert to the importance of illustrations in helping captivate the imagination? Yet apparently without realising it, Lewis had found the perfect visualisation of his imaginative world—perhaps most evocatively depicted in the drawing of a little girl walking arm in arm with a faun beneath an umbrella in a snowy wood.

In February 2008, the British educational charity Booktrust—"dedicated to encouraging people of all ages and cultures to enjoy books"—voted *The Lion, the Witch and the Wardrobe* the best children's book of all time. Lewis's winsome narrative may have laid the foundation for this award; many would say that Baynes's illustrations clinched it. Perhaps in the end Lewis would have agreed. After all, he replied to Baynes's letter of congratulation when *The Last Battle* won the Carnegie Medal for best children's book of 1956 by including her in his achievement: "Is it not rather 'our' Medal? I'm sure the illustrations were taken into consideration as well as the text."[17]

THE READING ORDER OF THE NARNIA SERIES

Lewis originally envisaged *The Lion, the Witch and the Wardrobe* as a stand-alone, self-contained work—and it can still be read and appreciated as such. The other Narnia novels radiate outwards from this work, even in the case of *The Magician's Nephew*, which is presented as chronologically prior to *The Lion, the Witch and the Wardrobe*. By allowing us to enter Narnia in the midst of its history, Lewis makes us want to know about its past, as well as its future. *The Magician's Nephew* is a flashback, a way of illuminating the present by looking back to the past.

The seven works can be read in three ways: according to their date of writing, their date of publication, or the internal chronology of the events the volumes describe. These three quite different approaches point to the following reading orders:

ORDER OF WRITING	ORDER OF PUBLICATION	INTERNAL CHRONOLOGY
1. The Lion, the Witch and the Wardrobe	1. The Lion, the Witch and the Wardrobe (1950)	1. The Magician's Nephew
2. Prince Caspian	2. Prince Caspian (1951)	2. The Lion, the Witch and the Wardrobe
3. The Voyage of the "Dawn Treader"	3. The Voyage of the "Dawn Treader" (1952)	3. The Horse and His Boy
4. The Horse and His Boy	4. The Silver Chair (1953)	4. Prince Caspian
5. The Silver Chair	5. The Horse and His Boy (1954)	5. The Voyage of the "Dawn Treader"
6. The Last Battle	6. The Magician's Nephew (1955)	6. The Silver Chair
7. The Magician's Nephew	7. The Last Battle (1956)	7. The Last Battle

The collected edition of the Chronicles of Narnia published by HarperCollins (2005) includes this statement: "Although *The Magician's Nephew* was written several years after C. S. Lewis first began The Chronicles of Narnia, he wanted it to be read as the first book in the series. HarperCollins is happy to present these books in the order in which

Professor Lewis preferred." This seemingly straightforward assertion is actually a questionable interpretation, rather than a direct statement, of Lewis's views.[18] Lewis made it clear that they could be read in any order, and was cautious about stipulating any prescribed order.

After all, Lewis's late essay "On Criticism" emphasises the importance of establishing the chronology of composition in the interpretation of a series of works—noting, for example, some influential misreadings of Tolkien's *Lord of the Rings* that arise on account of confusion on this matter.[19] Furthermore, Lewis is adamant that the author of a book is "not necessarily the best, and is never a perfect, judge" of how it is to be read and interpreted.[20]

These points should be given due weight, as the chronological approach raises considerable difficulties for readers. For example, the events of *The Horse and His Boy* actually occur during, not after, those of *The Lion, the Witch and the Wardrobe*. This makes the reading of the work quite problematic if strict internal chronology is used as the criterion for determining the correct order of reading.

The most significant difficulty concerns *The Magician's Nephew*, the last in the series to be written, which describes the early history of Narnia. To read this work first completely destroys the literary integrity of *The Lion, the Witch and the Wardrobe*, which emphasises the mysteriousness of Aslan. It introduces him slowly and carefully, building up a sense of expectation that is clearly based on the assumption that the readers know nothing of the name, identity, or significance of this magnificent creature. In his role as narrator within *The Lion, the Witch and the Wardrobe*, Lewis declares, "None of the children knew who Aslan was any more than you do."[21] But anyone who has read *The Magician's Nephew* already knows a lot about Aslan. The gradual disclosure of the mysteries of Narnia—one of *The Lion, the Witch and the Wardrobe*'s most impressive literary features—is spoiled and subverted by a prior reading of *The Magician's Nephew*.

Equally important, the complex symbolic structure of the Chronicles of Narnia is best appreciated through a later reading of *The Magician's Nephew*. This is most helpful when it is placed (following the order of publication) as the sixth of the seven volumes, with *The Last Battle* as the conclusion.

It is perfectly possible to read Tolkien's *Lord of the Rings* without needing to read its later prequel *The Silmarillion*; so it is with Lewis's *The Lion, the Witch and the Wardrobe*. Having read *The Lion, the Witch and the Wardrobe*, the reader naturally wants to move both forwards and backwards, exploring both what happens next and how Narnia came into being. Both options are open to readers; neither is to be imposed upon them.

Finally, there is a clear—and generally overlooked—literary clue to Lewis's true intentions in the subtitles of three of its novels. These subtitles are generally omitted in recent printings of the works. One of these is *Prince Caspian*, the full title of which is *Prince Caspian: The Return to Narnia*. Its illuminating subtitle clearly suggests that this work ought to be read immediately after *The Lion, the Witch and the Wardrobe*. Lewis provided only two of the remaining novels in the series with subtitles—the identical phrase *A Story for Children*. Significantly, these are *The Lion, the Witch and the Wardrobe* and *The Last Battle*.

Why is this important? Lewis, who as a professional scholar of English literature was well versed in literary and rhetorical devices, uses this subtitle as an *inclusio*—a literary device widely used in biblical and secular literature. The *inclusio* allows a writer to "bracket" material to indicate that what is enclosed constitutes a single or coherent unit.[22] The opening and closing of the bracket (or envelope) are indicated by the repetition of the same memorable term or phrase. Lewis uses the subtitle *A Story for Children* for two, and only two, works of the Chronicles of Narnia— namely, *The Lion, the Witch and the Wardrobe* and *The Last Battle*. This phrase, "a story for children," is Lewis's *inclusio*. The remaining five novels are thus bracketed or enfolded within these two bookends, which define the start and end of the series. The decision not to reproduce these subtitles in recent editions of the Chronicles of Narnia has obscured Lewis's use of this literary device, and thus somewhat concealed his purpose.

ANIMALS IN NARNIA

One of the most striking features of Narnia is the prominent role played in its narrative by animals. Some dismiss this as childish drivel, seeing it as a reversion to Lewis's childhood world of Boxen, populated by dressed, speaking animals. But there is rather more to Lewis's narrative than this.

The Chronicles of Narnia include criticisms of attitudes that were prevalent within the so-called "progressive" thought of Lewis's age—such as its widespread acceptance of the practice of vivisection in laboratory experiments. Lewis had no hesitation in criticising fashionable ideas of the 1930s and 1940s—such as H. G. Wells's enthusiastic advocation of eugenics and vivisection—which would today be rejected as dehumanizing and immoral. In Lewis's 1947 essay "Vivisection," he joined forces with the great Oxford children's novelist of the nineteenth century, Lewis Carroll (1832–1898), in protesting the infliction of torture on animals. For Lewis, the practice of vivisection exposed an inner contradiction within Darwinian naturalism. At one and the same time, it emphasised the biological proximity of humans and animals, while asserting the ultimate authority of human beings to do what they please with animals.[23]

Furthermore, as we discussed earlier (pages 235–237), Lewis shrewdly noted how support for eugenics and vivisection leads to some morally uncomfortable conclusions. The eugenics theories of the 1930s—which found embarrassingly wide support in socially liberal circles in western Europe at this time—involve the assumption that certain human beings are inferior to others, and that the survival of the human race thus demands that only the "best" be allowed to reproduce. The liberal elite of Europe loved this idea in the period between the two world wars. But where, Lewis wonders, does this dangerous idea take us?

Once the old Christian idea of a total difference in kind between man and beast has been abandoned, then no argument for experiments on animals can be found which is not also an argument for experiments on inferior men.[24]

It is easy to depict the Narnia novels as an infantile attempt to pretend that animals speak and experience emotion. Yet Lewis's narrative mounts a deceptively subtle critique of certain Darwinian ways of understanding the place of humanity within the natural order, and offers a corrective. Lewis's portrayal of animal characters in Narnia is partly a protest against shallow assertions of humanity's right to do what it pleases with nature.

The rich depictions of animals in the Chronicles of Narnia are partly informed by the "bestiaries" of the Middle Ages—classic accounts of animal life which emphasised their distinct identities and roles within the created order. Each was seen as witnessing to the complex interdependency of the natural world. Lewis adds to these by portraying animals as conscious moral agents.

Where vivisectionists saw animals—such as mice—simply as fodder for laboratory experiments, lacking any inner feelings or intrinsic value, Lewis portrays them as active, conscious agents in Narnia. The most obvious example of this is Reepicheep, a mouse of nobility and virtue, who ends up teaching Eustace Scrubb about honour, courage, and loyalty. This inversion of Darwinian hierarchies does not represent a lapse into irrational sentimentality, nor is it regression to the "Dressed Animals" of Lewis's childhood world of Boxen. For Lewis, the true mark of the primacy of humans over animals is "acknowledging duties to them which they do not acknowledge to us."[25] *Noblesse oblige*, as the French say. Human dignity demands that humans show respect for animals. More than that, animals can enable human beings to develop compassion and care. Lewis's theology of creation leads him to insist that human relationships with animals can be ennobling and fulfilling—both for animals and for humans. There is, of course, one animal in Narnia that stands out above all others—the mysterious and noble figure of Aslan, whom we shall consider in greater detail in the next chapter.

NARNIA AS A WINDOW ON REALITY

For Lewis, the narrative of Narnia has the capacity to re-enchant a dis-enchanted world. It helps us to imagine our world differently. This is not escapism, but is about discerning deeper levels of meaning and value in what we already know. As Lewis pointed out, the readers of such a children's book do not "despise real woods" because they have "read of enchanted woods"; instead, their new way of seeing things "makes all real woods a little enchanted."[26]

Lewis himself spoke about this process of "double seeing" at several points in his works—most notably, in concluding a lecture given at the Socratic Club in Oxford in 1945: "I believe that the Sun has risen, not only because I see it, but because by it I see everything else."[27] We can look at the sun itself; or we can look instead at what it illuminates—thus enlarging our intellectual, moral, and aesthetic vision. We see the true, the good, and the beautiful more clearly by being given a lens that brings them into focus. They are not invented by our reading of Narnia, but they are discerned, lit up, and brought into sharper focus. And more than that, we see *more*, and we see *farther*, by looking through the right lens.

We should read Narnia as Lewis asks us to read other works of litera-ture—as something that is to be enjoyed on the one hand, and something with the capacity to enlarge our vision of reality on the other. What Lewis wrote of *The Hobbit* in 1939 applies with equal force to his own Narnia books: they allow us into "a world of its own" which, once it has been encountered, "becomes indispensable." "You cannot anticipate it before you go there, as you cannot forget it once you have gone."[28]

The seven Chronicles of Narnia are often referred to (though not, it should be noted, by Lewis himself) as a religious allegory. Lewis's early work *The Pilgrim's Regress* is rightly described as a religious allegory. Each of its elements has a representational quality—in other words, they are all disguised yet specific ways of referring to something else. But within a decade, Lewis had moved away from this form of writing. It is possible to read Narnia as an allegory; however, as Lewis once noted, "the mere fact that you *can* allegorise the work before you is of itself no proof that it is an allegory."[29]

In 1958, Lewis made an important distinction between a "supposal" and an allegory. A supposal is an invitation to try seeing things in another way, and imagine how things would work out if this were true. To understand Lewis's meaning at this point, we need to consider the way in which he expresses this notion:

> If Aslan represented the immaterial Deity in the same way in which Giant Despair represents Despair, he would be an allegorical figure. In reality however he is an invention giving an imaginary answer to the question, "What might Christ become like if there really were a world like Narnia and He chose to be incarnate and die and rise again in *that* world as he actually has done in ours?" This is not allegory at all.[30]

Lewis thus invites his readers to enter into a world of supposals. Suppose God did decide to become incarnate in a world like Narnia. How would this work out? What would it *look* like? Narnia is a narrative exploration of this theological assumption. Lewis's own explanation of how the figure of Aslan is to be interpreted makes it clear that *The Lion, the Witch and the Wardrobe* is a supposal—the imaginative exploration of an interesting possibility. "Let us *suppose* that there were a land like Narnia and that the Son of God, as He became a Man in our world, became a Lion there, and then imagine what would happen."[31]

In *The Magician's Nephew*, Lewis describes a forest full of entrances to other worlds. One of these entrances leads to Narnia, a new world soon to be populated with sentient creatures, both animal and human. Yet Lewis is quite clear that there are worlds beyond Narnia. Narnia is, so to speak, a theological case study, capable of illuminating our own situation. It provokes thought, rather than answering questions. It demands that we work out the answers for ourselves, rather than accept them predigested. Lewis uses Narnia to *show* us something without really *arguing* for it, relying on the power of his imagery and narrative style to allow our imaginations to supplement what reason merely suggests.

NARNIA AND THE RETELLING OF THE GRAND NARRATIVE

It is impossible to understand the deep appeal of Narnia without appreciating the place of stories in shaping our understanding of reality, and our own place within that reality. The Chronicles of Narnia resonate strongly with the basic human intuition that our own story is part of something grander—which, once grasped, allows us to see our situation in a new and more meaningful way. A veil is lifted, a door is opened, a curtain is drawn aside—and we are enabled to enter a new realm. Our own story is now seen to be part of a much bigger story, which helps us both understand how we fit into a greater scheme of things and discover and value the difference we can make.

Like Tolkien, Lewis was deeply aware of the imaginative power of "myths"—stories that tried to make sense of who we are, where we find ourselves, what has gone wrong with things, and what can be done about it. Tolkien was able to use myth to saturate *The Lord of the Rings* with a mysterious "otherness," a sense of mystery and magic which hints at a reality beyond that which human reason can fathom. Lewis realized that good and evil, danger, anguish, and joy can all be seen more clearly when "dipped in a story." Through their "presentational realism," these narratives provide a way of grasping the deeper structures of our world at both the imaginative and rational levels.[32]

Lewis may also have come to realize the power of myth through reading G. K. Chesterton's *The Everlasting Man*, with its classic distinction between "imaginary" and "imaginative," and deft analysis of how the imagination reaches beyond the limits of reason. "Every true artist," Chesterton argues, feels "that he is touching transcendental truths; that his images are shadows of things seen through the veil."[33]

Steeped in the riches of medieval and Renaissance literature, and with a deep understanding of how myths work, Lewis managed to find the right voice and the right words to get past the suspicions of a "fully waking imagination of a logical mind."[34] Somehow, Narnia seems to provide a deeper, brighter, more wonderful, and more meaningful world than anything we know from our own experience. Though its readers all know that the Chronicles of Narnia are fictional, the books nevertheless seem far more true to life than many supposedly factual works.[35]

Lewis always recognised that the same story might be a "myth" to one reader, and not to another.[36] The stories of Narnia seem childish nonsense to some. But to others, they are utterly transformative. For the latter group, these evocative stories affirm that it is possible for the weak and foolish to have a noble calling in a dark world; that our deepest intuitions point us to the true meaning of things; that there is indeed something beautiful and wonderful at the heart of the universe, and that this may be found, embraced, and adored.

The contrast with Tolkien's *Lord of the Rings* is important here. The complex and dark narrative of *The Lord of the Rings* is about finding a master ring that rules the other rings—and then destroying it, because it turns out to be so dangerous and destructive. Lewis's Chronicles of Narnia are about finding a master story that makes sense of all other stories—and then embracing that story with delight because of its power to give meaning and value to life. Yet Lewis's narrative nevertheless subtly raises darker questions. Which story is the true story? Which stories are merely its shadows and echoes? And which are mere fabrications—tales spun to entrap and deceive?

At an early stage in *The Lion, the Witch and the Wardrobe*, the four children begin to hear stories about the true origins and destiny of Narnia. Puzzled, they find they have to make decisions about which people and which stories are to be trusted. Is Narnia *really* the realm of the White Witch? Or is she a usurper, whose power will be broken when two Sons of Adam and two Daughters of Eve sit on the four thrones at Cair Paravel? Is Narnia *really* the realm of the mysterious Aslan, whose return is expected at any time?

Gradually, one narrative emerges as supremely plausible—the story of Aslan. Each individual story of Narnia turns out to be part of this greater narrative. *The Lion, the Witch and the Wardrobe* hints at (and partially discloses) the big picture, expanded in the remainder of the Narnia series. This "grand narrative" of interlocking stories makes sense of the riddles the children see and experience around them. It allows the children to understand their experiences with a new clarity and depth, like a camera lens bringing a landscape into sharp focus.

Yet Lewis did not invent this Narnian narrative. He borrowed and adapted one that he already knew well, and had found to be true and trustworthy—the Christian narrative of Creation, Fall, redemption, and final consummation. Following his late-evening conversation with Tolkien and Dyson about Christianity as the true myth in September 1931, Lewis began to grasp the explanatory and imaginative power of an incarnational faith. As we saw (page 134), Lewis came to believe in Christianity partly because of the quality of its literary vision—its ability to give a faithful and realistic account of life. Lewis was thus drawn to Christianity not so much by the arguments in its favour, but by its compelling vision of reality, which he could not ignore—and, as events proved, could not resist.

The Chronicles of Narnia are an imaginative retelling of the Christian grand narrative, fleshed out with ideas Lewis absorbed from the Christian literary tradition. The basic theological themes that Lewis set out in *Mere Christianity* are transposed to their original narrative forms in Narnia, allowing the deep structure of the world to be seen with clarity and brilliance: a good and beautiful creation is spoiled and ruined by a fall, in which the creator's power is denied and usurped. The creator then enters into the creation to break the power of the usurper, and restore things through a redemptive sacrifice. Yet even after the coming of the redeemer, the struggle against sin and evil continues, and will not be ended until the final restoration and transformation of all things. This Christian metanarrative—which early Christian writers called the "economy of salvation"—provides both a narrative framework and a theological underpinning to the multiple stories woven together in Lewis's Chronicles of Narnia.

Lewis's remarkable achievement in the Chronicles of Narnia is to allow his readers to inhabit this metanarrative—to get inside the story, and feel what it is like to be part of it. *Mere Christianity* allows us to understand Christian ideas; the Narnia stories allow us to step inside and *experience* the Christian story, and to judge it by its ability to make sense of things, and "chime in" with our deepest intuitions about truth, beauty, and goodness. If the series is read in the order of publication, the reader enters this narrative in *The Lion, the Witch and the Wardrobe*, which concerns the coming—technically the "advent"—of the redeemer. *The Magician's Nephew* deals with the narrative of creation and fall, while *The Last Battle* concerns the ending of the old order, and the advent of a new creation.

The remaining four novels (*Prince Caspian*, *The Voyage of the "Dawn Treader," The Horse and His Boy*, and *The Silver Chair*) deal with the period between these two advents. Lewis here explores the life of faith, lived in the tension between the past and future comings of Aslan. Aslan is now at one and the same time an object of memory and of hope. Lewis speaks of an exquisite longing for Aslan, when he cannot be seen clearly; of a robust yet gracious faith, able to withstand cynicism and skepticism; of people of character who walk trustingly through the shadowlands, seeing "in a mirror darkly" and learning to deal with a world in which they are assaulted by evil and doubt.

The Screwtape Letters brought a fresh perspective to the Christian's struggles with temptation and doubt through its ingenious narrative framework of a master devil and his apprentice (page 217). The Chronicles of Narnia have a far greater scope and reach, using an imaginatively transposed version of the Christian narrative to enable its readers to understand and cope with the ambiguities and challenges of the life of faith. An imaginative engagement with Narnia prepares the way for, and helps give rise to, a more reasoned and mature internalization of the Christian grand narrative. Rarely has a work of literature combined such narrative power, spiritual discernment, and pedagogical wisdom.

In the following chapter, we shall both explore some rooms and open a few windows, focussing especially on the first and, in my estimation, best of the Narnia works—*The Lion, the Witch and the Wardrobe*.

CHAPTER 12

NARNIA: EXPLORING AN IMAGINATIVE WORLD

There are two main ways of exploring the Chronicles of Narnia. One—the easier, and by far the more natural—involves thinking of the individual novels as rooms in a house. We stroll around the rooms and their contents, enjoying working out how they are connected by corridors and doors. We are like tourists, wandering around a new town or country, taking in the sights and enjoying ourselves. And there is nothing wrong with this. Narnia, like any rich landscape, is worth exploring and getting to know. And, like most tourists, we might take a map of Narnia with us to help us make sense of what we see.

Yet there is a second way of reading the Narnian novels, which involves the imagination as the primary organ of investigation. This second way does not invalidate the first, but builds upon it and takes it further. Once more, we think of the Narnian novels as rooms in a house. Once more, we wander around the house, taking everything in. But we realise that the *rooms in this house have windows*. And when we look through them, we see things in a new way. We can see farther than before, as the landscape opens up in front of us. And what we come to see is not an accumulation of individual facts, but the bigger picture which underlies them. When seen in this way, our imaginative experience of Narnia enlarges our sense of reality. Living in our own world feels different afterwards.

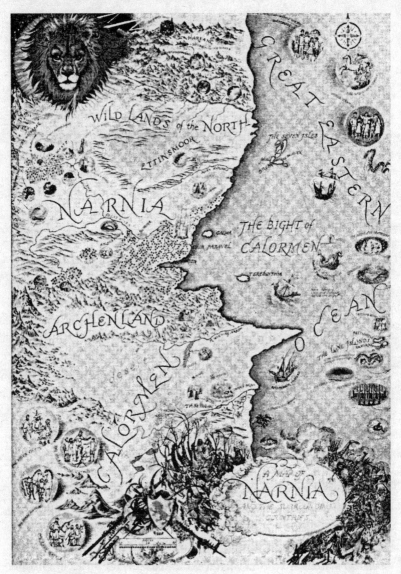

12.1 "Map of Narnia," drawn by Pauline Baynes.

Exploring Narnia is thus not just about encountering this strange and wonderful land; it is also about allowing it to shape the way we see our own land and our own lives. To use Lewis's way of speaking, we can see Narnia as a *spectacle*, something to be studied in its own right, or we can see it—whether additionally or alternatively—as a *pair of spectacles*, something that makes it possible to see everything else in a new way, as things are brought into sharp focus. The story captivates us, making us see things its way—setting to one side the ordinary, and seeing the extraordinary instead.

So let us enter the world of *The Lion, the Witch and the Wardrobe*, and explore both that strange place and the new ways of seeing things that it makes possible. And where better to begin than with its central character, the magnificent lion Aslan?

ASLAN: THE HEART'S DESIRE

How did Lewis develop the idea and image of a noble lion as his central character? Lewis himself seems to disclaim any privileged insight here. He once remarked, "I don't know where the Lion came from or why He came. But once He was there He pulled the whole story together." It is not, however, difficult to suggest possible explanations of how Aslan came "bounding into" Lewis's imagination.[1] Lewis's close friend Charles Williams had written a novel titled *The Place of the Lion* (1931), which Lewis had read with interest, clearly appreciating how the image could be developed further.

The use of the image of a lion as a central character made perfect literary and theological sense to Lewis. A lion was already used widely in the Christian theological tradition as an image of Christ, following the New Testament's reference to Christ as the "Lion of the tribe of Judah, the Root of David" (Revelation 5:5). Furthermore, a lion is the traditional symbol associated with Lewis's childhood church, St. Mark's Anglican Church in Dundela, located on the outskirts of Belfast. The church's rectory, which Lewis visited regularly as a child, had a door knocker in the form of a lion's head. The use of the image of a lion is relatively easy to understand. But what about the lion's name?

Lewis came across the specific name *Aslan* in the notes to Edward Lane's translation of the *Arabian Nights* (1838). The name *Aslan* is particularly significant in Ottoman colonial history. Until the end of the First World War, Turkey was an imperial power, exercising considerable political and economic influence in many parts of the Middle East. Although Lewis links his discovery of the term with the *Arabian Nights*, it is entirely possible that he also came to know of it through Richard Davenport's classic study of 1838, *The Life of Ali Pasha, of Tepeleni, Vizier of Epirus: Surnamed Aslan, or the Lion*. Davenport had earlier published an important life of Edmund Spenser (1822), which Lewis would have encountered while researching the poet. This Ottoman lineage explains how Lewis came to use the Turkish name "Aslan" for his great lion. "It is the Turkish for Lion. I pronounce it Ass-lan myself. And of course I meant the Lion of Judah."[2]

The most characteristic feature of Lewis's Aslan is that he evokes *awe and wonder*. Lewis develops this theme with relation to Aslan by emphasising the fact that he is *wild*—an awe-inspiring, magnificent creature, which has not been tamed through domestication, or had his claws pulled out to ensure he is powerless. As the Beaver whispers to the children, "He's wild, you know. Not like a *tame* lion."[3]

To understand the literary force of Lewis's depiction of Aslan, we need to appreciate the importance of Lewis's early reading of Rudolf Otto's classic religious work *The Idea of the Holy* (1923). This work, which Lewis first read in 1936 and regularly identified as one of the most important books he had ever read,[4] persuaded him of the importance of the "numinous"—a mysterious and awe-inspiring quality of certain things or beings, real or imagined, which Lewis described as seemingly "lit by a light from beyond the world."[5]

Lewis devotes a substantial part of the opening chapter of *The Problem of Pain* to an analysis of Otto's idea, and offers one specific literary illustration of its importance.[6] Lewis notes the passage in Kenneth Grahame's *The Wind in the Willows* (1908) in which Rat and Mole approach Pan:

> "Rat!" [Mole] found breath to whisper, shaking, "Are you afraid?"
>
> "Afraid?" murmured the Rat, his eyes shining with unutterable love. "Afraid? Of HIM? O never, never! And yet—and yet—O Mole, I am afraid!"[7]

This passage deserves to be read in full, as it had clearly influenced Lewis's depiction of the impact of Aslan on the children and animals in Narnia. For example, Grahame speaks of Mole's experiencing "an awe that smote and held him and, without seeing, he knew it could only mean that some august Presence was very, very near."[8]

Otto's account of numinous experience identifies two distinct themes: a *mysterium tremendum*, a sense of mystery which evokes fear and trembling; and *mysterium fascinans*, a mystery which fascinates and attracts. The numinous, for Otto, can thus terrify or energise, giving rise to a sense of either fear or delight, as suggested in Grahame's dialogue. Other writers reframed the idea in terms of a "nostalgia for paradise," which evokes an overwhelming sense of belonging elsewhere.

In describing the reaction of the children to the Beaver's softly whispered confidence that "Aslan is on the move—perhaps has already landed," Lewis offers one of the finest literary statements of the impact of the numinous:

> And now a very curious thing happened. None of the children
> knew who Aslan was any more than you do; but the moment
> the Beaver had spoken these words everyone felt quite different.
> Perhaps it has sometimes happened to you in a dream that
> someone says something which you don't understand but in the
> dream it feels as if it had some enormous meaning—either a
> terrifying one which turns the whole dream into a nightmare or
> else a lovely meaning too lovely to put into words, which makes

the dream so beautiful that you remember it all your life and
are always wishing you could get into that dream again. It was
like that now. At the name of Aslan each one of the children felt
something jump in its inside.[9]

Lewis then describes how this "numinous" reality impacts each of
the four children in a quite different manner. For some, it evokes fear and
trembling; for others, a sense of unutterable love and longing:

Edmund felt a sensation of mysterious horror. Peter felt suddenly
brave and adventurous. Susan felt as if some delicious smell or
some delightful strain of music had just floated by her. And Lucy
got the feeling you have when you wake up in the morning and
realize that it is the beginning of the holidays or the beginning
of summer.[10]

Susan's thoughts are clearly based on Lewis's classic analysis of "longing,"
found especially in his 1941 sermon "The Weight of Glory," which speaks
of this desire as "the scent of a flower we have not found" or "the echo of
a tune we have not heard."[11]

Lewis is here setting out, in a preliminary yet still powerful form, his
core theme of Aslan as the heart's desire. Aslan evokes wonder, awe, and
an "unutterable love." Even the name *Aslan* speaks to the depths of the
soul. What would it be like to meet him? Lewis captures this complex
sense of awe mingled with longing in the reaction of Peter to the Beaver's
declarations about this magnificent lion, who is "the King of the wood
and the son of the great Emperor-beyond-the-Sea." "'I'm longing to see
him,' said Peter, 'even if I do feel frightened.'"[12]

Lewis here transposes one of the central themes of works such as
Mere Christianity into an imaginative mode. There is indeed a deep emptiness within human nature, a longing which none but God can satisfy.
Using Aslan as God's proxy, Lewis constructs a narrative of yearning and
wistfulness, tinged with the hope of ultimate fulfilment. That this is no

misguided strategy is strongly suggested by a powerful passage in the writings of Bertrand Russell (1872–1970), easily one of the most articulate and influential British atheist writers of the twentieth century:

> The centre of me is always and eternally a terrible pain . . .
> a searching for something beyond what the world contains,
> something transfigured and infinite. The beatific vision—God.
> I do not find it, I do not think it is to be found—but the love of
> it is my life. . . . It is the actual spring of life within me.[13]

When, towards the end of *The Voyage of the "Dawn Treader,"* Lucy piteously declares that she cannot bear to be separated from Aslan, she echoes this theme of the longing of the human heart for God. If she and Edmund return to their own country, they fear they will never see Aslan again.

> "It isn't Narnia, you know," sobbed Lucy. "It's *you*. We shan't
> meet *you* there. And how can we live, never meeting you?"
>   "But you shall meet me, dear one," said Aslan.
>   "Are—are you there too, Sir?" said Edmund.
>   "I am," said Aslan. "But there I have another name. You must
> learn to know me by that name. This was the very reason why
> you were brought to Narnia, that by knowing me here for a little,
> you may know me better there."[14]

In using Aslan as a figure or type of Christ, Lewis stands within a long and continuing tradition of Christ figures in literature and film, such as Santiago, the "Old Man" in Ernest Hemingway's *The Old Man and the Sea* (1952).[15] Such Christ figures are found in literature of all genres, including children's books. The phenomenally successful Harry Potter series of novels incorporates a number of such themes. Gandalf is one of a number of Christ figures within Tolkien's *Lord of the Rings*, whose Christological role and associations are accentuated in Peter Jackson's recent film version of the epic series.[16]

Lewis develops many of the classic Christological statements of the New Testament in the Chronicles of Narnia, generally focussing these on the person of Aslan. Yet perhaps his most intriguing reworking of a classic theological theme concerns his depiction of the death and resurrection of Aslan in *The Lion, the Witch and the Wardrobe*. So what does Lewis understand by atonement?

THE DEEPER MAGIC: ATONEMENT IN NARNIA

One major theme in Christian theological reflection concerns how the death of Christ on the cross is to be interpreted, especially in relation to the salvation of humanity. These ways of interpreting the Cross, traditionally referred to as "theories of the Atonement," have played a major role in Christian discussion and debate through the ages. Lewis positions his account of the death of Aslan at the hands of the White Witch within the context of this stream of thinking. But what ideas does Lewis himself develop?

Before considering this question, we need to appreciate that Lewis was not a professional theologian, and did not have any expert knowledge of the historical debates within the Christian tradition on this question. While some have tried to relate Lewis to, for example, the medieval debate between Anselm of Canterbury and Peter Abelard, this is not a particularly profitable approach. Lewis tends to know theological ideas through their literary embodiments. It is therefore not to professional theologians that we must turn to explore Lewis's ideas on the Atonement, but to the English literary tradition—to works such as *Piers Plowman*, John Milton's *Paradise Lost*, or the medieval mystery plays. It is here that we will find the approaches that Lewis weaves into his Narnian narrative.

Lewis's first discussion of approaches to the Atonement is found in *The Problem of Pain* (1940). Lewis argues that any *theory* of the Atonement is secondary to the *actuality* of it. While these various theories may be useful to some, Lewis remarks, "they do no good to me, and I am not going to invent others."[17]

Lewis returns to this theme in his broadcast talks of the 1940s. Lewis here remarks that, before he became a Christian, he held the view that Christians were obliged to take a specific position on the meaning of Christ's death, and especially how it brought about salvation. One such theory was that human beings deserved to be punished for their sin, but "Christ volunteered to be punished instead, and so God let us off." After his conversion, however, Lewis came to realise that theories about redemption are of secondary importance:

> What I came to see later on was that neither this theory nor any other is Christianity. The central Christian belief is that Christ's death has somehow put us right with God and given us a fresh start. Theories as to how it did this are another matter.[18]

In other words, "theories of the Atonement" are not the heart of Christianity; rather, they are attempts to explain how it works.

We see here Lewis's characteristic resistance to the primacy of theory over theological or literary actuality. It is perfectly possible to "accept what Christ has done without knowing how it works." Theories are always, Lewis holds, secondary to what they represent:

> We are told that Christ was killed for us, that His death has washed out our sins, and that by dying He disabled death itself. That's the formula. That's Christianity. That's what has to be believed. Any theories we build up as to how Christ's death did all this are, in my view, quite secondary: mere plans or diagrams to be left alone if they don't help us, and, even if they do help us, not to be confused with the thing itself.[19]

These reflections are in no way inconsistent with actually adopting such a theory; they merely set a theory in context, insisting that it is like a plan or diagram, which is "not to be confused with the thing itself."

One of the most shocking and disturbing scenes in *The Lion, the Witch and the Wardrobe* is the death of Aslan. Where the New Testament speaks of the death of Christ as redeeming humanity, Lewis presents Aslan's death as initially benefitting one person, and one person only—Edmund. The easily misled boy falls into the hands of the White Witch. Alarmed that the presence of humans in Narnia is a portent of the end of her reign, she attempts to neutralise them, using Edmund as her unwitting agent. In his attempts to secure her goodwill (and more Turkish Delight), Edmund deceives his siblings. And that act of deception proves to be a theological turning point.

The White Witch demands a meeting with Aslan, at which she declares that Edmund, by committing such an act of betrayal, has come under her authority. She has a right to his life, and she intends to exercise that right. The Deep Magic built into Narnia at its beginning by the Emperor-beyond-the-Sea laid down "that every traitor belongs to me as my lawful prey and that for every treachery I have a right to a kill."[20] Edmund is hers. His life is forfeit. And she demands his blood.

Then a secret deal is done, of which the children know nothing. Aslan agrees to act as a substitute for Edmund. He will die, so that Edmund may live. Unaware of what is about to happen, Lucy and Susan follow Aslan as he walks towards the hill of the Stone Table, to be bound and to offer to die himself at the hands of the White Witch. This scene is as moving as it is horrific, and parallels at some points—but not at others—the New Testament accounts of Christ's final hours in the garden of Gethsemane and his subsequent crucifixion. Aslan is put to death, surrounded by a baying mob, who mock him in his final agony.

One of the most moving scenes in the entire Narnia series describes how Susan and Lucy approach the dead lion, kneeling before him as they "kissed his cold face and stroked his beautiful fur," crying "till they could cry no more."[21] Lewis here shows himself at his imaginative best, reworking the themes of the images and texts of medieval piety—such as the classic *Pietà* (the image of the dead Christ being held by his mother, Mary), and the text *Stabat Mater Dolorosa* (describing the pain and sorrow of Mary at Calvary, as she weeps at the scene of Christ's death).

Then everything is unexpectedly transformed. Aslan comes back to life. The witnesses to this dramatic moment are Lucy and Susan alone, paralleling the New Testament's insistence that the first witnesses to the resurrection of Christ were three women. They are astonished and delighted, flinging themselves upon Aslan and covering him with kisses. What has happened?

"But what does it all mean?" asked Susan when they were somewhat calmer.

"It means," said Aslan, "that though the Witch knew the Deep Magic, there is a magic deeper still which she did not know. Her knowledge goes back only to the dawn of time. But if she could have looked a little further back, into the stillness and the darkness before Time dawned, she would have read there a different incantation. She would have known that when a willing victim who had committed no treachery was killed in a traitor's stead, the Table would crack and Death itself would start working backward."[22]

Aslan thus lives again, and Edmund is liberated from any legitimate claim on the White Witch's part.

And there is still more to come. The courtyard of the White Witch's castle is filled with petrified Narnians, turned into stone by the Witch. Following his resurrection, Aslan breaks down the castle gates, romps into the courtyard, breathes upon the statues, and restores them to life. Finally, he leads the liberated army through the shattered gates of the once-great fortress to fight for the freedom of Narnia. It is a dramatic and highly satisfying end to the narrative.

But where do these ideas come from? They are all derived from the writings of the Middle Ages—not works of academic theology, which generally were critical of such highly visual and dramatic approaches, but the popular religious literature of the age, which took pleasure in a powerful narrative of Satan's being outmanoeuvred and outwitted by Christ.[23] According to these popular atonement theories, Satan had rightful possession over sinful human beings. God was unable to wrest humanity from Satan's grasp by any legitimate means. Yet what if Satan were to overstep his legitimate authority, and claim the life of a sinless person—such as Jesus Christ, who, as God incarnate, was devoid of sin?

The great mystery plays of the Middle Ages—such as the cycle performed at York in the fourteenth and fifteenth centuries—dramatised the way in which a wily and canny God tricked Satan into overstepping his rights, and thus forfeiting them all. An arrogant Satan received his comeuppance, to howls of approval from the assembled townspeople. A central theme of this great popular approach to atonement was the "Harrowing of Hell"—a dramatic depiction of the risen Christ battering the gates of hell, and setting free all who were imprisoned within its realm.[24] All of humanity were thus liberated by the death and resurrection of Christ. In Narnia, Edmund is the first to be saved by Aslan; the remainder are restored to life later, as Aslan breathes on the stone statues in the Witch's castle.

Lewis's narrative in *The Lion, the Witch and the Wardrobe* contains all the main themes of this medieval atonement drama: Satan having rights over sinful humanity; God outwitting Satan because of the sinlessness of Christ; and the breaking down of the gates of Hell, leading to the liberation of its prisoners. The imagery is derived from the great medieval popular religious writings which Lewis so admired and enjoyed.

So what are we to make of this approach to atonement? Most theologians regard Lewis's narrative depiction of atonement with mild amusement, seeing it as muddled and confused. But this is to misunderstand both the nature of Lewis's sources and his intentions. The great medieval mystery plays aimed to make the theological abstractions of atonement accessible, interesting, and above all *entertaining*. Lewis has brought his own distinct approach to this undertaking, but its historical roots and imaginative appeal are quite clear.

THE SEVEN PLANETS: MEDIEVAL SYMBOLISM IN NARNIA

Each of the seven Chronicles of Narnia has its own distinct literary identity—a "feel" or "atmosphere" that gives each novel its own place in the septet. So how did Lewis maintain the unity of the narrative as a whole, while giving each novel its own characteristic individuality?

It is a classic issue in literary history. Lewis would have known that Richard Wagner (1813–1883) managed to maintain the thematic unity of his massive operatic cycle *The Ring of the Nibelungs* by using musical motifs that recurred throughout the four operas of the drama, acting as threads that hold its fabric together. So what did Lewis do?

Lewis's reading of the Elizabethan Renaissance poet Edmund Spenser (ca. 1552–1599) led him to discover and appreciate the importance of a unifying device that allowed Spenser to bind together complex and diverse plots, characters, and adventures. Spenser's *Faerie Queene* (1590–1596) is a vast work, which Lewis realised maintained its unity and cohesion by a superb literary device—one that he himself would use in the Chronicles of Narnia.

What is this unifying device? Quite simply, according to Lewis, it is Faerie Land, which provides a place that is "so exceeding spatious and wide" that it can be packed full of adventures without loss of unity. "'Faerie Land' itself provides the unity—a unity not of plot, but of *milieu*."[25] A central narrative holds each of Spenser's seven books together, while at the same time providing space for "a loose fringe of stories," which are subordinate to its central structure.

The land of Narnia plays a role in Lewis's narrative which parallels that of Faerie Land for Spenser's. Lewis realised how a complex narrative can easily degenerate into a bundle of unrelated stories. Somehow, they had to be held together. It is perhaps no accident that there are seven books in the Chronicles of Narnia, paralleling the structure—though not the substance—of Spenser's *Faerie Queene*. The land of Narnia allows Lewis to give an overall thematic unity to the septet. But how did he give each novel its own distinct literary aura? How did he ensure that each constituent part of the Chronicles of Narnia had a coherent identity in its own right?

Lewis's critics and interpreters have devoted much attention to decoding the significance of the seven Narnia novels. Of the many debates, the most interesting is this: why are there *seven* novels? Speculation has been intense. We have already noted that Spenser's *Faerie Queen* has seven books, perhaps suggesting that Lewis saw his own work as paralleling this Elizabethan classic. And maybe it does—but if so, only in some very specific respects, such as the unifying role of Faerie Land for a complex narrative. Or perhaps it is an allusion to the seven sacraments? Possibly—but Lewis was an Anglican, not a Catholic, and recognised only two sacraments. Or perhaps there is an allusion to the seven deadly sins? Possibly—but any attempt to assign the novels to individual sins, such as pride or lust, seems hopelessly forced and unnatural. For example, which of the Narnia Chronicles majors on *gluttony*? Amidst the wreckage of these implausible suggestions, an alternative has recently emerged—that Lewis was shaped by what the great English seventeenth-century poet John Donne called "the Heptarchy, the seven kingdoms of the seven planets." And amazingly, this one seems to work.

The idea was first put forward by Oxford Lewis scholar Michael Ward in 2008.[26] Noting the importance that Lewis assigns to the seven planets in his studies of medieval literature, Ward suggests that the Narnia novels reflect and embody the thematic characteristics associated in the "discarded" medieval worldview with the seven planets. In the pre-Copernican worldview, which dominated the Middle Ages, Earth was understood to be stationary; the seven "planets" revolved around Earth. These medieval planets were the Sun, the Moon, Mercury, Venus, Mars, Jupiter, and Saturn. Lewis does not include Uranus, Neptune, and Pluto, since these were only discovered in the eighteenth, nineteenth, and twentieth centuries, respectively.

So what is Lewis doing? Ward is not suggesting that Lewis reverts to a pre-Copernican cosmology, nor that he endorses the arcane world of astrology. His point is much more subtle, and has enormous imaginative potential. For Ward, Lewis regarded the seven planets as being part of a poetically rich and imaginatively satisfying symbolic system. Lewis therefore took the imaginative and emotive characteristics which the Middle

Ages associated with each of the seven planets, and attached these to each of the seven novels as follows:

1. *The Lion, the Witch and the Wardrobe*: Jupiter
2. *Prince Caspian*: Mars
3. *The Voyage of the "Dawn Treader"*: the Sun
4. *The Silver Chair*: the Moon
5. *The Horse and His Boy*: Mercury
6. *The Magician's Nephew*: Venus
7. *The Last Battle*: Saturn

For example, Ward argues that *Prince Caspian* shows the thematic influence of Mars.[27] This is seen primarily at two levels. First, Mars was the ancient god of war (*Mars Gradivus*). This immediately connects to the dominance of military language, imagery, and issues in this novel. The four Pevensie children arrive in Narnia "in the middle of a war"—"the Great War of Deliverance," as it is referred to later in the series, or the "Civil War" in Lewis's own "Outline of Narnian History."

Yet in an earlier phase of the classical tradition, Mars was also a vegetation deity (known as *Mars Silvanus*), associated with burgeoning trees, woods, and forests. The northern spring month of March, during which vegetation comes back to life after winter, was named after this deity. Many readers of *Prince Caspian* have noted its emphasis on vegetation and trees. This otherwise puzzling association, Ward argues, is easily accommodated within the range of ideas associated with Mars by the medieval tradition.

If Ward is right, Lewis has crafted each novel in the light of the atmosphere associated with one of the planets in the medieval tradition. This does not necessarily mean that this symbolism determines the plot of each novel, or the overall series; it does, however, help us understand something of the thematic identity and stylistic tone of each individual novel.

Ward's analysis is generally agreed to have opened up important new ways of thinking about the Narnia series, although further discussion and evaluation will probably lead to modification of some of its details.

There is clearly more to Lewis's imaginative genius than his earlier interpreters appreciated. If Ward is right, Lewis has used themes drawn from his own specialist field of medieval and Renaissance literature to ensure the coherency of the Chronicles of Narnia as a whole, while at the same time giving each book its own distinct identity.

THE SHADOWLANDS: REWORKING PLATO'S CAVE

"It's all in Plato, all in Plato: bless me, what *do* they teach them at these schools!"[28] Lewis places these words in the mouth of Lord Digory in *The Last Battle*, as he tries to explain that the "old Narnia," which had a historical beginning and end, was really "only a shadow or a copy of the real Narnia which has always been here and always will be here."[29] A central theme of many of Lewis's writings is that we live in a world that is a "bright shadow" of something greater and better. The present world is a "copy" or "shadow" of the real world. This idea is found both in the New Testament in different forms—especially the letter to the Hebrews—and in the great literary and philosophical tradition which takes its inspiration from the classical Greek philosopher Plato (ca. 424–348 BC).

We see this theme developed in the climax of the epic of Narnia, *The Last Battle*. Lewis here invites us to imagine a room with a window that looks out onto a beautiful valley or a vast seascape. On a wall opposite this window is a mirror. Imagine looking out of the window, and then turning and seeing the same thing reflected in the mirror. What, Lewis asks, is the relationship between these two different ways of seeing things?

> The sea in the mirror, or the valley in the mirror, were in one sense just the same as the real ones: yet at the same time they were somehow different—deeper, more wonderful, more like places in a story: in a story you have never heard but very much want to know. The difference between the old Narnia and the new Narnia was like that. The new one was a deeper country: every rock and flower and blade of grass looked as if it meant more.[30]

We live in the shadowlands, in which we hear echoes of the music of heaven, catch sight of its bright colours, and discern its soft fragrance in the air we breathe. But it is not the real thing; it is a signpost, too easily mistaken for the real thing.

The image of a mirror helps Lewis explain the difference between the old Narnia (which must pass away) and the new Narnia. Yet perhaps the most important Platonic image used by Lewis is found in *The Silver Chair*—Plato's Cave. In his dialogue *The Republic*, Plato asks his readers to imagine a dark cave, in which a group of people have lived since their birth. They have been trapped there for their entire lives, and know about no other world. At one end of the cave, a fire burns brightly, providing them with both warmth and light. As the flames rise, they cast shadows on the walls of the cave. The people watch these shadows projected on the wall in front of them, wondering what they represent. For those living in the cave, this world of flickering shadows is all that they know. Their grasp of reality is limited to what they see and experience in this dark prison. If there is a world beyond the cave, it is something which they do not know and cannot imagine. They know only about the shadows.

Lewis explores this idea through his distinction between the "Overworld" and the "Underworld" in *The Silver Chair*. The inhabitants of the Underworld—like the people in Plato's Cave—believe that there is no other reality. When the Narnian prince speaks of an Overworld, lit up by a sun, the Witch argues that he is simply making it up, copying realities in the Underworld. The prince then tries to use an analogy to help his audience understand his point:

> "You see that lamp. It is round and yellow and gives light to the whole room; and hangeth moreover from the roof. Now that thing which we call the sun is like the lamp, only far greater and brighter. It giveth light to the whole Overworld and hangeth in the sky."
>
> "Hangeth from what, my Lord?" asked the Witch; and then,

while they were all still thinking how to answer her, she added, with another of her soft, silver laughs, "You see? When you try to think out clearly what this *sun* must be, you cannot tell me. You can only tell me it is like the lamp. Your *sun* is a dream; and there is nothing in that dream that was not copied from the lamp. The lamp is the real thing; the *sun* is but a tale, a children's story."[31]

Then Jill intervenes: what about Aslan? He's a *lion*! The Witch, slightly less confidently now, asks Jill to tell her about lions. What are they like? Well, they're like a big cat! The Witch laughs. A lion is just an imagined cat, bigger and better than the real thing. "You can put nothing into your make-believe without copying it from the real world, this world of mine, which is the only world."[32]

Most readers of this section of the book will smile at this point, realising that a seemingly sophisticated philosophical argument is clearly invalidated by the context within which Lewis sets it. Yet Lewis has borrowed this from Plato—while using Anselm of Canterbury and René Descartes as intermediaries—thus allowing classical wisdom to make an essentially Christian point.

Lewis is clearly aware that Plato has been viewed through a series of interpretative lenses—those of Plotinus, Augustine, and the Renaissance being particularly familiar to him. Readers of Lewis's *Allegory of Love*, *The Discarded Image*, *English Literature in the Sixteenth Century*, and *Spenser's Images of Life* will be aware that Lewis frequently highlights how extensively Plato and later Neoplatonists influenced Christian literary writers of both the Middle Ages and the Renaissance. Lewis's achievement is to work Platonic themes and images into children's literature in such a natural way that few, if any, of its young readers are aware of Narnia's implicit philosophical tutorials, or its grounding in an earlier world of thought. It is all part of Lewis's tactic of expanding minds by exposing them to such ideas in a highly accessible and imaginative form.

THE PROBLEM OF THE PAST IN NARNIA

Anyone reading *The Lion, the Witch and the Wardrobe* for the first time is likely to be impressed by its medieval imagery—its royal courts, castles, and chivalrous knights. It bears little relation to the 1939 world from which the four children come—or to that of subsequent readers. So is Lewis encouraging his readers to retreat into the past to escape the realities of modern life?

There are unquestionably points at which Lewis believes the past to be preferable to the present. For example, Lewis's battle scenes tend to emphasise the importance of boldness and bravery in personal combat. Battle is about hand-to-hand and face-to-face encounters between noble and dignified foes, in which killing is a regrettable but necessary part of securing victory. This is far removed from the warfare Lewis himself experienced in the fields around Arras in late 1917 and early 1918, where an impersonal technology hurled explosive death from a distance, often destroying friend as well as foe. There was nothing brave or bold about modern artillery or machine guns. You hardly ever got to see who killed you.

Yet Lewis is not expecting his readers to retreat to a nostalgic and imaginary re-creation of the Middle Ages; still less is he urging us to re-create its ideas and values. Rather, Lewis is giving us a way of thinking by which we can judge our own ideas, and come to realise that they are not necessarily "right" on account of being more recent. In the Narnia series, Lewis presents a way of thinking and living in which everything fits together into a single, complex, harmonious model of the universe—the "discarded image" which Lewis explores in so many of his later scholarly writings. In doing this, he invites us to reconsider our present ways of thinking in order to reflect on whether we have lost something on our journey, and might be able to recover it.

Yet there is a problem here. Today's readers of the Chronicles of Narnia have to make a double leap of the imagination—not simply to imagine Narnia, but to imagine the world from which its four original visitors come, shaped by the social presuppositions, hopes, and fears of

Britain in the aftermath of the Second World War. How many of today's readers of *The Lion, the Witch and the Wardrobe*—smiling at the lure of Turkish Delight for Edmund (while wondering what this mysterious substance might be)—realise that the rationing of sweets did not end in Britain until February 1953, four years after the book was written? The modest sumptuousness of Narnian feasts contrasts sharply with the austerity of postwar Britain, in which even basic foodstuffs were in short supply. To appreciate the full impact of the series on its original readers, we must try to enter into a bygone world, as well as an imagined one.

At several points, this becomes a problem for today's readers. The most obvious of these difficulties concerns the children in *The Lion, the Witch and the Wardrobe*, who are white, middle-class English boys and girls with somewhat stilted and "golly gosh" turns of phrase. Lewis's characters probably sounded a little stilted and unnatural even to his readers in the early 1950s. Many readers now need a cultural dictionary to make sense of Peter's schoolboy jargon, such as "Old chap!" "By Jove!" and "Great Scott!"

More problematically, some of the social attitudes of middle-class England during the 1930s and 1940s—and occasionally those of Lewis's own childhood during the 1910s—are deeply embedded within the Narnia novels. The most obvious of these concerns women. It is clearly unfair to criticise Lewis for failing to anticipate twenty-first-century Western cultural attitudes on this matter. Nevertheless, some have argued that Lewis allocates subordinate roles to his female characters throughout the Chronicles of Narnia, and wish he had broken free of the traditional gender roles of that age.

The case of Susan is often singled out for special comment. While playing a prominent role in *The Lion, the Witch and the Wardrobe*, she is conspicuously absent from the final volume in the series, *The Last Battle*. Philip Pullman, Lewis's most outspoken recent critic, declares that Susan "was sent to hell because she was getting interested in clothes and boys."[33] Pullman's intense hostility towards Lewis seems to subvert any serious attempt at objective evidential analysis on his part. As all readers of the

Narnia series know, at no point does Lewis suggest that Susan is "sent to hell," let alone because of an interest in "boys."

Yet Susan illustrates a concern that some recent commentators have expressed about the stories of Narnia—namely, that they tend to privilege male agents. Might Narnia have been different if Lewis had met a Ruth Pitter or a Joy Davidman in the 1930s?

It is, however, important to be fair to Lewis here. Despite the social predominance of male role models in his cultural context, the gender roles in the Chronicles of Narnia tend to be evenly balanced. Indeed, if there is a lead human character in the Chronicles of Narnia, this is played by a female. Lucy is the protagonist in *The Lion, the Witch and the Wardrobe*. She is the first to gain access to Narnia, and is the human who becomes closest to Aslan. She plays the lead role in *Prince Caspian*, and speaks the final words of human dialogue at the end of *The Last Battle*. Lewis was ahead of British views on gender roles during the 1940s, when the Chronicles of Narnia were conceived; he lags behind now—but not by as much as his critics suggest.

But we now must leave the imagined realm of Narnia, and return to the real world of Oxford in the early 1950s. As we noted earlier, Lewis was becoming increasingly beleaguered and isolated. But what could he do about it?

PART FOUR

CAMBRIDGE

THE MOVE TO CAMBRIDGE: MAGDALENE COLLEGE

I t was obvious to Lewis's friends that he did not fit readily or easily into postwar Oxford. Lewis himself was painfully aware that he was an isolated figure there in the early 1950s. He had been passed over for senior appointments on at least three occasions. Relationships within the faculty were often fractious and unpleasant. Lewis's correspondence of May 1954 speaks openly of a "crisis" within the Oxford University Faculty of English which tempted him "to hatred many times a day."[1]

A year earlier, the English faculty at Oxford had voted on extending the range of the undergraduate curriculum from 1830 to 1914, thus allowing Oxford students to study the literature of the Victorian Age. Looking back, many would feel that this represented an entirely reasonable development, particularly in the light of the literary creativity of that important age. Yet it was a development that was robustly opposed by Lewis, if somewhat less aggressively by J. R. R. Tolkien. The English faculty's challenge to the status quo—though ultimately unsuccessful— was nevertheless unsettling for Lewis, adding still further to his sense of isolation at Oxford. The Faculty of English increasingly coalesced around the "modernisers," leaving Lewis dangerously alone.

Although the Narnia series—written during Lewis's final years at Oxford, between 1949 and 1954—proved hugely successful, Lewis's correspondence suggests that he found himself at a low artistic ebb during the years 1949–1950. While his letters point to at least a partial recovery of his creative powers towards the end of 1951, Lewis remained imaginatively becalmed for some time. Despite its considerable commercial and reputational success, *Mere Christianity* was not a new book, but a reworking of four series of broadcast talks from the early 1940s. Lewis's most important work of this period was his *English Literature in the Sixteenth Century, Excluding Drama* (1954), which was a substantial work of literary scholarship, rather than a creative original composition. Furthermore, the writing of this mammoth work had exhausted him, draining him of both the energy and creativity that had characterised him as a younger man.

Lewis was also overworked. The postwar surge of students at Oxford University was creating serious difficulties for Lewis, whose tutorial responsibilities were now weighty. At Magdalen College, student numbers were escalating. Undergraduate levels had remained fairly constant at around forty during the 1930s, before slumping to record lows during the war years 1939–1945. In 1940, there were sixteen undergraduates; in 1944, only ten. After the war, the numbers soared. In 1948, there were eighty-four students; in 1952, there were seventy-six.[2] Lewis's workload became unbearable, and was clearly interfering with his academic research and writing. Although the BBC offered him an open door to make radio programmes, Lewis had to decline due to the pressure of work.[3]

But what else could he do? And where else could he go? There seemed no obvious way out of his dilemma.

THE NEW CAMBRIDGE CHAIR

Unknown to Lewis, one possible answer was emerging through developments at Oxford's great academic rival—the University of Cambridge.

Lewis had already been mentioned in the press as a possible candidate for the King Edward VII Professorship of English at Cambridge, following the death of Sir Arthur Quiller-Couch in May 1944. Late in 1944, rumours abounded that he had been offered this prestigious chair.[4] Even leading figures from the BBC wrote to ask when he was to take up the Cambridge chair.[5] Again, however, nothing came of this. In the end, the chair was filled in 1946 by Basil Willey (1897–1978), a highly regarded literary scholar and intellectual historian.

By the early 1950s, the University of Cambridge had one of the finest English faculties in the world. Its dominant personality was F. R. Leavis (1895–1978), whose approach to literary criticism Lewis detested. Yet Leavis was not popular at Cambridge. He had made enemies—including Henry Stanley Bennett (1889–1972), fellow of Emmanuel College and University Reader in English. A master of university politics and horse trading, Bennett had no doubt about what the Cambridge English faculty needed—a second chair, to supplement the existing King Edward VII Professorship. This new chair, Bennett believed, needed to be in medieval and Renaissance English. Perhaps more important, Bennett was quite clear who its first holder should be: Oxford's C. S. Lewis, a powerful and credible critic of Leavis's approach. And Bennett knew enough about university politics to make this happen.

The advertisement appeared on 31 March 1954, with a closing date for applications of 24 April.[6] On 10 May, Bennett joined seven other senior academics to elect Cambridge's first Professor of Medieval and Renaissance English in a meeting chaired by the vice-chancellor, Sir Henry Willink (1894–1973), who was also master of Magdalene College. Two of these electors were from Oxford: Lewis's former tutor at University College, F. P. Wilson, and Lewis's close colleague and (still) friend J. R. R. Tolkien.[7] Lewis, however, had not applied for the position. The committee chose to overlook this inconvenient formality. They enthusiastically and unanimously decided to offer the job to Lewis, with Helen Gardner—then fellow in English at St. Hilda's College, Oxford—as their second choice.[8]

Willink wrote personally to Lewis to offer him the position, emphasising its landmark importance. The electors, he declared, "were unanimous with a warmth and sincerity which could not have been exceeded, to invite you to become the first holder of what we feel will be a Chair of great value to the University."[9] The advantages of the position for Lewis were obvious. Moving to Cambridge would not merely extricate Lewis from a situation he was known to find difficult. It would also eliminate any responsibility on his part for undergraduate teaching, and free him to devote his time to research and writing. It would also triple Lewis's salary.

Lewis replied to Willink by return of post, declining the position.[10] In the manner of both its speed and its substance, Lewis's reply is somewhat puzzling. He responded with almost indecent haste to the offer, setting out reasons for refusing the position which seem less than compelling. Lewis suggested that he was not in a position to move to Cambridge, in that he would lose the services of Fred Paxford, his gardener and handyman. And he was, in any case, too old for a new chair; they needed someone younger and more energetic.

Yet Lewis did not trouble to ask anything about the conditions of the new position—including the critically important question of whether he would be required to move house to Cambridge. Nor does it seem to have occurred to him that the Cambridge electors were aware of his age, which was not unusual for such a senior appointment.

Willink was not impressed by Lewis's somewhat feeble reasons for declining, and was probably somewhat hurt at the speed with which Lewis had spurned Cambridge's advances. He wrote to Lewis again, urging him to reconsider his position.[11] Again, Lewis declined. There was now nothing that Willink could do, other than offer the position to Helen Gardner.

Tolkien, however, was made of sterner stuff. On the morning of 17 May, he confronted Lewis in the presence of Warnie over his reasons for declining the chair. The real problem, he soon discovered, was that Lewis had misunderstood the University of Cambridge's residence requirements for professors. He had assumed that he would have had to move lock, stock, and barrel to Cambridge, leaving behind his beloved Kilns, Paxford, and Warnie.

Tolkien had rightly discerned that there could be some flexibility here. Immediately after the meeting, Tolkien wrote two letters. First, he explained to Willink that Lewis needed to be able to keep his house in Oxford, and have college rooms in Cambridge that would be large enough to house most of his books.[12] Second, he penned a confidential letter to Bennett, expressing his faith that Cambridge would get Lewis, despite the unfortunate turn of events. They just needed to be patient. On 19 May, Lewis also wrote to Willink to clarify his situation. If he could indeed be allowed to retain his house in Oxford, while living in Cambridge during weekdays, then he would reconsider the offer.

But by then it was too late. On 18 May, Willink had written to offer the job to Helen Gardner, Cambridge's second choice.[13] Belatedly, he confirmed to Lewis that the university's residence requirements were perfectly open to allowing Lewis to live in Oxford at weekends during full term, and to reside in Oxford outside term. But this was now an academic issue. Willink informed him that a letter to "Choice No. 2"—Lewis never knew the identity of this person—had already been dispatched.[14] The matter was now closed.

But it wasn't. On 19 May, Professor Basil Willey—one of the Cambridge electors to the new chair—wrote confidentially to Willink. It now seemed "very probable" that Helen Gardner would decline the position that had just been offered to her.[15] Willey gave no indication of where this information came from, nor did he explain why Gardner was so likely to refuse Cambridge's offer.[16] But he was right.

After allowing the customary decent interval to pass to show that she was taking the offer seriously—something that Lewis had so conspicuously failed to do—Helen Gardner politely declined the chair on 3 June. She did not explain the reason for her decision. However, after Lewis's death, Gardner revealed that she had picked up rumours at that time that Lewis now wanted the chair, and that she herself had believed he was its ideal occupant.[17] Her refusal of the position reflected her knowledge of who would occupy the chair as a result. Relieved as much as delighted by Gardner's diplomatic masterstroke, Willink wrote again to Lewis: "No. 2 has declined, and I am filled with hope that after all Cambridge will obtain the acceptance of No. 1." He also mentioned that his own college, Magdalene, might be able to offer Lewis the rooms that he needed.[18]

It was enough. The deal was done. Lewis agreed to be appointed to the new chair effective 1 October 1954, but would not take up the position until 1 January 1955, allowing him time to settle his affairs in Oxford.[19] Lewis's departure from Magdalen created a vacancy in the fellowship, which had to be filled. His allies within the college quickly decided whom they wished to succeed him. Who better to follow Lewis than Owen Barfield?[20] This proposal, however, was defeated, and Lewis was eventually succeeded by Emrys L. Jones.

Was this move to Cambridge wise? Some certainly doubted it. John Wain, one of Lewis's former pupils, suggested that it was like "leaving an overblown and neglected rose-garden for a horticultural research station on the plains of Siberia."[21] Wain's meaning here was ideological, not meteorological. He was not thinking primarily of the icy east winds from the Urals that can make Cambridge so bitterly cold in winter, but of the clinically cool attitude towards literature that dominated the Cambridge English faculty at this time. Lewis was entering a lion's den—a faculty which prized "critical theory" and treated texts as "objects" for analytical dissection, rather than for intellectual enjoyment and enlargement.

Others wondered whether the commuting during full term would wear Lewis down. Yet, as things turned out, Lewis proved able to cope with his new routine. He resided in his comfortable wood-panelled rooms at Magdalene College during the week, and returned to Oxford for weekends, taking the direct train from Cambridge to the Rewley Road station in Oxford. This was popularly known as the "Cantab Crawler" (because it stopped at every station, and took three hours to cover the 80 miles [128 kilometres]) or the "Brain Line" (a pun on *main line*, in that the route was frequented by academics of the two universities). Neither the line nor the Oxford station of that name now remain in use.

Some felt that Lewis tried too hard to fit in at Magdalene, perhaps reflecting his nervousness that he would not be accepted in his newly adopted college. Richard Ladborough, fellow and Pepys Librarian of the college from 1949–1972, felt that Lewis was too eager to win acceptance at Magdalene, cultivating a booming voice and "jolly farmer" bonhomie as a way of obscuring his personal shyness and social anxiety. Might Lewis's shyness have been misunderstood as aggressiveness? Yet in the end, Lewis found acceptance more readily than he had dared to hope.

13.1 Magdalene College, Cambridge, seen from the River Cam in 1955.

By the end of his first complete calendar year in Cambridge, Lewis felt able to "pronounce the move to Cambridge a great success." Magdalene College Cambridge was a "smaller, softer and more gracious place" than Magdalen College Oxford. In comparison with the increasingly industrialised city of Oxford, Cambridge was a "delightfully small" market town, allowing Lewis to get "a real country walk" whenever he wanted. "All my friends say I look younger."[22]

RENAISSANCE: THE INAUGURAL LECTURE AT CAMBRIDGE

The success of Lewis's inaugural lecture as Cambridge's first Professor of Medieval and Renaissance English may have contributed to his buoyant mood. The lecture was delivered at 5.00 p.m. in the largest humanities lecture room Cambridge had at its disposal on Lewis's fifty-sixth birthday—Monday, 29 November 1954—while he was still resident in Oxford. Numerous reports of the lecture survive, emphasising the vast crowd that turned out to hear Lewis, and his remarkable competence as a lecturer.[23] The BBC Third Programme gave serious consideration to broadcasting the lecture—a rare honour for such an academic event.[24]

Lewis's theme was the periodization of literary history, an issue which he had explored during earlier lectures in Cambridge—a series of eight weekly lectures on Renaissance Literature delivered in Lent Term 1939, and the Clark Lectures, given at Trinity College in May 1944. Lewis reiterated a core theme of those lectures: "The Renaissance never happened." It was a theme he had been developing for some years. As he wrote to the Milton expert Douglas Bush in 1941, "My line is to *define* the Renaissance as 'an imaginary entity responsible for anything a modern writer happens to approve in the Fifteenth or Sixteenth Century.'"[25]

This challenging and bold statement needs careful nuancing. Lewis's fundamental objection was to the widespread notion that a period called "the Renaissance" cast aside the drab, old ways of the Middle Ages, introducing a new golden age of literature, theology, and philosophy. This, he suggested, was a myth, constructed by none other than the advocates of the Renaissance itself. By failing to challenge this myth, Lewis argued, scholarship was simply perpetuating this ideologically driven reading of the history of English literature. In making this point, Lewis quoted from the Cambridge historian George Macaulay Trevelyan (1876–1962), who had hosted Lewis's Clark Lectures at Trinity College, Cambridge, in 1944: "Unlike dates, 'periods' are not facts. They are retrospective conceptions that we form about past events, useful to focus discussion, but very often leading historical thought astray."[26]

In at least some important respects, Lewis is entirely correct. Recent studies of the European Renaissance have shown that its "narrative of identity" was deliberately constructed to emphasise its agenda. Renaissance writers coined the term "the Middle Ages" to denote and to denigrate what they regarded as being a drab and degenerate period between the glories of classical culture and their rebirth and renewal during the Renaissance. Lewis rightly pointed out that history simply could not be allowed to be shaped by such polemical agendas, which sought to minimise the continuity between medieval and Renaissance culture. "The barrier between those two ages has been greatly exaggerated, if indeed it was not largely a figment of Humanist propaganda."[27] The literature of the Middle Ages deserved to be treated with sympathy and respect, not to be summarily dismissed in the manner encouraged by Renaissance humanism.

It is significant that Lewis's lecture was primarily on the topic of "Renaissance." Did Lewis use this lecture as a way of reinventing himself? Did the move to Cambridge entail, at least in his mind, a change in his identity—a personal renaissance, in which he was "born again," as if emerging, transformed, from a cocoon? Was the Cambridge Lewis to be a *new* Lewis, drawing a line under some of the activities and issues that had been characteristic of his later Oxford years? It is, for example, significant that Lewis did not write anything substantial in the field of apologetics during his time at Cambridge. His popular writings of this period—such as *Reflections on the Psalms* and *The Four Loves*—are explorations of an assumed faith, not defences of a challenged faith.

Lewis now no longer saw himself primarily as an apologist, concerned to defend the Christian faith to its critics outside the church. His focus shifted to exploring and appreciating the depths of the Christian faith for the benefit of those who believed, or were close to believing. This new strategy is clearly set out in the opening pages of *Reflections on the Psalms*:

> This is not what is called an "apologetic" work. I am nowhere trying to convince unbelievers that Christianity is true. I address those who already believe it, or those who are ready, while reading, to "suspend their disbelief." A man can't be always defending the truth; there must be a time to feed on it.[28]

This final sentence needs to be read in the light of Lewis's frequently repeated assertions that he found defending Christian ideas draining and exhausting (page 258). He seems to be arguing that he ought to be allowed to *enjoy* these ideas, rather than be forced into battle constantly on their behalf.

Yet Lewis's concerns at Cambridge are best understood as representing a change in focus within Lewis's overall approach, rather than a significant—let alone radical—change from his basic commitments. Lewis represents an approach to the Christian faith in which the mind, heart, reason, and imagination are brought into creative interplay, with different audiences in mind. During the 1940s and early 1950s, Lewis developed works of rational apologetics—such as *Miracles* and *Mere Christianity*—which offered a rational defence of the Christian faith to unbelievers; during the later 1950s, Lewis tended to focus on works—such as *Surprised by Joy*—exploring the imaginative and relational dimensions of faith, with a presumed Christian audience in mind. The shift in envisaged readerships may reflect Lewis's changing perceptions of the needs of the moment; yet there is no loss of the comprehensive vision of the Christian faith that became so characteristic of Lewis, and was first seen in *The Pilgrim's Regress* (1933).

Lewis's inaugural lecture at Cambridge can certainly be read as the adept construction of an intellectual facade—not in the sense of something flimsy or deceitful, but rather in terms of shaping how one is seen. Just as Renaissance humanism developed its own narrative of identity, which Lewis skilfully deconstructed, so Lewis developed his own account of how he wished to be understood. Provocatively, he declared that he wished to be seen as an "intellectual dinosaur," prepared to challenge the "chronological snobbery" of his day. Although some interpreted Lewis's lecture otherwise—for example, as a manifesto for the reinvigoration of Christianity itself, or at least a Christian influence in literary studies—the ensuing controversy soon died down.

The perception that Lewis was a "dinosaur"—a massive beast whose values and working methods are ill-adapted to the modern world—has been reinforced by changing scholarly habits since the 1950s. Lewis's personal library shows signs of intense engagement. Annotations and underlinings, sometimes in different inks, indicate successive rereadings of already familiar texts. The British historian Keith Thomas (1933–) recently commented on the reading habits of the English Renaissance, noting the importance of annotation as a means of safeguarding the insights of extended periods of direct textual engagement:

> It was common for Renaissance readers to mark key passages by underlining them or drawing lines and pointing fingers in the margin—the early modern equivalent of the yellow highlighter. According to the Jacobean educational writer John Brinsley, "the choycest books of most great learned men, and the notablest students" were marked through, "with little lines under or above" or "by some prickes, or whatsoever letter or mark may best help to call the knowledge of the thing to remembrance."[29]

Thomas—who shares Lewis's commitment to the extended, active reading of primary sources—also remarked that he had now "become something of a dinosaur." Researchers no longer read books from cover to cover; they use search engines to find words or passages. But this approach has made researchers less sensitive to the deeper structures and inner logic of the texts they are discussing, and much less likely to make the "unexpected discoveries which come from serendipity." As Thomas ruefully remarked, the sad truth was that what once took a lifetime to learn by slow and painful accumulation can now "be achieved by a moderately diligent student in the course of a morning."

Nobody who has worked through Lewis's heavily annotated personal library can doubt the intensity or quality of his engagement with the texts he studied. Lewis illustrates precisely the detailed textual engagement and conceptual mastery that Thomas applauds—yet believes to be in terminal decline through the rise of technology. So is literary scholarship a dying art? In speaking of himself as a "dinosaur," was Lewis referring to his research methods, and not merely their outcomes? Lewis increasingly seems to witness to a lost age of scholarly methods, above all the mental inhabitation of primary sources, which does not appear to have survived his generation.

In the end, Lewis enjoyed a long and productive period at Cambridge, until ill health finally forced him to resign his chair with effect from October 1963. By my reckoning, Lewis wrote thirteen books and forty-four articles during his Cambridge years, not to mention numerous book reviews and several poems, and he edited three collections of essays. There were controversies, of course, perhaps most significantly the 1960 debate with F. R. Leavis and his supporters over the merits of literary criticism. Nevertheless, Lewis's Cambridge period—while not being anything like Bunyan's "Plain called Ease"—was certainly an oasis of creativity, resulting in some of his most significant works, including *Till We Have Faces* (1956), *Reflections on the Psalms* (1958), *The Four Loves* (1960), *An Experiment in Criticism* (1961), and *The Discarded Image* (published posthumously in 1964).

Yet Lewis's Cambridge period was dominated by an event in his personal life, which had a significant impact on his writings during this time. Lewis found a new—but rather demanding—literary stimulus: Helen Joy Davidman.

A LITERARY ROMANCE: ENTER JOY DAVIDMAN

On Monday, 23 April 1956, without any fanfare of advance publicity or courtesy of prior announcement, C. S. Lewis married Helen Joy Davidman Gresham, an American divorcée sixteen years his junior, in a civil ceremony at Oxford's Register Office at St. Giles. The ceremony was witnessed by Lewis's friends Dr. Robert E. Havard and Austin M. Farrer. Tolkien was not present; in fact, it would be some time before he learned of this development. It was, in Lewis's view, purely a marriage of convenience, designed to allow Mrs. Gresham and her two sons the legal right to remain in Oxford when their permission to reside in Great Britain expired on 31 May 1956.

After the brief ceremony, Lewis caught a train to Cambridge and resumed his normal pattern of weekly lectures. It was as if his marriage had made no difference to him. Lewis's close circle of friends knew nothing of this development. He had gone behind their backs. Most of them believed that Lewis was reconciled to remaining a bachelor for the rest of his life.

So who was this "Mrs. Gresham," whom Lewis married in such a furtive and secretive manner? And how did such a marriage come about? To understand this development, we need to appreciate the impact that Lewis had upon a specific audience—intelligent, literary women, who found Lewis to be both an effective apologist for the Christian faith and an enthusiastic and persuasive advocate of the use of literature in developing and communicating the themes of faith.

One such person was Ruth Pitter (1897–1992), a highly competent English poet who was awarded the Hawthornden Prize in 1937 for *A Trophy of Arms*, which she had published the previous year. During the Second World War, Pitter heard Lewis's broadcast talks on the BBC, and found them a source of spiritual inspiration and intellectual stimulation. Pitter was in a state of despair at this time, which nearly led her to throw herself off Battersea Bridge in the dead of night. Reading Lewis, however, persuaded her that the world made sense. Her rediscovery of faith was, she later insisted, due to Lewis.[30]

Having been influenced so much by him, Pitter sought to meet Lewis, using mutual friends as a means of bringing this about.[31] She asked Herbert Palmer (1880–1961) to help arrange a meeting. Lewis invited her to a lunch party at Magdalen College on 9 October 1946. It was the first of many such meetings, which led to a deep friendship and mutual respect on both sides. In 1953, Lewis even accorded her the rare honour of allowing her to address him as "Jack" in her letters. According to his friend and biographer George Sayer, Lewis once remarked that if he were the kind of man who was to get married, he would have wanted to wed the poet Ruth Pitter.[32] But though some saw Pitter as Lewis's obvious soul mate, nothing romantic resulted from this friendship.[33] With Joy Davidman, however, things were different.

Helen Joy Davidman was born in 1915 in New York City to Jewish parents of eastern European roots, who had by then ceased to practise their religion. In September 1930, at the early age of fifteen, she began attending Hunter College in New York City, taking courses in English and French literature. While at Hunter, Davidman formed a friendship with the future novelist Bel Kaufman (1911–), best known for her 1965 bestseller *Up the Down Staircase*. Kaufman recalls that Davidman tended to date "older men," particularly those who were "seriously interested in literature."[34] Davidman herself showed considerable talent as a writer, and was awarded the Bernard Cohen Short Story Prize while at Hunter for "Apostate," based on a story about nineteenth-century Russia her mother had told her. After taking an MA in English literature from Columbia University in 1935, she tried to make a career of freelance writing.

Initially, things seemed to go well. She won the prestigious Yale Younger Poets Series Award for her 1938 poetry collection, *Letter to a Comrade*. Then came an invitation to go to Hollywood. MGM, searching for new talent, recruited Davidman as a scriptwriter for a six-month trial period in 1939, paying her fifty dollars a week. During that time, Davidman worked on four scripts. MGM didn't like any of them, and sent Davidman back to New York. There she devoted herself to earning a living, developing her writing, and working for the Communist Party.

Like many during the Great Depression of the 1930s, Davidman had become an atheist and a Communist, believing that radical social action was the only solution to America's economic woes. She married fellow Communist and writer Bill Gresham, who fought on the socialist side in the Spanish Civil War. Their marriage was unstable. Gresham was prone to depression and alcoholism. And there were other women in his life. By February 1951, the marriage was in deep trouble.

By then Davidman's life had taken an unexpected turn. Having "sucked in atheism with [her] canned milk," Davidman encountered God suddenly and unexpectedly in the early spring of 1946. In a 1951 account of this dramatic event, Davidman suggested that God had, like a lion, been "stalking" her for a long time, awaiting an opportune moment to strike when she was unprepared. God "crept nearer so silently that I never knew he was there. Then, all at once, he sprang."[35]

Having discovered God, Davidman began to explore the new territory of her faith. Her chief guide was a British author who had recently acquired fame in America—C. S. Lewis. *The Great Divorce*, *Miracles*, and *The Screwtape Letters* became her gateway to an intellectually enriched and robust faith. Yet while others merely sought Lewis's advice, Davidman sought his soul.

In a series of newspaper reports in 1998, marking the centenary of Lewis's birth, Davidman's younger son, Douglas Gresham, declared that his mother had gone to England with one specific intention: "to seduce C. S. Lewis."[36] Although some questioned this statement at the time, there is a growing consensus that Douglas Gresham may have been quite accurate in his assessment of the situation.[37]

Davidman's intention to seduce Lewis is confirmed by a collection of papers bequeathed in 2010 by Jean Wakeman, Davidman's closest friend in England, to the Marion E. Wade Center, the premier research institution for Lewis studies based at Wheaton College in Wheaton, Illinois.[38] These newly acquired papers include forty-five sonnets, written by Davidman for Lewis over the period 1951–1954. As Don King has noted, these sonnets deal with Davidman's intentions of returning to England after her initial meeting with Lewis and forging a closer relationship with him. Twenty-eight of these sonnets set out in great detail how Davidman attempted to forge that relationship. Lewis is represented as a glacial figure, an iceberg that Davidman intends to melt through a heady mixture of intellectual sophistication and physical allure. But this is to rush ahead of our story, even if it sets subsequent developments in their proper context.

Some of those close to Davidman in America had already worked out what was going on. Renée Pierce, Davidman's cousin, was convinced that Davidman was falling in love with Lewis around 1950, despite never having met him—or even seen him.[39] But how could Davidman "seduce" Lewis? For a start, she needed to get in touch with him and meet him. How could she do that?

Happily for Davidman, an answer lay to hand. By that time, Chad Walsh was established as the leading American authority on Lewis. After befriending Walsh, Davidman asked his advice about befriending Lewis. As a result, Davidman then wrote to Lewis in January 1950, and received a promising and engaging reply. She kept writing to him. And he kept replying.

Encouraged, Davidman sailed to England, arriving on 13 August 1952, leaving her two sons—David and Douglas—with their father. Her cousin Renée went to help Bill look after the children. The declared purpose of Davidman's trip—funded by her parents—was to visit her penfriend Phyllis Williams and complete her book *Smoke on the Mountain*, a contemporary interpretation of the Ten Commandments. Yet the real objective of the visit was to befriend Lewis.

During the course of her extended visit to England, Davidman initiated correspondence that led to lunch with Lewis and some of his friends on two occasions in Oxford. Did Lewis have any idea of what was going on in Davidman's emotional world? Or how easily he might be drawn into it? It is interesting to note that Lewis brought colleagues with him to these occasions. The word *chaperone* was never mentioned, but that's what they were. When Warnie—the intended chaperone for one such lunch at Magdalen College—was unable to attend, Lewis hurriedly replaced him with George Sayer. Davidman clearly judged these occasions to be successful and interesting. Lewis seemed willing to allow the friendship to develop. Davidman made all the moves in the developing relationship; Lewis, however, seemed happy to go along with things. Up to this point, Davidman's relationship with Lewis paralleled that of Ruth Pitter.

Perhaps Lewis now felt safe in the company of this female admirer, whom he introduced to his circle as "Mrs. Gresham." Davidman lunched privately with Lewis in London in early December, an occasion which led to a further invitation to spend Christmas and the New Year with Lewis and Warnie at The Kilns. The experience, she later remarked to Walsh, made her into a "complete Anglo-maniac," who was desperate to "transplant."[40] Did she see Lewis as the possible vehicle of such a transplantation? Would Lewis be the knight in shining armour who delivered this maiden from the clutches of her evil husband in a noble act of courtly love? The evidence certainly suggests that Lewis was prepared to play some such role, especially when Davidman produced a letter from her husband, informing her that he wanted to marry her cousin Renée.

Davidman returned to America on 3 January 1953 to confront this situation. By the end of February, she and her husband had agreed to divorce. She remained in contact with Lewis as the situation unfolded. According to her immigration record, Davidman returned to England on 13 November 1953 with her two sons, Douglas and David, then aged eight and nine—a decision that deeply wounded Bill Gresham. This development clearly requires further comment. Why move to England, where she had no family connections? Her parents were both still alive; indeed, they even came to visit her in London in October 1954. Why not remain in the United States, where the cost of living was significantly lower, and her employment prospects so much better?

Many have argued that there is only one persuasive answer: Davidman clearly believed that she would be supported financially by Lewis. Her immigration documents explicitly stated that she was permitted to remain in the United Kingdom provided that she did not "enter any employment either paid or unpaid."[41] She had enrolled both boys at Dane Court School in Pyrford, Surrey (which closed in 1981). She needed money. It is likely (but not proved) that Lewis met most of Davidman's living costs and the school fees anonymously through the "Agapony Fund," a charitable trust set up in 1942 by Owen Barfield to administer some of Lewis's royalty earnings.[42] Warnie clearly knew nothing of any such arrangement.

Yet this is not the full story. Davidman's desire to remain in England was partly fuelled by anxiety about her employment prospects back home. Cold War fever was sweeping America, given added credibility by Soviet nuclear tests and the Korean War (1950–1953). Davidman could not have failed to notice that her active Communist past, which she never sought to hide, would cast a dark shadow over her chances of finding a job in Hollywood or the media. The House Un-American Activities Committee—an investigative committee of the United States House of Representatives—was actively pursuing people with Communist commitments and influence, especially those working in the media. Eventually more than three hundred artists with alleged Communist sympathies or connections—including movie directors, radio commentators, actors, and particularly screenwriters—were blacklisted, and boycotted by the Hollywood studios.[43]

Davidman's past was rapidly catching up with her. Who would be able to overlook her past membership with the Communist Party? Or her active involvement in its publications, such as the journal *New Masses*? She would be unlikely to secure employment as a Hollywood scriptwriter, or to make an impact as a writer anywhere in America. Davidman's conviction that her future as a writer lay outside the United States is perfectly plausible, given the political context of the time.

Davidman's relationship with Lewis gained new momentum in 1955, when she and her sons moved into a three-bedroom house at 10 Old High Street in Headington, not far from The Kilns. Lewis arranged for this lease and paid the rent. He visited Davidman for extended periods daily, clearly enjoying her company. Yet Davidman was more than good company for Lewis; she also helped stimulate his literary imagination—a matter which needs further comment.

Initially, Lewis was drawn to Davidman by her sense of humour and her obvious intellectual gifts. It soon became clear that she could be much more than this. It is likely that Davidman's influence lay behind Lewis's decision to start using a literary agent, rather than dealing directly with publishers. On 17 February 1955, Lewis informed Jocelyn Gibb (1907–1979), the managing director of Geoffrey Bles, that he had hired Spencer Curtis Brown (1906–1980) to represent him in future negotiations with publishers.[44] This decision appears to have been motivated by financial, rather than literary, considerations. Did Lewis suddenly realise he needed a greater income?

13.2 Joy Davidman Lewis in 1960.

Yet Davidman did more than suggest a way in which Lewis could make more money from his writings. She was midwife to three of Lewis's late books—including *Till We Have Faces* (1956), widely regarded as one of Lewis's most important novels. Davidman liked to compare herself to the "editor-collaborator" Maxwell Perkins (1884–1947), the great American literary editor who helped craft the finest novels of Ernest Hemingway, F. Scott Fitzgerald, and Thomas Wolfe. A respected writer himself, Perkins possessed the rare gift of enabling other authors to refine and perfect their art. Davidman had played this role already with Bill Gresham, and now brought her skills to bear on Lewis.

In March 1955, Davidman came to stay at The Kilns. Lewis had long been interested in the classical myth of Psyche, and had produced a poetic rewriting and interpretation of the story in the 1920s. But the project had stalled. Lewis could not work out how to develop the idea. Davidman began to deploy a collaborative strategy. She and Lewis "kicked a few ideas around till one came to life."[45]

It worked. Lewis suddenly saw how a book could be written on the Psyche theme. He was fired up with enthusiasm. By the end of the next day, Lewis had written the first chapter of the text that would become *Till We Have Faces*. Lewis dedicated the book to Davidman, and regarded it as one of his best pieces of writing. Commercially, however, it was something of a disaster. As Lewis himself ruefully remarked in 1959, the work that he himself considered "far and away the best I have written" turned out to be "my one big failure both with the critics and with the public."[46] Yet the Narnia Chronicles aside, it has become Lewis's most critically discussed piece of writing. Davidman's encouragement also lay behind two more of Lewis's later writings: *Reflections on the Psalms* (1958) and *The Four Loves* (1960).

Lewis worked collaboratively on many of his writing projects during his Oxford period. Although the Inklings were primarily concerned with the testing and improvement of works already under way, Lewis found that others provided him with the creative stimulus to write—probably most clearly Roger Lancelyn Green, who played a significant role in the genesis of the Chronicles of Narnia, especially *The Magician's Nephew*. Davidman can be seen to fit into this general pattern. Yet Davidman did rather more than join the ranks of those who stimulated Lewis's literary imagination. She also became his wife.

THE "VERY STRANGE MARRIAGE" TO JOY DAVIDMAN

It is usually suggested that Lewis's "very strange marriage" (the phrase came from Tolkien, who regarded their relationship with undisguised hostility)[47] to Joy Davidman was the result of a crisis which came to a head shortly after she moved to 10 Old High Street, Headington. Most biographies relate—often vaguely and without substantiation—that Davidman's right to reside in the United Kingdom was revoked by the Home Office in April 1956. This precipitated Lewis's decision to marry Davidman. Yet the situation is more complex than this.

Davidman was initially permitted to remain in England until 13 January 1955. However, this leave to stay was subsequently extended by the Home Office until 31 May 1956. There is no question of anything being "revoked." Davidman's permission to reside in the United Kingdom was simply due to expire at the end of May. The civil marriage might well have been planned with Lewis as a strategy of last resort to allow her and her sons to remain in Oxford.

Another possibility also needs to be noted. Davidman's permission to live in England was conditional; she was not permitted to undertake any employment, whether paid or unpaid. Warnie and many others in Lewis's circle assumed that Davidman was able to cover her living costs by undertaking writing or editing projects. In fact, she was explicitly forbidden to do this. Lewis's covert financial support for Davidman—carefully concealed from Warnie—was arguably a matter of necessity, in that she had no source of income while in England. A civil marriage to Lewis would remove this obstacle and allow Davidman to earn a living. Lewis may well have seen such a marriage as a legal formality enabling Davidman to make her own way in the world.

Yet this was not a sudden development. Lewis appears to have discussed the possibility of a civil marriage to Davidman months earlier, during a September 1955 visit to his confidant Arthur Greeves in Northern Ireland. Although we have no record of Greeves's reaction to this somewhat surprising proposal, it is clear that he raised significant concerns about it, which Lewis was unable to allay. When writing to Greeves a month after the visit, Lewis was defensive about the idea of a civil marriage to Davidman: it was merely a "legal formality," without any deeper religious or relational significance. Following the marriage, the Home Office removed any conditions on Davidman remaining in the United Kingdom. She applied for British citizenship on 24 April 1957, and was registered as a "Citizen of the United Kingdom and Colonies" on 2 August 1957.[48]

Lewis had earlier, to Tolkien's disquiet, set out such a view of civil marriage in his broadcast talks, and subsequently in *Mere Christianity*. A church marriage—the "reality"—was out of the question for Lewis, who held very traditional views on the matter. Such a religious "marriage" would have been adulterous from a religious perspective, since Davidman was divorced. Yet Lewis emphasised that this possibility was not even under discussion.[49]

To most of Lewis's close friends it seemed clear that Davidman had manipulated Lewis, putting him under moral pressure to enter into a marriage he did not want with someone whose interests in him were at least as mercenary as they were literary or spiritual. They took the view that Davidman was a gold digger, out to secure her own future and that of her sons. Davidman moved in on Lewis, whereas Pitter was so well bred she would never have dreamed of imposing herself in such a way. Lewis's furtiveness about his developing relationship with Davidman meant that members of his inner circle were unable to offer him advice and support, precisely because they were unaware of how serious matters had become. By the time Lewis announced his marriage, it was too late for them to do anything, other than to try to make the best of a messy situation. Lewis was out of his depth, and none of his friends had realised the extent to which he had become entangled with Davidman.

There is, of course, a second way of interpreting this relationship, favoured by Hollywood scriptwriters, which sees it as a late-blossoming love affair in Lewis's life, a fairy-tale romance which ultimately turned to tragedy. This romanticised reading of things—famously and uncritically presented in the movie *Shadowlands* (1993)—presents Lewis as a crusty, socially withdrawn old bachelor whose drab life was turned upside down by a feisty New York girl who knew a few things about the real world. The brash and breezy New Yorker brought a breath of fresh air to Lewis's dull existence, helping him to discover the good things in life and shake off his fusty old habits and dreary social conventions.

This view of the relationship has obvious problems. It is frankly some-what difficult to see how Lewis's social skills might have been enhanced by Davidman, whose lack of social or emotional intelligence was fre-quently noted by her irritated contemporaries. It is nonsense to suggest that Lewis was socially withdrawn; his colleagues remembered him as a social creature, possessed of an occasionally larger-than-life bonhomie, chiefly notable for his loud laughter.

In reality, Lewis had become—to put it bluntly, yet accurately—"an American divorcée's sugar daddy."[50] But Lewis seems to have been a willing victim, unquestionably benefitting from any such arrange-ment—perhaps most obviously in regaining his literary motivation and inspiration—however dubious the process by which it came about. Lewis had his own concerns and problems, and Davidman did much to help him engage with some of these.

It is also important to appreciate that Lewis was actively supporting other American women writers financially around this time. The most important of these was Mary Willis Shelburne (1895–1975), a poet and critic who kept in contact with Lewis over an extended period of time, and was clearly well regarded by Lewis.[51] She also had financial needs, which she did not conceal from Lewis. Initially, Lewis was not able to help her financially because of the strict regulation of foreign exchange by the British authorities, which prevented him (as a private British citizen) from sending money to America. In a letter to Shelburne on Christmas Day

1958, Lewis refers to a relaxation of foreign exchange regulations, which now allowed him to send her a regular stipend from the Agapony Fund.[52]

That Lewis saw his marriage to Davidman as a matter of chivalrous generosity, rather than as an exclusive passionate romance, is suggested by the fact that Davidman did not displace Pitter in Lewis's life. Lewis's enduring respect and affection for Pitter is obvious from his letter of July 1956—several months after his clandestine marriage—in which he invited her (rather than Davidman) to be his guest at a royal garden party at Buckingham Palace.[53] In the end, Pitter couldn't make it, so Lewis went on his own. He wrote to Pitter again a week later to tell her that the event was "simply ghastly," and invited her to lunch with him sometime soon, so that they could catch up with each other.[54] Lewis's correspondence and his meetings make it clear that Davidman did not dislodge other women who mattered to him.

Lewis's civil marriage to Davidman, which he so obviously regarded as a mere legal formality, was in reality a ticking time bomb, giving Davidman certain legal rights that Lewis seems to have assumed she would not choose to exercise. Lewis clearly believed that the marriage would make no difference to their lives or mutual relationships. Yet Lewis's gesture of solidarity towards Davidman and her sons turned out to be something of a Trojan horse. Davidman soon staked her claim to her rights, making it clear that she was not content to remain in her lodgings in Headington. The Kilns would soon be occupied by subterfuge rather than explicit invitation. If she was Lewis's wife—as she was in the eyes of the law—she and her sons had legal rights stretching far beyond the mere right to remain in England. For a start, they were entitled to live with her husband. Lewis had no options. By early October 1955, he had reluctantly agreed to install Davidman and her two sons at The Kilns.

Warnie had gloomily yet accurately foreseen such mercenary developments as soon as he was informed about the civil marriage. He had regarded it as inevitable that Davidman would "press for her rights"—a discreet allusion to the interest in Lewis's earnings and property that resulted from her new status as his wife. Davidman now regarded The Kilns as *her* house, clearly unaware of the complex arrangements for the legal ownership of the house stipulated in Mrs. Moore's will, by which Lewis was merely an occupant of The Kilns.

This became unpleasantly clear in a confrontation between Maureen Blake and Davidman, arising from Davidman's stated belief that her two boys would inherit The Kilns when Lewis and she were dead. Maureen (who had only recently found out that Lewis was married) promptly corrected her, making it clear that under Mrs. Moore's will, legal ownership of the house would pass to Maureen after the deaths of Lewis and Warnie.[55] Yet Davidman would have nothing of such legal niceties: "This house belongs to me and the boys."[56] Maureen, of course, was right. The conversation is important more in illuminating Davidman's mercenary motivations than her knowledge of English law. Davidman pressed Maureen on the matter, demanding that she yield her right to the property. Under some pressure, Maureen agreed to discuss the matter with her husband. Nothing further ensued.

Davidman's influence led to some much-needed renovation work at The Kilns. The blackout curtains, installed in 1940, were still in place in 1952.[57] The furniture needed replacement. The woodwork needed painting. Following Mrs. Moore's illness and death, Lewis and his brother had allowed the property to become decrepit. Davidman was determined to get it sorted out. The Kilns was renovated. New furniture began to appear.

In the end, however, events took a dramatic turn. Davidman had been suffering from pains in her leg, which Lewis's physician Robert Havard mistakenly diagnosed as a relatively minor case of fibrositis. (Havard here seems to have lived up to his nickname "The Useless Quack."[58]) On the evening of 18 October 1956, while Lewis was in Cambridge, Davidman fell over while trying to answer a telephone call from Katharine Farrer. She was admitted to the nearby Wingfield-Morris Orthopaedic Hospital, where X-rays showed a broken femur. But they revealed much more than a broken bone. Davidman had a malignant tumour in her left breast, as well as secondary manifestations elsewhere. Her days were numbered.

THE DEATH OF JOY DAVIDMAN

Davidman's serious illness seems to have brought about a change in Lewis's attitude towards her. The thought of Davidman's death made Lewis see their relationship in a new way. Perhaps the most important witness to this transformation in Lewis's thoughts is a letter to the novelist Dorothy L. Sayers, written in June 1957. Referring to Thanatos, the Greek god of death, Lewis comments on how Thanatos's approach galvanised Lewis's own feelings, converting friendship to love:

> My feelings had changed. They say a rival often turns a friend
> into a lover. Thanatos, certainly (they say) approaching but at
> an uncertain speed, is a most efficient rival for this purpose.
> We soon learn to love what we know we must lose.[59]

The realisation that Davidman might soon be taken from him concentrated Lewis's mind. As he commented grimly to one of his long-standing female correspondents, he might soon be "in rapid succession, a bridegroom and a widower. There may, in fact, be a deathbed marriage."[60] To others, however, he was more optimistic. Writing to Arthur Greeves in late November, he suggested that there was a "reasonable probability" that Davidman would enjoy "some years more of (tolerable) life."[61]

Lewis eventually realised that his furtive civil marriage to Davidman, which he had earlier referred to as their "innocent little secret,"[62] needed to be publicly acknowledged, not least because of rumours of other romantic entanglements around this time involving Lewis.[63] On 24 December 1956, the following announcement belatedly appeared in the *Times*:

> A marriage has taken place between Professor C. S. Lewis, of
> Magdalene College Cambridge, and Mrs. Joy Gresham, now a
> patient in the Churchill Hospital, Oxford. It is requested that
> no letters be sent.[64]

This profoundly ambiguous announcement made no mention of the date of the marriage, nor that it was a purely civil affair.

Behind the scenes, Lewis had been attempting to arrange a marriage in church, which he believed would place his relationship with Davidman on a firmly Christian footing. On 17 November 1956, Lewis asked the bishop of Oxford, Dr. Harry Carpenter, a former warden of Keble College, if this might be possible. Although sympathetic to Lewis's situation, Carpenter was clear that he could not sanction it within his diocese of Oxford. The Church of England did not then permit the remarrying of divorced persons, and Carpenter did not see why Lewis's celebrity status should allow him privileges that were denied to others. In any case, Lewis and Davidman were already married, in that the Church of England—as the established church of the land—recognised civil weddings as valid. He couldn't be married again in any parish church in the diocese. Lewis was angered by this ruling. On his view of things, Davidman's marriage to Bill Gresham was invalid, in that her husband had been married before. But none of his Oxford clerical friends would marry him in open defiance of their bishop, or the accepted position of the church at that time.

In March 1957, as Davidman's condition seemed to worsen, Lewis turned his thoughts to a student who had attended his lectures in the 1930s. Peter Bide, a former Communist, had studied English Language and Literature at Oxford from 1936 to 1939, and had attended Lewis's lectures. After serving in the Royal Marines in the Second World War, he had taken orders in the Church of England in 1949, and settled in the diocese of Chichester. In 1954, Bide was heavily involved in pastoral ministry during a polio outbreak in Sussex. Following his prayers for Michael Gallagher, a young boy believed to be terminally ill, the child recovered. Lewis heard of this miracle, and asked Bide to come and pray for his dying wife.[65]

Bide was apprehensive about this invitation. On the one hand, he did not particularly want to be thought of as a "priest with a gift of healing." On the other, he considered that he owed a "considerable intellectual debt" to Lewis, who had been a formative influence on him during his Oxford days. After much thought, he agreed to "lay hands"—a traditional Christian way of asking for God's blessing—on Davidman. Lewis's account of what happened next is found in a letter written three months later to Dorothy L. Sayers:

> Dear Father Bide (do you know him?) who had come to lay his hands on Joy—for he has on his record what looks v. like one miracle—without being asked and merely on being told the situation at once said he wd. marry us. So we had a bedside marriage with a nuptial Mass.[66]

Lewis's description does not ring completely true. Bide would have been aware of the position of the Church of England at this time, and known that it would have been a serious matter of ecclesiastical discipline and personal integrity to conduct any such service. Lewis's account of events implies that Bide saw such matters as being of little importance, and that he volunteered to marry Lewis and Davidman as if it were the most natural thing in the world.

It is instructive to compare Lewis's version of events with Bide's rather different recollection of what happened that day.[67] According to Bide, he arrived at The Kilns in preparation for laying hands on Davidman, when Lewis pleaded with him to marry them as well. "Look, Peter, I know this isn't fair, but do you think you could marry us?" Lewis seems to have believed that a priest of the Church of England from outside the diocese of Oxford was not necessarily subject to its bishop's ruling, and may not have realized that he was placing Bide in a very difficult position.

Bide asked for some time to think about this request, which was in his view out of order. In the end, Bide decided he would do whatever Jesus Christ would have done. "That somehow finished the argument." He agreed to marry them. But he had not volunteered to do so, and was clearly uneasy about both what he was being asked to do, and the manner in which he had been asked to do it.

It remains unclear why Lewis appears to have believed that Bide made an unprompted offer to marry them, which seems to be contradicted by Bide's vivid memory of being asked to do something that he regarded as irregular and improper. The balance of evidence would seem to lie in favour of Bide's account of things. It is possible that Lewis's belief that Davidman was about to die may have shaped the way he understood his conversation with Bide.

Yet we cannot overlook the fact that Lewis's entire relationship with Davidman was cloaked with subterfuge, recalling Lewis's earlier lack of transparency (particularly with his father) about his relationship with Mrs. Moore in 1918–1920. We do not know why Lewis failed to tell his friends the truth about this newer relationship, beginning with the civil marriage of April 1956, and ending with the religious marriage service of March 1957. There is no doubt that some of his closest acquaintances—most notably, Tolkien—were deeply hurt at being excluded from Lewis's confidence.

The Christian marriage service took place at eleven o'clock in the morning of 21 March 1957 in Davidman's ward at the Churchill Hospital, with Warnie and the ward sister as witnesses. Bide then laid hands on Davidman, and prayed for her healing. It was obviously a moment of great solemnity and significance for both Lewis and Davidman. It was also a moment of no small significance for Bide. He had crossed a Rubicon, deliberately flouting the discipline of his church. His forced choice had put his career on the line.

Bide decided to come clean with the church authorities immediately. He went to see Carpenter before leaving Oxford, and explained what he had just done. Carpenter was furious at this blatant breach of protocol, and ordered him to go straight back to his own diocese and confess everything. On his return home, Bide was alarmed to find that the bishop of Chichester, George Bell, had already asked to see him. Fearing the worst, Bide met Bell the next day and confessed his misdemeanour. Bell made it clear that he was not pleased with this development, and asked for a reassurance it wouldn't happen again. But that wasn't why he had summoned Bide. He wanted to offer him one of the best jobs in his diocese—the parish of Goring-by-Sea. And the offer, he reassured him, was still open. Would he accept it?[68]

13.3 Peter Bide in November 1960. Bide officiated at the "marriage service" between Lewis and Joy Davidman at the Churchill Hospital, Oxford, on 21 March 1957.

Davidman returned home to The Kilns in April, in the expectation of dying within weeks. Lewis himself was now suffering from osteoporosis, which caused him considerable pain in his legs and made it difficult for him to move around without the use of a surgical belt. Lewis took some small pleasure in the thought that as his pain had increased, Davidman's had decreased. This, he declared, was a "Charles Williams substitution,"[69] in which the lover bore the pain of the beloved. For Williams—and later for Lewis—"one had power to accept into one's own body the pain of someone else, through Christian love."[70]

In what Lewis regarded as a miracle, Davidman recovered sufficiently to allow her to start walking again by December 1957. In June of the following year, her cancer was diagnosed as being in remission. In July 1958, Lewis and Davidman flew to Ireland, where they spent ten days on a "belated honeymoon," visiting Lewis's family and friends, and drinking in the sights, sounds, and smells of his homeland—the "blue mountains, yellow beaches, dark fuchsia, breaking waves, braying donkeys, peat-smell and the heather just then beginning to bloom."[71]

In this late summer of his life, reassured about his wife's health, Lewis was able to turn to writing again. His *Reflections on the Psalms* (1958) and *The Four Loves* (1960) both date from this period, and reflect Davidman's influence. It is difficult to read the latter work without seeing at least something of Lewis's developing relationship with Davidman reflected in its chapters and some of its elegant phrases—such as the celebrated "Need-love cries to God from our poverty; Gift-love longs to serve, or even to suffer for, God; Appreciative love says: 'We give thanks to thee for thy great glory.'"[72]

Meanwhile, Lewis's lack of familiarity with the British tax system was causing him major headaches. In the postwar period, the United Kingdom imposed punitive tax rates of up to 90 percent on those who earned substantial amounts through royalties.[73] Both Lewis and Tolkien found themselves staggered by large and unexpected retrospective tax demands, resulting from the success of their books. Lewis does not appear to have employed an accountant, and was thus caught unawares by his legal obligations. In March 1959, Lewis told his confidant Arthur Greeves that he had been "knocked flat by a huge surtax on royalties earned 2 years ago," which forced him and Davidman to cut back drastically on expenditure.[74] Lewis became anxious about money, and was increasingly reluctant to buy new furniture or to continue renovating The Kilns, in case he would have to meet further massive demands from the Inland Revenue.

His finances seem to have recovered to some extent by September 1959, when—apparently at Davidman's instigation—Lewis and Roger Lancelyn Green planned an overseas trip together with their wives to explore some classical sites in Greece. But their plans were thrown into confusion by developments a few weeks later. On 13 October, following what was meant to be a routine hospital checkup, it was discovered that Davidman's cancer had returned.[75]

But the Greece trip still went ahead.[76] In April 1960, a week after the publication of *The Four Loves*, Lewis and Davidman flew with Roger and June Lancelyn Green to Greece, to visit the classical sites of the ancient world in Athens, Rhodes, and Crete. It was the first time Lewis had travelled outside the British Isles since setting out to fight on the killing fields of France in the Great War. It was to be the last trip Lewis and Davidman made together. Lewis's "very strange marriage" was soon to end in tragedy.

BEREAVEMENT, ILLNESS, AND DEATH: THE FINAL YEARS

Joy Davidman died of cancer at the age of forty-five at the Radcliffe Infirmary, Oxford, on 13 July 1960, with Lewis at her bedside. At her request, her funeral took place at Oxford's crematorium on 18 July. The service was led by Austin Farrer, one of the relatively few among Lewis's circle who had come to like Davidman. Her memorial plaque remains there, and is to this day one of the crematorium's best-known features.

Lewis was devastated. Not only had he lost his wife, whom he had nursed through her illness, and had come to love; he had also lost a personal Muse, a source of literary encouragement and inspiration. Davidman had been a significant influence on three of his late books—*Till We Have Faces*, *Reflections on the Psalms*, and *The Four Loves*. Now Davidman would be instrumental for one of Lewis's darkest and most revealing works. Her death unleashed a stream of thoughts which Lewis could not initially control. In the end, he committed them to writing as a way of coping with them. The result was one of his most distressing and disturbing books: *A Grief Observed*.

A GRIEF OBSERVED (1961): THE TESTING OF FAITH

In the months following Davidman's death, Lewis went through a process of grieving which was harrowing in its emotional intensity, and unrelenting in its intellectual questioning and probing. What Lewis once referred to as his "treaty with reality" was overwhelmed with a tidal wave of raw emotional turmoil. "Reality smashe[d] my dream to bits."[1] The dam was breached. Invading troops crossed the frontier, securing a temporary occupation of what was meant to be safe territory. "No one ever told me that grief felt so like fear."[2] Like a tempest, unanswered and unanswerable questions surged against Lewis's faith, forcing him against a wall of doubt and uncertainty.

Faced with these unsettling and disquieting challenges, Lewis coped using the method he had recommended to his confidant Arthur Greeves in 1916: "Whenever you are fed up with life, start writing: ink is the great cure for all human ills, as I have found out long ago."[3] In the days following Davidman's death in July 1960, Lewis began to write down his thoughts, not troubling to conceal his own doubts and spiritual agony. *A Grief Observed* is an uncensored and unrestrained account of Lewis's feelings. He found liberty and release in being able to write what he actually thought, rather than what his friends and admirers believed he ought to think.

Lewis discussed the manuscript with his close friend Roger Lancelyn Green in September 1960. What should he do with it? Eventually, they agreed that it ought to be published. Lewis, anxious not to cause his friends any embarrassment, decided to conceal his authorship of *A Grief Observed*. He did this in four ways:

1. By using the leading literary publisher Faber & Faber instead of Geoffrey Bles, his long-standing London publisher. Lewis handed the text over to his literary agent, Spencer Curtis Brown, who submitted it to Faber & Faber, without giving any indication that Lewis had any connection with the work. This was designed to lay a false trail for literary detectives.

2. By using a pseudonym for the author—"N. W. Clerk." Lewis originally suggested the Latin pseudonym *Dimidius* ("cut in half").
   T. S. Eliot, a director of Faber & Faber, who immediately guessed
   the true identity of the obviously erudite author on reading the
   text submitted by Curtis Brown, suggested that a more "plausible English pseudonym" would "hold off enquirers better than
   Dimidius."[4] Lewis had already used several pen names to conceal
   the authorship of his poems. The name he finally chose is derived
   from the abbreviation of *Nat Whilk* (an Anglo-Saxon phrase best
   translated as "I don't know who") and "Clerk" (someone who is
   able to read and write). Lewis had earlier used the Latinised form
   of this name—*Natwilcius*—to refer to a scholarly authority in his
   1943 novel *Perelandra*.

3. By using a pseudonym for the central figure of the narrative—"H.,"
   presumably an abbreviation of "Helen," a forename that Davidman
   rarely used yet which appeared on legal documents concerning her
   marriage and naturalisation as a British citizen, and her death certificate, which refers to her as "Helen Joy Lewis," "wife of Clive
   Staples Lewis."

4. By altering his style. *A Grief Observed* is deliberately written using a
   format and writing style which none of his regular readers would
   naturally associate with Lewis. By incorporating these "small stylistic disguisements all the way along," Lewis hoped to throw his
   readers off the scent.[5] Few early readers of the work appear to have
   made the connection with Lewis.

Even to those who recognised at least some telltale signs of Lewis's
style in the work (such as its clarity), *A Grief Observed* seemed quite unlike
anything else he had written. The book is about feelings, and their deeper
significance in subjecting any "treaty with reality" to the severe testing
which alone can prove whether it is capable of bearing the weight that is
placed upon it. Lewis was famously uncomfortable about discussing his

private emotions and feelings, having even apologised to his readers for the "suffocatingly subjective" approach he adopted at certain points in his earlier work *Surprised by Joy*.[6]

A Grief Observed engages emotions with a passion and intensity unlike anything else in Lewis's body of works, past or future. Lewis's earlier discussion of suffering in *The Problem of Pain* (1940) tends to treat it as something that can be approached objectively and dispassionately. The existence of pain is presented as an intellectual puzzle which Christian theology is able to frame satisfactorily, if not entirely resolve. Lewis was quite clear about his intentions in writing this earlier work: "The only purpose of the book is to solve the intellectual problem raised by suffering."[7] Lewis may have faced all the intellectual questions raised by suffering and death before. Yet nothing seems to have prepared him for the emotional firestorm that Davidman's death precipitated.

Suffering can only be little more than a logical riddle for those who encounter it from a safe distance. When it is experienced directly and immediately, firsthand—as when Lewis lost his mother, and again at the devastating death of Davidman—it is like an emotional battering ram, crashing into the gates of the castle of faith. To its critics, *The Problem of Pain* amounts to an evasion of the reality of evil and suffering as experienced realities; instead, they are reduced to abstract ideas, which demand to be fitted into the jigsaw puzzle of faith. To read *A Grief Observed* is to realise how a rational faith can fall to pieces when it is confronted with suffering as a personal reality, rather than as a mild theoretical disturbance.

Lewis seems to have realised that his earlier approach had engaged with the surface of human life, not its depths:

Where is God? . . . Go to Him when your need is desperate, when all other help is vain, and what do you find? A door slammed in your face, and a sound of bolting and double bolting on the inside. After that, silence.[8]

In June 1951, Lewis wrote to Sister Penelope to ask for her prayers. Everything was too easy for him. "I am (like the pilgrim in Bunyan) travelling across 'a plain called Ease.'" Might a change in his circumstances, he wondered, lead him to a deeper appreciation of his faith? Might a religious idea that he now understood only partly, if at all, suddenly take on new significance, becoming a new reality? "I now feel that one must never say one believes or understands anything: any morning a doctrine I thought I already possessed may blossom into this new reality."[9] It is difficult to read this without reflecting on how the somewhat superficial engagement with suffering in *The Problem of Pain* would "blossom" into the more mature, engaged, and above all *wise* account found in *A Grief Observed*.

Lewis's powerful, frank, and honest account of his own experience in *A Grief Observed* is to be valued as an authentic and moving account of the impact of bereavement. It is little wonder that the work has secured such a wide readership, given its accurate description of the emotional turmoil that results from a loved one's death. Indeed, some even recommended it to Lewis as an excellent account of the process of grieving, quite unaware of its true origins. Yet the work is significant at another level, in exposing the vulnerability and fragility of a purely rational faith. While Lewis undoubtedly recovered his faith after his wife's death, *A Grief Observed* suggests that this faith was some distance removed from the cool, logical approach to faith that he once set out in *The Problem of Pain*.

Some have mistakenly concluded that *A Grief Observed* is a tacit acknowledgement of the explanatory failure of Christianity, and that Lewis emerged from this process of grieving as an agnostic. This is a hasty and superficial conclusion, and shows a lack of familiarity with the text itself, or with Lewis's subsequent writings. It must be remembered that *A Grief Observed* describes what Lewis regards as a process of testing—not a testing *of God*, but a testing *of Lewis*. "God has not been trying an experiment on my faith or love in order to find out their quality. He knew it already. It was I who didn't."[10]

Those wishing to present Lewis as having become an agnostic at this time must selectively freeze that narrative, presenting one of its frames or phases as its final outcome. Lewis makes it clear that, in his distress, he sets out to explore every intellectual option open to him. No stone was to remain unturned, no path unexplored. Maybe there is no God. Maybe there is a God, but he turns out to be a sadistic tyrant. Maybe faith is just a dream. Like the psalmist, Lewis plumbs the depths of despair, relentlessly and thoroughly, determined to wrest the hidden meaning from their darkness. Finally, Lewis begins to recover a sense of spiritual balance, recalibrating his theology in light of the shattering events of the previous weeks.

A letter Lewis wrote a few weeks before his death both captures the argumentative flow of *A Grief Observed* and accurately summarises its outcome. Lewis had maintained a correspondence since the early 1950s with Sister Madeleva Wolff (1887–1964), a distinguished medieval literary scholar and poet who had recently retired as president of Saint Mary's College at the University of Notre Dame in South Bend, Indiana. Lewis speaks of expressing his grief "from day to day in all its rawness and sinful reactions and follies." He warns her that, though *A Grief Observed* "ends with faith," it nevertheless "raises all the blackest doubts *en route*."[11]

It is all too easy—especially for those predisposed towards depicting Lewis as having become an agnostic, or who lack the time to read him properly—to fix on these "sinful reactions and follies" as if they represent the final outcome of Lewis's no-holds-barred exploration of the entire gamut of theistic possibilities in response to his crisis of grief. Yet Lewis's judgement on his own writing is precisely the conclusion that will be reached by anyone who reads the work in its entirety.

It is difficult, and possibly quite improper, to seize on a single moment, a solitary statement, that represents a turning point in Lewis's grief-stricken meditations. Yet there seems to be a clear tipping point in Lewis's thinking, which centres around his desire to be able to suffer instead of his wife: "If only I could bear it, or the worst of it, of any of it, instead of her."[12] Lewis's line of thought is that this is the mark of the true lover—a willingness to take on pain and suffering, in order that the beloved might be spared its worst.

Lewis then makes the obvious, and critical, Christological connection: that this is what Jesus did at the Cross. Is it allowed, he "babbles," to take on suffering on behalf of someone else, so that they are spared at least something of its pain and sense of dereliction? The answer lies in the crucified Christ:

It was allowed to One, we are told, and I find I can now believe again, that He has done vicariously whatever can be so done. He replies to our babble, "You cannot and you dare not. I could and dared."[13]

There are two interconnected, yet distinct, points being made here. First, Lewis is coming to a realisation that, great though his love for his wife may have been, it had its limits. Self-love will remain present in his soul, tempering his love for anyone else and limiting the extent to which he is prepared to suffer for that person. Second, Lewis is moving towards, not so much a recognition of the self-emptying of God (that theological idea is readily found elsewhere in his writings), but a realisation of its existential significance for the problem of human suffering. God *could* bear suffering. And God *did* bear suffering. And that, in turn, allows us to bear the ambiguity and risks of faith, knowing that its outcome is secured. *A Grief Observed* is a narrative of the testing and maturing of faith, not simply its recovery—and certainly not its loss.

So why did Lewis react so severely to Davidman's death? There are clearly a number of factors involved. However questionably the relationship had been initiated, Davidman had become Lewis's lover and intellectual soul mate, who helped him retain his passion and motivation for writing. She played—or, more accurately, was *allowed* to play—a role unique among Lewis's female circle. Her loss was deeply felt.

In the end the storm was stilled, and the waves ceased to crash against Lewis's house of faith. The assault had been extreme, and the testing severe. Yet its outcome was a faith which, like gold, had passed through the refiner's fire.

LEWIS'S FAILING HEALTH, 1961–1962

Lewis's faith might have survived, perhaps even becoming more robust. But the same could not be said of his health. In June 1961, Lewis spent two days in Oxford with his childhood friend Arthur Greeves. It was, he later declared, "one of the happiest times." Yet Lewis's letter to Greeves thanking him for visiting him had a darker aspect. Lewis disclosed he would soon have to enter the hospital for an operation to deal with an enlarged prostate gland.[14] It is unlikely that Greeves would have been totally surprised by this news. Lewis, he had noted during his visit, "was looking very ill." Something was clearly wrong with him.

The operation was scheduled to take place on 2 July in the Acland Nursing Home, a private medical facility outside the National Health Service, close to the centre of Oxford. Yet it soon became clear to Lewis's medical team that any operation was out of the question. His kidneys and heart were both failing him. His condition was inoperable. It could only be managed; it could not be cured. By the end of the summer, Lewis was so ill that he was unable to return to Cambridge to teach in the Michaelmas Term of 1961.

Realising that he might not live much longer, Lewis drew up his will. This document, dated 2 November 1961, appointed Owen Barfield and Cecil Harwood as his executors and trustees.[15] Lewis bequeathed his books and manuscripts to his brother, along with any income arising from Lewis's publications during the period of his lifetime. After Warnie's death, Lewis's residuary estate was to pass to his two stepsons. The will made no provision for a literary executor. Warnie would receive income from Lewis's publications, but would have no legal rights over them.

Lewis also stipulated that four further individuals were to receive £100, if there were sufficient funds in Lewis's bank account at the time of his death: Maureen Blake and his three godchildren, Laurence Harwood, Lucy Barfield, and Sarah Neylan.[16] Shortly afterwards, Lewis seems to have realised that he had failed to give any recognition to those who had cared for him at The Kilns. In a codicil of 10 December 1961, Lewis added two further names to this list: his gardener and handyman Fred Paxford, who was to receive £100, and his housekeeper Molly Miller, who was to receive £50.

14.1 The Acland Nursing Home, 25 Banbury Road, Oxford, in 1900. The nursing home, founded in 1882, was named after Sarah Acland, wife of Sir Henry Acland, formerly Regius Professor of Medicine at Oxford University. It moved to its Banbury Road site in 1897.

These seem paltry sums, given that, after probate on 1 April 1964, Lewis's estate was valued at £55,869, with a death duty payable of £12,828. Yet Lewis had little idea of his personal worth, and was now constantly worried about large demands from the Inland Revenue, which might bring him close to bankruptcy. His will also reveals anxiety over what might happen if the death duty were to exceed his realisable assets.

Lewis had hoped to be able to return to his normal teaching responsibilities at Magdalene College the next term, in January 1962. Yet as the months passed, Lewis realised that he was simply not well enough to allow this to happen. He wrote to a student he was meant to be supervising to apologise for his enforced absence in the spring of 1962, and to explain the problem:

They can't operate on my prostate till they've got my heart and kidneys right, and it begins to look as if they can't get my heart & kidneys right till they operate on my prostate. So we're in what an examinee, by a happy slip of the pen, called "a viscous circle."[17]

Lewis was finally able to go back to Cambridge on 24 April 1962 and resume his teaching, giving biweekly lectures on Spenser's *Faerie Queene*.[18] Yet he had not been healed; his condition had merely been stabilised through a careful diet and exercise regimen. Apologizing to Tolkien for being unable to attend a celebratory dinner at Merton College the following month to mark the publication of a collection of essays dedicated to him, Lewis explained that he now had to "wear a catheter, live on a low protein diet, and go early to bed."[19]

The catheter in question was an amateurish contraption involving corks and pieces of rubber tubing, which was notoriously prone to leaks. It had been devised by Lewis's friend Dr. Robert Havard, whose failure to diagnose Davidman's cancer early enough to allow intervention ought to have raised some questions in Lewis's mind about his professional competence. Lewis grumbled about Havard's shortcomings in a letter of 1960, noting that he "could and should have diagnosed Joy's trouble when she went to him about the symptoms years ago before we were married."[20] Yet despite these misgivings, Lewis still seems to have allowed Havard to advise him on how to cope with his prostate troubles, including letting Havard design the catheter. The frequent malfunctions of this improvised device caused inconvenience and occasionally chaos to Lewis's social life, as at an otherwise dull Cambridge sherry party which was enlivened with a shower of his urine.

Lewis's declining last years were not peaceful. Warnie was increasingly prone to alcoholic binges, alleviated but not cured by the loving ministrations of the nuns of Our Lady of Lourdes in Drogheda. The sisters appear to have developed a sentimental soft spot for the routinely dipsomanic retired major, treating him with a well-intentioned indulgence that probably only encouraged his addiction. The Kilns was in poor repair, with damp and mould beginning to make their appearance.

Magdalene College,
Cambridge,
England

16 Jan. 1961

Gentlemen
In reply to your invitation I have
the honour of nominating as a candidate for
the Nobel Prize in literature for 1961

Professor J. R. R. Tolkien of Oxford
in recognition of his now celebrated romantic
trilogy The Lord of the Rings.
I remain
your obedient servant
C. S. Lewis
(C. S. LEWIS)

14.2 C. S. Lewis's unpublished letter of 16 January 1961, nominating J. R. R. Tolkien for the 1961 Nobel Prize in Literature. Copyright © C. S. Lewis Pte. Ltd.

A further concern was the continued cooling of the relationship between Tolkien and Lewis. This, it must be noted, was largely on Tolkien's side, reflecting his darkening views about Lewis. Yet Lewis never lost his respect or admiration for Tolkien. This is clear from an episode that has only recently come to light. Early in January 1961, Lewis wrote to his former student, the literary scholar Alastair Fowler, who had asked Lewis whether he ought to apply for a chair of English at Exeter University. Lewis told him he should. Then he asked Fowler's advice.

351

Whom did he think ought to get the 1961 Nobel Prize in Literature?[21] The reason for this curious request has now become clear.

When the archives of the Swedish Academy for 1961 were opened up to scholars in January 2012, it was discovered that Lewis had nominated Tolkien for the prize.[22] As a professor of English literature at the University of Cambridge, Lewis had received an invitation from the Nobel Committee for Literature in late 1960 to nominate someone for the 1961 prize. In his letter of nomination, dated 16 January 1961, Lewis proposed Tolkien, in recognition of his "celebrated romantic trilogy" *The Lord of the Rings*.[23] In the end, the prize went to the Yugoslavian writer Ivo Andriæ (1892–1975). Tolkien's prose was judged inadequate in comparison with his rivals, which included Graham Greene (1904–1991). Yet Lewis's proposal of Tolkien for this supreme literary accolade is an important witness to his continued admiration and respect for his friend's work, despite their increasing personal distance. If Tolkien ever knew about this development (and there is nothing in his correspondence that suggests he did), it did nothing to rebuild his deteriorating relationship with Lewis.

As if this were not enough, both of Davidman's sons—now entrusted to the care of Lewis and Warnie—had issues which needed to be resolved, not least concerning their schooling. David, apparently suffering a crisis of identity, had decided to become an observant Jew, reaffirming his mother's religious roots. This obliged Lewis to find kosher food to enable him to meet his new dietary requirements. (Lewis eventually tracked some down at Palm's Delicatessen in Oxford's covered market.) Lewis encouraged David's reassertion of his Jewish roots, including arranging for him to learn Hebrew rather than the more traditional Latin at Magdalen College School. He sought the advice of Oxford University's Reader in Post-Biblical Jewish Studies, Cecil Roth (1899–1970), about how to accommodate his stepson's growing commitment to Judaism.[24] It was on Roth's recommendation that David began his studies at North West London Talmudical College in Golders Green, London.

During the spring of 1963, Lewis's health recovered sufficiently to allow him to spend the Lent and Easter Terms teaching at Cambridge.

By May 1963, he was planning his lectures for the Michaelmas Term. He would deliver a lecture course at Cambridge on medieval literature on Tuesday and Thursday mornings in full term, beginning on 10 October.[25]

At this point, Lewis developed a friendship which would initially prove to be of critical importance in his final months, and subsequently in reviving interest in him after his death. Lewis had many American admirers with whom he corresponded over the years. One of these was Walter Hooper (1931–), a junior American academic from the University of Kentucky who had researched his writings and was interested in writing a book on him. Hooper had begun a correspondence with Lewis on 23 November 1954, while serving in the US army, and developed a long-standing interest in Lewis's work during his subsequent academic career. Hooper had been particularly impressed by a short preface Lewis had contributed to *Letters to Young Churches* (1947), a contemporary translation of the New Testament Epistles by the English clerical writer J. B. Phillips (1906–1982). Even as early as 1957, Lewis had agreed to meet Hooper if he should ever have cause to visit England.[26]

In the end, Hooper's visit was postponed, although their correspondence continued. In December 1962, Hooper sent Lewis a bibliography of Lewis's published works that he had compiled, which Lewis appreciatively corrected and expanded at several points. He once again agreed to meet with Hooper when Hooper was next in England, and suggested June 1963 as a time when he expected to be at home in Oxford.[27] The meeting was finally arranged for 7 June, when Hooper would be in Oxford to attend an International Summer School at Exeter College.

Lewis clearly enjoyed meeting Hooper, and invited him to come along to the next meeting of the Inklings the following Monday. These meetings now took place on the other side of St. Giles, the Inklings having reluctantly transferred from the Eagle and Child to the Lamb and Flag, following renovations which had ruined the privacy and intimacy of the "Rabbit Room."[28] Since Lewis had to be in residence at Magdalene College during term time, the meetings now took place on Mondays, allowing Lewis to take the afternoon "Cantab Crawler" to Cambridge. Hooper, who was an

Episcopalian at this point, accompanied Lewis to church at Holy Trinity, Headington Quarry, on Sunday mornings.

FINAL ILLNESS AND DEATH

Lewis had intended to travel to Ireland in late July 1963 to visit Arthur Greeves. Aware of his declining physical strength, Lewis had arranged for Douglas Gresham to join them, partly to help carry his luggage. On 7 June, when Lewis returned to Oxford at the end of Cambridge's summer term, Warnie had left for Ireland, assuming that Lewis would join him during the following month. But it was not to be. Lewis's health deteriorated sharply in the first week of July.

On 11 July, Lewis reluctantly wrote to Greeves to cancel his trip. He had had a "collapse as regards the heart trouble."[29] Lewis was now tired, unable to concentrate, and prone to falling asleep. His kidneys were not functioning properly, allowing toxins to build up in his bloodstream, causing him fatigue. The only solution was blood transfusions, which temporarily eased the situation. (The general use of kidney dialysis still lay some years in the future.)

When Walter Hooper arrived at The Kilns on the morning of Sunday, 14 July 1963 to take Lewis to church, he realised that Lewis was seriously ill. Lewis was exhausted, scarcely able to hold a cup of tea in his hands, and seemed to be in a state of confusion. Worried about his failure to maintain his correspondence in his brother's extended absence, Lewis invited Hooper to become his personal secretary. Hooper was already signed up to teach a course in Kentucky that fall, but agreed to take the position in January 1964. Lewis, however, possibly confused and unable to concentrate fully, failed to explain what kind of financial arrangement he had in mind to recompense Hooper for his work, or what formal expectations he had for his new employee.

On the morning of Monday, 15 July, Lewis wrote a short letter to Mary Willis Shelburne, explaining how he had lost all mental concentration, and would be going into the hospital that afternoon for an examination and evaluation of his condition.[30] Lewis arrived at the Acland Nursing Home at five o'clock that afternoon, and suffered a heart attack almost immediately after his arrival. He fell into a coma, and was judged to be close to death. The Acland informed Austin and Katharine Farrer, having failed in their efforts to contact Lewis's next of kin—Warnie.[31]

The next day, Austin Farrer made the decision that Lewis, who was being kept alive with an oxygen mask, would wish to receive the last rites. He arranged for Michael Watts, curate of the Church of St. Mary Magdalen, a few minutes' walk from the Acland Nursing Home, to visit Lewis for this purpose. At 2.00 p.m., Watts administered the last rites. An hour later, to the astonishment of the medical team, Lewis awoke from his coma and asked for a cup of tea, apparently unaware that he had been unconscious for the better part of a day.

Lewis later told his friends that he wished he had died during the coma. The "whole experience," he later wrote to Cecil Harwood, was "very gentle." It seemed a shame, "having reached the gate so easily, not to be allowed through."[32] Like Lazarus, he would have to die again. In a more extended comment in his final letter to his confidant Arthur Greeves, he remarked:

> Tho' I am by no means unhappy I can't help feeling it was rather a pity I did revive in July. I mean, having been glided so painlessly up to the Gate it seems hard to have it shut in one's face and know that the whole process must some day be gone thro' again, and perhaps far less pleasantly! Poor Lazarus! But God knows best.[33]

Lewis had remained in regular correspondence with Greeves since June 1914—one of the most significant and intimate relationships of his life, which few of his circle knew anything about until the publication of *Surprised by Joy* revealed their youthful friendship (though not its prolonged extension into the present). Characteristically, Lewis apologised for the consequences of his condition: "It looks as if you and I shall never meet again in this life."

Although Lewis enjoyed two days of mental clarity after awakening from his coma, he then entered a dark period of "dreams, illusions, and some moments of tangled reason."[34] On 18 July, the day on which these delusions began, Lewis was visited by George Sayer, who was disturbed to find him so very confused. Lewis told Sayer that he had just been appointed Charles Williams's literary executor, and urgently needed to find a manuscript hidden under Mrs. Williams's mattress. The problem was that Mrs. Williams wanted a vast sum of money for the manuscript, and Lewis didn't have the ten thousand pounds she was demanding. When Lewis began to talk about Mrs. Moore as if she were still alive, Sayer realised that Lewis was delusional. When Lewis then told him that he had asked Walter Hooper to be his temporary secretary to handle his correspondence, Sayer not unreasonably assumed this was also a delusion.[35]

Once Sayer realised that there really was a Walter Hooper, outside the dark hallucinatory realm that Lewis was occupying at that time, and that Hooper would be able to help look after Lewis, he decided that he ought to travel to Ireland to track down Warnie. In the end, Warnie turned out to be in such a bad state of alcohol poisoning that he was incapable of understanding what had happened to Lewis, let alone contributing to the amelioration of the situation. Sayer returned alone to Oxford.

On 6 August, Lewis was allowed to return to The Kilns, under the care of Alec Ross, a nurse provided by the Acland. Ross was used to caring for wealthy patients in their well-appointed homes, and was shocked by the squalid conditions he found at The Kilns, particularly its filthy kitchen. A major cleanup began, to make the house habitable. Lewis was forbidden to climb stairs, and so had to be accommodated on the ground floor. Hooper took over Lewis's old upstairs bedroom and acted as secretary to Lewis. Among the more pathetic missives Hooper wrote on behalf of Lewis at this point were Lewis's letters of resignation from his chair at Cambridge University and his fellowship at Magdalene College.

But how was Lewis to move all his books from Cambridge? He was totally unable to travel. On 12 August, Lewis wrote to Jock Burnet, the bursar of Magdalene College, informing him that Walter Hooper would be coming to Cambridge on his behalf to remove all the possessions from his room. The following day, Lewis penned an even more pathetic missive, telling Burnet that he was free to sell anything that remained. Walter Hooper and Douglas Gresham turned up at Magdalene on 14 August, armed with seven pages of detailed instructions from Lewis concerning his possessions. It took them two days to sort things out. On 16 August, they returned to The Kilns in a truck containing thousands of books, which were stacked in piles on the floor until space could be found for them in bookcases.

In September, Hooper returned to the United States to resume his teaching responsibilities, leaving Lewis to be cared for by Paxford and Mrs. Molly Miller, Lewis's housekeeper. Lewis was clearly anxious about his own situation. Where was Warnie, and when would he return? Sadly, Lewis concluded that Warnie had "completely deserted" him, despite knowing the seriousness of his condition. "He has been in Ireland since June and doesn't even write, and is, I suppose, drinking himself to death."[36] Warnie had still not returned by 20 September, when Lewis wrote a somewhat furtive letter to Hooper to clarify the nature of his future employment.

It is clear that Lewis had not given proper thought to what he wished Hooper to do in his role as his private secretary, nor how he would pay for this.[37] When Hooper wrote to broach the subject of a salary for his proposed employment, Lewis somewhat shamefacedly confessed that he just didn't have the funds to pay him, offering plausible yet weak excuses. Having resigned his chair, he no longer had a salary. And what if one of the Gresham boys needed money?[38] Having Hooper as a "paid secretary" would be a luxury that he just couldn't afford. But if Hooper could afford to come over in June 1964, he would be most welcome. The unspoken assumption seems to have been that Hooper would be funding himself.

We see here one of the matters that preyed heavily on Lewis's mind after the resignation of his Cambridge chair—money. Lewis continued to live in fear of tax demands that he might not be able to pay. His income was limited to royalties from his books. This was quite substantial at the time; yet Lewis was convinced that they would soon decline as interest in his works waned. His anxieties about his financial future were clearly fuelled in September by his loneliness. He had no soul mate with whom to share his worries.

A month later, Lewis wrote again to Hooper, bringing the good news that Warnie had finally returned.[39] Lewis, it soon became clear, was still anxious about his finances. He was not sure what he could pay Hooper—if anything. His best offer was that Hooper could live at The Kilns, where they would have to share a fire and a table. Then there was the problem of Warnie, who might resent Hooper's presence. The most Lewis could afford to pay Hooper was five pounds a week—fourteen dollars.[40] It was hardly an attractive prospect. In the end, however, Hooper agreed to come. His arrival was scheduled for the first week of January 1964.[41]

In the middle of November, Lewis received a letter from Oxford University which can be seen as a sign—if a sign were indeed needed—marking a rehabilitation of his reputation there. He was invited to deliver the Romanes Lecture in the Sheldonian Theatre, perhaps the most prestigious of Oxford University's public lectures. With great regret, Lewis asked Warnie to write a "very polite refusal."[42]

Friday, 22 November 1963, began as usual in the Lewis household, Warnie later recalled: after they had breakfast, they turned to the routine answering of letters, and tried to solve the crossword puzzle. Warnie noted that Lewis seemed tired after lunch, and suggested that he go to bed. At 4.00, Warnie brought him a cup of tea, and found him "drowsy but comfortable." At 5.30, Warnie heard a "crash" from Lewis's bedroom. He ran in to find Lewis collapsed, unconscious, at the foot of the bed. A few moments later, Lewis died.[43] His death certificate would give the multiple causes of his death as renal failure, prostate obstruction, and cardiac degeneration.

At that same time, President John F. Kennedy's motorcade left Dallas's Love Field Airport, beginning its journey downtown. An hour later, Kennedy was fatally wounded by a sniper. He was pronounced dead at

Parkland Memorial Hospital. Media reports of Lewis's death were completely overshadowed by the substantially more significant tragedy that unfolded that day in Dallas.

Warnie was overwhelmed by his brother's death, which triggered another alcoholic binge. He refused to let anyone know when the funeral was taking place.[44] In the end, Douglas Gresham and others telephoned a few key friends to let them know the arrangements. While Warnie spent Tuesday, 26 November in bed drinking whisky, others gathered on that cold, frosty, sunlit morning to bury Lewis at Holy Trinity Church, Headington Quarry, Oxford. There was no funeral procession into the church; Lewis's coffin had been brought to the church the previous evening. No public announcement was made of the funeral. It was a private affair, attended by Lewis's circle of friends—including Barfield, Tolkien, Sayer, and the president of Magdalen College. The service was led by the vicar of Holy Trinity, Ronald Head. Austin Farrer read the lesson. There being no immediate family present, the small funeral procession from the church into the graveyard was headed by Maureen Blake[45] and Douglas Gresham, who followed the candle bearers and processional cross into the churchyard, where the freshly dug grave awaited them.[46]

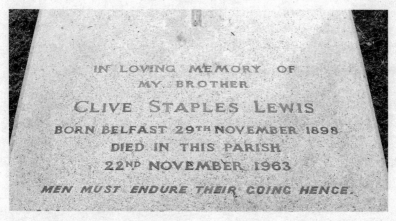

IN LOVING MEMORY OF
MY BROTHER
CLIVE STAPLES LEWIS
BORN BELFAST 29TH NOVEMBER 1898
DIED IN THIS PARISH
22ND NOVEMBER 1963
MEN MUST ENDURE THEIR GOING HENCE.

14.3 The inscription on Lewis's gravestone in the churchyard of Holy Trinity, Headington Quarry, Oxford.

The rather melancholic text Warnie chose for his brother's gravestone was that displayed on the Shakespearean calendar in Little Lea on the day of their mother's death in August 1908: "Men must endure their going hence." Yet perhaps some of Lewis's own words, penned a few months earlier, capture both his style and his hope in the face of his inevitable death somewhat better than this severe and forbidding epitaph. We are, Lewis suggested, like

> a seed patiently waiting in the earth: waiting to come up a flower in the Gardener's good time, up into the *real* world, the real waking. I suppose that our whole present life, looked back on from there, will seem only a drowsy half-waking. We are here in the land of dreams. But cock-crow is coming.[47]

PART FIVE

AFTERLIFE

CHAPTER 15

THE LEWIS PHENOMENON

T owards the end of his life, Lewis remarked to Walter Hooper that he expected to be forgotten within five years of his death. That was the judgement of many in the 1960s, who saw Lewis as hopelessly wedded to the cultural outlook of an earlier generation. Cometh the hour, cometh the man—yet Lewis's hour now seemed to lie in the past. The "High Sixties" (1960–1973) witnessed rapid cultural change, as a rising younger generation sought to distance themselves from the culture and values of their parents.[1] And Lewis was on the wrong side of that watershed.

THE 1960S: A FADING STAR

In 1965, Chad Walsh (1914–1991), the American literary scholar who published the first book on Lewis in 1949, declared that Lewis's influence was now "on the wane in America."[2] Lewis's rise to fame in the United States was linked with the wartime revival of interest in religious questions, which persisted until late in the 1950s—but then began to fade. During the 1960s, religious interest and concern switched from theoretical questions to practical issues. Lewis seemed "much too theoretical and abstract" to the younger generation. He had little to say in the face of the great debates of that age—the Vietnam War, the sexual revolution, and the "death of God."

Lewis was beached, as the tide that had brought him to prominence receded in the 1960s. This was the wisdom of that turbulent age. In its obituary for Lewis, *Time* magazine declared him to be "one of the church's minor prophets," a defender of the faith who "with fashionable urbanity justified an unfashionable orthodoxy against the heresies of his time."[3] But the tone of the obituary was that of marking his passing, not anticipating his resurrection. Lewis would be remembered as "an impressive scholar"—by those who looked backwards.

15.1 Lewis at home at The Kilns in 1960. This is one of the best-known images of the later Lewis. It depicts him sitting at his desk, complete with the materials he used when writing—on the left, a large cup of tea, a bottle of Quink ink, an ashtray, and a box of matches; on the right, a pipe, a tin of tobacco, and a second box of matches.

So what lay ahead? Walsh was rightly cautious here, warning it was not possible to determine what Lewis's future standing in America might be. Walsh's own hunch was that Lewis's more "straightforward books"—such as *Mere Christianity*—would dwindle in their appeal. After all, such works of "religious journalism" appealed primarily to their own day and age. Walsh, himself a literary scholar, suggested that Lewis's "more imaginative books"—such as his "superb series of seven Narnia novels for children"—might live on, and "become a permanent part of the literary and religious heritage." Yet that would lie in the future, if it were to happen at all. For the moment, Lewis was entering a period of "relative obscurity."[4]

Lewis had indeed few champions in North America during the 1960s. Lewis was then read and advocated chiefly by Episcopalians—such as Chad Walsh and Walter Hooper—even though there were signs of an emerging interest on the part of some influential Catholics. Evangelicals—a growing religious constituency in the United States during the 1960s—clearly regarded him with suspicion, in that he violated both their social norms and their religious concerns. Theologically, evangelicals had little in common with Lewis, who offered a literary explanation of the observed centrality of the Bible to the Christian faith, not a theological defence of its right to occupy that place. Apart from a loose connection with the Oxford Pastorate through the Socratic Club, Lewis did not associate with British evangelicals, even in Oxford or Cambridge. In the year of Lewis's death, Martyn Lloyd-Jones (1899–1981), one of the most influential British evangelical preachers of that time, pronounced him to be unsound on a number of issues, chiefly relating to the doctrine of salvation.[5]

Lewis seemed a total outsider to American evangelicals in the late 1950s and early 1960s, when most within the movement regarded even watching movies as spiritually dangerous. What evangelical would want to be associated with someone who smoked heavily, drank copious quantities of beer, and held views on the Bible, the Atonement, and purgatory which were out of place in the evangelical community of that age? While some evangelicals warmed to Lewis's apologetic writings in the 1960s, most regarded him with distrust.

It would be unfair to suggest that Lewis was written off by 1970.

Perhaps a more reliable judgement would be that the surging tide that had once swept Lewis to public attention now withdrew, seemingly leaving him washed up and beached. Lewis was not discredited; he was simply sidelined. The rebirth of interest in religious questions between 1942 and 1957, which originally brought Lewis to prominence, was replaced by a new cultural mood that was inclined to reject religion as an outdated habit of thought and practice and was anxious to break free from any lingering influence of the past. The great sociological predictions of the 1960s envisaged religion as losing its intellectual and social traction. A secular age lay ahead.

The cultural mood of the High Sixties was well captured by Tom Wolfe in his 1987 essay "The Great Relearning." Everything was to be swept aside, so that culture could be reconstructed by an "unprecedented start from zero."[6] Other religious and literary prophets arose in America and Europe, and Lewis fell by the wayside. Lewis was a distinctly religious voice in a coming secular age, and more important, he advocated taking the past seriously, when most wanted to abandon it altogether as an embarrassing liability.

On the literary front, the impact of Lewis's imaginative writings—including the Narnia series—was overshadowed by the astonishing success of Tolkien's *Lord of the Rings*, which achieved cult status during the 1960s, especially once cheap paperback editions began to appear in the United States. Tolkien waxed as Lewis waned. The intricate structure and deep backstory of *The Lord of the Rings* pointed to a sophistication and profundity that seemed lacking in Narnia.

Tolkien's epic narrative of the pathology of power chimed in with the anxieties of that age concerning nuclear holocausts. Though conceived long before the advent of the atom bomb, Tolkien's "one ring to rule them all" seemed a powerful image of the lure of a weapon of supreme destructive force, and the power it conveyed on its apparent masters—who were, in reality, its slaves. Much to Tolkien's surprise, he now found himself idolised by exactly the sort of students he would have once thrown out of his Oxford lectures.

REDISCOVERY: THE NEW INTEREST IN LEWIS

Yet Lewis bounced back. It is relatively straightforward to account for Lewis's rise to fame, first in the dark wartime period of the early 1940s, and then again as Narnia wove its imaginative magic throughout the 1950s. But that does not explain the *resurgence* of interest in Lewis a generation later. Many popular writers of the 1940s and 1950s simply sank without a trace. For example, consider the five American top fiction bestsellers of 1947:

1. Russell Janney, *The Miracle of the Bells*
2. Thomas B. Costain, *The Moneyman*
3. Laura Z. Hobson, *Gentleman's Agreement*
4. Kenneth Roberts, *Lydia Bailey*
5. Frank Yerby, *The Vixens*[7]

All of these books can still be purchased today, generally from specialist, secondhand dealers. But despite their initial blaze of glory, they have all faded. Why is Lewis different?

We can map out some possible lines of exploration that at least help us understand—even if they do not really "explain" in the stronger sense of the term—the resurgence of interest in Lewis. It is relatively easy to identify some pieces of the jigsaw; the problem is that we do not fully understand how they fit into a bigger picture.

First, collections of previously unpublished or inaccessible material by Lewis began to appear. These were largely the result of the dedicated editorial work of Walter Hooper, who had acted as a private secretary to Lewis in the summer of 1963, and subsequently served as Lewis's literary executor after the death of Cecil Harwood in 1975. Hooper had consulted with Lewis during his lifetime on developing a complete bibliography of his works. When this was first published in 1965, it ran to 282 items, not including letters.[8]

In the early 1970s, the leading British publisher William Collins &

Sons bought the rights to Lewis's publications, and established the Fount imprint to give them a distinct identity within the company. Over the next decade, Hooper brought out a steady trickle of collected essays with Collins—such as *Screwtape Proposes a Toast* (1965); *Of This and Other Worlds* (1966); *Christian Reflections* (1967); *Fern-Seed and Elephants* (1975); and *God in the Dock* (1979).[9] These new collections expanded the horizons of those who already knew Lewis, while introducing him to others. Hooper insisted that the publication of any new collection of Lewis's material should be matched by the reprint of two of his earlier works, thus ensuring that his less popular works—such as *The Pilgrim's Regress* and *The Abolition of Man*—remained in print.[10]

Most recently, and possibly most significantly, Hooper edited the 3,500 pages of Lewis's correspondence (2000–2006), allowing Lewis's intellectual, social, and spiritual trajectory to be tracked in detail. These letters, essential to Lewis scholarship, form the narrative backbone of this biography.

Second, a series of significant societies were formed in the United States, dedicated to preserving Lewis's memory and legacy. The first of these was the New York C. S. Lewis Society, founded in 1969. Others soon followed, creating associations through which devotees of Lewis could gather to discuss his work. Those who were enthused about Lewis in the 1940s and 1950s sought to pass that enthusiasm on to others in the 1970s. In 1974, the Marion E. Wade Center, dedicated to the life and works of Lewis and his circle, was established at Wheaton College, Wheaton, Illinois, building on an earlier collection of material brought together by Clyde S. Kilby (1902–1986), a former professor of English at Wheaton College. Lewis's homeland was somewhat slow to follow suit: the Oxford C. S. Lewis Society was established as late as 1982. The institutionalisation of the Lewis legacy had begun. Networks were established that facilitated the intergenerational transmission of his legacy.

Third, well-written biographies began to appear from the pens of those close to Lewis, allowing their readers to grasp what he was like. The first was *C. S. Lewis: A Biography* (1974), written jointly by Roger

Lancelyn Green and Walter Hooper. Green (1918–1987), a former student of Lewis's at Oxford, had gone on to write children's books himself, and had authored important biographies of British children's writers—most notably, his studies of J. M. Barrie (1960) and Lewis Carroll (1960). Hooper and Green's biography was followed by *Jack* (1988) by George Sayer, another close friend. These remain landmarks in Lewis studies. Though inevitably lacking critical distance, both of these biographies revealed details of Lewis's personal life which portrayed him as a human being and gave added depth to a reading of some of his works.

Finally, we might note how the great surge of interest in Tolkien in the United States in the late 1960s and early 1970s indirectly benefitted Lewis. As it became increasingly clear that Tolkien was not a solitary Oxford writer, but was linked with the group now generally known as the Inklings, attention was paid once more to the most prominent member of that group—C. S. Lewis. The always large number of American graduate students studying at Oxford began to explore the haunts of Tolkien and Lewis, the students taking both their memories and their enthusiasm home with them. (With this trend in mind, tourist maps of Oxford now show the precise location of the Eagle and Child.)

Lewis has always been appreciated more in the United States than in England, despite never once setting foot stateside. This is partly due to the intellectual and cultural prestige of Oxford University in American eyes. Lewis is one of the elite group of bestselling children's authors who were also Oxford dons—including Lewis Carroll and J. R. R. Tolkien. Lewis's Cambridge period tends to be glossed over by many American commentators, who often refer to him simply as an "Oxford don."

Yet Lewis now rides high in America only partly for cultural reasons; there is a significant religious element to his appeal. Lewis is trusted and respected by many American Christians, who treat him as their theological and spiritual mentor. Engaging both heart and mind, Lewis opened up the intellectual and imaginative depths of the Christian faith like nobody else. As Lewis himself pointed out in his broadcast talks during the Second World War, he was simply an educated layman, who spoke directly and accessibly to ordinary Christians over the heads of their clergy. Lewis proved ideally attuned to the pedagogical needs and abilities of laypeople, irrespective of their denomination, who wanted to explore their faith further.

Irrespective of their denomination. We must linger over this crucial point. During the 1960s, the first signs began to emerge of an erosion of denominationalism in American Protestantism. Protestant Christians began to define themselves primarily as Christians, and secondarily by denomination, reflecting an increasingly loose commitment to a denomination as a marker of religious identity.[11] A Presbyterian might become a Methodist upon moving to a new town or state, if the local Methodist church offered better child care or preaching. A church's denomination came to be seen as of lesser importance than the quality of its preaching and pastoral care. Seminaries began to drop denominationally specific titles. Thus the Protestant Episcopal Theological Seminary in Virginia became Virginia Theological Seminary. Lewis's notion of "mere Christianity" spoke powerfully into this trend, with Lewis achieving a high degree of acceptance across denominations precisely because he avoided advocating any specific form of Christianity. Lewis's *Mere Christianity* became the manifesto for a form of Christianity that exulted in essentials, regarding other matters as secondary.

American Catholics began to read Lewis in the aftermath of the Second Vatican Council (1962–1965). This landmark council, convened by Pope John XXIII (1881–1963), aimed to reconnect Catholicism with other Christian churches, and encourage a deeper engagement with contemporary culture. Before this, Catholics tended to regard the works of other Christian writers as being of questionable orthodoxy and utility. The council opened the way for Catholics to read and respect non-Catholic authors—such as Lewis. Lewis now gained a growing Catholic readership both as a close friend of J. R. R. Tolkien and as an admirer of G. K. Chesterton, neither of whose Catholic credentials could be questioned. Leading American Catholics, such as Cardinal Avery Dulles (1918–2008) and Peter Kreeft (1937–), began to champion Lewis as a "mere

Christian" whom Catholics could take seriously. Many who converted to Catholicism in the last two decades have cited Lewis as an important influence, despite Lewis's original Ulster Protestant cultural roots.[12]

Yet there is another point, too easily overlooked, which is of especial importance for American Catholics today. "Mere Christianity" avoids more than "denominational imperialism"; it also avoids the abuses of power and privilege that too easily arise when denominations and their leaders see their own preservation as taking priority over the well-being of the Christian faith itself. Lewis represents a lay form of Christianity which has no special place for clergy or ecclesiastical institutions. My conversations with American Catholics suggest that many of them, increasingly disenchanted with the failings of their bishops and dioceses, find in Lewis a voice that allows them to reclaim their faith without having also to affirm the institutions they believe to have tarnished that faith in recent years. Will Lewis become the voice of those who are demanding reform and renewal of overclericalised churches?

It is clear that Lewis's writings have now found a new audience far beyond his original admirers. He has come to be seen as a trustworthy, intelligent, and above all *accessible* representative of a theologically and culturally attractive vision of the Christian faith. The fact that Lewis was an outsider to the United States worked to his advantage, in that it allowed him to be seen as a unifying figure, rising above local American denominational disputes and debates. Lewis has become that rarest of phenomena—a modern Christian writer regarded with respect and affection by Christians of all traditions.

LEWIS AND AMERICAN EVANGELICALS

A growing number of those Americans who profited from reading Lewis in the 1970s were evangelicals. A generation after his death, Lewis has become a cultural and religious icon for the movement. Some have now even spoken of Lewis as the "patron saint" of American evangelicalism. So how did a movement that initially regarded Lewis with intense suspicion come eventually to embrace him, and then to enthrone him? To understand the somewhat unexpected rise of Lewis's influence within the American evangelical constituency, we need to reflect on the changing face of American evangelicalism since 1945.

During the 1920s, American evangelicalism was shaped by the rise of fundamentalism, which led to evangelicals developing a significant degree of cultural disengagement and isolationism. The mood within the movement began to change in the late 1940s, partly through the influence of writers such as Billy Graham (1918–) and Carl F. H. Henry (1913–2003), who strongly advocated engagement with mainstream American culture. This "new evangelicalism," initially a minority trend, grew apace, taking its lead from individuals such as Graham, publications such as *Christianity Today*, and institutions such as Fuller Theological Seminary in Pasadena, California.[13] This new form of American evangelicalism was a strongly populist movement, capturing the hearts and wills of many. But many noted that it had yet to engage the mind, or see the importance of connecting with the intellectual subculture.

As American evangelicals sought refreshment of the mind as well as the soul, they found what they lacked in British writers—above all, from within the Church of England. During the 1950s and 1960s, the leading British evangelical John R. W. Stott (1921–2011) developed an intellectually rigorous approach to evangelicalism, which was warmly received in the United States. Stott's approach itself may have lacked populist appeal, but it was strong on rational reflection on faith. Stott became a hero for American evangelicals who wanted to love God with all their minds. His *Basic Christianity* (1958) was a masterpiece of reasoned argument, setting out to demonstrate the "intellectual respectability" of Christian faith.

Then evangelicals started reading Lewis. It is difficult to date this development with any precision, but anecdotal evidence suggests it dates from the mid-1970s. Hints of an evangelical recognition of Lewis's wisdom can, however, be seen much earlier, particularly on the part of its leaders. Though few knew of it, both John Stott and Billy Graham sought

Lewis's counsel as they prepared for Graham's mission to the University of Cambridge in 1955.[14] In that same year, Carl F. H. Henry had invited Lewis to write some apologetic pieces for the flagship evangelical journal *Christianity Today*.[15]

Evangelical leaders who came to faith from a secular background in the 1970s often cited Lewis's *Mere Christianity* as a core influence in their conversion—such as Charles "Chuck" Wendell Colson (1931–2012), the special adviser to President Richard Nixon, who became implicated in the Watergate scandal and rose to prominence within evangelical circles after his conversion in 1973. Evangelical writers now began to cite Lewis in their works, especially his *Mere Christianity*, encouraging their readers to value this important author and explore him further.

As evangelicalism intensified its commitment to cultural engagement, the importance of apologetics became increasingly clear. Lewis was rapidly recognised by evangelicals as a master of that art. John Stott's apologetic approach in *Basic Christianity* relied on its readers already knowing something about the Bible, and being willing to have biblical passages explained to them. Lewis made few such demands in *Mere Christianity*, basing his apologetic approach on general principles, fine observation, and an appeal to shared human experience.

Evangelical student organisations, such as InterVarsity Christian Fellowship, now began to make Lewis's works part of their staple diet, valuing both their accessibility and their rhetorical power. Those in the know forgave Lewis for not being an evangelical; most evangelicals, however, simply saw Lewis as one of their own. After all, had he not been converted from atheism? That, for many, was enough to allow Lewis to be seen as a "born-again" Christian.

As American evangelicals read Lewis, they encountered a vision of the Christian faith that they found to be intellectually robust, imaginatively compelling, and ethically fertile. Those who initially valued Lewis for his rational defence of the Christian faith now found themselves appreciating his appeal to the imagination and emotions. Lewis's multilayered conception of Christianity enabled evangelicals to realise that they could enrich their faith without diluting it, and engage secular culture in ways other than through reasoned argument.

Yet Lewis's growing acceptance within evangelicalism reflects more than his winsome and accessible presentation of the Christian faith. A major cultural transition made Lewis even more attractive and significant. Nobody really knows when modernity finally lost out to postmodernity in the United States—or why. Some argue it happened in the 1960s; others in the 1980s. Yet there is no doubt about the outcome of this cultural shift. Intuitive modes of reflection, shaped by images and stories, have trumped logical argument, based solely on reason.

John Stott's strongly didactic approach to faith in *Basic Christianity* had many modernist virtues; yet with the rise of postmodernism, its approach increasingly seemed to belong to a previous generation. *Basic Christianity* was virtually devoid of any appeal to the imagination, or any recognition of the emotional dimensions of faith. As American evangelicals came to realise the importance of narrative and imagination in the life of faith, they turned instead to Lewis as their guide.

Lewis allowed his readers to grasp and benefit from the importance of images and stories for the life of faith, without losing sight of the robustly reasonable nature of the Christian gospel. Where older American evangelicals spent their time taking potshots at postmodernity during the 1980s and early 1990s, the writings of Lewis allowed younger evangelicals to connect with this new cultural mood. Where the Old Guard urged their younger followers to shun this trend, Lewis allowed them to engage it powerfully and persuasively.

In a 1998 article marking the centenary of Lewis's birth, *Christianity Today* declared that Lewis had come to be "the Aquinas, the Augustine, and the Aesop of contemporary evangelicalism."[16] There is no doubt that Lewis has been instrumental in changing the cultural outlook of American evangelicalism. In the 1950s, evangelicalism was suspicious of literature, movies, and the arts.[17] Evangelical admiration for Lewis may have begun with respect for his ideas; it soon developed into a respect for the modes and manners in which Lewis expressed those ideas.

By the mid-1980s, evangelical colleges—such as the flagship Wheaton College in Wheaton, Illinois—were encouraging evangelicals to engage with literature as a means of enriching their faith, appealing to Lewis as an exemplar. To date, evangelical engagement has focussed primarily on a group of writers clustered around Lewis or historically linked with him—namely, Owen Barfield, G. K. Chesterton, George MacDonald, J. R. R. Tolkien, Dorothy L. Sayers, and Charles Williams. It remains to be seen where this development will lead; there are, however, now clear signs that evangelicalism has begun to grasp the potential of literature to enrich, communicate, and commend faith.

Since 1985, I have taught at summer schools in Oxford attended by large numbers of young American evangelicals. Lewis has been a topic of conversation throughout that entire period. At the time of writing, there is not the slightest sign of any loss of interest. On the basis of those extended conversations over a quarter of a century, I have come to my own conclusion about why Lewis appeals so powerfully to a rising evangelical generation in the United States: Lewis is seen to enrich and extend faith, without diluting it. In other words, evangelicals tend to see Lewis as a catalyst, who opens up a deeper vision of the Christian faith, engaging the mind, the feelings, and the imagination, without challenging fundamental distinctives. Lewis supplements, without displacing, evangelical basics. While this involves a selective reading of Lewis, this does not seem to cause any fundamental concern. Lewis is grafted on to evangelical essentials, engaging weaknesses without compromising strengths. For many young evangelicals, reading Lewis gives added depth and power to their evangelical commitments.

Yet some fundamentalist Protestant Christians in the United States continue to regard Lewis as a dangerous heretic. The strident tone of such criticisms of Lewis can be judged from the following:

> C.S. Lewis was an imposter, who corrupted the Gospel of Jesus Christ, and led multitudes of victims into Hellfire with his doctrines of devils. Lewis used profanities, told lewd stories, and frequently got drunk with his students.[18]

Other fundamentalists argue that the modern evangelical admiration for Lewis is a sign that evangelicalism has lost its way and forfeited its birthright.[19] While this is a minority viewpoint, it is indicative of anxiety on the part of some older evangelicals about the recent directions the movement has taken in America. Yet theology may be of secondary importance here; some would suggest that the real issue is power and influence. Lewis has displaced some who would see themselves as natural authority figures within the American evangelical movement.

LEWIS AS A LITERARY LANDMARK

It is Lewis's imaginative works, particularly his Chronicles of Narnia, that now attract the greatest following, both in American culture at large and within Christian circles in particular. Chad Walsh's 1965 intuition about Lewis's possible future appeal can now be seen to have been justified. Lewis is now regarded as one of the finest authors of fantasy literature, standing alongside—and in most cases well above—J. M. Barrie, L. Frank Baum, Lewis Carroll, Neil Gaiman, Kenneth Grahame, Rudyard Kipling, Madeleine L'Engle, Ursula K. Le Guin, Terry Pratchett, Philip Pullman, J. K. Rowling, and J. R. R. Tolkien.

The literary convention of fantasy is not restricted to any specific ideology. It can be used to champion—or subvert—secular humanism or Christianity. As a secular humanist, the British writer Philip Pullman loathes Lewis, recently suggesting that he was "tempted to dig him up and throw stones at him."[20] This will probably strike most people as slightly weird, but it is completely consistent with what one critic has described as the "virulent theological hatred" that Pullman displays towards those he disagrees with.[21]

In fact, far from dismissing Lewis's Chronicles of Narnia, Pullman's His Dark Materials trilogy implicitly recognises them as representing the definitive statement of the position he wishes to reject. The more Pullman criticises Lewis, the more he affirms Lewis's cultural significance. In the end, Pullman's appeal is parasitic, depending precisely upon the cultural impact of Narnia that he wishes to subvert. As recent studies have noted, Pullman offers "a kind of inverted homage to his predecessor, deliberately composing a kind of 'anti-Narnia,' a secular humanist alternative to Lewis's Christian fantasy."[22]

Literary scholars have pointed out how Pullman draws extensively on Lewis in many respects—for example, his affirmation of the importance of the story, his description of the creative process, his fascination with the mythic dimension of certain literary works, and his "high Romantic view of the imagination."[23] Lewis's most strident critic, paradoxically, turns out to be one of the most important witnesses to his present-day influence and importance.

There is no doubt of Lewis's current status as a literary figure and religious writer. Lewis's books began to appear on the religion bestseller lists of secular bookstores in the early 1990s, and they have remained there ever since. The 1994 release of the Hollywood version of *Shadowlands*, starring Anthony Hopkins and Debra Winger, generated a new interest in Lewis as a human being, leading to increased sales of his works.

By the time of the centenary of his birth—1998—it was obvious that Lewis was not merely back in business; he had reached new heights of influence. The British Royal Mail, for example, issued a set of commemorative postage stamps based on characters from Narnia. In 2011, they followed through with a further release of eight postage stamps featuring magical figures from British literature. Two of these stamps featured characters from *The Lion, the Witch and the Wardrobe*—Aslan and the White Witch.[24]

The production of successful blockbuster movie versions of the Narnia novels, beginning with *The Lion, the Witch and the Wardrobe* in 2005, has raised Lewis's profile still further, giving him a broader and deeper reach than before. The international success of the movies has led to Lewis's more religious works being freshly translated or republished in languages other than English. In the United States, polls of American Christians show that *Mere Christianity* is regularly cited as the most influential religious book of the twentieth century, just as polls of ordinary readers continue to affirm the abiding popular affection for *The Lion, the Witch and the Wardrobe*, and its canonical status in the children's literature of the twentieth century.

CONCLUSION

So how are we to judge Lewis, fifty years after his death? Lewis himself had no doubt about the identity of the judge, or the criterion to be used in such an assessment. For Lewis, the only reliable critic of a writer's value is *time*, and the only reliable measure is the *enjoyment* that results from reading that writer's works. As Lewis himself remarked, nobody is ultimately able to "suppress" an author who is "obstinately pleasurable."[25] Lewis has made the most difficult transition an author can hope to make—being read by more people a generation after his death than before it.

What the next generation will make of him remains to be seen. Contrary to the expectations of the 1960s, belief in God has not gone away, and has become resurgent as a factor in personal and public life since about 2000. The recent rise of the so-called "New Atheism" has simply increased public interest in religious questions, creating a new appetite for discussions about God that simplistic and superficial slogans such as "God is a delusion" fail to satisfy. Lewis is thus likely to remain a controversial figure, in that he is now—and will be in the future—widely seized upon as both a champion and a villain in these new debates, pointing once more to his abiding importance. The volume and tone of the criticism of Lewis from fundamentalisms of the left and right is ultimately to be seen as a reflection of his iconic cultural status, rather than a reliable gauge of his personal and literary defects.

Some will doubtless continue to accuse Lewis of writing disguised religious propaganda, crudely and cruelly dressed up as literature. Others will see him as a superb, even visionary, advocate and defender of the rationality of faith, whose powerful appeals to imagination and logic expose the shallowness of naturalism. Some will hold him to defend socially regressive viewpoints, based on the bygone world of England in the 1940s. Others will see him as a prophetic critic of cultural trends that were widely accepted in his time, but are now recognised as destructive, degrading, and damaging. Yet whether you agree with Lewis or not, you cannot ignore his landmark significance. As Oscar Wilde once so shrewdly remarked, "The only thing worse than being talked about is not being talked about."

Most, however, will see Lewis simply as a gifted writer who brought immense pleasure to many and illumination to some—and who, above all, celebrated the classic art of good writing as a way of communicating ideas and expanding minds. For Lewis, the best art hinted at the deeper structures of reality, helping humanity in its perpetual quest for truth and significance.

Let the last word go to a charismatic, young American president, who died shortly after Lewis on 22 November 1963. In a speech given at Amherst College four weeks before his death, John F. Kennedy, honouring the great American poet Robert Frost (1874–1963), paid a handsome tribute to the work of poets and writers. "We must never forget," he declared, "that art is not a form of propaganda; it is a form of truth."[26] Lewis, I think, would agree.

Timeline

N ote that all publication dates refer to the British editions of Lewis's works.

1898	*29 November*	Birth of Clive Staples Lewis
1899	*29 January*	Baptised at St. Mark's, Dundela, Belfast
1905	*18 April*	Lewis family moves into Little Lea
1908	*23 August*	Death of Flora Lewis
	18 September	Begins studies at Wynyard School
1910	*September*	Begins studies at Campbell College, Belfast
1911	*January*	Begins studies at Cherbourg School, Great Malvern
1913	*September*	Begins studies at Malvern College, Great Malvern
1914	*19 September*	Begins private study with William Thompson Kirkpatrick at Great Bookham
1916	*13 December*	Learns he has been accepted at University College, Oxford

1917	25 April	Applies to join Oxford University Officers' Training Corps
	29 April	Takes up place at University College
	7 May	Joins E Company, No. 4 Officer Cadet Battalion, stationed at Keble College, Oxford, and meets Paddy Moore
	26 September	Commissioned as second lieutenant in 3rd Somerset Light Infantry
	17 November	Crosses to France and joins British front line near Arras
1918	1–28 February	Hospitalised at Le Tréport, near Dieppe
	15 April	Wounded in battle at Riez du Vinage
	25 May	Repatriated to England for convalescence
1919	13 January	Returns to Oxford to resume studies at University College
	20 March	*Spirits in Bondage* published
1920	31 March	Gains First Class Honours in Classical Moderations
1921	24 May	Wins Chancellor's Essay Prize
1922	4 August	Gains First Class Honours in *Literae Humaniores*
1923	16 July	Gains First Class Honours in English Language and Literature
1925	1 October	Takes up tutorial fellowship in English Language and Literature at Magdalen College, Oxford
1926	18 September	*Dymer: A Poem* published
1929	25 September	Death of Albert Lewis
1930	23–24 April	Visits Little Lea for the last time, along with Warnie

	10 October	Moves into The Kilns
	29 October	Informs Arthur Greeves that he has begun to attend college chapel
1931	19 September	Realises, after a conversation with Tolkien, that Christianity is a "true myth"
	25 December	Attends Holy Communion for the first time as an adult at Holy Trinity Church, Headington Quarry, Oxford
1932	15–29 August	Writes *The Pilgrim's Regress* while staying with Arthur Greeves
	21 December	Warnie moves into The Kilns
1933	25 May	*The Pilgrim's Regress* published
1936	21 May	*The Allegory of Love* published
1939	2 September	Warnie recalled to active military service
	3 September	Britain declares war on Germany
1940	18 October	*The Problem of Pain* published
1941	6–27 August	Gives four live broadcast talks on the BBC Home Service from Broadcasting House, London
1942	11 January–15 February	Gives five more live broadcast talks on the BBC Home Service from Broadcasting House, London
	9 February	*The Screwtape Letters* published
	13 July	*Broadcast Talks* published
	20 September–8 November	Gives eight more live talks on the BBC Home Service from Broadcasting House, London
1943	20 April	*Perelandra* published
1944	22 February–4 April	Gives seven more live broadcast talks

		on the BBC Home Service from Broadcasting House, London
1945	*9 May*	End of Second World War in Europe
	15 May	Death of Charles Williams
	16 August	*That Hideous Strength* published
1946	*14 January*	*The Great Divorce* published
1947	*12 May*	*Miracles* published
	8 September	Appears on cover of *Time* magazine
1948	*2 February*	Elizabeth Anscombe criticises Lewis's argument against naturalism at the Socratic Club
	17 March	Elected fellow of the Royal Society of Literature
1950	*16 October*	*The Lion, the Witch and the Wardrobe* published
1951	*12 January*	Death of Mrs. Moore
1954	*4 June*	Accepts professorship of Medieval and Renaissance English at University of Cambridge
	16 September	*English Literature in the Sixteenth Century, Excluding Drama* published
1955	*7 January*	Takes up residence at Magdalene College, Cambridge
	July	Elected fellow of the British Academy
	19 September	*Surprised by Joy* published
1956	*23 April*	Marries Joy Davidman in civil ceremony at Oxford Register Office
1957	*21 March*	Marriage ceremony to Joy Davidman in Churchill Hospital, Oxford, conducted by Reverend Peter Bide
1960	*28 March*	*The Four Loves* published

	13 July	Death of Joy Davidman
		Writes *A Grief Observed*
1961	*24 June*	Diagnosed with enlarged prostate gland
1963	*22 November*	Death of C. S. Lewis

Acknowledgements

It is always a pleasure to acknowledge indebtedness to others, especially since this represents a celebration of the collegiality of scholarship. My greatest debt is to archivists who have opened their collections to me, occasionally uncovering items for the first time. I owe particular thanks to the following: the BBC Written Archives Collection, Caversham Park; the Bodleian Library, Oxford; Cambridge University Library; Craigavon Historical Society; Exeter College, Oxford; Holy Trinity Church, Headington Quarry, Oxford; Keble College, Oxford; King's College, Cambridge; Lambeth Palace Library, London; Magdalen College, Oxford; Magdalene College, Cambridge; Merton College, Oxford; Methodist College, Belfast; National Archives (Public Records Office), Kew; Oxford University Officers' Training Corps; Oxfordshire History Centre; the Royal Society of Literature; the Swedish Academy; University College, Oxford; and the Marion E. Wade Center, Wheaton College, Wheaton, Illinois.

I gratefully acknowledge the award of a Clyde S. Kilby Research Grant for 2011 at the Marion E. Wade Center, Wheaton College, Wheaton, Illinois. I also wish to acknowledge helpful and perceptive conversations with leading Lewis authorities Walter Hooper, Don King, Alan Jacobs, and especially Michael Ward. I also benefitted from discussions with my editor, Mark Norton, as well as with Charles Bressler, Joanna Collicutt, J. R. Lucas, Roger Steer, Robert Tobin, and Andrew Walker. Among those who have helped me with archival work, I would especially like to thank Dr. Robin Darwall-Smith, archivist of both Magdalen College and University College, Oxford, and Laura Schmidt and Heidi Truty of the Marion E. Wade Center, Wheaton College. I am also grateful for the help of many others in checking facts and tracing photographs and other records, particularly Rachel Churchill, the Comité Départemental de Tourisme en Pas de Calais, Andreas Ekström, Michaela Holmström, Monica Thapar, the Ulster Museum, and Adrian Wood. Jonathan Schindler provided invaluable assistance at the copyediting stage. I myself remain responsible for any errors of fact or judgement.

The author and publishers gratefully acknowledge permission to reproduce extracts from copyrighted material, as follows. COLLECTED LETTERS by C. S. Lewis, copyright © C. S. Lewis Pte. Ltd 2004, 2006; SURPRISED BY JOY by C. S. Lewis, copyright © C. S. Lewis Pte. Ltd 1955; ALL MY ROAD BEFORE ME by C. S. Lewis, copyright © C. S. Lewis Pte. Ltd 1992; ESSAYS by C. S. Lewis, copyright © C. S. Lewis Pte. Ltd 2000; THE LION, THE WITCH AND THE WARDROBE by C. S. Lewis, copyright © C. S. Lewis Pte. Ltd 1950; REFLECTIONS ON THE PSALMS by C. S. Lewis, copyright © C. S. Lewis Pte. Ltd 1958; THE SILVER CHAIR by C. S. Lewis, copyright © C. S. Lewis Pte. Ltd 1953; THE LAST BATTLE by C. S. Lewis, copyright © C. S. Lewis Pte. Ltd 1956; THE MAGICIAN'S NEPHEW by C. S. Lewis, copyright © C. S. Lewis Pte. Ltd 1955; THE PILGRIM'S REGRESS by C. S. Lewis, copyright © C. S. Lewis Pte. Ltd 1933; THE PROBLEM OF PAIN by C. S. Lewis, copyright © C. S. Lewis Pte. Ltd 1940; A GRIEF OBSERVED by C. S. Lewis, copyright © C. S. Lewis Pte. Ltd 1961; REHABILITATIONS by C. S. Lewis, copyright © C. S. Lewis Pte. Ltd 1979; SPIRITS IN BONDAGE by C. S. Lewis, copyright © C. S. Lewis Pte. Ltd 1984; illustrations by Pauline Baynes © C. S. Lewis Pte. Ltd 1950. C. S. Lewis's unpublished letter of 16 January 1961, nominating J. R. R. Tolkien for the 1961 Nobel Prize in Literature (illustration 14.2), copyright © C. S. Lewis Pte. Ltd. The letters of J. R. R. Tolkien © The J. R. R. Tolkien Copyright Trust 1981, reprinted by permission of HarperCollins Publishers Ltd. Archive material is cited with the permission of the warden and fellows of Keble College, Oxford; the president and fellows of Magdalen College, Oxford; the master and fellows of University College, Oxford; and the Marion E. Wade Center, Wheaton College, Wheaton, Illinois.

Permission to reproduce photographs and other illustrations is gratefully acknowledged as follows. The president and fellows of Magdalen College (5.1; 5.2; 6.1); the master and fellows of University College (3.1); Oxfordshire History Collection (3.2; 4.1; 6.3; 8.1); Billet Potter, Oxford (5.5); the Francis Frith Collection (1.1; 2.3; 4.2; 4.3; 4.5; 6.2; 7.1; 7.3; 8.3; 13.1; 14.1); C. S. Lewis Pte. Ltd (11.1; 11.2; 12.1; 14.2); Penelope Bide (13.3); Holy Trinity Church, Headington

Quarry, Oxford (14.3); the Marion E. Wade Center, Wheaton College, Wheaton, Illinois (1.3; 1.5; 2.1; 2.2; 3.3; 4.4; 5.3; 5.4; 7.2; 8.2; 10.1; 13.2; 15.1). Other illustrations used in this book are taken from the author's personal collection.

Every effort has been made to identify and contact the copyright holders of material reproduced in this work. The author and publisher apologise for any omissions or errors.

Works Consulted

I. WORKS BY C. S. LEWIS

Full bibliographical details of Lewis's known works are provided in Walter Hooper, *C. S. Lewis: The Companion and Guide*, 799–883. This is an authoritative resource for Lewis studies. The editions used in researching this work are identified below.

A. Published Works

The Abolition of Man. New York: HarperCollins, 2001.

All My Road before Me: The Diary of C. S. Lewis, 1922–1927. Edited by Walter Hooper. San Diego: Harcourt Brace Jovanovich, 1991.

The Allegory of Love: A Study in Medieval Tradition. London: Oxford University Press, 1936.

Boxen: Childhood Chronicles before Narnia. London: HarperCollins, 2008. [Jointly authored with W. H. Lewis.]

Broadcast Talks. London: Geoffrey Bles, 1943; US edition published as *The Case for Christianity*. New York: Macmillan, 1943.

C. S. Lewis's Lost Aeneid: Arms and the Exile. Edited by A. T. Reyes. New Haven, CT: Yale University Press, 2011.

The Collected Letters of C. S. Lewis. Edited by Walter Hooper. 3 vols. San Francisco: HarperOne, 2004–2006.

The Discarded Image. Cambridge: Cambridge University Press, 1994.

Dymer: A Poem. London: Dent, 1926. [Originally published under the pseudonym "Clive Hamilton."]

English Literature in the Sixteenth Century, Excluding Drama. Vol. 3 of *Oxford History of English Literature*. Edited by F. P. Wilson and Bonamy Dobrée. Oxford: Clarendon Press, 1954.

Essay Collection and Other Short Pieces. Edited by Lesley Walmsley. London: HarperCollins, 2000.

An Experiment in Criticism. Cambridge: Cambridge University Press, 1992.

The Four Loves. London: HarperCollins, 2002.

The Great Divorce. London: HarperCollins, 2002.

A Grief Observed. New York: HarperCollins, 1994. [Originally published under the pseudonym "N. W. Clerk."]

The Horse and His Boy. London: HarperCollins, 2002.

The Last Battle. London: HarperCollins, 2002.

Letters to Malcolm: Chiefly on Prayer. London: HarperCollins, 2000.

The Lion, the Witch and the Wardrobe. London: HarperCollins, 2002.

The Magician's Nephew. London: HarperCollins, 2002.

Mere Christianity. London: HarperCollins, 2002.

Miracles. London: HarperCollins, 2002.

Narrative Poems. Edited by Walter Hooper. London: Fount, 1994.

On Stories and Other Essays on Literature. Edited by Walter Hooper. Orlando, FL: Harcourt Brace Jovanovich, 1982.

Out of the Silent Planet. London: HarperCollins, 2005.

Perelandra. London: HarperCollins, 2005.

The Personal Heresy: A Controversy. London: Oxford University Press, 1939. [Jointly authored with E. M. W. Tillyard.]

The Pilgrim's Regress. London: Geoffrey Bles, 1950.

Poems. Edited by Walter Hooper. Orlando, FL: Harcourt, 1992.

A Preface to "Paradise Lost." London: Oxford University Press, 1942.

Prince Caspian. London: HarperCollins, 2002.

The Problem of Pain. London: HarperCollins, 2002.

Reflections on the Psalms. London: Collins, 1975.

Rehabilitations and Other Essays. London: Oxford University Press, 1939.

The Screwtape Letters. London: HarperCollins, 2002.

Selected Literary Essays. Edited by Walter Hooper. Cambridge: Cambridge University Press, 1969.

The Silver Chair. London: HarperCollins, 2002.

Spenser's Images of Life. Edited by Alastair Fowler. Cambridge: Cambridge University Press, 1967.

Spirits in Bondage: A Cycle of Lyrics. London: Heinemann, 1919. [Originally published under the pseudonym "Clive Hamilton."]

Studies in Medieval and Renaissance Literature. Cambridge: Cambridge University Press, 2007.

Surprised by Joy. London: HarperCollins, 2002.

That Hideous Strength. London: HarperCollins, 2005.

Till We Have Faces. Orlando, FL: Harcourt Brace Jovanovich, 1984.

The Voyage of the "Dawn Treader." London: HarperCollins, 2002.

B. Unpublished Works

Lewis, W. H. "C. S. Lewis: A Biography" (1974). Unpublished typescript held in the Wade Center, Wheaton College, Wheaton, IL, and the Bodleian Library, Oxford.

———, ed. "The Lewis Papers: Memoirs of the Lewis Family 1850–1930." 11 vols. Unpublished typescript held in the Wade Center, Wheaton College, Wheaton, IL, and the Bodleian Library, Oxford.

II. SECONDARY STUDIES OF LEWIS

Adey, Lionel. *C. S. Lewis's "Great War" with Owen Barfield*. Victoria, BC: University of Victoria, 1978.

Aeschliman, Michael D. *The Restitution of Man: C. S. Lewis and the Case against Scientism*. Grand Rapids, MI: Eerdmans, 1998.

Alexander, Joy. "'The Whole Art and Joy of Words': Aslan's Speech in the Chronicles of Narnia." *Mythlore* 91 (2003): 37–48.

Arnell, Carla A. "On Beauty, Justice and the Sublime in C. S. Lewis's *Till We Have Faces*." *Christianity and Literature* 52 (2002): 23–34.

Baggett, David, Gary R. Habermas, and Jerry L. Walls, eds. *C. S. Lewis as Philosopher: Truth, Beauty and Goodness*. Downers Grove, IL: InterVarsity Press, 2008.

Barbour, Brian. "Lewis and Cambridge." *Modern Philology* 96 (1999): 439–484.

Barker, Nicolas. "C. S. Lewis, Darkly." *Essays in Criticism* 40 (1990): 358–367.

Barrett, Justin. "Mostly Right: A Quantitative Analysis of the *Planet Narnia* Thesis." *VII: An Anglo-American Literary Review* 27 (2010), online supplement.

Beversluis, John. *C. S. Lewis and the Search for Rational Religion*. Grand Rapids, MI: Eerdmans, 1985.

Bingham, Derek. *C. S. Lewis: A Shiver of Wonder*. Belfast: Ambassador Publications, 2004.

Bleakley, David. *C. S. Lewis at Home in Ireland: A Centenary Biography*. Bangor, Co. Down: Strandtown Press, 1998.

Bowman, Mary R. "A Darker Ignorance: C. S. Lewis and the Nature of the Fall." *Mythlore* 91 (2003): 64–80

———. "The Story Was Already Written: Narrative Theory in *The Lord of the Rings*." *Narrative* 14, no. 3 (2006): 272–293.

Brawley, Chris. "The Ideal and the Shadow: George MacDonald's *Phantastes*." *North Wind* 25 (2006): 91–112.

Brazier, P. H. "C. S. Lewis and the Anscombe Debate: From *analogia entis* to *analogia fidei*." *The Journal of Inklings Studies* 1, no. 2 (2011): 69–123.

———. "C. S. Lewis and Christological Prefigurement." *Heythrop Journal* 48 (2007): 742–775.

———. "'God . . . Or a Bad, or Mad, Man': C. S. Lewis's Argument for Christ—A Systematic Theological, Historical and Philosophical Analysis of *Aut Deus Aut Malus Homo*." *Heythrop Journal* 51, no. 1 (2010): 1–30.

———. "Why Father Christmas Appears in Narnia." *Sehnsucht* 3 (2009): 61–77.

Brown, Devin. *Inside Narnia: A Guide to Exploring "The Lion, the Witch and the Wardrobe."* Grand Rapids, MI: Baker, 2005.

Brown, Terence. "C. S. Lewis, Irishman?" In *Ireland's Literature: Selected Essays*, 152–165. Mullingar: Lilliput Press, 1988.

Campbell, David C., and Dale E. Hess. "Olympian Detachment: A Critical Look at the World of C. S. Lewis's Characters." *Studies in the Literary Imagination* 22, no. 2 (1989): 199–215.

Carnell, Corbin Scott. *Bright Shadow of Reality: Spiritual Longing in C. S. Lewis*. Grand Rapids, MI: Eerdmans, 1999.

Carpenter, Humphrey. *The Inklings: C. S. Lewis, J. R. R. Tolkien, Charles Williams, and Their Friends*. London: Allen & Unwin, 1981.

Caughey, Shanna, ed. *Revisiting Narnia: Fantasy, Myth and Religion in C. S. Lewis's Chronicles*. Dallas, TX: Benbella Books, 2005.

Charles, J. Daryl. "Permanent Things." *Christian Reflection* 11 (2004): 54–58.

Christopher, Joe R. "C. S. Lewis: Love Poet." *Studies in the Literary Imagination* 22, no. 2 (1989): 161–174.

Clare, David. "C. S. Lewis: An Irish Writer." *Irish Studies Review* 18, no. 1 (2010): 17–38.

Collings, Michael R. "Of Lions and Lamp-Posts: C. S. Lewis' *The Lion, the Witch and the Wardrobe* as a Response to Olaf Stapledon's *Sirius*." *Christianity and Literature* 32, no. 4 (1983): 33–38.

Como, James. *Branches to Heaven: The Geniuses of C. S. Lewis*. Dallas, TX: Spence Publishing Company, 1998.

———, ed. *C. S. Lewis at the Breakfast Table, and Other Reminiscences*. San Diego: Harcourt Brace Jovanovich, 1992.

Connolly, Sean. *Inklings of Heaven: C. S. Lewis and Eschatology*. Leominster: Gracewing, 2007.

Constable, John. "C. S. Lewis: From Magdalen to Magdalene." *Magdalene College Magazine and Record* 32 (1988): 42–46.

Daigle, Marsha A. "Dante's *Divine Comedy* and C. S. Lewis's *Narnia Chronicles*." *Christianity and Literature* 34, no. 4 (1985): 41–58.

Dorsett, Lyle W. *And God Came In: The Extraordinary Story of Joy Davidman: Her Life and Marriage to C. S. Lewis*. New York: Macmillan, 1983.

———. *Seeking the Secret Place: The Spiritual Formation of C. S. Lewis*. Grand Rapids, MI: Brazos Press, 2004.

Downing, David C. "From Pillar to Postmodernism: C. S. Lewis and Current Critical Discourse." *Christianity and Literature* 46, no. 2 (1997): 169–178.

———. *Into the Wardrobe: C. S. Lewis and the Narnia Chronicles*. San Francisco: Jossey-Bass, 2005.

———. *The Most Reluctant Convert: C. S. Lewis's Journey to Faith*. Downers Grove, IL: InterVarsity Press, 2002.

Duriez, Colin. *Tolkien and C. S. Lewis: The Gift of Friendship*. Mahwah, NJ: HiddenSpring, 2003.

Edwards, Bruce L., ed. *C. S. Lewis: Life, Works and Legacy*. 4 vols. Westport, CT: Praeger, 2007.

———. *Not a Tame Lion: Unveil Narnia through the Eyes of Lucy, Peter, and Other Characters Created by C. S. Lewis*. Carol Stream, IL: Tyndale House, 2005.

———. *A Rhetoric of Reading: C. S. Lewis's Defense of Western Literacy*. Provo, UT: Brigham Young University Press, 1986.

Edwards, Michael. "C. S. Lewis: Imagining Heaven." *Literature and Theology* 6 (1992): 107–124.

Fernandez, Irène. *Mythe, Raison Ardente: Imagination et réalité selon C. S. Lewis*. Geneva: Ad Solem, 2005.

———. "Un rationalisme chrétien: le cas de C. S. Lewis." *Revue philosophique de la France et de l'étranger* 178 (1988): 3–17.

Fowler, Alastair. "C. S. Lewis: Supervisor." *Yale Review* 91, no. 4 (2003): 64–80.

Fredrick, Candice. *Women among the Inklings: Gender, C.S. Lewis, J. R. R. Tolkien, and Charles Williams*. Westport, CT: Greenwood Press, 2001.

Gardner, Helen. "Clive Staples Lewis, 1898–1963." *Proceedings of the British Academy* 51 (1965): 417–428.

Gibb, Jocelyn, ed. *Light on C. S. Lewis*. London: Geoffrey Bles, 1965.

Gibbs, Lee W. "C. S. Lewis and the Anglican *Via Media*." *Restoration Quarterly* 32 (1990): 105–119.

Gilchrist, K. J. *A Morning after War: C. S. Lewis and WWI*. New York: Peter Lang, 2005.

Glover, Donald E. "'The Magician's Book: That's Not Your Story." *Studies in the Literary Imagination* 22 (1989): 217–225.

Glyer, Diana. *The Company They Keep: C. S. Lewis and J. R. R. Tolkien as Writers in Community*. Kent, OH: Kent State University Press, 2007.

Graham, David, ed. *We Remember C. S. Lewis: Essays & Memoirs*. Nashville, TN: Broadman & Holman, 2001.

Gray, William. "Death, Myth and Reality in C. S. Lewis." *Journal of Beliefs & Values* 18 (1997): 147–154.

———. *Fantasy, Myth and the Measure of Truth: Tales of Pullman, Lewis, Tolkien, MacDonald, and Hoffman*. London: Palgrave, 2009.

Green, Roger Lancelyn, and Walter Hooper. *C. S. Lewis: A Biography*, rev. ed. London: HarperCollins, 2002.

Griffin, William. *Clive Staples Lewis: A Dramatic Life*. New York: Harper & Row, 1986.

Hardy, Elizabeth Baird. *Milton, Spenser and the Chronicles of Narnia: Literary Sources for the C. S. Lewis Novels*. Jefferson, NC: McFarland & Co., 2007.

Harwood, Laurence. *C. S. Lewis, My Godfather: Letters, Photos and Recollections*. Downers Grove, IL: InterVarsity Press, 2007.

Hauerwas, Stanley. "Aslan and the New Morality." *Religious Education* 67 (1972): 419–429.

Heck, Joel D. *Irrigating Deserts: C. S. Lewis on Education*. St. Louis, MO: Concordia, 2005.

Hein, David, and Edward Henderson, eds. *C. S. Lewis and Friends: Faith and the Power of Imagination*. London: SPCK, 2011.

Holmer, Paul L. *C. S. Lewis: The Shape of His Faith and Thought*. New York: Harper & Row, 1976.

Holyer, Robert. "The Epistemology of C. S. Lewis's *Till We Have Faces*." *Anglican Theological Review* 70 (1988): 233–255.

Honda, Mineko. *The Imaginative World of C. S. Lewis*. New York: University Press of America, 2000.

Hooper, Walter. *C. S. Lewis: The Companion and Guide*. London: HarperCollins, 2005.

Huttar, Charles A. "C. S. Lewis, T. S. Eliot, and the Milton Legacy: The Nativity Ode Revisited." *Texas Studies in Literature and Language* 44 (2002): 324–348.

Jacobs, Alan. *The Narnian: The Life and Imagination of C. S. Lewis*. New York: HarperCollins, 2005.

———. "The Second Coming of C. S. Lewis." *First Things* 47 (1994): 27–30.

Johnson, William G., and Marcia K. Houtman. "Platonic Shadows in C. S. Lewis' Narnia Chronicles." *Modern Fiction Studies* 32 (1986): 75–87.

Johnston, Robert K. "Image and Content: The Tension in C. S. Lewis' Chronicles of Narnia." *Journal of the Evangelical Theological Society* 20 (1977): 253–264.

Keeble, N. H. "C. S. Lewis, Richard Baxter, and 'Mere Christianity.'" *Christianity and Literature* 30 (1981): 27–44.

Kilby, Clyde S. *The Christian World of C. S. Lewis*. Grand Rapids, MI: Eerdmans, 1964.

King, Don W. "The Anatomy of a Friendship: The Correspondence of Ruth Pitter and C. S. Lewis, 1946–1962." *Mythlore* 24, no. 1 (2003): 2–24.

———. *C. S. Lewis, Poet: The Legacy of His Poetic Impulse*. Kent, OH: Kent State University Press, 2001.

———. "The Distant Voice in C. S. Lewis's Poems." *Studies in the Literary Imagination* 22, no. 2 (1989): 175–184.

———. "Lost but Found: The 'Missing' Poems of C. S. Lewis's *Spirits in Bondage*." *Christianity and Literature* 53 (2004): 163–201.

———. "The Poetry of Prose: C. S. Lewis, Ruth Pitter, and *Perelandra*." *Christianity and Literature* 49, no. 3 (2000): 331–356.

Knight, Gareth. *The Magical World of the Inklings*. Longmead, Dorset: Element Books, 1990.

Kort, Wesley A. *C. S. Lewis Then and Now*. New York: Oxford University Press, 2001.

Kreeft, Peter. *C. S. Lewis for the Third Millennium: Six Essays on the "Abolition of Man."* San Francisco: Ignatius Press, 1994.

———. "C. S. Lewis's Argument from Desire." In *G. K. Chesterton and C. S. Lewis: The Riddle of Joy*, edited by Michael H. MacDonald and Andrew A. Tadie, 249–272. Grand Rapids, MI: Eerdmans, 1989.

Lacoste, Jean-Yves. "Théologie anonyme et christologie pseudonyme: C. S. Lewis, *Les Chroniques de Narnia*." *Nouvelle Revue Théologique* 3 (1990): 381–393.

Lawlor, John. *C. S. Lewis: Memories and Reflections*. Dallas, TX: Spence Publishing Co., 1998.

Lawyer, John E. "Three Celtic Voyages: Brendan, Lewis, and Buechner." *Anglican Theological Review* 84, no. 2 (2002): 319–343.

Leiva-Merikakis, Erasmo. *Love's Sacred Order: The Four Loves Revisited*. San Francisco: Ignatius Press, 2000.

Lewis, W. H. "Memoir of C. S. Lewis." In *The Letters of C. S. Lewis*, edited by W. H. Lewis, 1–26. London: Geoffrey Bles, 1966.

Lindskoog, Kathryn. *Finding the Landlord: A Guidebook to C. S. Lewis's "Pilgrim's Regress."* Chicago: Cornerstone Press, 1995.

Lindskoog, Kathryn Ann, and Gracia Fay Ellwood. "C. S. Lewis: Natural Law, the Law in Our Hearts." *Christian Century* 101, no. 35 (1984): 1059–1062.

Linzey, Andrew. "C. S. Lewis's Theology of Animals." *Anglican Theological Review* 80, no. 1 (1998): 60–81.

Loades, Ann. "C. S. Lewis: Grief Observed, Rationality Abandoned, Faith Regained." *Literature and Theology* 3 (1989): 107–121.

———. "The Grief of C. S. Lewis." *Theology Today* 46, no. 3 (1989): 269–276.

Lobdell, Jared. *The Scientifiction Novels of C. S. Lewis: Space and Time in the Ransom Stories*. Jefferson, NC: McFarland, 2004.

Loomis, Steven R., and Jacob P. Rodriguez. *C. S. Lewis: A Philosophy of Education*. New York: Palgrave Macmillan, 2009.

Lucas, John. "The Restoration of Man." *Theology* 58 (1995): 445–456.

Lundin, Anne. "On the Shores of Lethe: C. S. Lewis and the Romantics." *Children's Literature in Education* 21 (1990): 53–59.

MacSwain, Robert, and Michael Ward, eds. *The Cambridge Companion to C. S. Lewis*. Cambridge: Cambridge University Press, 2010.

Manley, David. "Shadows That Fall: The Immanence of Heaven in the Fiction of C. S. Lewis and George MacDonald." *North Wind* 17 (1998): 43–49.

McBride, Sam. "The Company They Didn't Keep: Collaborative Women in the Letters of C. S. Lewis." *Mythlore* 29 (2010): 69–86.

McGrath, Alister E. *The Intellectual World of C. S. Lewis*. Oxford and Malden, MA: Wiley-Blackwell, 2013.

Meilander, Gilbert. "Psychoanalyzing C. S. Lewis." *Christian Century* 107, no. 17 (1990): 525–529.

———. *The Taste for the Other: The Social and Ethical Thought of C. S. Lewis*. Grand Rapids, MI: Eerdmans, 1998.

———. "Theology in Stories: C. S. Lewis and the Narrative Quality of Experience." *Word and World* 1, no. 3 (1981): 222–230.

Menuge, Angus J. L. "Fellow Patients in the Same Hospital: Law and Gospel in the Works of C. S. Lewis." *Concordia Journal* 25, no. 2 (1999): 151–163.

Miller, Laura. *The Magician's Book: A Skeptic's Adventures in Narnia*. New York: Little, Brown and Co., 2008.

Mills, David, ed. *The Pilgrim's Guide: C. S. Lewis and the Art of Witness*. Grand Rapids, MI: Eerdmans, 1998.

Morris, Francis J., and Ronald C. Wendling. "C. S. Lewis: A Critic Recriticized." *Studies in the Literary Imagination* 22, no. 2 (1989): 149–160.

———. "Coleridge and 'the Great Divide' between C. S. Lewis and Owen Barfield." *Studies in the Literary Imagination* 22, no. 2 (1989): 149–159.

Morris, Richard M. "C. S. Lewis as a Christian Apologist." *Anglican Theological Review* 33, no. 1 (1951): 158–168.

Mueller, Steven P. "C. S. Lewis and the Atonement." *Concordia Journal* 25, no. 2 (1999): 164–178.

Myers, Doris T. "The Compleat Anglican: Spiritual Style in the Chronicles of Narnia." *Anglican Theological Review* 66 (1984): 148–180.

———. *Bareface: A Guide to C. S. Lewis's Last Novel.* Columbia, MO: University of Missouri Press, 2004.

Nelson, Michael. "C. S. Lewis and His Critics." *Virginia Quarterly Review* 64 (1988): 1–19.

———. "'One Mythology among Many': The Spiritual Odyssey of C. S. Lewis." *Virginia Quarterly Review* 72, no. 4 (1996): 619–633.

Nicholi, Armand M. *The Question of God: C. S. Lewis and Sigmund Freud Debate God, Love, Sex, and the Meaning of Life.* New York: Free Press, 2002.

Nicholson, Mervyn. "C. S. Lewis and the Scholarship of Imagination in E. Nesbit and Rider Haggard." *Renascence: Essays on Values in Literature* 51 (1998): 41–62.

———. "What C. S. Lewis Took from E. Nesbit." *Children's Literature Association Quarterly* 16, no. 1 (1991): 16–22.

Noll, Mark A. "C. S. Lewis's 'Mere Christianity' (the Book and the Ideal) at the Start of the Twenty-First Century." *Seven: An Anglo-American Literary Review* 19 (2002): 31–44.

Odero, Dolores. "La 'experiencia' como lugar antropológico en C. S. Lewis." *Scripta Theologica* 26, no. 2 (1994): 403–482.

Osborn, Marijane. "Deeper Realms: C. S. Lewis' Re-Visions of Joseph O'Neill's *Land under England*." *Journal of Modern Literature* 25 (2001): 115–120.

Oziewicz, Marek, and Daniel Hade. "The Marriage of Heaven and Hell? Philip Pullman, C. S. Lewis, and the Fantasy Tradition." *Mythlore* 28, no. 109 (2010): 39–54.

Patrick, James. *The Magdalen Metaphysicals: Idealism and Orthodoxy at Oxford, 1901–1945.* Macon, GA: Mercer University Press, 1985.

Pearce, Joseph. *C. S. Lewis and the Catholic Church.* Fort Collins, CO: Ignatius Press, 2003.

Phillips, Justin. *C. S. Lewis in a Time of War.* San Francisco: HarperSanFrancisco, 2006.

Poe, Harry L., ed. *C. S. Lewis Remembered.* Grand Rapids, MI: Zondervan, 2006.

———. "Shedding Light on the Dark Tower: A C. S. Lewis Mystery Is Solved." *Christianity Today* 51, no. 2 (2007): 44–45.

Prothero, Jim. "The Flash and the Grandeur: A Short Study of the Relation among MacDonald, Lewis, and Wordsworth." *North Wind* 17 (1998): 35–39.

Purtill, Richard L. *C. S. Lewis's Case for the Christian Faith.* San Francisco: Harper & Row, 1985.

———. *Lord of the Elves and Eldils: Fantasy and Philosophy in C. S. Lewis and J. R. R. Tolkien.* 2nd ed. San Francisco: Ignatius Press, 2006.

Reppert, Victor. *C. S. Lewis's Dangerous Idea: In Defense of the Argument from Reason.* Downers Grove, IL: InterVarsity Press, 2003.

Root, Jerry. *C. S. Lewis and a Problem of Evil.* Cambridge: James Clarke, 2009.

Rossow, Francis C. "Giving Christian Doctrine a New Translation: Selected Examples from the Novels of C. S. Lewis." *Concordia Journal* 21, no. 3 (1995): 281–297.

———. "Problems in Prayer and Their Gospel Solutions in Four Poems by C. S. Lewis." *Concordia Journal* 20, no. 2 (1994): 106–114.

Sayer, George. *Jack: A Life of C. S. Lewis.* London: Hodder & Stoughton, 1997.

Schakel, Peter J. "Irrigating Deserts with Moral Imagination." *Christian Reflection* 11 (2004): 21–29.

———. *Reading with the Heart: The Way into Narnia.* Grand Rapids, MI: Eerdmans, 1979.

———. *Reason and Imagination in C. S. Lewis: A Study of "Till We Have Faces."* Grand Rapids, MI: Eerdmans, 1984.

———. "The Satiric Imagination of C. S. Lewis." *Studies in the Literary Imagination* 22, no. 2 (1989): 129–148.

Schakel, Peter J., and Charles A. Huttar, eds. *Word and Story in C. S. Lewis: Language and Narrative in Theory and Practice*. Columbia, MO: University of Missouri Press, 1991.

Schwartz, Sanford. *C. S. Lewis on the Final Frontier: Science and the Supernatural in the Space Trilogy*. New York: Oxford University Press, 2009.

———. "Paradise Reframed: Lewis, Bergson, and Changing Times on Perelandra." *Christianity and Literature* 51, no. 4 (2002): 569–602.

Seachris, Joshua, and Linda Zagzebski. "Weighing Evils: The C. S. Lewis Approach." *International Journal for Philosophy of Religion* 62 (2007): 81–88.

Segura, Eduardo, and Thomas Honegger, eds. *Myth and Magic: Art According to the Inklings*. Zollikofen, Switzerland: Walking Tree, 2007.

Smietana, Bob. "C. S. Lewis Superstar: How a Reserved British Intellectual with a Checkered Pedigree Became a Rock Star for Evangelicals." *Christianity Today* 49, no. 12 (2005): 28–32.

Smith, Robert Houston. *Patches of Godlight: The Pattern of Thought of C. S. Lewis*. Athens, GA: University of Georgia Press, 1981.

Stock, Robert Douglas. "Dionysus, Christ, and C. S. Lewis." *Christianity and Literature* 34, no. 2 (1985): 7–13.

Taliaferro, Charles. "A Narnian Theory of the Atonement." *Scottish Journal of Theology* 41 (1988): 75–92.

Tennyson, G. B., ed. *Owen Barfield on C. S. Lewis*. Middletown, CT: Wesleyan University Press, 1989.

Terrasa Messuti, Eduardo. "Imagen y misterio: Sobre el conocimiento metafórico en C. S. Lewis." *Scripta Theologica* 25, no. 1 (1993): 95–132.

Tynan, Kenneth. "My Tutor, C. S. Lewis." *Third Way* (June 1979): 15–16.

Van Leeuwen, Mary Stewart. *A Sword between the Sexes?: C. S. Lewis and the Gender Debates*. Grand Rapids, MI: Brazos Press, 2010.

Walker, Andrew. "Scripture, Revelation and Platonism in C. S. Lewis." *Scottish Journal of Theology* 55 (2002): 19–35.

Walker, Andrew, and James Patrick, eds. *A Christian for All Christians: Essays in Honor of C. S. Lewis*. Washington, DC: Regnery Gateway, 1992.

Walsh, Chad. *C. S. Lewis: Apostle to the Skeptics*. New York: Macmillan, 1949.

———. *The Literary Legacy of C. S. Lewis*. London: Sheldon, 1979.

Ward, Michael. "The Current State of C. S. Lewis Scholarship." *Sewanee Theological Review* 55, no. 2 (2012): 123–144.

———. *Planet Narnia: The Seven Heavens in the Imagination of C. S. Lewis*. Oxford: Oxford University Press, 2008.

Watson, George. "The Art of Disagreement: C. S. Lewis (1898–1963)." *Hudson Review* 48, no. 2 (1995): 229–239.

Wheat, Andrew. "The Road before Him: Allegory, Reason, and Romanticism in C. S. Lewis' *The Pilgrim's Regress*." *Renascence: Essays on Values in Literature* 51, no. 1 (1998): 21–39.

Williams, Donald T. *Mere Humanity: G. K. Chesterton, C. S. Lewis, and J. R. R. Tolkien on the Human Condition*. Nashville, TN: B & H Publishing Group, 2006.

Williams, Rowan. *The Lion's World: A Journey into the Heart of Narnia*. London: SPCK, 2012.

Wilson, A. N. *C. S. Lewis: A Biography*. London: Collins, 1990.

Wolfe, Judith, and Brendan N. Wolfe, eds. *C. S. Lewis and the Church*. London: T & T Clark, 2011.

Wood, Naomi. "Paradise Lost and Found: Obedience, Disobedience, and Storytelling in C. S. Lewis and Phillip Pullman." *Children's Literature in Education* 32, no. 4 (2001): 237–259.

Wood, Ralph C. "The Baptized Imagination: C. S. Lewis's Fictional Apologetics." *Christian Century* 112, no. 25 (1995): 812–815.

———. "C. S. Lewis and the Ordering of Our Loves." *Christianity and Literature* 51, no. 1 (2001): 109–117.

———. "Conflict and Convergence on Fundamental Matters in C. S. Lewis and J. R. R. Tolkien." *Renascence: Essays on Values in Literature* 55 (2003): 315–338.

Yancey, Philip. "Found in Space: How C. S. Lewis Has Shaped My Faith and Writing." *Christianity Today* 57, no. 7 (2008): 62.

III. OTHER WORKS CONSULTED

Aston, T. S., ed. *The History of the University of Oxford*. 8 vols. Oxford: Oxford University Press, 1984–1994.

Bartlett, Robert. *The Natural and the Supernatural in the Middle Ages*. Cambridge: Cambridge University Press, 2008.

Brockliss, Laurence W. B., ed. *Magdalen College Oxford: A History*. Oxford: Magdalen College, 2008.

Cantor, Norman F. *Inventing the Middle Ages: The Lives, Works and Ideas of the Great Medievalists of the Twentieth Century*. New York: William Morrow, 1991.

Carpenter, Humphrey. *J. R. R. Tolkien: A Biography*. London: Allen & Unwin, 1977.

Ceplair, Larry, and Steven Englund. *The Inquisition in Hollywood: Politics in the Film Community, 1930–1960*. Urbana, IL: University of Illinois Press, 2003.

Chance, Jane, ed. *Tolkien and the Invention of Myth*. Lexington, KY: University Press of Kentucky, 2004.

Collins, John Churton. *The Study of English Literature: A Plea for Its Recognition and Organization at the Universities*. London: Macmillan, 1891.

Cunich, Peter, David Hoyle, Eamon Duffy, and Ronald Hyam. *A History of Magdalene College Cambridge 1428–1988*. Cambridge: Magdalene College Publications, 1994.

Dal Corso, Eugenio. *Il Servo di Dio: Don Giovanni Calabria e i fratelli separati*. Rome: Pontificia Università Lateranense, 1974.

Darwall-Smith, Robin. *A History of University College, Oxford*. Oxford: Oxford University Press, 2008.

Davidman, Joy. "The Longest Way Round." In *These Found the Way: Thirteen Converts to Christianity*, edited by David Wesley Soper, 13–26. Philadelphia: Westminster Press, 1951.

———. *Out of My Bone: The Letters of Joy Davidman*. Edited by Don W. King. Grand Rapids, MI: Eerdmans, 2009.

Dearborn, Kerry. "The Baptized Imagination." *Christian Reflection* 11 (2004): 11–20.

———. "Bridge over the River Why: The Imagination as a Way to Meaning." *North Wind* 16 (1997): 29–40, 45–46.

Drout, Michael D. C. "J. R. R. Tolkien's Medieval Scholarship and Its Significance." *Tolkien Studies* 4 (2007): 113–176.

Eagleton, Terry. *Literary Theory: An Introduction*. Oxford: Blackwell, 2008.

Fitzgerald, Jill. "A 'Clerkes Compleinte': Tolkien and the Division of Lit. and Lang." *Tolkien Studies* 6 (2009): 41–57.

Flieger, Verlyn. *Splintered Light: Logos and Language in Tolkien's World*. Kent, OH: Kent State University, 2002.

Foster, Roy. *The Irish Story: Telling Tales and Making It Up in Ireland*. London: Allen Lane, 2001.

Freeden, Michael. "Eugenics and Progressive Thought: A Study in Ideological Affinity." *Historical Journal* 22 (1979): 645–671.

Garth, John. *Tolkien and the Great War*. London: HarperCollins, 2004.

Goebel, Stefan. *The Great War and Medieval Memory: War, Remembrance and Medievalism in Britain and Germany, 1914–1940*. Cambridge: Cambridge University Press, 2008.

Haldane, J. B. S. *Possible Worlds*. London: Chatto & Windus, 1927.

Harford, Judith. *The Opening of University Education to Women in Ireland*. Dublin: Irish Academic Press, 2008.

Hart, Trevor, and Ivan Khovacs, eds. *Tree of Tales: Tolkien, Literature, and Theology*. Waco, TX: Baylor University Press, 2007.

Hassig, Debra. *Medieval Bestiaries: Text, Image, Ideology*. Cambridge: Cambridge University Press, 1995.

Hatlen, Burton. "Pullman's *His Dark Materials*: A Challenge to Fantasies of J. R. R. Tolkien and C. S. Lewis, with an Epilogue on Pullman's Neo-Romantic Reading of *Paradise Lost*." In *His Dark Materials Illuminated: Critical Essays on Philip Pullman's Trilogy*, edited by Millicent Lenz and Carole Scott, 75–94. Detroit: Wayne State University Press, 2005.

Hennessey, Thomas. *Dividing Ireland: World War I and Partition*. London: Routledge, 1998.

Herford, C. H. *The Bearing of English Studies upon the National Life*. Oxford: Oxford University Press, 1910.

James, William. *The Varieties of Religious Experience: A Study in Human Nature*. New York: Longmans Green, 1902.

Jeffery, Keith. *Ireland and the Great War*. Cambridge: Cambridge University Press, 2000.

Ker, Ian. *G. K. Chesterton*. Oxford: Oxford University Press, 2011.

Kerry, Paul E., ed. *The Ring and the Cross: Christianity and the Writings of J. R. R. Tolkien*. Madison, NJ: Fairleigh Dickinson University Press, 2011.

King, Don W. *Hunting the Unicorn: A Critical Biography of Ruth Pitter*. Kent, OH: Kent State University Press, 2008.

Littledale, R. F. "The Oxford Solar Myth." In *Echoes from Kottabos*, edited by R. Y. Tyrrell and Sir Edward Sullivan, 279–290. London: E. Grant Richards, 1906.

Majendie, V. H. B. *A History of the 1st Battalion Somerset Light Infantry (Prince Albert's)*. Taunton, Somerset: Phoenix Press, 1921.

Mangan, J. A. *Athleticism in the Victorian and Edwardian Public School: The Emergence and Consolidation of an Educational Ideology*. London: Frank Cass, 2000.

McGarry, John. *Northern Ireland and the Divided World*. Oxford: Oxford University Press, 2001.

McMurtry, Jo. *English Language, English Literature: The Creation of an Academic Discipline*. Hamden, CT: Archon Books, 1985.

O'Brien, Conor Cruise. *Ancestral Voices: Religion and Nationalism in Ireland*. Chicago: University of Chicago Press, 1995.

Oddie, William. *Chesterton and the Romance of Orthodoxy*. Oxford: Oxford University Press, 2008.

Padley, Jonathan, and Kenneth Padley. "'From Mirrored Truth the Likeness of the True': J. R .R. Tolkien and Reflections of Jesus Christ in Middle-Earth." *English* 59, no. 224 (2010): 70–92.

Parsons, Wendy, and Catriona Nicholson. "Talking to Philip Pullman: An Interview." *The Lion and the Unicorn* 23, no. 1 (1999): 116–134.

Rhode, Deborah L. *In Pursuit of Knowledge: Scholars, Status, and Academic Culture*. Stanford, CA: Stanford University Press, 2006.

Roberts, Nathan. "Character in the Mind: Citizenship, Education and Psychology in Britain, 1880–1914." *History of Education* 33 (2004): 177–197.

Shaw, Christopher. "Eliminating the Yahoo: Eugenics, Social Darwinism and Five Fabians." *History of Political Thought* 8 (1987): 521–544.

Shippey, Tom. *Roots and Branches: Selected Papers on Tolkien*. Zollikofen, Switzerland: Walking Tree, 2007.

Teichmann, Roger. *The Philosophy of Elizabeth Anscombe*. Oxford: Oxford University Press, 2008.

Thomson, G. Ian F. *The Oxford Pastorate: The First Half Century*. London: The Canterbury Press, 1946.

Tolkien, J. R. R. *The Letters of J. R. R. Tolkien*. Edited by Humphrey Carpenter. London: HarperCollins, 1981.

Townshend, Charles. *Easter 1916: The Irish Rebellion*. London: Allen Lane, 2005.

Wain, John. *Sprightly Running: Part of an Autobiography*. London: Macmillan, 1962.

Watson, Giles. "Dorothy L. Sayers and the Oecumenical Penguin." *Seven: An Anglo-American Literary Review* 14 (1997): 17–32.

Watson, G. J. *Irish Identity and the Literary Revival: Synge, Joyce, Yeats and O'Casey*. 2nd ed. Washington, DC: Catholic University of America Press, 1994.

Werner, Maria Assunta. *Madeleva: Sister Mary Madeleva Wolff, CSC: A Pictorial Biography*. Notre Dame, IN: Saint Mary's College, 1993.

Williams, Charles. *To Michal from Serge: Letters from Charles Williams to his Wife, Florence, 1939–45*. Edited by Roma A. King, Jr. Kent, OH: Kent State University Press, 2002.

Wilson, Ian. "William Thompson Kirkpatrick (1848–1921)." *Review: Journal of the Craigavon Historical Society* 8, no. 1 (2000–2001): 33–40.

Winter, Jay. *Sites of Memory, Sites of Mourning: The Great War in European Cultural History*. Cambridge: Cambridge University Press, 1995.

Wolfe, Kenneth M. *The Churches and the British Broadcasting Corporation 1922–1956: The Politics of Broadcast Religion*. London: SCM Press, 1984.

Worsley, Howard. "Popularized Atonement Theory Reflected in Children's Literature." *Expository Times* 115, no. 5 (2004): 149–156.

Wyrall, Everard. *The History of the Somerset Light Infantry (Prince Albert's) 1914–1919*. London: Methuen and Co., 1927.

Notes

PREFACE

1. Edna St. Vincent Millay, *Collected Sonnets* (New York: Harper, 1988), 140.
2. *Surprised by Joy*, 266. Elsewhere in *Surprised by Joy*, Lewis refers to this as a "reconversion": ibid., 135.
3. Alister E. McGrath, *The Intellectual World of C. S. Lewis* (Oxford and Malden, MA: Wiley-Blackwell, 2013).

1. THE SOFT HILLS OF DOWN: AN IRISH CHILDHOOD, 1898–1908

1. *Surprised by Joy*, 1.
2. W. H. Lewis, "C. S. Lewis: A Biography," 27.
3. Available online at http://www.census.nationalarchives.ie/reels/nai000721989/. The entry "Cannot Read" is in a different hand.
4. *Lloyds Register of Shipping*, No. 93171.
5. Wilson, "William Thompson Kirkpatrick," 33.
6. Since the late nineteenth century, these roles have become fused in American legal practice. An American attorney can act in either or both capacities.
7. Harford, *The Opening of University Education to Women in Ireland*, 78.
8. J. W. Henderson, *Methodist College, Belfast, 1868–1938: A Survey and Retrospect*. 2 vols. (Belfast: Governors of Methodist College, 1939), vol. 1, 120–30. Note that the school, though founded in 1865, did not open until 1868.
9. Ibid., vol. 1, 127. First Class Honours (often referred to simply as a "First") in the British university examination system is equivalent to a GPA of 4.0 in the American system.
10. *Belfast Telegraph*, 28 September 1929.
11. See especially Lewis's letter to Warren Lewis, 2 August 1928; *Letters*, vol. 1, 768–777, which is rich in such references.
12. W. H. Lewis, "Memoir of C. S. Lewis," 2.
13. Letter to Arthur Greeves, 30 March 1915; *Letters*, vol. 1, 114.
14. *All My Road before Me*, 105.
15. Letter to Warren Lewis, 12 January 1930; *Letters*, vol. 1, 871.

16. Bleakley, *C. S. Lewis at Home in Ireland*, 53. Elsewhere Lewis suggests transferring Oxford to County Donegal, rather than Down: see, for example, his letter to Arthur Greeves, 3 June 1917; *Letters*, vol. 1, 313.

17. *Studies in Medieval and Renaissance Literature*, 126.

18. For other examples, see Clare, "C. S. Lewis: An Irish Writer," 20–21.

19. Letter to Arthur Greeves, 8 July 1917; *Letters*, vol. 1, 325.

20. Letter to Arthur Greeves, 24 July 1917; *Letters*, vol. 1, 330.

21. Letter to Arthur Greeves, 31 August 1918; *Letters*, vol. 1, 394.

22. *Surprised by Joy*, 9.

23. W. H. Lewis, "Memoir of C. S. Lewis," 1.

24. *The Lion, the Witch and the Wardrobe*, 10–11.

25. *Surprised by Joy*, 6.

26. Ibid., 16.

27. Ibid., 17.

28. Ibid.

29. Ibid., 18.

30. Ibid.

31. James, *The Varieties of Religious Experience*, 380–381.

32. See the dedication of Tolkien's poem "Mythopoiea": Tolkien, Tree and Leaf, 85. The context of this poem makes it clear that this is a reference to Lewis: see Carpenter, *J. R. R. Tolkien: A Biography*, 192–199.

33. Letter to Albert Lewis, 16 February 1918; *Letters*, vol. 1, 356.

34. Warnie would later have the same quotation inscribed on his brother's gravestone in Oxford in 1963.

35. *Surprised by Joy*, 23.

36. *The Magician's Nephew*, 166.

37. *Surprised by Joy*, 20.

38. Ibid., 22.

2. THE UGLY COUNTRY OF ENGLAND: SCHOOLDAYS, 1908–1917

1. Letter to Francine Smithline, 23 March 1962; *Letters*, vol. 3, 1325. The two "horrid" schools were Wynyard School and Malvern College.

2. Sayer, *Jack*, 86.

3. *Surprised by Joy*, 26.

4. Letter to Arthur Greeves, 5 June 1914; *Letters*, vol. 1, 60.

5. *Surprised by Joy*, 37.

6. "Lewis Papers," vol. 3, 40.

7. *Surprised by Joy*, 56.

8. Cherbourg School became part of Malvern College in 1992. The original site has since been sold for development.

9. *Surprised by Joy*, 82.

10. Ibid., 82.

11. Richard Wagner, *Siegfried* and *The Twilight of the Gods*, translated by Margaret Armour, illustrated by Arthur Rackham (London: Heinemann, 1911).

12. *Surprised by Joy*, 83.

13. Ibid., 38.

14. Letter to Albert Lewis, 8 July 1913; *Letters*, vol. 1, 28.

15. *Surprised by Joy*, 71.

16. Letter to Albert Lewis, 7 June 1913; *Letters*, vol. 1, 23.

17. Ian Wilson, "William Thompson Kirkpatrick," 39.

18. The narrative can be found in *Surprised by Joy*, 95–135, taking up 18 percent of the text of the book.

19. This often led to boys regarded as effete "intellectuals"—such as Lewis—being victimised and bullied: see Mangan, *Athleticism in the Victorian and Edwardian Public School*, 99–121.

20. See Roberts, "Character in the Mind."

21. *Surprised by Joy*, 11. Lewis and Warnie inherited this defect from their father. The condition (a form of metacarpophalangeal synostosis) is now sometimes referred to as *symphalangism (Lewis type)* on account of its association with Lewis: see Alessandro Castriota–Scanderbeg and Bruno Dallapiccola, *Abnormal Skeletal Phenotypes: From Simple Signs to Complex Diagnoses* (Berlin: Springer, 2006), 405.

22. Letter to Arthur Greeves, 5 June 1914; *Letters*, vol. 1, 59.

23. *Surprised by Joy*, 117.

24. The text of the poem is found in "Lewis Papers," vol. 3, 262–263.

25. W. H. Lewis, "Memoir of C. S. Lewis," 5.

26. Letter to Albert Lewis, 17 July 1929; *Letters*, vol. 1, 802.

27. Letter to Albert Lewis, 18 March 1914; *Letters*, vol. 1, 51.

28. Warren Lewis to Albert Lewis, 29 March 1914; "Lewis Papers," vol. 4, 156.

29. Ibid., 157.

30. *Surprised by Joy*, 151.

31. Letter to Warren Lewis, 18 May 1907; *Letters*, vol. 1, 3–4.

32. *Surprised by Joy*, 151.

33. Letter to Arthur Greeves, 5 June 1914; *Letters*, vol. 1, 60.

34. Letter to Albert Lewis, 29 June 1914; *Letters*, vol. 1, 64.

35. *Surprised by Joy*, 158.

36. See Ian Wilson, "William Thompson Kirkpatrick."

37. Queen's College, Belfast, was incorporated into the Royal University of Ireland in 1879. It was reestablished as a separate institution by the Irish Universities Act of 1908, which dissolved the Royal University of Ireland and replaced it with the National University of Ireland and the Queen's University of Belfast.

38. *Surprised by Joy*, 171.

39. Letter to Albert Lewis, 8 February 1917; *Letters*, vol. 1, 275.

40. Letter to Arthur Greeves, 12? October 1916; *Letters*, vol. 1, 230–231.

41. "Lewis Papers," vol. 10, 219. Lewis's comments are found in a three-page reflection on Greeves, possibly written around 1935, on pages 218–220.

42. Letter to Arthur Greeves, 18 October 1916; *Letters*, vol. 1, 235.

43. Lewis's own account in *Surprised by Joy* incorrectly dates this as taking place in August 1915. See Hooper, *C. S. Lewis: The Companion and Guide*, 568.

44. *Surprised by Joy*, 208–209.

45. Letter to Albert Lewis, 28? May 1915; *Letters*, vol. 1, 125.

46. Letter to Arthur Greeves, 7 March 1916; *Letters*, vol. 1, 171.

47. Letter from Albert Lewis to William Kirkpatrick, 8 May 1916; "Lewis Papers," vol. 5, 79–80. For Kirkpatrick's earlier letter, dated 5 May, see "Lewis Papers," vol. 5, 78–79.

48. *Surprised by Joy*, 214.

49. Letter to Albert Lewis, 7 December 1916; *Letters*, vol. 1, 262.

50. Letter to Albert Lewis, 28 January 1917; *Letters*, vol. 1, 267.

51. Aston, *The History of the University of Oxford*, vol. 6, 356.

3. THE VASTY FIELDS OF FRANCE: WAR, 1917–1918

1. Letter to Francine Smithline, 23 March 1962; *Letters*, vol. 3, 1325.

2. *Surprised by Joy*, 226.

3. Ibid., 183.

4. See Darwall-Smith, *A History of University College, Oxford*, 440–447.

5. Ibid., 443.

6. Letter to Albert Lewis, 28 April 1917; *Letters*, vol. 1, 296.

7. Letter to Arthur Greeves, 8 July 1917; *Letters*, vol. 1, 324.

8. *Surprised by Joy*, 216.

9. Lewis's military record is held in the National Gallery (Public Records Office): War Office 339/105408.

10. Letter to Albert Lewis, 3 May 1917; *Letters*, vol. 1, 299.

11. Letter to Albert Lewis, 12 May 1917; *Letters*, vol. 1, 302.

12. Letter to Albert Lewis, 8 June 1917; *Letters*, vol. 1, 316.

13. Letter to Albert Lewis, 17 May 1917; *Letters*, vol. 1, 305.

14. Letter to Arthur Greeves, 13 May 1917; *Letters*, vol. 1, 304.

15. Letter to Albert Lewis, 3? June 1917; *Letters*, vol. 1, 315.

16. Winifred Mary Letts, *The Spires of Oxford and Other Poems* (New York: Dutton, 1917), 3. Letts was "passing by" Oxford on a train.

17. War Office 372/4 12913.

18. *King Edward VII School Magazine* 15, no. 7 (May 1961).

19. *Surprised by Joy*, 217. Detailed records survive for C Company: Oxford University Officers' Training Corps, Archive OT 1/1/1-11; OT 1/2/1-4. Little documentation has survived about E Company, in which Lewis served.

20. Oxford University Officers' Training Corps Archives, Archive OT 1/1/1-11.

21. Strictly speaking, Keble was a "New Foundation," with tutors rather than fellows. It was not until 1930 that Keble's internal governance fell into line with that of other Oxford colleges.

22. Letter to Albert Lewis, 10? June 1917; *Letters*, vol. 1, 317.

23. Moore was born on 17 November 1898; Lewis on 29 November 1898.

24. Letter to Albert Lewis, 17? November 1918; *Letters*, vol. 1, 416. In fact, although Lewis did not know it, one of the four he believed to have been killed (Denis Howard de Pass) actually survived the war, becoming a dairy farmer in Sussex until his death in 1973.

25. Letter to Albert Lewis, 10? June 1917; *Letters*, vol. 1, 317; Letter to Arthur Greeves, 10 June 1917; *Letters*, vol. 1, 319.

26. Letter to Albert Lewis, 18 June 1917; *Letters*, vol. 1, 322.

27. "Lewis Papers," vol. 5, 239.

28. Now held in the archives of Keble College, Oxford.

29. Battalion Orders No. 30, 15 June 1917, sheet 4.

30. See the instructions for platoon exercises issued in 1917 by the General Head-Quarters Small Arms School: Oxford University Officers' Training Corps, Archive OT 1/8.

31. Battalion Orders No. 31, 20 June 1917, Part 2, sheet 1.

32. Battalion Orders No. 35, 13 July 1917, Part 2, sheet 5.

33. Battalion Orders No. 59, 30 November 1917, Part 2, sheet 1.

34. Letter to Albert Lewis, 24 July 1917; *Letters*, vol. 1, 329–330.

35. *"C" Company No. 4 O. C. B. 1916–19* (Oxford: Keble College, 1920), 34. Keble College, KC/JCR H1/1/3.

36. In late July 1917, Lewis wrote to his father, remarking that the War Office had at last discovered his existence, and paid him seven shillings: Letter to Albert Lewis, 22 July 1917; *Letters*, vol. 1, 327. Perhaps this can be taken as an indication of the inadequate paperwork associated with this Cadet Battalion.

37. *All My Road before Me*, 125.

38. Note especially his letters to Arthur Greeves dated 3 June 1917 and 10 June 1917; *Letters*, vol. 1, 313, 319–320. The references to the "Visconte de Sade" were originally deleted by Greeves.

39. Letter to Arthur Greeves, 10 June 1917; *Letters*, vol. 1, 319. "s." is an abbreviation of "shilling."

40. Letter to Arthur Greeves, 28 January 1917; *Letters*, vol. 1, 269. This section of the letter was later deleted by Greeves.

41. Lewis hints at this in a letter of January 1917, in which he fantasises about "punishing" an unnamed member of Greeves's family: Letter to Arthur Greeves, 31 January 1917; *Letters*, vol. 1, 271.

42. Letters to Arthur Greeves, 31 January 1917, 7 February 1917, 15 February 1917; *Letters*, vol. 1, 272, 274, 278. The significant letter of 28 January 1917, which discusses whipping, is not signed "Philomastix": *Letters*, vol. 1, 269.

43. Letter to Arthur Greeves, 15 February 1917; *Letters*, vol. 1, 276.

44. Greeves's pocket diaries (11.5 cm x 8 cm) for January 1917 to December 1918 are preserved in the Wade Center, Wheaton College, Wheaton, IL. For this prayer, see entry for 8 July 1917; Arthur Greeves Diaries, 1–2.

45. Entry for 18 July 1917; Arthur Greeves Diaries, 1–2.

46. Lewis comments on this change in letters to his father, dated 18 September 1918 and 18 October 1918: *Letters*, vol. 1, 399–400, 408–409.

47. For comment and analysis, see King, *C. S. Lewis, Poet*, 52–97.

48. *Spirits in Bondage*, 25.

49. Walter Hooper, who edited the manuscript of this diary, later came to the view that the character he had transcribed as *D* was actually the Greek letter Delta, Δ. This suggests that Lewis had a private name for Mrs. Moore based on a Greek term beginning with this letter. Lewis is known to have used this device in other contexts. For example, in 1940, Lewis read a paper to an Oxford society titled "The *Kappa* Element in Romance." Kappa is the initial letter of the Greek word *kryptos*, meaning "concealed" or "hidden."

50. This battalion was designated as a "Special Reserve" unit, concerned primarily with military training, and remained in the United Kingdom throughout the Great War.

51. Battalion Orders No. 30, 15 June 1917, sheet 4. As noted earlier (page 59), these incorrect initials were altered to "E. F. C." a week later. Note that the British system of dating, used in this entry, refers to "day/month/year" rather than the American reference to "month/day/year."

52. "Lewis Papers," vol. 5, 239.

53. Letter to Albert Lewis, 22 October 1917; *Letters*, vol. 1, 338.

54. Letter to Albert Lewis, 3 October 1917; *Letters*, vol. 1, 337.

55. Letter to Arthur Greeves, 28? October 1917; *Letters*, vol. 1, 339.

56. Letter to Arthur Greeves, 14 December 1917; *Letters*, vol. 1, 348.

57. Letter to Albert Lewis, 5 November 1917; *Letters*, vol. 1, 344.

58. Albert Lewis wondered if this was because Lewis was Irish: "Lewis Papers," vol. 5, 247.

A document of 22 May 1918 indicates that he was assigned to the 11th Brigade, 4th Division, of the 1st Somerset Light Infantry.

59. For detailed accounts from 1914, see Wyrall, *The History of the Somerset Light Infantry*; from 1916, see Majendie, *History of the 1st Battalion Somerset Light Infantry*. The 2nd Battalion of the Somerset Light Infantry was stationed in India throughout the Great War.

60. Telegram to Albert Lewis, 15 November 1917; *Letters*, vol. 1, 345.

61. "Lewis Papers," vol. 5, 247.

62. Letter to Albert Lewis, 13 December 1917; *Letters*, vol. 1, 347–348.

63. Letter to Albert Lewis, 4 January 1918; *Letters*, vol. 1, 352.

64. *Surprised by Joy*, 227.

65. Letter to Arthur Greeves, 3 June 1918; *Letters*, vol. 1, 378.

66. Darwall-Smith, *History of University College, Oxford*, 437.

67. Letter to Arthur Greeves, 30 May 1916; *Letters*, vol. 1, 187.

68. Letter to Albert Lewis, 16 February 1918; *Letters*, vol. 1, 356.

69. Letter to Arthur Greeves, 21 February 1918; *Letters*, vol. 1, 358–360.

70. Entry in the "memorandum" section of the diary for the week 17–23 March 1918; Arthur Greeves Diaries, 1-4.

71. Entry for 11 April 1918; Arthur Greeves Diaries, 1-4.

72. Entry for 31 April 1918; Arthur Greeves Diaries, 1-4.

73. For this assault, see Majendie, *History of the 1st Battalion Somerset Light Infantry*, 76–81; Wyrall, *History of the Somerset Light Infantry*, 293–295.

74. Letter to Arthur Greeves, 4? November 1917; *Letters*, vol. 1, 341–342.

75. *Surprised by Joy*, 229.

76. Majendie, *History of the 1st Battalion Somerset Light Infantry*, 81; Wyrall, *History of the Somerset Light Infantry*, 295.

77. "Lewis Papers," vol. 5, 308. In a later letter to the War Office, Lewis stated that he was "severely wounded" on this occasion: Letter to the War Office, 18 January 1919; *Letters*, vol. 1, 424.

78. Warnie was promoted to captain on 29 November 1917, and retained this rank until his retirement in 1932, suggesting his subsequent military career was perhaps undistinguished.

79. "Lewis Papers," vol. 5, 309.

80. For example, his remark that Greeves's handwriting "is so like a girl's": Letter to Arthur Greeves, 14 June 1916; *Letters*, vol. 1, 193.

81. Letter to Arthur Greeves, 23 May 1918; *Letters*, vol. 1, 371. Text enclosed thus "< >" was deleted by Greeves, and subsequently restored on editing by Walter Hooper.

82. Entry for 27 May 1918; Arthur Greeves Diaries, 1-5.

83. Entry in the "memorandum" section of the diary for the week 5–11 May 1918; Arthur Greeves Diaries, 1-5.

84. Entry for 31 December 1918; Arthur Greeves Diaries, 1-6.

85. Greeves kept a diary recording a visit to Oxford to meet Lewis in 1922, which is buoyant in tone, taking particular pleasure in the fact that Lewis suggested that he extend his visit. See his diary for 28 June–28 August 1922; Arthur Greeves Diaries, 1–7. This diary takes the form of an "Oxford Series" notebook, in which Greeves provides extended description of his artistic work and reflections, making no reference to any of the issues that so troubled him in 1917–1918.

86. Letter to Albert Lewis, 20? June 1918; *Letters*, vol. 1, 384–387.

87. For comment, see W. H. Lewis, "Memoir of C. S. Lewis," 9–10.

88. *Poems*, 81. The exact date of composition of this poem is unclear.

89. *Surprised by Joy*, 197.

90. Sayer, *Jack*, xvii–xviii.
91. Letter to Albert Lewis, 29 June 1918; *Letters*, vol. 1, 387.
92. Letter to Albert Lewis, 18 October 1918; *Letters*, vol. 1, 409.
93. "Lewis Papers," vol. 6, 79.

4. DECEPTIONS AND DISCOVERIES: THE MAKING OF AN OXFORD DON, 1919–1927

1. See Fred Bickerton, *Fred of Oxford: Being the Memoirs of Fred Bickerton* (London: Evans Bros, 1953).
2. Letter to Albert Lewis, 27 January 1919; *Letters*, vol. 1, 428.
3. *Spirits in Bondage*, 82–83.
4. Note Lewis's explicit and immediate statement of his "wish to get a fellowship": Letter to Albert Lewis, 27 January 1919; *Letters*, vol. 1, 428.
5. Oxford University did not divide the Second Class into "Lower Second (2:2)" and "Upper Second (2:1)" until the 1990s. Oxford awarded Fourth Class Honours until the late 1960s.
6. *Oxford University Calendar 1918* (Oxford: Oxford University Press, 1918), xiv.
7. Letter to Arthur Greeves, 26 January 1919: *Letters*, vol. 1, 425–426. One of the postwar reforms introduced by most Oxford colleges after the Great War was the abolition of compulsory chapel; Lewis's enforced attendance at chapel did not last long.
8. Bickerton, *Fred of Oxford*, 5–9.
9. The village of Headington became part of the city of Oxford in 1929.
10. For example, see Lewis's letter to Arthur Greeves, 9 February 1919; *Letters*, vol. 1, 433: "'The family' has been greatly taken with your photo." Or his letter to Arthur Greeves, 18 September 1919; *Letters*, vol. 1, 467: "The family sends their love."
11. Earlier letters use the more formal "Mrs Moore"; for example, his letters to Greeves of 6? October 1918 and 26 January 1919; *Letters*, vol. 1, 404, 425. The first (unexplained) use of this nickname is in the letter to Greeves of 14 July 1919; *Letters*, vol. 1, 460. It is used regularly thereafter: see, for example, *Letters*, vol. 1, 463, 465, 469, 473. By the early 1920s, "The Minto" simply became "Minto."
12. Lady Maureen Dunbar, OH/SR-8, fol. 11, Wade Center Oral History Collection, Wheaton College, Wheaton, IL. For the history of "the Minto," see *Doncaster Gazette*, 8 May 1934.
13. Letter to Arthur Greeves, 2 June 1919; *Letters*, vol. 1, 454.
14. See the correspondence between Warren and Albert Lewis on this question: "Lewis Papers," vol. 6, 118, 124–125, 129.
15. "Lewis Papers," vol. 6, 161.
16. Letter to Arthur Greeves, 20 February 1917; *Letters*, vol. 1, 280.
17. Letter to Albert Lewis, 4 April 1920; *Letters*, vol. 1, 479.
18. Letter to Albert Lewis, 8 December 1920; *Letters*, vol. 1, 512.
19. Letter to Warren Lewis, 1 July 1921; *Letters*, vol. 1, 556–557.
20. Letter to Albert Lewis, 17 June 1921; *Letters*, vol. 1, 551.
21. I am very grateful to colleagues in the Oxford University Archives and the "Special Collections" of the Bodleian Library, Oxford, for their exhaustive searches for this document.
22. Letter to Albert Lewis, 9 July 1921; *Letters*, vol. 1, 569.
23. Letter to Warren Lewis, 7 August 1921; *Letters*, vol. 1, 570–573.
24. Letter to Albert Lewis, 18 May 1922; *Letters*, vol. 1, 591.
25. Darwall-Smith, *History of University College Oxford*, 447. These changes were implemented in 1926.
26. Letter to Albert Lewis, 18 May 1922; *Letters*, vol. 1, 591–592.

27. Letter to Albert Lewis, 20 July 1922; *Letters*, vol. 1, 595.
28. Following the incorporation of Headington into the city of Oxford in 1929, this road was eventually renamed "Holyoake Road" in 1959, to avoid confusion with another "Western Road" in the southern Oxford suburb of Grandpont. The house numbering was also changed, so that the new address of "Hillsboro" is 14 Holyoake Road.
29. *All My Road before Me*, 123.
30. Some biographies suggest it was a fellowship in philosophy. The Magdalen College archives clearly indicate that it was a "Classical Fellowship." See *The President's Notebooks*, vol. 20, fols. 99–100. Magdalen College Oxford: MS PR 2/20.
31. For the list of eleven candidates, see President's Notebook for 1922: *The President's Notebooks*, vol. 20, fol. 99.
32. *All My Road before Me*, 110.
33. Ibid., 117.
34. Letter from Sir Herbert Warren to Lewis, 4 November 1922; Magdalen College Oxford, MS 1026/III/3.
35. *All My Road before Me*, 151.
36. See John Bowlby, *Maternal Care and Mental Health* (Geneva: World Health Organization, 1952). For a fuller statement, see John Bowlby, *A Secure Base: Parent-Child Attachment and Healthy Human Development* (New York: Basic Books, 1988). Bowlby's personal narrative shows similarities to Lewis's at important points: see Suzan van Dijken, *John Bowlby: His Early Life; A Biographical Journey into the Roots of Attachment Theory* (London: Free Association Books, 1998).
37. *Surprised by Joy*, 22.
38. *Allegory of Love*, 7.
39. Letter to Albert Lewis, 27 June 1921; *Letters*, vol. 1, 554.
40. *All My Road before Me*, 240.
41. Such as John Churton Collins, *The Study of English Literature: A Plea for Its Recognition and Organization at the Universities* (London: Macmillan, 1891).
42. The view of Edward Augustus Freeman (1823–1892), Oxford's Regius Professor of History, in 1887: see Alvin Kernan, *The Death of Literature* (New Haven, CT: Yale University Press, 1990), 38.
43. Eagleton, *Literary Theory*, 15–46.
44. *All My Road before Me*, 120.
45. Ibid., 53.
46. *The Allegory of Love*, v.
47. *Surprised by Joy*, 262.
48. Ibid., 239. For the full text of the "Great War" letters, including illustrations, see *Letters*, vol. 3, 1600–1646.
49. The best study of this phase in Lewis's life is Adey, *C. S. Lewis's "Great War" with Owen Barfield.*
50. *Surprised by Joy*, 241.
51. Ibid., 243.
52. For a detailed analysis of this approach, see McGrath, "The 'New Look': Lewis's Philosophical Context at Oxford in the 1920s," in *The Intellectual World of C. S. Lewis*, 31–54.
53. Ibid., 237.
54. Ibid., 243.
55. "The Man Born Blind," in *Essay Collection*, 783–786.
56. Gibb, *Light on C. S. Lewis*, 52.

57. *All My Road before Me*, 256.
58. Letter to Albert Lewis, 1 July 1923; *Letters*, vol. 1, 610.
59. Peter Bayley, "Family Matters III: The English Rising," *University College Record* 14 (2006): 115–116.
60. Darwell-Smith, *History of University College*, 449.
61. Ibid., 447–452.
62. Letter to Albert Lewis, 11 May 1924; *Letters*, vol. 1, 627–630.
63. *All My Road before Me*, 409–410. The plot developed further a few days later: 413–414.
64. Letter to Arthur Greeves, 4? November 1917; *Letters*, vol. 1, 342.
65. Lewis noted the comment in his diary for 26 January 1927: *All My Road before Me*, 438.
66. Letter to Albert Lewis, 15 October 1924; *Letters*, vol. 1, 635.
67. A copy of the original announcement is bound into the President's Notebook for 1927: *The President's Notebooks*, vol. 21, fol. 11. Magdalen College Oxford: MS PR 2/21.
68. See letters to Albert Lewis, April 1925 and 26 May 1925; *Letters*, vol. 1, 640, 642–646.
69. President Warren, as events made clear, was perfectly prepared to sack even senior fellows who failed to deliver their promised performance.
70. "University News: New Fellow of Magdalen College," *Times*, 22 May 1925. There is an error in this report. As we saw in the previous chapter, Lewis actually won his scholarship to University College in 1916 (not 1915), and took up his place at the college in 1917.

5. FELLOWSHIP, FAMILY, AND FRIENDSHIP: THE EARLY YEARS AT MAGDALEN COLLEGE, 1927–1930

1. Letter to Albert Lewis, 14 August 1925; *Letters*, vol. 1, 647–648.
2. Brockliss, *Magdalen College Oxford*, 593–594.
3. Lewis commented on this in a letter to his father, written shortly after his arrival at Magdalen: Letter to Albert Lewis, 21 October 1925; *Letters*, vol. 1, 651.
4. Brockliss, *Magdalen College Oxford*, 601. The practice of "procession by seniority" was not abandoned until 1958, some years after Lewis had left the college.
5. Ibid., 602.
6. For the salaries of fellows at this time, see Brockliss, *Magdalen College Oxford*, 597.
7. Letter to Albert Lewis, 21 October 1925; *Letters*, vol. 1, 650.
8. See Lewis's diary entries for 23 June and 1 July 1926: *All My Road before Me*, 416, 420.
9. For Lewis's emerging understanding of the value of education, see Heck, *Irrigating Deserts*, 23–48.
10. W. H. Lewis, *C. S. Lewis: A Biography*, 213.
11. Letter to Owen Barfield, 9 September 1929; *Letters*, vol. 1, 820.
12. Lewis's correspondence with his brother about his father's death seems confused about the dates: see Walter Hooper's annotations to the letter to Warren Lewis, 29 September 1929; *Letters*, vol. 1, 823–824.
13. Warnie was in Shanghai, China, on military service; Lewis had arrived back in Oxford on 22 September after being reassured that his father was in no imminent danger.
14. Cromlyn [John Barry], in *Church of Ireland Gazette*, 5 February 1999. "Cromlyn" was Barry's pen name when writing for this journal.
15. Letter to Rhona Bodle, 24 March 1954; *Letters*, vol. 3, 445.
16. Letter to Warren Lewis, 29 September 1929; *Letters*, vol. 1, 824–825.
17. Warnie's diary entry for 23 April 1930; "Lewis Papers," vol. 11, 5.
18. Letter to Dom Bede Griffiths, 8 February 1956; *Letters*, vol. 3, 703.

19. *Surprised by Joy*, 231.

20. Ibid., 251.

21. "On Forgiveness," in *Essay Collection*, 184–186.

22. *Surprised by Joy*, 266.

23. Letter to Warren Lewis, 12 January 1930; *Letters*, vol. 1, 865.

24. Ibid., 870.

25. See Warren Lewis's letter to Lewis, dated 9 December 1931, confirming these details: Bodleian Library, Oxford, MS. Eng. Lett. c. 200/7 fol. 5. The UK Land Registry reference for this property is ON90127.

26. Mrs. Moore's will was drawn up by Barfield and Barfield, Solicitors, on 13 May 1945, with Maureen and Lewis as executors. By that time, Maureen was married, and her husband was incorporated into the inheritance stipulation.

27. Letter to Warren Lewis, 12 December 1932; *Letters*, vol. 2, 90. The letter was sent to Le Havre in France, where the *Automedon* would dock before the final stage of its journey to Liverpool.

28. Maureen Moore was of the view that Warnie did not "retire," but was thrown out of the army because of an emerging drink problem: Wade Center Oral History Collection: Lady Maureen Dunbar, OH/SR-8, fol. 19.

29. Warnie indicates that his often poor relationship with Mrs. Moore led him to prepare an "exit strategy" involving relocation to the Republic of Ireland. However, this was never put into action. W. H. Lewis, "Memoir of C. S. Lewis," 24.

30. In 1925, the Merton Chair of English Language and Literature was held by H. C. K. Wyld (1870–1945), and the Merton Chair of English Literature by George Stuart Gordon (1881–1942).

31. *All My Road before Me*, 392–393.

32. Lewis's personal library, now held in the Wade Center (Wheaton College, Wheaton, IL), included a copy of the 1926 edition of Geir T. Zoëga, *A Concise Dictionary of Old Icelandic*, in which Lewis has added notes concerning the conjugation of irregular verbs, as well as Guðbrandur Vigfússon's *Icelandic Prose Reader* (1879).

33. Letter to Arthur Greeves, 30 January 1930; *Letters*, vol. 1, 880.

34. Letter to Arthur Greeves, 26 June 1927; *Letters*, vol. 1, 701.

35. Letter to Arthur Greeves, 17 October 1929; *Letters*, vol. 1, 838. This section of the letter was actually written on 3 December.

36. Tolkien eventually abandoned work on this poem in September 1931, and returned to it only in the 1950s.

37. Members of the TCBS ("Tea Club, Barrovian Society"). This club was integral to Tolkien's literary development, and in some ways anticipates the Inklings: see Carpenter, *J. R. R. Tolkien*, 67–76; Garth, *Tolkien and the Great War*, 3–138.

38. Cited in J. R. R. Tolkien, *The Lays of Beleriand* (Boston: Houghton Mifflin, 1985), 151.

6. THE MOST RELUCTANT CONVERT: THE MAKING OF A MERE CHRISTIAN, 1930-1932

1. Joseph Pearce, *Literary Converts: Spiritual Inspiration in an Age of Unbelief* (London: HarperCollins, 1999).

2. *Surprised by Joy*, 221–222.

3. Graham Greene, *Collected Essays* (New York: Penguin, 1966), 91–92.

4. Donat Gallagher, ed., *The Essays, Articles and Reviews of Evelyn Waugh* (London: Methuen, 1983), 300–304.

5. Letter to Edward Sackville-West, cited in Michael de-la-Noy, *Eddy: The Life of Edward Sackville-West* (London: Bodley Head, 1988), 237.

6. *Surprised by Joy*, 249.

7. Ibid.

8. Ibid., 248.

9. *Allegory of Love*, 142

10. *The Discarded Image*, 206.

11. *Surprised by Joy*, 252–260.

12. Henri Poincaré, *Science and Method* (London: Nelson, 1914), 129.

13. *Surprised by Joy*, 197.

14. Ibid., 260–261.

15. For the issues arising, see McGrath, "The Enigma of Autobiography: Critical Reflections on *Surprised by Joy*," in *The Intellectual World of C. S. Lewis*, 7–29.

16. *Surprised by Joy*, 264.

17. Letter to Leo Baker, 25 September 1920; *Letters*, vol. 1, 509.

18. *Surprised by Joy*, 265.

19. Ibid., 261.

20. Ibid., 265. For further comment on this "treaty with reality," see McGrath, "The 'New Look': Lewis's Philosophical Context at Oxford in the 1920s," in *The Intellectual World of C. S. Lewis*, 39–42.

21. Ibid., 266.

22. Ibid., 271.

23. Letter from Paul Elmer More to Lewis, 26 April 1935; cited in *Letters*, vol. 2, 164 n. 37.

24. *Surprised by Joy*, 272.

25. Ibid., 270.

26. Ibid.

27. Letter to Laurence Krieg, 21 April 1957; *Letters*, vol. 3, 848.

28. W. H. Lewis, "C. S. Lewis: A Biography," 43.

29. *Surprised by Joy*, x.

30. These dates are confirmed in official university publications of the period: see *Oxford University Calendar, 1928* (Oxford: Oxford University Press, 1928), xx–xxii; *Oxford University Calendar, 1929* (Oxford: Oxford University Press, 1929), viii–x. Note that Lewis invariably refers to the eight-week "Full Term" during which tutorials and lectures took place.

31. Letter to Arthur Greeves, 22 September 1931; *Letters*, vol. 1, 969–972.

32. Letter to Owen Barfield, 3? February 1930; *Letters*, vol. 1, 882–883.

33. *Surprised by Joy*, 268.

34. Owen Barfield, in Poe, *C. S. Lewis Remembered*, 25–35.

35. Letter to Arthur Greeves, 29 October 1930; *Letters*, vol. 1, 942.

36. *Surprised by Joy*, 267.

37. Ibid., 268.

38. For an engaging comparison of Lewis and Freud on this point, see Nicholi, *The Question of God*.

39. *Surprised by Joy*, 265.

40. Ibid., 270.

41. Letter to Arthur Greeves, 22 September 1931; *Letters*, vol. 1, 969–972.

42. Lewis seems to have the imagery of the nighttime conversation between Christ and Nicodemus (John 3) in mind in later reflections on this conversation.

43. Letters to Arthur Greeves, 1 October and 18 October 1931; *Letters*, vol. 1, 972–977.

44. Letter to Arthur Greeves, 1 October 1931; *Letters*, vol. 1, 974.

45. Letter to Arthur Greeves, 18 October 1931; *Letters*, vol. 1, 976.

46. Ibid., 977.
47. *Miracles*, 218. For the importance of this notion, see McGrath, "A Gleam of Divine Truth: The Concept of 'Myth' in Lewis's Thought," in *The Intellectual World of C. S. Lewis*, 55–81.
48. "Myth Became Fact," in *Essay Collection*, 142.
49. J. R. R. Tolkien, *The Silmarillion* (London: Allen & Unwin, 1977), 41.
50. *Surprised by Joy*, 267.
51. Ibid., 275. Whipsnade Park Zoo, located near Dunstable in Bedfordshire, about 50 miles (80 kilometres) from Oxford, opened in May 1931.
52. See, for example, Downing, *Most Reluctant Convert*, 155.
53. W. H. Lewis, "Memoir of C. S. Lewis," 19.
54. Holmer, *C. S. Lewis: The Shape of His Faith and Thought*, 22–45.
55. For example, see the letter to Warren Lewis, 24 October 1931; *Letters*, vol. 2, 1–11. This letter suggests that Lewis has not yet resolved certain theological issues.
56. Letter to Warren Lewis, 24 October 1931; *Letters*, vol. 2, 2. Warnie had left England for his last tour of duty in China on 9 October, 1931, arriving in Shanghai on 17 November.
57. W. H. Lewis, "Memoir of C. S. Lewis," 19.
58. *Surprised by Joy*, 276.
59. Since about 1960, the Spanish bluebell (*Hyacinthoides hispanica*) has become increasingly widespread in England. Lewis's reference is clearly to the traditional English bluebell.
60. ZSL Whipsnade Zoo, "Beautiful Bluebells," press release, 17 May 2004.
61. *Surprised by Joy*, 6.
62. Note the cornflower theme in the early part of E. M. Forster's classic *Room with a View* (1908).
63. See his letter to Warren Lewis, 14 June 1932; *Letters*, vol. 2, 84.
64. Letter to Warren Lewis, 25 December 1931; *Letters*, vol. 2, 30.
65. This chapel, which took its name from the street on which it was located, no longer exists. "Bubbling Well Street" was renamed "Nanjing Road West" in 1945.
66. *The Pilgrim's Regress*, 5.

7. A MAN OF LETTERS: LITERARY SCHOLARSHIP AND CRITICISM, 1933–1939

1. Letter to Arthur Greeves, 4 February 1933; *Letters*, vol. 2, 95.
2. Letter to Arthur Greeves, 12 September 1933; *Letters*, vol. 2, 125.
3. Letter to Warren Lewis, 22 November 1931; *Letters*, vol. 2, 14–16.
4. Letter to Thomasine, 14 December 1959; *Letters*, vol. 3, 1109.
5. Sayer, *Jack*, 198.
6. Lawlor in Gibb, *Light on C. S. Lewis*, 71–73. See further Lawlor, *C. S. Lewis: Memories and Reflections*. Lawlor later became Professor of English Language and Literature at the University of Keele.
7. John Wain in Gibb, *Light on C. S. Lewis*, 72.
8. Wain, *Sprightly Running*, 138.
9. Hooper, *C. S. Lewis: A Companion and Guide*, 42.
10. Letter to Cynthia Donnelly, 14 August 1954; *Letters*, vol. 3, 503.
11. Wilson, *C. S. Lewis: A Biography*, 161.
12. Letter to Albert Lewis, 28 August 1924; *Letters*, vol. 1, 633.
13. This image is used of Lewis by John Wain, in Roma Gill (ed.), *William Empson* (London: Routledge, 1977), 117.
14. See the "faculty lecturer lists" published in *Oxford University Calendar 1935* (Oxford: Oxford University Press, 1935), 12.

15. *Oxford University Calendar 1936* (Oxford: Oxford University Press, 1936), 423 n. 9.

16. *The Discarded Image*, 216.

17. *The Four Loves*, 166.

18. Letter to Guy Pocock, 17 January 1933; *Letters*, vol. 2, 94.

19. *The Pilgrim's Regress*, 5.

20. Ibid., 5.

21. "The Vision of John Bunyan," in *Selected Literary Essays*, 149.

22. *Poems*, 81.

23. *Pilgrim's Regress*, 11–12.

24. Ibid., 8.

25. Ibid., 10.

26. For Lewis's exploration of the significance of desire and longing, see McGrath, "Arrows of Joy: Lewis's Argument from Desire," in *The Intellectual World of C. S. Lewis*, 105–128.

27. *The Pilgrim's Regress*, 10.

28. Ibid., 177.

29. Acts 9:9-19; 2 Corinthians 3:13-16.

30. Letter to Warren Lewis, 22 November 1931; *Letters*, vol. 2, 16.

31. Tolkien mentions this in a letter to Christopher Tolkien, 30 January 1945; Tolkien, *Letters*, 108.

32. Letter to Arthur Greeves, 4 February 1933; *Letters*, vol. 2, 96.

33. Warnie's best books, in my view, are *The Splendid Century: Some Aspects of French Life in the Reign of Louis XIV* (1953) and *Levantine Adventurer: The Travels and Missions of the Chevalier d'Arvieux, 1653–1697* (1962).

34. J. R. R. Tolkien to W. L. White, 11 September 1967; Tolkien, *Letters*, 388.

35. Williams, *To Michal from Serge*, 227.

36. J. R. R. Tolkien to W. L. White, 11 September 1967; Tolkien, *Letters*, 388.

37. Letter to Charles Williams, 11 March 1936; *Letters*, vol. 2, 183.

38. Letter to Janet Spens, 16 November 1934; *Letters*, vol. 2, 147–149.

39. Owen Barfield; J. A. W. Bennett; David Cecil; Nevill Coghill; James Dundas-Grant; Hugo Dyson; Adam Fox; Colin Hardie; Robert E. Havard; C. S. Lewis; Warren Lewis; Gervase Mathew; R. B. McCallum; C. E. Stevens; Christopher Tolkien; J. R. R. Tolkien; John Wain; Charles Williams; C. L. Wrenn.

40. Tolkien to Stanley Unwin, 4 June 1938; Tolkien, *Letters*, 36. It is not clear whether Tolkien is here referring to the Inklings or "The Cave," a related group which was mainly concerned with English faculty politics. For "The Cave," see Lewis's letter to Warren Lewis, 17 March 1940; *Letters*, vol. 2, 365.

41. Wain, *Sprightly Running*, 185.

42. Letter to Leo Baker, 28 April 1935; *Letters*, vol. 2, 161.

43. Letter to Albert Lewis, 10 July 1928; *Letters*, vol. 1, 766–767.

44. The Clarendon Press is an imprint of Oxford University Press.

45. Letter to Guy Pocock, 27 February 1933; *Letters*, vol. 2, 98.

46. Bodleian Library, Oxford, MS. Eng. c. 6825, fols. 48–49.

47. *Allegory of Love*, 1.

48. Ibid., 2. The phrase *courtly love* is the traditional English translation of the French term *amour courtois*, somewhat tenuously derived from the Provençal term *fin' amors*.

49. See, for example, John C. Moore, "'Courtly Love': A Problem of Terminology," *Journal of the History of Ideas* 40, no. 4 (1979): 621–632.

50. See, for example, C. Stephen Jaeger, *The Origins of Courtliness: Civilizing Trends and the Formation of Courtly Ideals, 937–1210* (Philadelphia: University of Pennsylvania Press, 1991).

51. David Hill Radcliffe, *Edmund Spenser: A Reception History* (Columbia, SC: Camden House, 1996), 168.

52. *Oxford University Calendar 1938* (Oxford: Oxford University Press, 1938), 460 n. 12.

53. Gardner, "Clive Staples Lewis, 1898–1963," 423.

54. See Lewis's *Rehabilitations*. Lewis here seeks to rehabilitate both individuals and schools, and offers a particularly interesting assessment of differences in style between Shakespeare and Milton.

55. "On the Reading of Old Books," in *Essay Collection*, 439.

56. Ibid., 440.

57. Ibid., 439.

58. "Learning in War-Time," in *Essay Collection*, 584.

59. "De Descriptione Temporum," in *Selected Literary Essays*, 13.

60. "De Audiendis Poetis," in *Studies in Medieval and Renaissance Literature*, 2–3.

61. *Experiment in Criticism*, 140–141.

62. Ibid., 137.

63. Ralph Waldo Emerson, *Essays and Lectures* (New York: Library of America, 1983), 259.

64. *Experiment in Criticism*, 85.

65. *The Personal Heresy*, 11.

8. NATIONAL ACCLAIM: THE WARTIME APOLOGIST, 1939–1942

1. Now known by the title "Learning in War-Time," in *Essay Collection*, 579–586. Quote at page 586.

2. Letter to Warren Lewis, 2 September 1939; *Letters*, vol. 2, 270–271.

3. Letter to Arthur Greeves, 27 December 1940; *Letters*, vol. 3, 1538.

4. Letter to Warren Lewis, 11 August 1940; *Letters*, vol. 2, 433.

5. Letter to Warren Lewis, 24 November 1939; *Letters*, vol. 2, 296.

6. J. R. R. Tolkien to Christopher Bretherton, 16 July 1964; Tolkien, *Letters*, 349.

7. Letter to Arthur Greeves, 27 December 1940; *Letters*, vol. 3, 1538.

8. Letter to Warren Lewis, 11 November 1939; *Letters*, vol. 2, 287.

9. Ibid., 288–289.

10. Williams, *To Michal from Serge*, 253.

11. J. R. R. Tolkien to Rayner Unwin, 12 September 1965; Tolkien, *Letters*, 362. A similar point was made in 1954 on the publication of *The Fellowship of the Ring*: J. R. R. Tolkien to Rayner Unwin, 9 September 1954; Tolkien, *Letters*, 184. Both these letters were written at a time when Tolkien's friendship with Lewis had cooled, giving added significance to his warm commendations.

12. Letter to Warren Lewis, 3 December 1939; *Letters*, vol. 2, 302.

13. See J. R. R. Tolkien to Christopher Tolkien, 31 May 1944; Tolkien, *Letters*, 83.

14. *The Problem of Pain*, 91.

15. "On Science Fiction," in *Essay Collection*, 451.

16. *The Problem of Pain*, 3.

17. Ibid., 16.

18. Ibid., 39.

19. Ibid., 80.

20. Letter to Warren Lewis, 3 December 1939; *Letters*, vol. 2, 302. Emphasis in original.

21. Letter to Arthur Greeves, 3 April 1930; *Letters*, vol. 1, 889.

22. Lewis discusses Adams primarily in his correspondence with Mary Neylan (1908–1997), his former student. Lewis was godfather to Neylan's daughter, Sarah.

23. Letter to Sister Penelope, 24 October 1940; *Letters*, vol. 2, 452.

24. Letter to Mary Willis Shelburne, 31 March 1954; *Letters*, vol. 3, 449.

25. The best study is Dorsett, *Seeking the Secret Place*, 85–107.

26. Letter to Mary Neylan, 30 April 1941; *Letters*, vol. 2, 482.

27. The BBC suspended local radio transmissions in 1939, and did not resume them until 1946.

28. See Wolfe, *The Churches and the British Broadcasting Corporation 1922–1956*.

29. See Justin Phillips, *C. S. Lewis at the BBC* (New York: HarperCollins, 2002), 77–94.

30. All correspondence between the BBC and Lewis is held at the BBC Written Archives Centre [WAC], Caversham Park. James Welch to Lewis, 7 February 1941, file 910/TAL 1a, BBC Written Archives Centre, Caversham Park.

31. Letter to James Welch, 10 February 1941; *Letters*, vol. 2, 470.

32. Eric Fenn to Lewis, 11 February 1941, 910/TAL 1a, BBC Written Archives Centre, Caversham Park.

33. Letter to Sister Penelope, 15 May 1941; *Letters*, vol. 2, 485.

34. "Christian Apologetics," in *Essay Collection*, 153.

35. Ibid., 155.

36. Eric Fenn to Lewis, 21 February 1941, 910/TAL 1a, BBC Written Archives Centre, Caversham Park.

37. Letter to Sister Penelope, 15 May 1941; *Letters*, vol. 2, 484–485.

38. Letter to Arthur Greeves, 25 May 1941; *Letters*, vol. 2, 486.

39. Letter to J. S. A. Ensor, 13 March 1944; *Letters*, vol. 2, 606.

40. Eric Fenn to Lewis, 13 May 1941, 910/TAL 1a, BBC Written Archives Centre, Caversham Park.

41. Eric Fenn to Lewis, 9 June 1941, 910/TAL 1a, BBC Written Archives Centre, Caversham Park.

42. Eric Fenn to Lewis, 24 June 1941, 910/TAL 1a, BBC Written Archives Centre, Caversham Park.

43. Internal Circulating Memo HG/PVH, 15 July 1941, file 910/TAL 1a, BBC Written Archives Centre, Caversham Park.

44. Eric Fenn to Lewis, 22 July 1941, file 910/TAL 1a, BBC Written Archives Centre, Caversham Park.

45. Eric Fenn to Lewis, 4 September 1941, file 910/TAL 1a, BBC Written Archives Centre, Caversham Park.

46. Eric Fenn to Lewis, 5 December 1941, file 910/TAL 1a, BBC Written Archives Centre, Caversham Park.

47. *Miracles*, 218. For the importance of this notion, see McGrath, "A 'Mere Christian': Anglicanism and Lewis's Religious Identity," in *The Intellectual World of C. S. Lewis*, 147–161.

48. For an exploration of this point, see Wolfe and Wolfe, *C. S. Lewis and the Church*.

49. *Broadcast Talks*, 5.

50. Eric Fenn to Lewis, 18 February 1942, file 910/TAL 1a, BBC Written Archives Centre, Caversham Park.

51. Eric Fenn to Lewis, 15 September 1942, file 910/TAL 1a, BBC Written Archives Centre, Caversham Park.

52. Letter to Eric Fenn, 25 March 1944; *Letters*, vol. 2, 609.

9. INTERNATIONAL FAME: THE MERE CHRISTIAN, 1942–1945

1. Letter to Warren Lewis, 20 July 1940; *Letters*, vol. 2, 426.

2. These comments are found in a preface written by Lewis in May 1960 for a later edition of this work, explaining more about its composition: *The Screwtape Letters and Screwtape Proposes a Toast* (London: Geoffrey Bles, 1961), xxi.

3. *The Screwtape Letters*, 88.

4. J. R. R. Tolkien to Michael Tolkien, November 1963?; Tolkien, *Letters*, 342.

5. Oliver Quick to William Temple, 24 July 1943; William Temple Papers, vol. 39, fol. 269, Lambeth Palace Library. For the significance of Lewis's approach to theology, see McGrath, "Outside the 'Inner Ring': Lewis as a Theologian," in *The Intellectual World of C. S. Lewis*, 163–183.

6. Lillian Lang to J. Warren MacAlpine, 16 June 1948, file 910/TAL 1b, BBC Written Archives Centre, Caversham Park.

7. "On the Reading of Old Books," in *Essay Collection*, 439.

8. Richard Baxter, *The Church History of the Government by Bishops* (London: Thomas Simmons, 1681), folio b.

9. *English Literature in the Sixteenth Century*, 454.

10. *Mere Christianity*, 11–12. See further McGrath, "A 'Mere Christian': Anglicanism and Lewis's Religious Identity," in *The Intellectual World of C. S. Lewis*, 147–161.

11. W. R. Inge, *Protestantism* (London: Nelson, 1936), 86 (Wade Center, Wheaton College, Wheaton, IL).

12. For a good analysis, see Giles Watson, "Dorothy L. Sayers and the Oecumenical Penguin."

13. Farrer, "The Christian Apologist," in Gibb, *Light on C. S. Lewis*, 37. For further discussion of Lewis's approach to apologetics, see McGrath, "Reason, Experience, and Imagination: Lewis's Apologetic Method," in *The Intellectual World of C. S. Lewis*, 129–146.

14. *Mere Christianity*, 21.

15. Ibid., 24.

16. Ibid., 8.

17. Ibid., 25.

18. Ibid., 135.

19. Ibid., 137. For a careful evaluation of this line of argument, see McGrath, "Arrows of Joy: Lewis's Argument from Desire," in *The Intellectual World of C. S. Lewis*, 103–128.

20. Ibid., 136–7.

21. *A Preface to "Paradise Lost,"* 80.

22. "Is Theology Poetry?" in *Essay Collection*, 21. For Lewis's use of the image of the sun, see McGrath, "The Privileging of Vision: Lewis's Metaphors of Light, Sun, and Sight," in *The Intellectual World of C. S. Lewis*, 83–104.

23. Letter to Arthur Greeves, 11 December 1944; *Letters*, vol. 3, 1555.

24. *Mere Christianity*, 52.

25. Ibid., 123.

26. Lewis's views on this matter can be found in *Mere Christianity*, 104–113.

27. The text, which was found tucked into Tolkien's copy of Lewis's pamphlet *Christian Behaviour*, is included in Tolkien's published correspondence: Tolkien, *Letters*, 59–62.

28. Lewis to Emrys Evans [Principal, University College of North Wales], 30 October 1941; *Letters*, vol. 2, 494.

29. *A Preface to "Paradise Lost,"* 1.

30. Ibid., 62–63.

31. The Newcastle campus of the University of Durham formally became a university in its own right in 1963, with the ownership of the Riddell Memorial Lectures being transferred to the new University of Newcastle.

32. *The Abolition of Man*, 18.

33. Ibid., 1–4.

34. Ibid., 18.

35. The best study is Lucas, "The Restoration of Man."
36. George Macaulay Trevelyan to Lewis, 2 February 1945, MS Eng. c. 6825, fol. 602, Bodleian Library, Oxford.
37. J. R. R. Tolkien to Christopher Tolkien, 13 April 1944; Tolkien, *Letters*, 71.
38. For example, Pearce, *C. S. Lewis and the Catholic Church*, 107–112.
39. *Surprised by Joy*, 38.
40. "On Science Fiction," in *Essay Collection*, 456–457.
41. Ibid., 459.
42. Letter to Roger Lancelyn Green, 28 December 1938; *Letters*, vol. 2, 236–237.
43. Haldane, *Possible Worlds*, 190–197.
44. For further details, see Harry Bruinius, *Better For All the World: The Secret History of Forced Sterilization and America's Quest for Racial Purity* (New York: Knopf, 2006).
45. "Vivisection," in *Essay Collection*, 693–697.
46. Ibid., 696.
47. Ibid., 695.

10. A PROPHET WITHOUT HONOUR?: POSTWAR TENSIONS AND PROBLEMS, 1945-1954

1. "Religion: Don v. Devil," *Time*, 8 September 1947.
2. J. R. R. Tolkien to Christopher Tolkien, 1 March 1944; Tolkien, *Letters*, 68.
3. Lewis made little effort to conceal his home telephone number: Oxford 6963.
4. J. R. R. Tolkien to Joy Hill, 10 May 1966; Tolkien, *Letters*, 368–369.
5. J. R. R. Tolkien to Christopher Tolkien, 28 October 1944; Tolkien, *Letters*, 102.
6. J. R. R. Tolkien to Rayner Unwin, 9 September 1954; Tolkien, *Letters*, 184.
7. MS RSL E2, C. S. Lewis file, Cambridge University Library.
8. A. N. Wilson, *Lewis: A Biography*, 191.
9. Letter to Jill Flewett, 17 April 1946; *Letters*, vol. 2, 706.
10. Letter to Lord Salisbury, 9 March 1947; *Letters*, vol. 2, 766.
11. Letter to Owen Barfield, 4 April 1949; *Letters*, vol. 2, 929.
12. Letter to Arthur Greeves, 2 July 1949; *Letters*, vol. 2, 952.
13. Letter to J. R. R. Tolkien, 27 October 1949; *Letters*, vol. 2, 990–991.
14. Letter to Don Giovanni Calabria, 13 September 1951; *Letters*, vol. 3, 136. My translation of Lewis's Latin.
15. Letter to the Prime Minister's Secretary, 4 December 1951; *Letters*, vol. 3, 147. The British cabinet office finally confirmed this information following a "Freedom of Information" request on 26 January 2012.
16. Tolkien, *Letters*, 125–129.
17. Stella Aldwinckle, OH/SR-1, fol. 9, Wade Center Oral History Collection, Wheaton College, Wheaton, IL.
18. Per. 267 e.20, no. 1, fol. 4, Bodleian Library, Oxford.
19. Stella Aldwinckle Papers, 8/380; Wade Center, Wheaton College, Wheaton, IL.
20. "Evil and God," in *Essay Collection*, 93.
21. J. B. S. Haldane, "When I Am Dead," in *Possible Worlds and Other Essays* (London: Chatto and Windus, 1927), 209.
22. This conclusion was printed in italics in the original first edition: C. S. Lewis, *Miracles* (London: Geoffrey Bles, 1947), 27.
23. The text of her critique of Lewis is to be found in *Socratic Digest* 4 (1948): 7–15. This was

later reprinted in *The Collected Philosophical Papers of G. E. M. Anscombe*, vol. 2 (Oxford: Blackwell, 1981), 224–232.

24. A. N. Wilson, *C. S. Lewis: A Biography*, 220.

25. John Lucas, personal communication to author, dated 14 October 2010. Lucas (born 1929) was studying *Literae Humaniores* at Balliol College at the time of the Anscombe debate.

26. "Christian Apologetics," in *Essay Collection*, 159.

27. Letter to Mary van Deusen, 18 June 1956; *Letters*, vol. 3, 762.

28. The Italian translation was titled *Le Lettere di Berlicche*. The book's two chief characters—Screwtape and Wormwood—were renamed Berlicche and Malacoda.

29. The best study of this correspondence is Dal Corso, *Il Servo di Dio*, 78–83.

30. Letter to Don Giovanni Calabria [in Latin; my translation], 14 January 1949; *Letters*, vol. 2, 905. Although Lewis was able to read Dante's Italian, it is interesting to note that he did not use this language when writing to Don Giovanni.

31. Letter to Robert C. Walton, 10 July 1951; *Letters*, vol. 3, 129.

32. Letter to Stella Aldwinckle, 12 June 1950; *Letters*, vol. 3, 33–35.

33. Letter to Carl F. H. Henry, 28 September 1955; *Letters*, vol. 3, 651. For Lewis's approach to apologetics, see McGrath, "Reason, Experience, and Imagination: Lewis's Apologetic Method," in *The Intellectual World of C. S. Lewis*, 129–146.

11. REARRANGING REALITY: THE CREATION OF NARNIA

1. "C. S. Lewis's Handwriting Analysed," *Times*, 27 February 2008. Lewis did indeed have a "garden shed of sorts": see his "Meditation in a Toolshed," in *Essay Collection*, 607–610.

2. Letter to Eliza Marian Butler, 25 September 1940; *Letters*, vol. 2, 444–446.

3. J. R. R. Tolkien to W. H. Auden, 7 June 1955; Tolkien, *Letters*, 215.

4. *Miracles*, 44.

5. Letter to Sister Penelope, 20 February 1943; *Letters*, vol. 2, 555. Lewis's Greek phrase *ex hypokeimenōn* (mistranscribed by the editor of *Letters*) literally means "out of those things that lie to hand," although it is better understood as "out of underlying realities."

6. This memory is not dated, but must precede Maureen's marriage to Leonard Blake on 27 August 1940, when she moved out of The Kilns.

7. Lady Maureen Dunbar, OH/SR-8, fol. 35, Wade Center Oral History Collection, Wheaton College, Wheaton, IL.

8. Green and Hooper, *Lewis: A Biography*, 305–306.

9. We later learn that their family name is "Pevensie." This is not disclosed in *The Lion, the Witch and the Wardrobe*, but only appears in a later volume in the series, *The Voyage of the "Dawn Treader."*

10. *The Lion, the Witch and the Wardrobe*, 11.

11. *A Preface to "Paradise Lost,"* v.

12. "On Three Ways of Writing for Children," in *Essay Collection*, 512.

13. *Surprised by Joy*, 14.

14. E. Nesbit, *The Enchanted Castle* (London: Fisher Unwin, 1907), 250.

15. E. Nesbit, *The Magic World* (London: Macmillan, 1924), 224–225.

16. J. R. R. Tolkien to Allen & Unwin, 16 March 1949; Tolkien, *Letters*, 133.

17. Letter to Pauline Baynes, 4 May 1957; *Letters*, vol. 3, 850.

18. HarperCollins's statement is clearly based on—even if it does not accurately summarise the substance of—Lewis's letter to Laurence Krieg, 21 April 1957; *Letters*, vol. 3, 847–848. It is essential to appreciate the tentative note of Lewis's comments in this letter, and

especially his revealing remark that "perhaps it does not matter very much in which order anyone reads them."

19. "On Criticism," in *Essay Collection*, 543–544.

20. Ibid., 550.

21. *The Lion, the Witch, and the Wardrobe*, 67.

22. For a good example, see Jack R. Lundbom, "The *Inclusio* and Other Framing Devices in Deuteronomy I–XXVIII," *Vetus Testamentum* 46 (1996): 296–315.

23. "Vivisection," in *Essay Collection*, 693–697.

24. Ibid., 695–696.

25. Ibid., 695.

26. "On Three Ways of Writing for Children," in *Essay Collection*, 511.

27. "Is Theology Poetry?" in *Essay Collection*, 21.

28. "The Hobbit," in *Essay Collection*, 485. See also Williams, *The Lion's World*, 11–29.

29. "On Criticism," in *Essay Collection*, 550.

30. Letter to Mrs. Hook, 29 December 1958; *Letters*, vol. 3, 1004.

31. Letter to a fifth grade class in Maryland, 24 May 1954; *Letters*, vol. 3, 480.

32. "Tolkien's *The Lord of the Rings*," in *Essay Collection*, 525.

33. G. K. Chesterton, *The Everlasting Man* (San Francisco: Ignatius Press, 1993), 105.

34. See *An Experiment in Criticism*, 40–49, which identifies six characteristics of myths—all of which can be found in the Chronicles of Narnia. See also "The Mythopoeic Gift of Rider Haggard," in *Essay Collection*, 559–562.

35. See Lewis's comments in *An Experiment in Criticism*, 57–73. For comment, see Fernandez, *Mythe, Raison Ardente*, 174–389; Williams, *The Lion's World*, 75–96.

36. *An Experiment in Criticism*, 45.

12. NARNIA: EXPLORING AN IMAGINATIVE WORLD

1. "It All Began with a Picture . . .," in *Essay Collection*, 529.

2. Letter to Carol Jenkins, 22 January 1952; *Letters*, vol. 3, 160.

3. *The Lion, the Witch and the Wardrobe*, 166.

4. See the list of ten works Lewis identified in 1962, the year before his death: *Christian Century*, 6 June 1962.

5. *Surprised by Joy*, 274.

6. *The Problem of Pain*, 5–13.

7. Kenneth Grahame, *The Wind in the Willows* (New York: Charles Scribner, 1908), 156.

8. Ibid., 154. This section is omitted from some modern popular editions of Grahame's classic story.

9. *The Lion, the Witch and the Wardrobe*, 65.

10. Ibid.

11. "The Weight of Glory," in *Essay Collection*, 98–99.

12. *The Lion, the Witch and the Wardrobe*, 75. See the excellent discussion in Williams, *The Lion's World*, 49–71.

13. Bertrand Russell to Colette O'Niel, 21 October 1916; Bertrand Russell, *The Selected Letters of Bertrand Russell*, ed. Nicholas Griffin, vol. 2, *The Public Years 1914–1970* (London: Routledge, 2001), 85.

14. *The Voyage of the "Dawn Treader,"* 188.

15. On film, see Christopher Deacy, "Screen Christologies: Evaluation of the Role of Christ-Figures in Film," *Journal of Contemporary Religion* 14 (1999): 325–338.

16. Mark D. Stucky, "Middle Earth's Messianic Mythology Remixed: Gandalf's Death and Resurrection in Novel and Film," *Journal of Religion and Popular Culture* 13 (2006); Padley and Padley, "From Mirrored Truth the Likeness of the True."

17. *The Problem of Pain*, 82.

18. *Broadcast Talks*, 52.

19. Ibid., 53–54.

20. *The Lion, the Witch and the Wardrobe*, 128–129.

21. Ibid., 142.

22. Ibid., 148.

23. See, for example, C. William Marx, *The Devil's Rights and the Redemption in the Literature of Medieval England* (Cambridge: D. S. Brewer, 1995); John A. Alford, "Jesus the Jouster: The Christ-Knight and Medieval Theories of Atonement in Piers Plowman and the 'Round Table' Sermons," *Yearbook of Langland Studies* 10 (1996): 129–143.

24. See Karl Tamburr, *The Harrowing of Hell in Medieval England* (Cambridge: D. S. Brewer, 2007).

25. *English Literature in the Sixteenth Century*, 380.

26. Ward, *Planet Narnia*, 3–41.

27. Ibid., 77–99.

28. *The Last Battle*, 160.

29. Ibid., 159.

30. Ibid., 160.

31. *The Silver Chair*, 141–142.

32. Ibid., 143.

33. John Ezard, "Narnia Books Attacked as Racist and Sexist," *The Guardian*, 3 June 2002. Pullman did not specifically name Susan, referring merely to "one girl" in the story of Narnia.

13. THE MOVE TO CAMBRIDGE: MAGDALENE COLLEGE, 1954–1960

1. Letter to Sheldon Vanauken, 14 May 1954; *Letters*, vol. 3, 473.

2. Figures for students reading for honour degrees from Brockliss, *Magdalen College Oxford*, 617.

3. Letter to James W. Welch, 24 November 1945; *Letters*, vol. 2, 681.

4. See letter to Arthur Greeves, 11 December 1944; *Letters*, vol. 3, 1554.

5. Roy S. Lee to Lewis, 29 August 1945, file 910/TAL 1b, BBC Written Archives Centre, Caversham Park.

6. *Cambridge University Reporter* 84, no. 30 (31 March 1954), 986. See Barbour, "Lewis and Cambridge," 459–465.

7. Tolkien dates the loss of intimacy between Lewis and himself to around this time: J. R. R. Tolkien to Michael Tolkien, November 1963?; Tolkien, *Letters*, 341.

8. G. M. Trevelyan, master of Trinity College, later recalled that this was the only time an electing committee had voted unanimously in his long experience at Cambridge: W. H. Lewis, "Memoir of C. S. Lewis," 22.

9. Henry Willink to Lewis, 11 May 1954; Group F, Private Papers, F/CSL/1, Magdalene College, Cambridge.

10. Letter to Henry Willink, 12 May 1954; *Letters*, vol. 3, 470–471.

11. Henry Willink to Lewis, 14 May 1954; Group F, Private Papers, F/CSL/1, Magdalene College, Cambridge.

12. J. R. R. Tolkien to Henry Willink, 17 May 1954; Group F, Private Papers, F/CSL/1, Magdalene College, Cambridge. Neither this letter nor his accompanying letter to H. S. Bennett are included in existing published collections of Tolkien's correspondence.

13. On receiving Lewis's letter, dated 19 May, reopening negotiations, Willink penned these words on its first page: "I wrote to Miss Gardner, May 18."

14. Henry Willink to Lewis, 24 May 1954; Group F, Private Papers, F/CSL/1, Magdalene College, Cambridge.

15. Basil Willey to Henry Willink, 19 May 1954; Group F, Private Papers, F/CSL/1, Magdalene College, Cambridge.

16. The most obvious source would be Gardner's Oxford colleague Tolkien. But Tolkien did not make any statement to this effect in either of his letters of 17 May 1954 to Willink and Bennett.

17. Gardner makes this clear in her obituary notice of Lewis for the British Academy: Gardner, "Clive Staples Lewis, 1898–1963." The reader needs to know that Gardner was Cambridge's second choice to make sense of her intriguing comments.

18. Henry Willink to Lewis, 3 June 1954; Group F, Private Papers, F/CSL/1, Magdalene College, Cambridge. A link between Magdalen College Oxford and Magdalene College Cambridge already existed: an "amicable accord" was agreed upon in March 1931, based on a pairing arrangement by which members of each college had shared dining rights: Brockliss, *Magdalen College Oxford*, 601.

19. Two letters to Sir Henry Willink, one in his capacity as vice-chancellor of the University of Cambridge, and one in his capacity as master of Magdalene College, both dated 4 June 1954; *Letters*, vol. 3, 483–484. The official history of Magdalene College incorrectly records Lewis's election to a fellowship at Magdalene as taking place in 1953: Cunich et al., *A History of Magdalene College Cambridge*, 258.

20. Brockliss, *Magdalen College Oxford*, 593.

21. John Wain, *The Observer*, 22 October 1961, 31.

22. Letter to Edward A. Allen, 5 December 1955; *Letters*, vol. 3, 677–678.

23. Barbara Reynolds, OH/SR-28, fols. 49–50, Wade Center Oral History Collection, Wheaton College, Wheaton, IL.

24. See the exchanges between Christopher Holme and P. H. Newby, 3 March 1945, file 910/TAL 1b, BBC Written Archives Centre, Caversham Park. The "Third Programme," established in 1946, provided comment on intellectual and cultural issues, and was often parodied as "two dons talking."

25. Letter to Douglas Bush, 28 March 1941; *Letters*, vol. 2, 475.

26. G. M. Trevelyan, *English Social History: A Survey of Six Centuries from Chaucer to Queen Victoria* (London: Longman, 1944), 92.

27. "De Descriptione Temporum," in *Selected Literary Essays*, 2.

28. *Reflections on the Psalms*, 7.

29. Keith Thomas, "Diary," *London Review of Books* 32, no. 11 (10 June 2010), 36–37.

30. Her views are best studied from her unpublished journals: see MS. Eng. lett. c. 220/3, Bodleian Library, Oxford.

31. For an excellent study, see King, "The Anatomy of a Friendship."

32. Sayer, *Jack*, 347–348.

33. Pitter herself was quite unaware of any suggestion that she was the obvious choice for Lewis's wife: Ruth Pitter, OH/SR-27, fol. 30, Wade Center Oral History Collection, Wheaton College, Wheaton, IL.

34. Dorsett, *And God Came In*, 17.

35. Davidman, "The Longest Way Round," 23–24.

36. *Observer*, 20 September 1998; *Belfast Newsletter*, 12 October 1998.

37. Davidman's correspondence is revealing at this point, particularly her interest in Madame de Maintenon (née Françoise d'Aubigné, 1635–1719), the second wife of the French king Louis XIV. Though "born in the workhouse," she secured a dramatic rise in her social status through marrying a poet, and finally the king. See Davidman, *Out of My Bone*, 197.

38. For a discussion of these papers, see the forthcoming study of Don W. King, *Yet One More Spring: A Critical Study of Joy Davidman* (Grand Rapids, MI: Eerdmans, 2013).

39. Dorsett, *And God Came In*, 87.

40. Davidman, *Out of My Bone*, 139.

41. Davidman's Certificate of Registration, No. A 607299, under the Aliens Order (1920) is held at the Wade Center, Wheaton College, Wheaton, IL: Joy Davidman Papers 1-14.

42. Also referred to as the "Agape Fund" in some documents. Barfield closed the fund in 1968, when all the funds had been disbursed according to Lewis's general directions.

43. Ceplair and Englund, *The Inquisition in Hollywood*, 361–397.

44. See Gibb's letter to Lewis, 18 February 1955; MS Facs. B. 90 fol. 2, Bodleian Library, Oxford.

45. Davidman, *Out of My Bone*, 242.

46. Letter to Anne Scott, 26 August 1960; *Letters*, vol. 3, 1181.

47. J. R. R. Tolkien to Christopher Bretherton, 16 July 1964; Tolkien, *Letters*, 349.

48. Correspondence, Joy Davidman Papers 1-14, Wade Center, Wheaton College, Wheaton, IL.

49. Letter to Arthur Greeves, 30 October 1955; *Letters*, vol. 3, 669.

50. Jacobs, *The Narnian*, 275.

51. Lewis's letters to Shelburne were published in 1967 as *Letters to an American Lady* (Grand Rapids, MI: Eerdmans, 1967).

52. Lewis to Mary Willis Shelburne, 25 December 1958; *Letters*, vol. 3, 1004. For the regulatory change, see Paul Addison and Harriet Jones, *A Companion to Contemporary Britain 1939–2000* (Oxford: Blackwell, 2005), 465.

53. Letter to Ruth Pitter, 9 July 1956; *Letters*, vol. 3, 769.

54. Letter to Ruth Pitter, 14 July 1956; *Letters*, vol. 3, 771.

55. Mrs. Moore's will was executed by Barfield & Barfield Solicitors on 16 July 1951.

56. A. N. Wilson, *C. S. Lewis: A Biography*, 266.

57. R. E. Head, OH/SR-15, fols. 14-5, Wade Center Oral History Collection, Wheaton College, Wheaton, IL.

58. Tolkien uses this form of reference in a letter to his son Christopher, dated 13 April 1944; Tolkien, *Letters*, 71.

59. Letter to Dorothy L. Sayers, 25 June 1957; *Letters*, vol. 3, 861–862. Lewis's *The Four Loves*, written around this time, explores this theme in more detail.

60. Letter to Mary Willis Shelburne, 16 November 1956; *Letters*, vol. 3, 808.

61. Letter to Arthur Greeves, 25 November 1956; *Letters*, vol. 3, 812.

62. Letter to Katharine Farrer, 25 October 1956; *Letters*, vol. 3, 801.

63. The most interesting of these appeared in the *Daily Mail* on 26 October 1956, which reported a rumour—hastily denied by Lewis—that he was due to marry a forty-six-year-old antique dealer in London the following day.

64. Lewis refers to this announcement in a letter to Dorothy L. Sayers, written on the day on which it appeared: "You may see in the *Times* a notice of my marriage to Joy Gresham." Letter to Dorothy L. Sayers, 24 December 1956; *Letters*, vol. 3, 819. Wilson incorrectly dates this "notice" to 22 March 1957: Wilson, *C. S. Lewis: A Biography*, 263–264.

65. For this episode, see Hooper, *C. S. Lewis: A Companion and Guide*, 631–635.

66. Letter to Dorothy L. Sayers, 25 June 1957; *Letters*, vol. 3, 861.

67. Hooper, *C. S. Lewis: The Companion and Guide*, 82, 633. Bide related much the same story to the present author at Oxford in 1978.

68. He did. Sadly, Bide's wife, Margaret, died of cancer in September 1960. Bide subsequently returned to Oxford as chaplain and tutor in theology at Lady Margaret Hall from 1968–1980.

69. Letter to Sheldon Vanauken, 27 November 1957; *Letters*, vol. 3, 901.

70. The (slightly perplexed) comment of Nevill Coghill, in Gibb, *Light on C. S. Lewis*, 63.

71. Letter to Jessie M. Watt, 28 August 1958; *Letters*, vol. 3, 966–967.

72. *The Four Loves*, 21.

73. Tom Clark and Andrew Dilnot, *Long-Term Trends in British Taxation and Spending* (London: Institute for Fiscal Studies, 2002).

74. Letter to Arthur Greeves, 25 March 1959; *Letters*, vol. 3, 1033.

75. Letter to Chad Walsh, 22 October 1959; *Letters*, vol. 3, 1097.

76. Full details in Green and Hooper, *C. S. Lewis: A Biography*, 271–276.

14. BEREAVEMENT, ILLNESS, AND DEATH: THE FINAL YEARS, 1960–1963

1. *A Grief Observed*, 38.

2. Ibid., 3.

3. Letter to Arthur Greeves, 30 May 1916; *Letters*, vol. 1, 187.

4. T. S. Eliot to Spencer Curtis Brown, 24 October 1960; MS Eng. lett. C. 852, fol. 62, Bodleian Library, Oxford.

5. Letter to Laurence Whistler, 4 March 1962; *Letters*, vol. 3, 1320.

6. *Surprised by Joy*, x.

7. *The Problem of Pain*, xii.

8. *A Grief Observed*, 5–6.

9. Letter to Sister Penelope, 5 June 1951; *Letters*, vol. 3, 123.

10. *A Grief Observed*, 52.

11. Letter to Sister Madeleva, CSC, 3 October 1963; *Letters*, vol. 3, 1460.

12. *A Grief Observed*, 44.

13. Ibid.

14. Letter to Arthur Greeves, 27 June 1961; *Letters*, vol. 3, 1277.

15. Lewis had known Barfield and Harwood since the 1920s and went on annual walking tours with both men. See Lewis's comments in *Surprised by Joy*, 231–234. *Miracles* was dedicated to Harwood and his wife, *The Allegory of Love* to Barfield.

16. Laurence Harwood was the second son of Cecil Harwood; Lucy Barfield was Owen Barfield's adopted daughter. Lewis had earlier dedicated *The Lion, the Witch and the Wardrobe* to her. Sarah Neylan, who married Christopher Patrick Tisdall on 31 December 1960, was the daughter of Mary Neylan, to whom Lewis had dedicated his George MacDonald anthology.

17. Letter to Francis Warner, 6 December 1961; *Letters*, vol. 3, 1301–1302.

18. Published posthumously as *Spenser's Images of Life* (1967).

19. Letter to J. R. R. Tolkien, 20 November 1962; *Letters*, vol. 3, 1382.

20. Letter to Phoebe Hesketh, 14 June 1960; *Letters*, vol. 3, 1162.

21. Letter to Alastair Fowler, 7 January 1961; *Letters*, vol. 3, 1223–1224.

22. Andreas Ekström, "Greene tvåa på listan 1961" *Sydsvenska Dagbladet*, 3 January 2012. The Nobel archives are embargoed to the public for fifty years.

23. Letter to the Nobel Committee for Literature, 16 January 1961, held in the archives of the Swedish Academy, released to the author on request.

24. Letter to Cecil Roth, 20 March 1962; *Letters*, vol. 3, 1323.

25. Letter to Evelyn Tackett, 23 May 1963; *Letters*, vol. 3, 1428.

26. Letter to Walter Hooper, 2 December 1957; *Letters*, vol. 3, 902–903.

27. Letter to Walter Hooper, 15 December 1962; *Letters*, vol. 3, 1393–1394.

28. On the reasons for the move, see Lewis's letter to Roger Lancelyn Green, 28 January 1963; *Letters*, vol. 3, 1408–1409. The Eagle and Child was registered as a Grade II Listed Building in December 1954. This prevented any alterations to its external appearance, but not to certain parts of its interior.

29. Letter to Arthur Greeves, 11 July 1963; *Letters*, vol. 3, 1440.

30. Letter to Mary Willis Shelburne, 15 July 1963; *Letters*, vol. 3, 1442.

31. Walter Hooper wrote two reports of Lewis's time in the Acland, both mentioning these specific dates and times; Walter Hooper to Roger Lancelyn Green, 5 August 1963; *Letters*, vol. 3, 1445–1446; and Walter Hooper to Mary Willis Shelburne, 10 August 1963; *Letters*, vol. 3, 1447–1448.

32. Letter to Cecil Harwood, 29 August 1963; *Letters*, vol. 3, 1452.

33. Letter to Arthur Greeves, 11 September 1963; *Letters*, vol. 3, 1456.

34. Walter Hooper to Mary Willis Shelburne, 10 August 1963; *Letters*, vol. 3, 1448.

35. Sayer, *Jack*, 404–405.

36. Letter to Arthur Greeves, 11 September 1963; *Letters*, vol. 3, 1455.

37. Letter to Walter Hooper, 20 September 1963; *Letters*, vol. 3, 1457.

38. David had moved to a Talmudical college in New York, and was short of money: see Lewis's letter to Jeannette Hopkins, 18 October 1963; *Letters*, vol. 3, 1465.

39. Letter to Walter Hooper, 11 October 1963; *Letters*, vol. 3, 1461–1462.

40. For most of 1964—when Hooper's proposed employment would begin—£1 converted to $2.80. The sterling crisis of 1964–1967 was yet to come.

41. Letter to Walter Hooper, 23 October 1963; *Letters*, vol. 3, 1469–1470.

42. W. H. Lewis, "C. S. Lewis: A Biography," 468.

43. Ibid., 470.

44. R. E. Head, OH/SR-15, fol. 13, Wade Center Oral History Collection, Wheaton College, Wheaton, IL.

45. Earlier that year, Maureen had inherited the title of Baronetess of Hempriggs, and was generally known as "Dame Maureen Dunbar."

46. Contrary to some accounts, there was no candle on Lewis's coffin. Ronald Head, who organised and led the funeral, suggested that the acolytes' candles may have reflected off the coffin in the church or graveyard, creating such an impression.

47. Letter to Mary Willis Shelburne, 28 June 1963; *Letters*, vol. 3, 1434.

15. THE LEWIS PHENOMENON

1. See Arthur Marwick, *The Sixties: Cultural Revolution in Britain, France, Italy, and the United States, c. 1958–c. 1974* (Oxford: Oxford University Press, 1999); Francis Beckett, *What Did the Baby Boomers Ever Do for Us? Why the Children of the Sixties Lived the Dream and Failed the Future* (London: Biteback, 2010).

2. Walsh, "Impact on America," in Gibb, *Light on C. S. Lewis*, 106–116.

3. "Defender of the Faith," *Time*, 6 December 1963.

4. Chad Walsh in Gibb, *Light on C. S. Lewis*, 115.

5. *Christianity Today*, 20 December 1963.

6. Tom Wolfe, "The Great Relearning," in *Hooking Up* (London: Jonathan Cape, 2000), 140–145.

7. Source: *Publishers Weekly*.

8. Hooper, "A Bibliography of the Writings of C. S. Lewis," in Gibb, *Light on C. S. Lewis*, 117–148.

9. Titles of British editions.

10. Collins was acquired by Rupert Murdoch in 1989. The HarperCollins imprint, under which most Lewis works are now published, was established in 1990.

11. See, for example, Donald E. Miller, *Reinventing American Protestantism: Christianity in the New Millennium* (Berkeley, CA: University of California Press, 1997).

12. Pearce, *C. S. Lewis and the Catholic Church*.

13. George M. Marsden, *Reforming Fundamentalism: Fuller Seminary and the New Evangelicalism* (Grand Rapids, MI: Eerdmans, 1987).

14. Roger Steer, *Inside Story: The Life of John Stott* (Nottingham: Inter-Varsity Press, 2009), 103–104.

15. As noted earlier (page 260), Lewis declined this invitation: Letter to Carl F. H. Henry, 28 September 1955; *Letters*, vol. 3, 651.

16. J. I. Packer, "Still Surprised by Lewis," *Christianity Today*, 7 September 1998.

17. For the historical background, see Alister E. McGrath, *Christianity's Dangerous Idea: The Protestant Revolution* (San Francisco: HarperOne, 2009), 351–372.

18. David J. Stewart, "C. S. Lewis Was No Christian!" http://www.jesus-is-savior.com/Wolves/cs_lewis.htm.

19. John W. Robbins, "Did C. S. Lewis Go to Heaven?" *The Trinity Review*, November/December 2003, http://www.trinityfoundation.org/journal.php?id=103.

20. Parsons and Nicholson, "Talking to Philip Pullman."

21. Gray, *Fantasy, Myth and the Measure of Truth*, 171.

22. Hatlen, "Pullman's *His Dark Materials*," 82.

23. Oziewicz and Hade, "The Marriage of Heaven and Hell?"

24. Royal Mail commissioned research from experts in British folklore and cultural history to determine the eight most appropriate characters to be used. In the end, two were taken from the Harry Potter series, two from the Chronicles of Narnia, two from traditional British folktales, and two from Terry Pratchett's Discworld books.

25. *Selected Literary Essays*, 219–220.

26. John F. Kennedy, address at Amherst College, 26 October 1963, transcript at the John F. Kennedy Presidential Library, http://www.jfklibrary.org/Research/Ready-Reference/JFK-Speeches/Remarks-at-Amherst-College-October-26-1963.aspx.

Index